Obama Elected Trump

political opinions & history, 2011-2016

Carol Headrick
Kathleen Tompkins
Mary T. Hardy

Library of Congress
U.S. Copyright Office Catalog

Copyright © 2018 Carol Headrick

ISBN: 0-9600213-1-0
ISBN-13: 978-0-9600213-1-4

DEDICATION

*To the Silent Majority who waited patiently for November 8, 2016,
to elect Donald J. Trump as our president.*

You changed the course of history.
MAGA

Table of Contents

V

VII

IX

X

XIII

INTRODUCTION

Obama Elected Trump starts with the third year of the Obama presidency and ends two years into the Trump presidency. You will see how conservatives view a radical liberal administration and the thrill felt at finally electing a fighter for conservative views. Liberals were in absolute shock that we didn't want Hillary to complete Obama's promised transformation of our country. My guest authors and I paid attention to what truly was happening during the Obama years. We were absolutely not shocked that Trump was elected.

My political journey started in 1984, the first year I was eligible to vote for president of the United States. Before I left for the polling booth, I asked my dad who I should vote for. He told me to do my own research. Not the answer I wanted but good advice. I heard what he said: my vote counts and only I am responsible for it. Cram-session time. Research for me was the editorial section in the local newspaper, the St. Louis Post-Dispatch. Unlike today, TV viewing for news included three major stations; DVRs with recorded shows and 24-hour cable news were yet to invade TV viewing. Our family computer of the day sat in the basement out of sight and used only for typing and playing Pong (the very first video game ever). Internet would not become mainstream for another ten years. Life happened without email, social media, twitter, blogging, podcasts and texting. Everyone's thoughts and opinions were not posted for the world to see. I didn't own a cell phone until 1995. If we were out of the house and needed to make a phone call, we used a phone booth for a quarter. The Rush Limbaugh radio program nationalized four years later in 1988. What I had at my fingers was the editorial section. I read about the Democrat candidate Walter Mondale and Republican incumbent President Ronald Reagan. Both sounded good to me. I had watched the debate and recalled President Reagan being asked if he was too old to be president (he was 73 at the time). He was prepared for the age question and responded, "I will not make age an issue of this campaign. I am not going to exploit, for political purposes, my opponent's youth and inexperience."

1

His comment made everyone laugh, including his opponent Mondale. I pulled the lever for Reagan, went to bed and woke up to hear that Reagan won 49 states with 525 electoral college votes to Mondale's 13.

Looking back, I was 20 years old and working at a frozen custard stand for $10 an hour, 55-65 hours per week in the summer, 20-30 hours during school weeks. (There was no Obamacare liberal mess encouraging companies to limit working hours to part-time.) Money was great. I was paying for my own college tuition at Mizzou, which cost a total of $4000 per year, including room and board. These were the 80's and I was clueless that President Ronald Reagan brought prosperity and left the Misery Index behind with the Carter years. Imagine paying 12-18% for a home mortgage which people did in the 1970's. My mortgage rate in the late nineties was 3 to 4%. President Carter earned the reputation as the Worst President Ever. And Mondale? He ran on raising taxes and predicted that Reagan would also raise taxes. Back then, I did not place much importance on the presidency and politics. What did this really matter to me? Taxes, regulations, and the economy didn't seem to affect my personal life and were just things to expect, good or bad, high or low. Since then, I have learned that politics affect every aspect of our lives.

After the first George Bush, Vice-President to President Reagan, folded on his campaign promise of No New Taxes, he lost a second term to Bill Clinton who brought his wife Hillary into the White House as First Lady, kind of. Clinton campaigned on getting two presidents for the price of one. Sure enough, Hillary took control of healthcare reform and put together a bill for government-controlled healthcare. HillaryCare was so awful that it never came to a vote. She also took on the women who claimed that her Arkansas governor husband had raped and/or sexually assaulted them. The Clinton's spokesman James Carville got away with saying, "Drag a hundred-dollar bill through a trailer park, you never know what you'll find." Not to stop philanderer Bill, he fooled around with a young intern in the oval office and the country had to deal with all the lurid details for years. It was Hillary on national TV who defended her husband, crucified the abused women, and named the vast right-wing conspiracy as the culprit.

Clinton's VP Al Gore ran against George W. Bush in 2000. Gore boasted about inventing the internet which he didn't. He had a mentor, Roger Revelle, known as the father of global warming. When Gore chose global warming as his pet cause, his mentor warned him that it was not factual, and that climate has variability on its own. No reason to stop Gore's global warming scare. He lost to W, who won two terms, second time against John Kerry. Gore got filthy rich on the global warming scare and probably will until his last dying, hot breath. Back to Bush, his approval ratings were sky high after the 9-11 Islamic terror attacks on American soil. Democrats persistently tried to get his ratings down and finally did with the slogan War for Oil. The 3,000 people that died 9-11 on American soil were forgotten by the Democrats.

2

Fast-forward to 2008, and Obama was elected president over RINO Senator John McCain, and in 2012 over Governor Romney. The smooth prompter-reading Democrat candidate Barrack Obama was elected by speaking about a united America and then went about dividing America. Despite Obama claiming his administration as the most transparent and scandal-free, the opposite was true. Obama easily earned the title of Worst President Ever by wasting eight years hurting the US and its citizens. Our first black president could have been a truly transformational president who built up urban communities, turning lives away from poverty, drugs and crime.

At one point during the earlier Clinton years, a friend of mine tried to convince me that President Clinton was fooling around in the Oval Office. I refused to believe her that our President could be that stupid. I was wrong. Later, when the Obamas came along talking about fundamentally transforming our country and the need for new traditions and history, it surprised me that no one cared to question their intentions. The Obama years were nearly impossible to have rational discussions about politics and best to avoid any discussions altogether. After all, the Obamas were black, and racism was being thrown around to silence anyone with differing views or appearing to be racist. A simple example of this time: a Washington, DC mayor's aide, who knows correct English, used the term niggardly in referring to how he would manage a tight budget. The definition is miserly, originating from the Middle English origin nygg. The aide should have been applauded for watching the budget closely. But the word sounded like a racial slur, a stink was made, and the mayor asked for his resignation. He lost his job because he used a word that sounded racist. Anyone who criticized Obama or his policies, appeared to, or accused, was RACIST, no question.

The articles in this book share history and information that define the stark differences between liberals and conservatives. Mind you, I didn't say between Democrats and Republicans, because together, these long-term politicians (some for more than 30 years) have become the elite politicians, also known as the Swamp, who are drunk on their power and ignore the citizens who elected them. Anyway, Obama did one absolutely great thing.

Obama's greatest achievement was getting Trump elected, no doubt about it. His policies, actions and inactions were so bad, leaving us miserable and definitely wanting change. He left office with cities burned by blacks after igniting hatred for whites and the police. He stole our healthcare choices and forced us to buy his healthcare with excessive premiums and deductibles. He bragged about leading from behind and told us to get used to the dying economy as the new normal, for manufacturing jobs would not come back. He was not aware of Trump's magical wand. Oddly, near the end of Obama's eight years, his focus became transgenderism, ridiculously and dangerously allowing men into little girls' restrooms and to compete in sports as women, and vice versa. Obama claimed (threatened) that his policies were on the ballot so that we had to vote for Hillary. The media were purely clueless for reporting that Hillary would be our next president. Obama foisted his liberal ideology on the American electorate and expected us to just take it and like it. Liberals live in a bubble of their own creation that ignores everyone and everything else.

Donald Trump arrived as a breath of fresh air. The non-politician, billionaire real estate developer tycoon and executive producer of the successful Celebrity Apprentice TV show, campaigned with an everyday man attitude on common sense instead of political correctness, beating 17 good Republican candidates. The election of President Donald John Trump was a true blessing. Hopefully, videos of the media and snowflake Millennials bawling their eyes out on election night are still available to view, truly great entertainment. My personal favorite is a video compilation of the media laughing about candidate Trump as a joke.

Obama's Millennial supporters earned the nickname Snowflakes who live by the words offended and diversity. They cried, crumbled and melted when Hillary lost; they literally thought they would die without the old hag Hillary as president. College campuses have become liberal-indoctrination Snowflake havens. Our younger generations appear to be brainwashed into believing liberal politician-infused hatred for, name anything: US Constitution, white men, water bottles, cows, cheeseburgers, gas cars, Barbie dolls, big families, police, etc. Alpha male Trump was America's answer to leave the Obama years behind as a bad joke. Trump supporters also earned their nickname, the Deplorables. Instead of being outraged at Hillary for calling half of Trump's supporters deplorable, we laughed at her and said bring it on. Call us whatever you want. We won't cry. We won't demand a phony apology. And we will never, ever vote for liberals.

I am in awe of the quiet conservatives who waited patiently, having to hear Obama's arrogant, condescending voice for eight long years, for November 8, 2016, to elect Donald J. Trump as our 45th president. Read on for those of you who missed the Trump Train or are interested in conservative thought during the Obama years. It really is eye-opening to what liberal progressives are truly pushing on America, the greatest country in the world.

One more note, Trump was not my first pick. (Sorry!) Back to November 2011.

We Are All Equal

November 9, 2011

My sister congratulated her son on getting an A on his project which was extremely detailed and well thought out. His response was simply, "We all got A's because we are all equal." I can still picture the steam coming from my sister's ears. The teacher failed to teach the kids that skill and effort separate the successful from the unsuccessful. It's probably fair to say that every student did not put in the time and effort to receive an A. This is the beginning of what we call socializing our children. They learn early that no one is better than anyone else and that we are all equal. Next project, whatever is turned in gets an A.

Compare this lesson to communism. Everyone receives the same pay because no one deserves more than anyone else. In communism, everyone works for the collective good. You are not working for yourself, but you work for others by demand, also called slavery. How hard are you going to work (or study) if you can never get ahead? If you work hard, you still do not deserve anything more than the next guy. If you did, you would not all remain equal. Democrat mobs have been yelling the commie saying, "Workers unite for equality!" While the government promotes equality to the workers, the top government bureaucrats are going to accumulate more power and money and will definitely not adhere to the principles of equality for themselves. Have you ever heard of a benevolent communist leader?

In communism, the government owns everything. It is the government that determines who gets what. A jerk politician decides your housing, your food, your education, your job, your news and your medical care. Individual property rights do not exist. The individual with Constitutionally protected rights does not exist. Read any of the great books written by North Korean defectors. Their lives are unimaginable to us.

The opposite of communism is a country where individuals have economic freedom to control their own destinies. People get to work for their self-interests. If they are lucky, they do it for a profit. Imagine that, a country where your hard work is valued and rewarded. This is capitalism. It is a country where children should be taught that A work earns an A and F work earns an F. I know how far-fetched it seems that someone might want to fundamentally change the United States, but can you think of anyone who has said this?

Obama's Greed

November 9, 2011

Can we please call out Obama on his greed? He rails on the rich and then has $25,000.00 per plate lunches with them. Receiving obscene amounts of money for a lunch is not greedy; it is smart fundraising. However, the payouts Obama donors are receiving in return are obscene. The difference in receiving fundraising money and doling out taxpayer money as payback is criminal to me. What kind of game is he playing with our taxpayer dollars? 2008 fundraising total: $745 million, 2012 fundraising goal: $1 billion

Can we call the One Trillion Stimulus Package for what it really is? A GARGANTUAN THANK YOU to his donors who got him elected. Really, could he have been elected on his past experiences? Obama's past, in review:

- Harvard Law Editor - zero papers written
- College Transcripts - unavailable
- Birth Document - unavailable
- Community Organizer Accomplishments - Any?
- Religion - Twenty years of Black Liberation Theology from Reverend Wright. Whites must give back what they took from blacks - not a religion.
- Illinois Senate - 129 present votes - avoided voting on some very controversial bills. He did vote to let babies die that were born from failed abortions.

Election Theme: Hope and Change. What kind of change did Obama hope for? He let it slip a few times. Spoken words off teleprompter, with my paraphrasing:

"Hey, little businessman, you didn't build your business. The government did. Ya know, we built the roads and bridges. OK, we built it from your tax money but still."

"Hey, little businessman who hires people and pays them for their work, you are going to be taxed more because I want to spread the money you keep for yourself. You sure are selfish."

"We are five days away from transforming your country which is the most prosperous country ever. I know no one will ask me what kind of transformation I mean. Progressive sounds so hip, but I mean progress away from your constitutional rights," which leads to another off-teleprompter remark:

"Your Constitution is just an old piece of paper written by old, white men that just tells you your rights. It doesn't say that I can take those rights away and make my own rules. How selfish, restraining and outdated from oh so long ago."

And this guy is our president and has a chance of being reelected in 2012?!? Wake up, America. He is stealing from small business and using our tax dollars as his personal bank account. Greedy? Definitely. Criminal? We'll see.

Leveling the Playing Field and Social Justice and Greed, by Kithy

November 9, 2011

I'm amazed at how many idiots are participating in the Occupy hippie groups. I think if someone told them that they are standing up for principles that led to Hitler Germany, they wouldn't understand it. Obviously, they wouldn't understand it. They don't know why they are there, except for the ones who are being paid to be there. Those ones are there for the paycheck.

I worked with a communist at my last job. I was stunned, but his philosophy was that since we won't help others on our own, it is our Christian moral duty to have the government take care of everyone. I don't understand how a corrupt government (I don't trust anyone with tons of other people's money) can possibly distribute resources in an efficient manner, or even in the manner utopian believers think it should be distributed.

Anyway, there are certain code phrases that are repeated like a mantra, and the people quoting them don't even know what they are saying. Things like: let's level the playing field. That is code word for we don't like capitalism, we want socialism. In general, someone is doing well, and someone is jealous and wants a handout to start out at the top where the first person doing well worked his way up or wants to stifle competition. Leveling the playing field establishes excessive regulations to prevent new competition.

I remember hearing about the cornrowers. Some people who were good at fixing people's hair in cornrows opened a shop. Someone else with connections got upset because customers were going to the cornrowers instead of to her shop. So, to "level the playing field", she got some legislation passed which originated a licensing fee and many regulations. To cornrow hair. Kids cornrow each others' hair, yet this type of business needs all kinds of regulations. Customers needed to be protected from the evil cornrowers who might, what, cornrow too tightly? Whatever. Leveling the playing field sounds good because everyone wants a fair chance. However, when it is instituted at the government level, it does the exact opposite.

Social justice generally is referring to communism. I sat through a presentation on social justice and the presenter had us say a prayer that she provided. It was just about word for word out of the Marxist manifesto. I couldn't read along with the prayer because I was sick to my stomach. The rest of the group were reading it and going along with it. The presenter said she believed in

7

communism, everything for the greater good. We should give our resources to others because it is the right thing to do. She said the difference between what she spouted and Marxism is the reason for it. She said Marxism is to strengthen the government. But since her reason was the right reason, communism is better. She absolutely did not see the connection that bad economic policy is bad, regardless of the reason for it. And the sheeple followed. Greed is code word for evil capitalism. Just because some people have found a legitimate way to make a profit by doing business, certain other people are jealous and therefore must attribute the profit making to greed. So, please, figure out what the code words are and how they are used. I'm sure new words will pop up, but these seem to be staples.

Theory on Occupy, by Kithy

November 9, 2011

This is my theory: the people who are taking part in Occupy are doing so because 1. they are too dumb to realize they are standing up for communist ideals. 2. they are there for sex, drugs and rock 'n roll, and want their turn at a Woodstock type party. 3. they are being paid to be there, or 4. they are part of SEIU (Service Employees International Union) thuggery.

The dummies don't know why communism is unattainable (duh, someone has to make the decisions – the ruling class, the more power they get, the less power they share). They don't know that it has never worked anywhere, and there is no reason to think it will work because we will implement it properly. They probably don't even know the difference between communism and capitalism, except that for some reason they think that capitalism is bad. Here's a clue, dummies: capitalism is an efficient way to distribute goods. Communism is an inefficient way to distribute goods. Either their education was woefully inadequate, or their brains are woefully inadequate.

Why I Don't Like the President, by Kithy

November 9, 2011

Why I don't like the current president: I didn't like his first victory – expanding abortions to an unbelievable extent. I don't like his positions on the economy, America, religion, or jobs. I don't like his arrogance and his attempt to become a dictator. I see his position on the economy as the exact opposite of mine. I'm a capitalist, we need to be free from excessive regulation to be able to do our best if we so choose. I see his desire to "equal the playing field", which is code word for socialism, as a jobs and business destroying effort. He wants the government to be able to provide everything for everyone. Which in the end means that no one gets anything, because there is no incentive to provide anything. It appears to me as though he thinks he is on a high podium, looking down on us, telling us everything that is wrong (which is everything to him). I love America and believe it is the greatest country on earth.

His position on religion is that it just doesn't matter, and preachers who spread hate are the same as all other preachers. I teach religion to public school kids because I believe in God, and I believe that learning about your religion is important. I believe that people who want their children to make up their own minds about religion, and then don't give them any information about their religion, are doing a disservice. Kids, especially, need the information before they can make a choice this important.

Well, it seems that just about everyone agrees with me that he doesn't know how to create jobs. His jobs bill was defeated in the Senate; he can't even get his own party to agree with him. I do support Herman Cain's plan, not necessarily two different kinds of taxes, but that cutting taxes and regulations will help with growth and therefore, jobs.

I am worried that the recent public announcement that government isn't working and those in charge should have more power to make decisions is an effort to shift our government from democracy to dictatorship. I don't think they know that the reason the changes they want to make are being thwarted is because our government is working properly, and that what they are advocating is opposite of the Republic that our founding fathers designed. There's a lot more, but those are some of the reasons.

Occupiers' Modus Operandi

November 11, 2011

Do the Occupiers have a point? From what I gather from posted videos and MSM (MainStream Media), the protests are against social and economic inequality and corporate greed. Corporate greed is not a reality. You might think they charge too much, but that's where you decide if parting with your money is worth it. If nobody buys the product, the corporation can either lower the price or go out of business. If everybody buys the product, competition comes in and helps lower prices. Corporations are small businesses that have grown because of their success, a common goal of businesses. If you steal the product, steal from your boss, or embezzle, that's greedy (and criminal). Protesting someone's success and demanding that government take that success (money through higher taxes) define greed.

Social and economic inequality is a reality and always will be. And the beautiful thing about the United States is that you can move in and out of the poor class, middle class and upper class. And everyone has the opportunity to do so. I hate seeing poverty and would like everyone to do well. However, it is up to each capable individual to go about working for what he or she wants.

I see the Occupiers' protesting as begging. Their modus operandi is begging to get what they want, because they sure are not working for what they want. We will all see how this pans out for them. They might find out that this only gets them so much. They may find out that getting jobs or creating their own destinies works best. I love my 16-year-old nephew's story. He could not wait to get a job at McDonald's. His friends ripped him for being a hamburger flipper. He didn't care; he wanted to save for a car. He recently purchased a $1200 car and he is proud.

There are two clashing mindsets in America today. They can easily be summed up as I want what you have, and I am either going to complain about it or I am going to work for it. Occupiers, what really are you protesting? Are you willing to work for what you want?

Why does President Obama despise rich people? by Tbird

November 12, 2011

President Obama is a rich man, yet he seems to despise rich people and thinks they should give more of their money to the government to spend. Does he not realize that most people with money earned their money the old-fashioned way, by creating a good or service other people are willing to buy with their own money? Well, no, I don't think he does. For Obama, money is easy come, easy go.

Obama's first job out of college in New York was copy editor for a small company that published international business publications. He rewrote copy other people had written, which is legitimate work. The company produced newsletters. This seems to be the only real job he ever held.

The next step for Obama was community organizer for the Developing Communities Project in Chicago, funded by Bill Ayers, former domestic terrorist (who just three years ago still had not apologized for blowing up buildings). His job was to stir up poor minority people to believe that they were miserable and that their misery was due to unresponsive governments or greedy corporations and then get them to bond together to demand what they deserved and make such an almighty stink that the government or corporation will grant them whatever will make them stop harassing them. After three years, he became a consultant and then trainer for the Gamaliel network of church-based community organizers (of which DCP was a part). Obama finally joined a church, as people repeatedly asked him what church he belonged to. His church was Trinity United Church of Christ headed by Reverend Jeremiah Wright, who preached a separatist, anti-American liberation theology, which doesn't seem to have much relationship to Christianity. It was the church of choice for black politicians, and Obama needed the street cred if he was to enter politics.

While attending Harvard Law School, Obama interned at Sidley Austin, where he met wife Michelle and Bernadine Dohrn. He was elected president of Harvard Law Review and wrote nothing. A literary agent asked him to write a book for her publishing company and gave him a $125,000 advance. He wrote nothing and got another contract with a $40,000 advance. He and Michelle went to Bali so he could write, and he wrote nothing. He turned in Dreams of My Father, which was very well-written in the style of Bill Ayres, using a lot of imagery and phrases in Ayres own writings, leading writer Jack Cashill to determine that Ayres, not Obama, wrote it. His next book, The Audacity of Hope, published just before he started his US senatorial campaign, was not nearly as well-written, but it had a lot of passages identical to stump speeches he gave that were written by his speechwriter Jon Favreau. Obama made millions off books he did not write himself and didn't even credit his ghostwriters.

After Harvard, Obama went to work for Davis Miner, a very politically well-connected law firm in Chicago. The partners were counsel to Mayor Harold Washington and partners with slum-redeveloper Tony Rezko. Obama worked on cases relating to discrimination, such as the Citibank case, in which the bank supposedly did not loan money to enough black applicants; as a result, banks were forced to comply with a Jimmy Carter-era law (Community Reinvestment Act) that set quotas for minority loans, whether the customer could pay back loans or not.

ACORN (Association of Community Organizations for Reform Now) used the law along with intimidating tactics such as public charges of racism and loud sit-ins to force banks to give more bad loans. The community organizers got lots of government money they didn't earn. Obama also lectured part time at the University of Chicago law school in constitutional law; he said the Constitution was written wrong because it didn't guarantee a minimum standard of living. Other lecturers and professors hated him, complaining that he was unqualified, lazy, and never attended faculty meeting.

Obama joined Project Vote to get more blacks to vote, something they hadn't been very involved in. He was wildly successful. Running this mini-political campaign made him a political star. He served on the board of directors for Woods Fund with Ayres, giving out grants to Trinity, ACORN, and low-income housing construction. They used Northern Trust, which provided his mortgage in 2005 for his $1.65 million house.

State senator was Obama's first elected position, which he won unopposed after disqualifying four other candidates from the ballot (evidently, candidates in

Illinois cheat with lots of fake ballot petition signatures). He steered state funding to churches and community groups. His wife, who worked for the University of Chicago hospitals, got her salary tripled; her employer had donated campaign money. Her position was so important that it was simply discontinued when she left for Washington a few years later. After a failed bid for Congress, the Obamas were in debt, but Barry got an $8,000 a month retainer as a consultant to a tech entrepreneur and long-time political supporter Robert Blackwell.

Obama wanted more. He wanted to be US Senator. He went to Emil Jones, Illinois state senate majority leader, who became his kingmaker. In his last year as senator, Obama was appointed to sponsor a slew of high-profile bills, which more senior senators had been working on for years. Otherwise, Obama left no paper trail. Hillary Clinton had a list compiled of how often the state legislature met; it averaged 1 to 1 ½ days a week. Obama won in 2004, owing in part to his main competitors imploding due to previously secret divorce details. As US Senator, Obama gave tens of millions of dollars to Jones' district. Obama gave a very well-received speech at the Democratic National Convention, which brought him national attention. He sponsored a bill to send money to the Congo and another bill to name a post office. He requested almost $800 million in earmarks.

Obama wanted more. He wanted to be president. He won the Nobel Peace Prize for getting elected, which came with $1.4 million, which he donated to charities. Next step, president of the world? His political career needs to end in January 2013. Obama will never have to work another day in his life. Except for his first year out of college, he never produced anything, yet he has always had money, money from royalties from the writings of others, money from rich political donors, money from taxpayers. He hasn't really had to work for his money, which explains his cavalier attitude towards other people's money. He just knows how to spend it, as does his grifter wife. As everybody knows, it means less to get something you haven't earned than it does to get something you worked hard to earn.

Community Organizer President of the People

November 14, 2011

A President of the United States should represent all the citizens of the United States, not just specific groups over the other. I will never consider Obama my president. Obama acts as if he is the community organizer of our country. He should go down in history as the warfare president, pitting one against the other: rich vs. poor, government vs. private, corporations vs. workers, union vs. non-union, blacks vs. whites. As the most powerful man in the world, why does he want everyone hating one another?

The means justify the ends. By everyone hating one another, Obama is getting closer to the end he wants. The unions and Occupiers are helping Obama towards his goal. We have seen the violence and anger in Wisconsin with the unions and we continue to see the violence and anger of the Occupiers. What happens if these cities are uncontrollably overrun by chaos and violence? A revolution, perhaps?

Obama told us what he wants. Remember these two quotes before he was elected president: "We are five days away from fundamentally transforming the United States of America." "We cannot continue to rely only on our military in order to achieve the national security objectives that we've set. We've got to have a civilian national security force that's just as powerful, just as strong, just as well funded." How many voters asked what he meant? He meant transforming the United States economy from capitalism to communism and having the might to accomplish this.

Enough chaos and violence would require Obama's civilian force to take over. This is straight out of Marxism class struggle with the theme 'workers unite', transforming capitalism into communism through revolution. Capitalist money is moved to the State (government.) Obama is already destroying the rich through his taxation and regulations. The rich will eventually stop producing or leave the United States if this continues. The middle class is on its way to being destroyed by this, leaving what the Marxist calls a classless society – all poor.

Believe it that this administration wants to rule your life. They have taken over an auto company, banks, student loans and health care. They continue to spend money we don't have creating US credit downgrades. A second term for Obama may result in this ultimate transformation he promised. Why in God's name would you give that power to anyone, much less your government?

Workers of All Lands Unite

November 16, 2011

Karl Marx, (1818-1883) the man behind Marxism, was born into an upper middle-class family with Jewish ancestry and married an upper-class woman of nobility. He organized revolutions and wrote for radical newspapers criticizing established society, politics and religion. He lived mostly off his inheritance and a friend's family business. Four of his seven children died before adulthood due partly to living in extreme poverty.

Karl Marx co-wrote *The Communist Manifesto* which expresses communist views and lists a ten-point plan on how to transition from capitalism to communism. He believed that workers were not free because they had to 'sell' their labor to the capitalist producer owner. Workers should overthrow the capitalist producer and own the production together. In turn, the workers would all work together and class differences would be eliminated. No classes – no exploiting the worker – no inequality. No thought on how the business would continue to run without leadership or money, just minor details ignored.

Marxist concepts that may sound familiar today:

- Class Struggle
- Proletariat vs. Bourgeois (Workers vs. Rich Capitalists)
- Capitalist Oppression
- Workers of All Lands Unite
- Religion as the Opiate of the People
- Revolution
- Socialist Transformation
- Collective Production

On the tombstone of Karl Marx is written, 'WORKERS OF ALL LANDS UNITE.' Next time you hear the mantra of Marxism, think of the atheist Karl Marx announcing, 'From each according to his ability, to each according to his need.' His children's basic need of food was not met because their father was busy protesting the establishment. He never had a plan on how communism would function. His classless communist society envisioned would run on a political economy. Isn't that the same as relying on the government for all your needs, the same government that would depend on successful companies for taxes to pay for every need? When the businesses in communist countries fail because they always do, what then?

Abortion Losing Steam, by Tbird

November 18, 2011

Abortion has been legal in all fifty states during all nine months of pregnancy since 1973. In the last couple of decades, however, abortion has been losing ground as more and more people have come to realize that a pregnancy involves an unborn baby who should have its life protected from deliberate killing. All the states (except Vermont) have enacted laws restricting abortion, such as parental consent laws and clinic safety laws. More importantly, hearts and minds have been changing. There is still a long way to go, but I think we're generally on the right track.

Roe v. Wade in 1973 repealed all state laws prohibiting and restricting abortion. The Supreme Court found an implied "right to privacy" in the "penumbra" of the Bill of Rights. This means that they wanted abortion and made up a constitutional right. Never mind the Tenth Amendment, which provides that powers not granted to the federal government nor prohibited to the states by the

14

Constitution are reserved respectively, to the states or the people. Doe v. Bolton, the same year, made abortion on demand legal during the entire nine months of pregnancy. The Supreme Court made up pregnancy trimesters: during the first three months, there are no restrictions on abortion; during the fourth through sixth months, there may be restrictions regarding safety only; during the last three months, the states can impose restrictions if the state found it in its interest to protect the child, but the states have a broad and meaningless exception for health of the mother, which includes any condition that might impact a woman's physical, emotional, psychological or financial "health". I remember a story of a teenager getting a late abortion because it would be too embarrassing to appear at the pool in a bikini if she were obviously pregnant.

Ironically, both Doe and Roe later became pro-life spokesmen. Doe (Sandra Cano) wanted to reclaim her children, who had been taken from her when she couldn't provide for them. She was pregnant, and her lawyers used her in their efforts to legalize abortion in Georgia, though she didn't want an abortion.

She had to flee the state when her lawyers and her family tried to force her to have a late term abortion. She tried to publicize her opposition to abortion right after the 1973 decision, but the media ignored her. Roe (Norma McCorvey) wanted an abortion in Texas, claiming she had been gang raped. Her lawyer knew it was a lie but didn't tell the Supreme Court. McCorvey had the baby before the case was decided, and she became a pro-lifer in 1995.

Since 1973, 50 million unborn babies have been slaughtered legally, most of them during the first nine weeks. The first time I heard of partial-birth abortion, a late-term abortion technique, I thought it was a gruesome joke. It wasn't. One of my cousins was born when her mother was five and a half months along; she is now an adult working in the army reserves. She was born earlier than many of the babies killed by abortionists.

Abortion is a very divisive topic in America. Before 1973, the states had written their own laws based on what their citizens wanted. The Supreme Court nullified all that and basically said it didn't matter what people wanted, and it didn't matter that so many people consider abortion to be the killing of unborn children. Pro-abortion people said no one should be forced to carry an unwanted pregnancy to term because the mother's wishes should trump a baby's life. They claimed it was only a clump of cells, anyway. My clump of cells is a baby because I want it, but yours isn't a baby because you don't want it? What if we change our minds? Does the character of the cells change then? That doesn't make sense; it either is or is not a baby. (I have never heard of a human woman pregnant with a puppy; she's always pregnant with a human baby.) Besides, a baby would ruin people's lives by interrupting their schooling or their jobs. Or people couldn't afford to care for a baby, etc, etc. Pro-life people consider a baby in its mother's womb to be an individual unique child worthy of protection from deliberate killing. Most people can agree that abortion kills a human baby; the dispute centers on whether it is good or bad, and should it be allowed or not.

I think more and more people are leaning to protect the unborn. The abortion rates have been going down. In 1973, 16.3% of pregnancies were aborted (abortions were legal in some states, but they have always been done). In 1981, the rate was 29.3%. Since 2008, it has leveled off to just under 20%. The yearly number of abortions peaked at 1.6 million in 1990 and is now about 1.2 million. Chemical abortions done with RU 486 account for 1 to 2 % of abortions, despite the hype when they first came out: women said they were too expensive, took too many doctor visits, and were too dangerous. Thirty years ago, 50% of hospitals did abortions, but now only 6% do. There are fewer abortionists now, and fewer young doctors want anything to do with them. Young people in their twenties are the most likely age group to favor limits on abortion. They came of age during the partial birth debate, were in the first group to grow up with pictures of sonograms on their refrigerators, and the major reproductive development during their lifetimes was IVF, which help create pregnancies rather than terminate them.

Crisis pregnancy centers now outnumber abortion providers, and 86% of counties have no abortion providers. In 1992, in Planned Parenthood v. Casey, the justices extended states' ability to protect fetal life and maternal health throughout pregnancy, as long as the restrictions do not present an undue burden for women seeking abortions. In 2007, the Supreme Court upheld the Partial Birth Abortion Ban Act of 2003 without an exception to protect women's health. Since then, states can have laws requiring doctors to notify patients of the potential dangers of abortion, alternatives, and waiting periods, and some states have written partial-birth abortion ban laws. I am optimistic that more and more babies will be protected from abortion.

It Was Never About the Environment

November 18, 2011

The US Department of Energy, October 2000, reported the percentages of the makeup of Greenhouse Gases without water vapor:

Carbon Dioxide 99.438%
Methane 0.471%
Nitrous Oxide 0.084%.

The left has used the term greenhouse gases scaring people about the dangers of global warming for decades. 99% carbon dioxide sounds scary. We must be bad humans for allowing this to happen to our environment. Obama's EPA has even gone so far as to label carbon dioxide a dangerous pollutant and warns that

16

global warming is a worse threat than terrorists. If you paid any attention in science class, you learned that CO2 is one-part carbon and two parts oxygen. We breathe it and plants absorb it in photosynthesis.

Same report with the title Anthropogenic (Man-made) Contribution to the Greenhouse Effect, Greenhouse Gases including water vapor:

Water Vapor 95%, 94.999% natural, 0.001 man-made
Carbon Dioxide 3.618%, 3.502% natural, 0.117% man-made
Methane 0.360%, 0.294% natural, 0.066 man-made
Nitrous Oxide 0.950%, .903 natural, 0.047% man-made

Sane people have determined that 0.117% man-made carbon dioxide is not going to kill the planet, much less have any effect on it at all. Greenhouse gases are mostly water. Minor details are not to stop Obama. His solution to this non-problem was a cap and trade energy bill which he named the American Clean Energy and Security Act of 2009. Surprising to me, the Democrat-controlled Senate refused to vote on the already passed Democrat-controlled House bill, possibly realizing this bill would destroy our energy sector? I would have named it the Steal Directly from Businesses, Halt Energy Producers and Hurt Americans Legally bill. America dodged a bullet.

Blame the Republicans, Again, by SH

November 22, 2011

Mr. President –

How dare you?! You go on live television blaming Republicans for the failed debt deadline. Do you not realize Republicans and Democrats work for the same company (i.e., the United States federal government)? While I was working at a growing company, a director said to a vice president, "What an idiot our one director, Joe Public, is." The VP responded, "That may be true, but he is our idiot."

In other words, all those people represented the same company and until the 'idiot' caught on, changed positions, or no longer worked at that company, you stand behind your company and its representatives. (criminal activity being an exception.) I do not view the Republicans as "idiots" but apparently you do, Mr. President. Please keep in mind when you go on live television and point the finger at a group of people who are working for the same entity, we come across as an incompetent, screwed up country. You have had over 900 days to work on this debt crisis, with your party's majority for over half that time period, and you did not get the job done. Your incompetence is helping to bring down this country.

On a side note to TransCanada (owner of the Keystone XL pipeline) – Please do not write the Keystone XL pipeline off in the United States. We would love to purchase your oil instead of shipping it in from faraway places, but as you have seen on live TV, our country's leadership is lacking. Apparently, the administration does not know what the best interests of our country are (i.e., 20,000 jobs from the pipeline project, working with a close and friendly country – we hope still – regarding its oil exports, etc). Pandering to special interest groups for political purposes (read: votes) is more important to our current administration, but we are working to change that.

Easy Election Decision: Conservative Republican or Liberal Democrat

November 22, 2011

2012 is an easy election decision. You either vote Republican or for Obama, the liberal Democrat. If a third party hops in, ignore it. If you want more of Obama's accomplishments, vote for him. If you don't, vote Republican, whoever that may be. If you conduct an internet search on Obama's accomplishments, you will find lists that go on and on. One thing that Obama has accomplished better than any other president in history is spending your tax dollars. He did this at the expense of America's credit rating, which has been downgraded for the first time ever and is threatened to be downgraded again. For the first time in 70 years, US finances are less stable and less predictable affecting increased borrowing costs and increased interest rates for people and companies.

Obama's accomplishment lists start with: Investing, Double fund, Increase funding, Significantly expand, Increase budget, Fully fund, Create fund, Expand and Fund. All of these mean the same exact thing, spend, and we are not talking about Obama's stash of money as his supporters believe. Obama is on his way to spending $5 trillion that America does not have.

Obama recently stood in front of African American leaders touting that he is trying to lay a solid economic foundation for the nation. In February 2011, Obama presented his budget plan. It went for a vote in the Senate and was unanimously rejected, even by the 57 Democrats. Obama's budget plan did not receive one vote. It called for $3.73 trillion in spending for 2012. How many people are aware of this? We have a president who does the opposite of what he says. No solid economic plan here. And his supporters will believe him when he lays the blame on those obstructionist Republicans.

Again, 2012 is an easy election decision. You either vote for Obama to continue spending tax-payer dollars and destroy our economy, or you vote for the Republican who wants less government, less spending and a free economy.

18

Is Mr. Gore a liar? by TH

November 22, 2011

Is Al Gore's man-made global warming real? Al Gore is trying to pull the sheep's wool over everyone's eyes to sell carbon coupons and get richer off the global warming scare rather than tell the truth. Could a volcano underneath the ice caps explain why they are melting? Can we trust the Democrats to tell us the truth? Can we trust the Democrats not to choose money (their own wealth), over us, the American public?

Financial Meltdown, by Kithy

November 27, 2011

I just read Trillion Dollar Meltdown by Charles Morris. He understands the recent meltdown and high finance a lot better than me. After reading this, here is my understanding: Every financial meltdown has been the result of high leverage. The new regulations post meltdown cause new unregulated products to be developed, so that over-leveraging can again occur. Apparently, there's a lot of money to be made in over-leveraging. Individuals were making $48 million a year, $52 million a year, etc. There's the incentive. For the last incident, computers and statistics came into play. The computers allow people to make money on every little discrepancy in the market. The statistics allowed people the false security of thinking they had no risk by hedging. I don't really understand hedging, but it sounds to me like placing a bet on both sides of an issue. For instance, a company was selling lots of MBS (mortgage backed securities) at the same time betting that they would default. Since they had bets on both sides, they figured they couldn't lose.

It's kind of like gun control. As soon as AK47s were banned, AK47 lookalikes were made. They were different by a small technicality, but that made them exempt from the regulations. That's how banks and investment companies get themselves into trouble over and over. They take advantage of the technicality, instead of realizing that there is a certain amount of leveraging that prevents crisis. Leveraging can be done with little risk, and the investors were assured that these were AAA investments. That's the paradox that brought our economy down. If you think you have little risk, why not invest? The investments turned out to be risky, so any amount of leverage was "over-leverage".

From the beginning, banks used to hold a percentage of capital for each loan they made. When they made enough loans for their capital, they were done lending. Then Fannie and Freddie came in, and bought the loans the banks had already made, replenishing the capital. The banks could lend to more borrowers, which was a good thing, because there were more people who wanted to borrow.

Financiers looked at this and said, hey we can make money buying the F&F loans and slicing and dicing the loans into chunks that wouldn't have any risk. I'm still not sure how the statisticians figured that they had removed the risk, but that's how they looked at it. This also worked in commercial lending. Company A could buy Company B and borrow money against Company B's balance sheet. Company A didn't need more than about 1/10 of the money it needed to purchase, because it was borrowing against the company it was purchasing. There are estimates that this lending was done at 100:1, meaning that the borrower only needed $1 for every $100 it borrowed. New money was hatched, where none existed before. I'm still researching this, because it's still over my head at this point. I'll report back later.

Insuranced to Death, by Kithy

November 27, 2011

I am sick to death of paying for insurance. I know I need it, but does it have to be so darn expensive? What happened to catastrophic insurance? The cheap stuff that only pays for exorbitant expenses that rarely occur?

I have to carry an additional car payment worth of auto insurance. Not only do I have to carry insurance on my husband and me, but the insurance companies are force placing insurance on children as soon as they get a driver's license, regardless of whether they own a car or not. My cars are free and clear junkers, yet I pay enough for a brand-new car payment and get nothing in return. I hope to get nothing in return – I don't want to have a huge accident in my family. But, for the cost of a new car?

I have to carry medical insurance, in the range of $400-1100/ month. I have been on COBRA, which is around $1100/mo. Why? Because my husband has a medical issue, and $1100/mo is what he costs whether or not we have insurance. Might as well have the additional coverage in case we need it. Lab fees and medicine and doctor visits add up. $1100/mo is just barely lower than my house payment. Really, I have to pay for a 2nd home and a car, but I don't get either of these? That's crap.

I do not know the answer to the high medical cost problem. However, I do know that we are going broke trying to keep up with his medical costs. Are we supposed to pay way more than everyone else because he has an expensive medical condition which is not his fault?

I have to carry homeowners and life insurance, both of which I think are exorbitant. My husband didn't qualify for term life, so we had to get a rated universal (read more expensive) policy. We needed it when the kids were young and we were one income. It's the responsible thing to do. But it sure is difficult to afford all the darn insurances we need.

Collective Bargaining with Government Unions

November 29, 2011

We the taxpayers have been left out of the collective bargaining with our government workers and I think it's time we take part.

Union Rep: We want raises. We want gold-plated benefits and we do not want to pay very much for them. We want to be paid for life. We also want to keep our health insurance for life and, redundant here, but we don't want to pay very much for them. Also, management would like large, one-time pay-outs upon retiring. And we still want to collect pensions for life. Base our pensions on the last year's salary, which may or may not include a large last year bonus and unused sick and vacation pay.

Taxpayer: You have got to be kidding. This is unaffordable in the long term, as opposed to Politician: All I need is your vote.

Union Rep: You will pay up because you care about police, firemen, teachers and the rest of us.

Taxpayer: I do care, but I work for a paycheck all my life and no company will continue paying me for the rest of my life when I retire. Why do you think all of us taxpayers want to pay you full wages for life? You sure have a lot of nerve. You should save your money from your paycheck like the rest of us try to do in 401Ks or mutual funds.

Union Rep: Well, we'll just tell everyone that you want to cut services in your community.

Taxpayer: We are the community and we won't fall for that line anymore.

The actual collective bargaining with public union reps is through our elected representatives. Union campaign contributions help elect these representatives. We are talking astronomical campaign donations: $85 million in 2008 by SEIU (Service Employees International Union), $96 million in 2008 by NEA (National Education Association) and AFT (American Federation of Teachers) and $87.5 million in 2010 by AFSCME (American Federation of State, County & Municipal Employees). These millions come from union member dues which are automatically deducted from their paychecks. Every single government worker's check is paid courtesy of the taxpayers. You can say that the Post Office supports itself but when taxpayer subsidies, tax breaks and legal

21

monopolies add up to $18 billion annually, I include the USPS, too. We the taxpayers are funding this scam against ourselves. Government unions should be illegal.

What's the next McDonalds' toy going to be?

November 30, 2011

The government wants McDonalds to stop selling Happy Meals because the toys make kids fat. Weird since the kids can't eat the toy. Nonetheless, San Francisco passed the Healthy Meal Incentive Ordinance which bans free toys with fast food meals effective December 1, 2011.

McDonalds wants to continue selling their popular Happy Meals with toys. To do this legally, they will offer the toy for 10 cents only with the purchase of the now toy-less Happy Meal. I love corporations and how they think.

Update on the Trillion Dollar Meltdown, by Kithy

November 30, 2011

I'm a little closer to understanding the meltdown. Here's the key to the meltdown. Financiers borrowed money against products they didn't own to bet whether or not the borrowers would pay. They invented a fantasy football type of finance. Fantasy football is bets using actual statistics, however the people who own fantasy teams have no ownership of the players on their teams. To use this in finance, people who play use the statistics of certain loans (which were subprime but can now be just about any statistic whatsoever on any product) and make bets on whether or not the borrowers will pay. The financiers do not own any of the loans, yet they borrow against them and they get insurance for the statistics they buy. They borrow money against the loans that they do not own and bet that these will pay. They also are hedged, which means they borrowed money against the loans they do not own and buy insurance on their bets. The key number that was priced incorrectly in the subprime mess was the risk involved. When the risk was underpriced, the insurance failed.

Say that I borrowed $99,900 to buy $100,000 of bets against the statistics of some subprime loans. (I didn't buy the loans; I'm just betting on the statistics.) Say that I borrowed $100 to pay for insurance to cover $100,000 of my bet on the statistics of some subprime loan. I'm covered either way, if the borrowers keep paying, or if they default. I have no risk, and a lot of profit, since I borrowed the money at a low interest rate, and the loans are paying at a higher interest rate than I borrowed against. I will never have to come up with the money that I borrowed because either way, I win. Either the borrowers will pay this, or the insurance will. I only paid $100 for the insurance because the risk was so low. The statisticians told me it was for a 2-3% default rate. But, let's say the default ended up being $30,000. My insurance company only collected $100 from me and doesn't have anywhere near $30,000 to pay up. Now, I'm on the hook for the $30,000, which I don't have, because I thought I was covered. Now, my original $100,000 of statistics is only worth $10,000 because nobody wants it. I have to pay on my loans. The insurance company defaulted because the risk was priced too low. Who could have guessed that lowering the underwriting standards on loans would cause the default rate to increase? The bets on the statistics were the synthetic CDO's (collateralized debt obligations). The insurance was the CDS's (credit default swaps).

Keep in mind that the bets that I'm talking about do not involve actual sales of products. Instead, we have added an additional $100,000 of bets that do not increase the value of anything other than money. There was not an additional $100,000 of loans being made. We increased the money supply by $100,000, without printing money. We do this over and over, and basically, we are counterfeiters. That's why we didn't have hyperinflation with the bust. There wasn't any paper money that needed to rush back into our hands. It never existed.

The statistics showed that there was no risk involved in the subprime loans. The financiers had eradicated risk on the riskiest product around. Yippee! Lots of money to be made by people who knew how to borrow large amounts of money to bet on statistics. The ratings agencies agreed with the statisticians, who said there was no risk. Oops. Someone made a mistake on the risk factor. Instead of using 30-40% for the default rate, they used 2-3%. When you're using big $ for bets, an incorrect number like that can make you go bankrupt. Oops. Just a mistake. Bail us out. You need us. I say, go bankrupt and go to jail for criminal electronic counterfeiting. Then, maybe you'll learn your lesson and stop betting money on statistics. Use money for real products that you own. Don't borrow money against someone else's assets. Only borrow against real products. Don't borrow against my balance sheet, borrow against your own. Don't buy insurance against things that you don't own. Call insurance insurance, not CDS. Call bets, not synthetic CDO's.

The term fantasy finance and the football analogy come from *The Looting of America* by Les Leopold. I loved the explanation of the problem through chapter 10, but I vehemently disagree with his solution in the following chapters. Wage controls brought us employer paid health insurance, a system which I absolutely abhor.

Energy and ANWR. Can we survive one more year of Obama?

December 1, 2011

Just when I start to see the light at the end of the tunnel, it starts flickering out. As ordinary Americans go about their days, the Obama administration is busy destroying our country. Some of us haven't felt it yet because we still have jobs and the gas price is the lowest in recent years. But this administration is after power and control of our lives and the money that comes with it.

One of the most powerful agencies in Obama's hands is the EPA (Environmental Protection Agency). This agency, designed to protect us from pollution, is now 17,000 employees working towards destroying our energy producers. Expensive regulations are being forced on our coal industry which supplies half of our energy. Obama personally threatened to bankrupt the entire coal industry. Nuclear industry supplies 20% of our energy with 104 nuclear reactors in 31 states and is now stifled with red tape and regulations. The solar and wind industries power less than 2% of our energy and being propped up with billions of tax dollars.

And then we have oil and gas. Obama recently delayed the Keystone XL Pipeline that would send Canadian crude to the Gulf Coast refineries. The EPA has requested more studies to protect us and mentioned global warming as an excuse. The United States already has 168,000 miles of pipelines that work 24 hours a day and doing just fine. Obama initiated a moratorium on Gulf Coast offshore drilling. After Obama was ordered by a judge to end the moratorium, the EPA stood in and halted drilling by refusing to issue permits, adding restrictions and regulatory changes. Obama objected to Alaskan drilling in ANWR (Arctic National Wildlife Refuge) and used environmental issues as his reason. The proposed development is 2000 acres, or 3.13 square miles, in the northeast coast of Alaska. It is a barren refuge teeming with animals that would not be disrupted in any capacity. The nearby Prudhoe Bay area accounts for 17% of US domestic oil production.

When Republicans talk about energy independence, they mean it, and the jobs come with it, along with the improvement of our economy. When Obama says he wants energy independence, he's lying. He is destroying our energy production through the EPA, and with the turmoil in the Mideast, he is setting the United States up for disaster. Can we survive one more year of Obama?

Fire Obama with his Volts and Occupoopers

December 2, 2011

Voters were persuaded by Obama's smile, his smooth teleprompter reading and his slogan of hope and change. These were the same voters who listened to liberals for close to eight years telling them how awful George Bush was. Sure enough, when asked why they voted for Obama, they regurgitated how awful George Bush was. I have had enough of the Obama administration. Although Obama deserves to be impeached on Fast and Furious gunrunning alone, I'm more concerned with how terrible a job Obama is doing day-to-day. I would like to plain fire him right now.

Everyday something more awful is reported than the day before. With Obama facing a possible one term, I think more and more outright thievery will be occurring. Doling out the so-called Stimulus (trillion dollars of taxpayer money) to his friends is thievery. Obama has been using this stimulus money as his personal slush fund and still has billions to give away.

I've heard my friends say they like his green ideas. What Obama has done and continues to do is borrow money that the United States does not have to fund his green pet projects. These are terrible investments that individuals refuse to invest with their own money. However, his top donor bundler George Kaiser and Al Gore each received over half a billion taxpayer dollars for their green projects.

A one-word reason to fire Obama is Volt. GM (General Motors) was bankrupt but Obama wanted it, bought it with $50 billion taxpayer dollars, and now we the taxpayers are subsidizing a loser green car. We are paying to build a $41,000 priced car that has a $10,000 battery, goes about 35 miles on a charge and needs premium fuel to continue. Of the 6,000 Volts sold with taxpayers funding the $7,500 tax credit per car, hundreds were purchased as fleet cars for government agencies. We pay again and have a 2012 goal of producing 50,000 more! The absolute worst is that the batteries catch fire after crash tests so GM (remember, owned by us the taxpayers) has offered to buy back all 6,000 Volts. To put us at ease, GM claims that they will be repaired once they figure out what causes the fires.

Obama should also be fired just on the fact that he claimed to stand with the Occupiers, more recently nicknamed the Occupoopers. Their little encampments are being de-occupied and sanitation workers are coming in and sweeping away the excrement. At least the sanitation workers have a job to do and will receive paychecks for it. Imagine these Occupoopers' next move, interviewing for entry level jobs. How can they justify dissing big, evil corporations for months? They didn't even leave the parks green.

25

Obamacare Must Die, by Tbird

December 2, 2011

The Senate passed its version of Obamacare on Christmas Eve 2009 with a 60-39 vote. In March 2010, the House passed the Senate version 219-212. Not a single Republican voted for it. Parts of Obamacare are already in effect, such as covering children up to age 26 even if they are married, and the rest of it is supposed to go into effect in 2014. We can't let it.

Our health care is the best in the world, but it is expensive. Americans make more important health-related discoveries, invent more drugs, come up with new and better surgical techniques, and have better cancer cure rates than any other country. That will all change when Obamacare makes it even more expensive.

We were promised that healthcare costs would slow down significantly and that we could keep our own health plans and doctors. Then again, we were also told we had to pass the bill to find out what was in it, as at 2700 pages (I have seen 2000 to 3000 pages estimated) it was too long for any one person to read in the short time before the House vote. Betsy McCaughey, former lieutenant governor of New York, did go through the monstrosity, and she found all sorts of nasty things in it. I tried, but I gave up when so many different parts in just the first few pages referred to other bills that weren't available for me to read. Michele Bachmann found a $100 million slush fund embedded in the bill to get the ball rolling—bills are not supposed to include funding mechanisms.

The House vote was very close. Many of the Representatives knew it was a bad, bad bill and intended to vote against it. Enough Democrats allowed themselves to be bribed that the bill passed anyway. Bart Stupak was one of twelve pro-life Democrats who at first resisted; seven of them caved when Obama told them that abortion coverage would not be part of the bill by promising to issue an executive order saying so; he knew that an executive order can't change a law. It came out later that Stupak had accepted $700,000 in grants for three airports in his district. Do you remember the Cornhusker Kickback ($100 million to help Nebraska with expanded Medicaid), the Louisiana Purchase ($300 million), the Connecticut Hospital ($100 million to build a hospital)? How about $600 million each to Massachusetts and Vermont to help with Medicaid?

The Obamacare law is all about government control of Americans and their healthcare. John Dingell (D-NY) said the healthcare law will control the people. Slip of the tongue? No. The law mandates that everyone must buy health insurance and that those who don't will have to pay a fine, up to 2.5% of their income; 16,000 IRS agents will be hired to enforce the fines. It grants the Department of Health and Human Services (HHS) the authority to set and periodically revise essential health benefits. Kathleen Sebelius is the Secretary, and she and other unelected federal officials get to decide what benefits all insurance companies and health plans must offer. She is considering suggestions, among them, plastic surgery, chiropractic, and acupuncture. She chooses the winners and losers. The law creates 159 new federal agencies. It requires mental health coverage without financial incentives or treatment limitations. Plans will have to cover so many new things, and they can use reasonable medical management techniques to determine details, but if a patient disputes his treatment and wins, the plan can be heavily fined for not complying with the extremely comprehensive but at the same time vague rules.

The law tells insurance companies they must pay out 80 to 85% of the premiums they collect in claims (this is the medical loss ratio), 85% for large group policies and 80% for individual and small group policies. The remaining 15-20% is spent on administrative costs, such as commissions, salaries and advertising. Individual and small group policies typically pay out 55-75%, and large ones 70-90% or so due to economies of scale, and the profit margin is just 2.2%. The smaller percentage ordered by Obamacare must also cover the newly mandated preventive care such as colonoscopies and birth control pills and morning-after pills, for which insurance companies cannot charge any co-pays or deductibles. Yes, we must pay for other people's birth control pills. Obviously, many insurance companies will be put out of business, for they are not allowed to raise their rates to cover the new costs. Many of them have already dropped all individual child policies because they cannot not cover children with pre-existing conditions. Smaller insurance companies cannot compete with larger companies, so many smaller group policies are being rescinded and the smaller companies are leaving. If the purpose of Obamacare is to drive private insurance companies out of business (if?), it is succeeding. Obama has said that he wants a government-run health system (single-payer) but that since he can't get it yet, he'll just get private insurers to get themselves out of the way.

Once the law was passed, Obama granted 1800 waivers to organizations so they wouldn't have to abide by onerous regulations and go out of business. 50% were given to unions, including SEIU, which had campaigned for Obamacare and resisted any efforts to repeal it. Senate Majority Leader Harry Reid got his state exempted. Speaker of the House Nancy Pelosi got 20% of the waivers issued in April for luxury businesses in her district. Large corporations such as McDonald's and Jack in the Box got waivers; they said otherwise they'd have to drop the health care they already offered their employees. Health care companies such as AARP, who campaigned for Obamacare, got a waiver. Walmart, which was recently denied a waiver (after all, this evil corporation isn't unionized), says it will have to rescind healthcare coverage for part-timers and raise the rates on full-timers.

To help pay for Obamacare, the government took over the student loan business. My son, who is a recent college graduate and newly employed, gets to repay his loans with an interest rate twice that of today's mortgages and car loans. It also

27

takes $500 million out of Medicare (old folks) to cover, instead, new people added to Medicaid (poor folks). Medicare reimbursement rates are already so low that a lot of doctors dropped their Medicare patients or limit the number they treat. Smoke and mirrors, anyone?

The CLASS Act was made part of the Obamacare law despite warnings in emails released by congressional investigators that it would require either sizeable federal bailout or mandates, as it was unsustainable. Its purpose is to fund long term nursing home care with a minimum $50 per day coverage. It is voluntary, and participants are likely to be disabled, part-time workers and those expecting to need nursing home care. To be sustainable, there would need to be 234 million enrollees (more than our entire workforce) in order to be funded with contributors' premiums. The CBO, using just information handed to it by Congress, said the CLASS Act would help pay for Obamacare because for the first six years, premiums would be collected but no benefits would be paid out. HHS Secretary Sebelius effectively killed the CLASS Act by reassigning or letting go all its staffers. She says they are still analyzing it. To be on the safe side, Congress needs to repeal the CLASS Act now. Actually, to make sure the CLASS Act and the entire Obamacare law is not merely dead but really most sincerely dead (to paraphrase the coroner in The Wizard of Oz), Congress must repeal it in its entirety.

We need a new president and a Congress that will protect us from government intrusion into our healthcare, since our current Democrat president and democratic Senate won't.

Thanks, Herman for 9-9-9! by Tbird

December 6, 2011

Herman Cain effectively dropped out of the Republican presidential primary this weekend. All the allegations of sexual harassment and infidelities did him in, whether there is any truth in them or not. I liked Cain, but I never thought he was quite ready for prime time. He had lots of private sector experience but very little government experience other than a stint at the Federal Reserve. He seems like a happy, positive man, and I hope those allegations do not destroy his private life.

Regardless of Cain's chances, he helped the field of prospective nominees by boldly putting forth a straightforward, simple plan to fix the tax code, which encouraged them to do the same. Our current horrendous tax code grew from 9000 pages in 1947 to over 72,000 today. Cain's 9-9-9 plan called for a 9% rate for individuals and businesses and a national 9% sales tax; he would get rid of all or most deductions. He would then eventually move to a consumption tax and get rid of the income taxes altogether. We would pay tax on what we buy, not on how much we make. That incentivizes savings, which right now are woefully small. Simple and bold, but not easy.

Once Cain came out with his 9-9-9 plan, most of the other candidates also came out with simplified tax plans, mostly involving a relatively flat tax. Why should one person pay a higher rate on his income than another pays on his, when the person with more income already pays more tax anyway? Perry's plan calls for a 20% flat tax on individual and corporate income, dumps all corporate deductions and most individual deductions, and puts no tax on capital gains, dividends, and interest income. Gingrich's plan calls for a 15% individual rate and a 12.5% corporate rate, but he keeps most deductions. Romney's timid plan keeps things pretty much the same with a little tweaking, though he does lower the corporate rate to 25%.

The Republican presidential contenders are all talking about simplifying our horrible tax code, and that is a big first step. Thanks, Herman.

Born in the USA, by SH

December 10, 2011

I'm so glad I was born in the United States. I'm still enjoying my day from yesterday. I went to the Old Cathedral in downtown St. Louis for mass (it was a Holy Day of obligation for Catholics). The church was built in the 1830s and is just a really pretty church down on the riverfront. Now I realize that how a church looks is not important (the people make up a church) but it just really hit me how beautiful the Old Cathedral is and how beautiful the United States is. I had dozens of choices for mass yesterday (St. Louis is a pretty Catholic town), but there are tons of different churches/religions around St. Louis and throughout the United States. I can't imagine living in a country where one risks his/her life to practice one's religion. So, especially with Christmas headed our way, enjoy your freedom of religion. For any atheists out there, you might want to visit some churches just for the history, architecture, etc. And if you start believing in God, that's a bonus for you!

Obama's Latest Speech of Lies

December 10, 2011

President Obama recently gave a campaign speech in Kansas stating that limited government has never worked and that we should want a more activist government. To preserve the middle class, we need more taxes, more spending and more regulations.

He also claimed that all of America's problems are due to the rich. Obama's only solution is to tax the rich more. He wants to transfer money from private citizens who earned it to the government. It won't come close to covering the $15 trillion debt. This year's deficit alone is $1.3 trillion. The rich tax would have brought this down to $1.22 trillion. Obama doesn't believe this class warfare rhetoric, but it works really well on the poor.

While rubbing shoulders at his fundraising event with New York's elite, Obama recently stated, "Our kids are going to be fine ... even if the country as a whole is not successful." He's right. The elites' kids will be fine with their piles of money. The elites know that this inequality talk doesn't pertain to them. As for the rest of his quote, what kind of a president of the United States contemplates our country failing? His job is to make sure this does not happen. However, if you are a Marxist, you relish it.

In 2008, Argentina seized individual retirement accounts to raise cash to cover its debts. Back in the 1990's, Hillary wrote up her government-run healthcare plan and proposed to pay for it with a one-time 15% tax on personal IRAs and 401Ks. Anyone who saved money for retirement, Hillary was going to take 15%. Obama has proposed converting personal IRAs and 401Ks to annuities to pay down Treasury debt. One would basically receive a promise of later returns with a government-run investment plan. This directly affects the middle class. If Obama gets another four years, your savings will not be yours. They will belong to the government.

Republican Primary Debate on ABC, by Kithy

December 12, 2011

I hated the ABC TV debate this weekend because I can't stand the moderators or the post-debate reviewer they chose. The moderators are the lefties who picked questions like "were you ever poor?" Instead of focusing on some meaty substance, they latched onto an innocuous comment about a bet. Both have nothing to do with the issues, but they met one of their main objectives: make Romney look like a loser. I have never liked Romney, but I certainly don't want the lefties to make the choice for me. He will lose votes if he maintains consistency with their image of him as out of touch, as they will crucify him for any comments that fit with that image now. That's their version of Mitt.

I think it was good to bring up character, and that is a real issue that needs to be considered. I liked Bachmann's response that the founders considered it the most important virtue in a politician. I liked the way Gingrich responded, short and sweet, essentially: I have made mistakes and learned from them. He has stated his viewpoint previously, immediately get rid of Obamacare and the new finance law, which I wholeheartedly agree with, and I believe he would pursue that, and get it done. His viewpoints are in line with mine. If he is the strongest politician, as in will get things that I want done, maybe he is the right choice. Bachmann has the same idea, but I don't believe as strongly that she can get it done.

I suppose the difference between Cain and Gingrich, in the character department, is that Gingrich's discrepancies were in the past, and Cain's were alleged to be ongoing. Cain couldn't say he learned from his mistakes, if the media brought out a current event that he hasn't presented to his wife yet. I liked Cain, but he bowed out when the media was relentless on him. I wonder what advice Sarah Palin would have been able to give him.

I think that because we have debates, and Gingrich is good at them, he is on top. If, instead, we were to see essays or single one-hour interviews with each candidate, Santorum may be on top. Santorum has the conservative viewpoint, and has the character, but he does not have stage presence in a debate setting. I have heard that if Abe Lincoln was on TV, he never would have won the presidency. He looked and sounded unintelligent. I do not think stage presence should be the main reason to choose a candidate. On the other hand, with TV so prevalent, I would hate to have to see a whiner on the TV every day. Not calling Santorum a whiner, but he has that defensive voice he uses in the debates.

Oh yeah, and the President was on TV today saying that the free market does not work and never has. I guess he's rooting for communism instead? Please tell me that the leftie TV media is listening to him, and that they know their jobs are over if he remains in office. The un-free market has no place for a free press.

Republican Primary Election Time

December 14, 2011

Political commentator Glenn Beck is trying to discourage us from voting for Newt Gingrich. Newt has said things in the past that are questionable. But haven't we all? If we required all the relevant information before we spoke our thoughts, surely we would never speak again. I'm sure Newt will explain his liking Andy Stern comment. Conservatives cringed when they saw Newt on the couch with Democrat Speaker of the House Nancy Pelosi. Sorry, but I like Newt. I like that he can communicate his original thoughts. I always learn something from listening to him. A huge positive is that the teleprompter along with the head moving back and forth will become obsolete in a Newt presidency. Google Obama without his teleprompter and what you'll hear is painful to listen to unless you really like uh, uh, uhs and stuttering.

Here are some ideas for the Left to disparage my Newt. Of course, if these are used, they will backfire on our Lefty friends. Newt is fat. Newt is rich and has

31

rich in his name. He even wants young children to learn the value of the dollar and of work. Stop the presses! The Left will continue to attack Republican candidates, some may have a grain of truth, but most will be blatant lies. Maybe we should stop listening to what has formerly been known as the mass media.

America is tired of the Destroy the Competition elections. Let Obama win or lose on his record. This time the Republican candidate, hopefully Newt, will tell us like it is, even the truth about Obama. This is the election that I want. Unfortunately, I recall when Obama was elected, my trusty confidante stated that this (2008) would be our last presidential election. A Marxist, once in power in the United States, will not let it go. Let's hope that statement was overly pessimistic.

My Crystal Ball, by Tbird

December 14, 2011

I asked my crystal ball who will be the Republican nominee for President in 2012. It was really foggy, but I could see some lights floating around.

Huntsman winked out, and I couldn't find him again. Paul keeps flaring up, but he goes black just as fast; I like his strict constructionist views, but his Why Can't They All Just Get Along foreign policy is something I cannot support because it is dangerous. Bachman and Santorum are bright but very small, and I don't see them getting enough traction to win, although either one would be a very competent commander-in-chief. Perry was almost ashes, but he throws out some sparks; I hope he can catch fire and make a comeback, but chances are small. Romney and Gingrich are chasing each other around, but Romney's light hasn't grown any at all since the beginning; unless he can completely disavow Massachusetts healthcare, Romneycare, and do it convincingly, I can't get behind him (although I would hold my nose and vote for him against Obama). Gingrich grows brighter and bigger and just may overtake everyone else as long as he doesn't crash and burn; he's got lots of baggage, but he's forceful enough to stand up for a lot of my conservative views and not back down.

My crystal ball is not crystal-clear right now, but so far, within the fog, it seems to show Gingrich as the leader. I'll check it again once in a while.

Is "Party of No" supposed to be an insult? by Kithy

December 22, 2011

The left keeps harping on Republicans as the party of no. I am proud to be a part of the party of no. I do not see it as an insult. I am proud to say no to the health insurance debacle now taking place due to Obamacare.

I am proud to say no to a two-month budget fix from Congress. What's that about? How on earth can Congress take so long to make a decision that covers such a short time frame? It reminds me of my daughter whining for hours and then taking 10 minutes to do the chore she's been whining about. I say no to expanding abortions. I say no to the Frank Dodd financial fiasco (I think they called it reform). I say no to the socialization of the United States. I say no to spending money the United States does not have and raising our debt another five trillion.

What disturbs me are the judges who say no to a guaranteed Constitutional right to free speech when it refers to Christianity, specifically telling congressmen not to say Merry Christmas in emails. No blaming this on Conservative judges or the Tea Party. Democrats also say no to long term solutions and no to interstate insurance competition. It was Obama who said no to Canadian oil and the jobs that go with the pipeline. Both parties have earned the name 'Party of No.' It is not an insult to me. Have yourselves a very Merry Christmas.

JANUARY 2012

Get Rid of Dodd-Frank, by Kithy

January 2, 2012

I read an article today about Verizon trying to charge customers $2 for every online or telephone payment, but no fee for e-checks. E-checks are cheaper because Dodd-Frank does not apply to e-checks. Dodd-Frank applies to ATM and debit fees. I didn't even know what an e-check was, but yesterday I filed my property tax online and I would have had to pay $5.75 to use my debit card, or $2.75 for an e-check. Technically, there is very little difference between an e-check and a debit card, but I have to give out my bank account # for an e-check. I'd rather use my debit card, but I was not happy about the higher fee. Apparently, the technical difference is enough to make it not an ATM or a debit that is regulated. Thanks, Congress for making payments inconvenient!

Should we just go back to cash, and carry around sacks of change? Here's the deal. Congress passed Dodd-Frank, and in their great wisdom threw in some regulations on ATM/debit card fees, to rescue we the people from greedy banks.

33

I would think this is unconstitutional, because Congress does not have the right to dictate to any business how much it can charge for any item or service. If they have that right, they shouldn't have it. That is central planning, and our government is not supposed to be a central planning unit. We have the free market to decide what the right price is to pay. Banks were making a ton of money on fees, and someone (Obama) saw the dollar signs, and turned green with envy, and made sure he could take their GREEDY PROFIT away from them. Well, in general, if someone's making a lot of money (think Bill Gates), it's because he's providing something that people are willing to pay for. Banks provided us with a convenient way to pay, and we were willing to pay it. With so many banks competing for our debit fees, we had a pretty good thing going. The fees were lower than they are now- $1.25 vs $5.75. We were able to pull out a card, pay for something and be on our happy ways. Now, we cannot pull out these cards, because they are not profitable. The banks have found a way to get around the new fees, obviously, by making us use e-checks. Throw away your debit cards and pull out your checkbooks again. When the e-checks get regulated, throw away your checkbook, because we are headed back to cash! Help! Save me from Congress! Get rid of the liberals and get rid of Dodd-Frank!

Resolutions for 2012

January 2, 2012

If you write your resolutions down, they are more likely to come true. Here are mine: 1) help elect a conservative president, 2) help elect a conservative president and 3) help elect a conservative president. Obviously, I like to improve my odds. See, I don't want Obama as president and I surely don't want to see him ping-ponging his head back and forth reading a speech anymore. Even when he says the right thing, it isn't heartfelt and he believes the opposite of what he prompter-reads, especially when referring to his hard work for the middle class. When the opposite happens as he wanted, he blames those darn Republicans. If you have browsed my past articles, you know that I think Obama is a communist and wants to transform the United States into a third world. As president, he has that power through inflation.

The following three causes of inflation will sound very familiar: government prints too many dollar bills, production costs rise – i.e. gas prices, increased international lending and national debts, and dealing with interest. The unanswered question is how much inflation will occur due to Obama. The higher the inflation imposed upon us, the more the middle class gets wiped out, savings and all.

Despite this information, I have high hopes for the United States. Obama is making a fatal error in his ideology calculations – he underestimates the people of the United States. We will fight for our freedoms and way of life. And we do

34

it peacefully through voting. That's what the Tea Party has been all about. Bring on 2012 and good luck, Rick Santorum.

Conservatives on Conservation, by Kithy

January 17, 2012

My friend argued that conservatives should not alienate the greenies, because regardless of our opinion on global warming, we should be accountable for the resources we are using. Here's the problem with that.

We already know that we are accountable and should take care of mother earth, but we don't think we should have to tell you exactly what we are doing. We are not keeping score, like the greenies. According to greenies, we have to recycle our trash in recycle bins separately from our other litter. We have to use water bottles. Oops, that one changed, bad plastic! We have to bring in processed food for our kids for birthdays at schools because of germs. Etc. Well, I'd rather pass clothes from one kid to the next until they are totally worn out. I'd like to pass the clothes they don't wear onto someone who will through Goodwill. I'd like to serve leftovers. I like to garage sale. I compost. I use laundry lint as fire starter. I save jars and use them to store food.

There are certain things that people have been doing forever that are foreign to greenies and don't count in the greenie scorekeeper's guide but are far greener than what the greenies suggest. How is having several trucks going through my neighborhood (one for regular trash, one for recyclables) and all the gasoline and emissions involved supposed to be green? Not to mention the effort it takes to separate trash and clean it and then send it somewhere where it will pile up as mountains of trash instead of filling a landfill.

MLK Would Not Approve of Obama

January 17, 2012

It's Martin Luther King, Jr. Day, 2012, and the running joke told by a famous black comedian goes something like this: If you find yourself on Martin Luther King Blvd., Any City, USA, Run! Inner city MLK Boulevards are known for violence. This past week in New Orleans, 15 people were shot within a 24-hour period, all black on black crime.

The United States is celebrating Martin Luther King, Jr. because he stood for non-violence and for judging someone not on the color of one's skin but on the content of one's character. I don't see the point of celebrating when the black community doesn't follow his ideals. It's almost like they don't deserve

35

ownership of MLK. The violent crime is undeniable in the black community and the election of Obama showed us just how important skin color is.

When Barack Obama was elected president, pictures on TV panned over black people bawling their eyes out. It was all about the color of his skin. If they had truly listened to his words, blacks should have come out in numbers to vote against him. Instead, Obama received approximately 96% of the black vote. This is a man who voted to deny medical care to infants who survived abortion. According to Obama, breathing, living babies should not get care from a doctor because they were meant to die. Skin color trumps this slaughter? Obama also supports $10 per gallon gasoline. His reasoning is that we would drive less because we would not be able to afford it. That should have been the major reason NOT to vote for him.

As blacks were celebrating Obama's election, I know plenty of people who were crying over the real newly elected president, a communist community organizer who has no respect for the people of the United States of America. Who can forget what he said five days before being elected, "We are five days away from fundamentally transforming the USA?" What is fundamentally unique for all the citizens of the USA is our Constitution. The oath of the office of president is clear: "I do solemnly swear (or affirm) that I will faithfully execute the office of President of the United States, and will to the best of my ability, preserve, protect and defend the Constitution of the United States."

If a community organizer came forward with the backing of unlimited funding such as a George Soros to fundamentally change the USA to a communist country, our president would protect us by stopping this. When that community organizer is our president and he is ignoring our Constitution with seemingly innocent platitudes of hope and change, who is left to protect our basic rights?

Addiction to Politics

January 19, 2012

I admit to a problem. I have evolved into a political junky. I used to post political articles on my Facebook page, but no one seemed interested except for a liberal union retiree. We didn't agree much. As a matter of fact, I lost those Facebook friends who only like fluff like recipes and cute animals. I need an outlet and that's why I started blogging on my own website. Ironically, I did not promote it because my husband's job was in New Orleans, you know, a Chocolate City as described by the mayor after Katrina. If you are against Obama policies, everyone knows that means you're a racist.

I watch Fox News' O'Reilly, Hannity and Greta most nights and I listen to Rush during the day. And, yes, I do fit in some housework, PTA president duties, assisting my golf pro husband and my chauffeuring duties. My DVR records my non-guilty pleasure shows. *Revenge* is good. Politics will come up among friends and I find many are just not into it. The main reason is that they think the politicians are a bunch of jokers and liars. So, these are middle-class, smart people and they don't care what's going on politically. I am envious of them because I am unable to turn off my brain politically. The irony is that we should not have to worry about what our politicians are doing. They are supposed to have our best interests at heart and let us just live our lives in peace. With what I have learned about Obama and his administration, I can't do that.

Everyday something in the news changes the game. For instance, today Obama rejected Canadian oil. He said no to the Keystone Pipeline. His EPA is working on regulations that will close coal mines. Obama is succeeding on this campaign promise – electricity and energy rates will necessarily skyrocket. I hate to say this, but the people who did not listen nor care what their presidential candidate said have no room to complain when our electricity bills rise and when they drive up to the pump and see $5.00 plus gallon of gas.

One of my daughter's science teachers told her class that she voted for Obama because she liked his energy policy ideas on wind and solar. She should realize that wind and solar will not run her car any time in the near future nor run her air conditioning this summer. It will continue to be the coal and gasoline that her president promised the costs would necessarily skyrocket under his plan. Imagine if our president believed in energy independence and approved Keystone, drilling in the gulf and shale fracturing on federal lands.

The election is shaping up and soon Republicans will have their candidate. May the truth about Obama come to light for enough Americans to say no thanks to his Hope and Change, Yes We Can and Change We Can Believe In slogans. Wonder if my union retiree friend will see the light. I already know the answer to that one. Not in this lifetime.

Republican Primary Debates with Newt

January 19, 2012

I like debates with Newt. He says what I want to hear, no politically correct talk, no coddling the poor, no bowing to liberals, and no sugar-coating. As candidate, he wants to debate Obama seven times – even allowing Obama to bring his teleprompter! Too funny. We already suspect he has the questions beforehand. Obama would not agree to this so Newt already has plans to follow Obama on the campaign trail just as Lincoln did to Douglas. Wherever Obama goes on his campaign speech, Newt will be right on his heels and refute Obama's words directly to the TV cameras.

Obama will not win this next campaign on slogans and big, perfect teeth smiles. Nope, Newt wants to challenge his record. Maybe independents will listen this time and really hear the difference between a radical liberal and a conservative. At Saturday's debate, Newt expanded on hiring kids as janitors. My liberal friends laughed earlier at this as hiring kids for hard labor. With Newt, the facts come out. A New York union janitor's salary could employ over thirty kids with part-time jobs within a school – light janitorial, in the cafeteria, front office and library. Newt had to remind Juan Williams that poor kids would like to make money. This work isn't demeaning. It's work that not only pays money but teaches a work ethic and builds a resume.

This Saturday is South Carolina's primary. If Mitt Romney wins and follows this with a win in Florida, Romney will be the Republican candidate. Again, Newt is right. If the conservative vote is split among Santorum, Perry and himself, it is a vote for Romney. We need to continue hearing Newt.

Savings in Obamacare

January 20, 2012

We were told by Speaker Nancy Pelosi that we had to pass Obamacare to find out what was in it. It's the same as if she said that they had to pass Obamacare BEFORE we find out what is in it. If we knew what was in it, it would have NEVER passed. Then again, they did not have the votes to pass this until hundreds of thousands of dollars were promised to Nebraska, Louisiana, and Vermont politicians.

Here is a major savings point in Obamacare. Neurosurgery will be denied to patients over 70 years old. Ethics panels comprised of administrators will tell neurosurgeons that their patients will be approved for comfort care. See the savings? A 71-year-old with a bleed out or stroke will be denied life-saving surgery but will be given a pill like presidential candidate Obama proposed. In other words, we will have Obama to thank for killing our parents and elderly for the greater good of saving money. Thank you, Mr. President. I thought those old people would hang around for another 20 or 30 years using OUR healthcare!

GOP Debate Primaries, by Kithy

January 23, 2012

So, Newt won yesterday. I'm glad that it wasn't Mitt, because I don't much care for him. But between Newt, who is a good debater with questionable morals, or Rick, with a strong moral record, I'd pick Rick. It seems to me that we want someone who we can trust, first and foremost. What I'd like to see is Rick as the nominee, and Newt as his press secretary. If Newt wins the nomination, he'll need to have a strong moral compass for his second in command. Anyway, I'm pretty sure that we'll find out in Florida some of Newt's lesser qualities. It's the nature of the game - attack the leader.

Free Contraceptives

January 24, 2012

Obama is giving everyone free contraceptives! How progressive! But, before we celebrate, why exactly are we paying for everyone's contraceptives? Free isn't free. We all know that, well, not the Millennials; they love this! Someone is paying and that someone is the American taxpayer. I learned in marketing that it is all in the wording. Try this one on. Obama is forcing every business and American taxpayer to fund contraceptives for whoever wants them.

I personally do not want to pay for my neighbors' and strangers' contraceptives. The Catholic Church agrees. They not only do not want to, but they condemn artificial contraception. The Obama administration will not exempt Catholic churches or hospitals. Catholic hospitals will also be required to perform abortions. They would close their doors rather than be forced to do this.

When conservatives talk about losing our liberties, this is a clear-cut case. Your freedom whether to support something or not will be over if Obamacare is fully implemented. It is a government directive – no choice! We have been teased by "helping the children". Twenty-six-year-old children (or rather adults), married or not, can stay on their parents' policy. Newt took a swipe at this by saying he would help 26-year-olds get jobs so they can buy their own.

Obamacare will be the basis for full government control over our healthcare. As an option, Obama promised that we can keep our own insurance. When these insurance companies are forced to close due to paying for all the free stuff, we will not have this option. In the future, when your loved one is told by a doctor that he or she requires surgery and it is not your decision but a bureaucrat's, remember the 2012 election and how you voted. A vote for Obama is a vote to take your liberty over your healthcare away from you.

Nun Sense Politics, by SH

January 24, 2012

Discussing politics in an inquisitive, calm manner can be quite the eye opener. I asked a Catholic nun the other day if the other nuns she knew voted predominantly Democrat or Republican. She replied that they definitely vote

Democrat. I asked about the abortion issue and she stated that they thought the Democrat's overall view on social justice was more important. Really?! I know people who are not religious who will vote for a candidate just because they are pro-abortion. They don't care about any of the other views that candidate may have. And yet, here are some devout religious ladies who will overlook the killing of babies because their view is that the means justify the end.

When I mentioned that Obama's views on abortion were so extreme, she did state that some nuns will vote based on the man (the individual candidate). She wouldn't go so far as to state that some nuns vote Republican. Those mean, rich Republicans couldn't possibly love your neighbor as yourself was my impression that they believed.

Everybody is entitled to an opinion. I personally think the federal government's most important jobs are national security and to protect and defend the Constitution. I think the government should help the people in times of need to an extent. I think it is much more important to have a country that allows opportunities and freedom for people to succeed in their endeavors, whether that's becoming a successful businessman providing hundreds/thousands of jobs or a person devoting his/her life to his/her religion. I think it is much more important to teach a person to fish than to dole out fish at the taxpayers' expense for life. I think very few things in life should be free – how many times have you taken something because it was free but didn't end up using it or even threw it away? I believe social justice is something people need to participate in…from their hearts and not because government decides which endeavors should be considered social justice and enforced as such.

Having said that, I believe in social security disability for those individuals who are physically and/or mentally unable to provide for themselves. I believe in an America where people can make money and do with it what they want after paying realistic taxes. As Mitt Romney's tax returns were released last night, I know some people will be outraged that he had so much income. Hey, he paid taxes on it and he gave roughly 16 percent of his income to charity. If he was taxed at 100 percent, along with all the other super wealthy folk, it won't get the US out of debt. Spending is out of control! Lastly, I believe in Americans' freedom to vote for whoever they believe in … however wrong they may be!

FEBRUARY 2012

My Crystal Ball, by Tbird

February 5, 2012

My crystal ball says Newt drops out soon, Romney stays as does Paul, and Santorum keeps trudging along until he wins. I hope so.

Today are the Nevada caucuses. Newt says he will hold a press conference this evening. I think he will either drop out tonight or drop out after the next contest, which is Tuesday. My state of Missouri is holding a primary Tuesday, but no delegates will be assigned because we defied the establishment Republicans and held it earlier than they wanted us to. We usually get to hold our primary after the clear winner has already been determined. Ha. We told them. Actually, on March 17, Missouri will hold caucuses and pick our delegates then. I got a call from a pollster yesterday who asked me who I intended to vote for on Tuesday, and when I replied Santorum, she laughed happily and said everyone she had talked to so far said the same. Today, I saw a Rasmussen poll that shows Santorum beating Obama 45 to 44. The Democrats are sending out their minions to vote for Santorum figuring he is such a homophobe that he will handily lose to Obama; I guess they didn't see the latest poll.

I am more and more disgusted with Romney, the chosen one. He won Florida's primary last Saturday after outspending Newt something like 15 to 1 (big surprise). The next things I heard him say were that he wasn't concerned with the really poor (because there are welfare safety nets, which have infantilized many of them into thinking they can never support themselves and their families so they don't even bother trying—not a conservative position!) and that he thinks the minimum wage should be indexed for inflation (Missouri tried that a few years ago, but it was overturned when it came out that teenagers were losing work hours after the first increase and others couldn't get that first job—also, not conservative!). Romney is a mushy moderate who can't speak conservative because that's not who he is; his instincts are all wrong.

Newt was best described in a recent Jonah Goldberg article. Goldberg said Romney, if he became president, would know that he was on a very short leash and would do as he promised. Newt, however, would chew through his leash in ten minutes flat and who knows where he'd head next. I never thought Newt had the right temperament to be president, although he articulates our views fantastically at times. Ron Paul won't drop out because he knows he won't win anyway. He's an old man having fun on the campaign trail. I like his views on constitutional government where the government does only what it is mandated to do by the Constitution and nothing else, but his "why can't everyone get along" foreign policy is the deal breaker.

True Separation of Church and State

February 8, 2012

The true meaning of Separation of Church and State is that the state cannot dictate to a religious entity on doctrine. Government can make no law establishing a religion nor prohibit the freedom of exercising one's religion. Here comes a seemingly innocent law bestowed upon the American people, the

Patient Protection and Affordable Care Act. For our own good, liberals have decided that everyone should fund abortions, sterilizations, contraceptives and abortion pills. Everyone does exclude certain entities who received waivers, mostly because of the added expense of Obamacare. Look up who received waivers and you'll find plenty in Nancy 'you have to pass this bill to find out what is in it' Pelosi's district and Obama union supporters. The Catholic Church asked for waivers because of its religious beliefs and was denied. I imagine if Muslims asked for waivers on the same ground that they would be granted.

Everyone's hair on the back of the neck should be sending off signals that something very bad is happening through Obamacare. Like I told a liberal friend who complained about taking Christ out of Christmas, you can't blame this one on the Tea Party or conservatives. His reply was that true Democrats don't believe that. Well, my friend, it IS your party that wants to take Christ out of Christmas and deny religious rights. By standing with your liberal party-mates, you, too, are guilty of trampling on the first amendment, the right to freedom of religion and freedom of expression from government interference.

Proof of Global Warming Lie

February 9, 2012

Embarrassingly, the global warming experts now state that the official United Nations forecasts on the severity of climate change are overstated and supported by weak science. In other words, the facts prove that global warming is not happening. That's right, global warming really is just a manufactured fear. How many experts must come forward to claim that man-made global warming is and will always be a lie, one of the biggest scams perpetuated on the public?

Winter started out warm and the newsmakers beat the global warming drum to death. Now that January has ended and February has begun with winter setting in, the drum is silenced. Did the media report the incredible amounts of snow that have fallen in Alaska, the record heights of snow in Japan and Rome's biggest snowfall in 26 years? No chance.

The two largest ice caps in Greenland and Antarctica have lost no ice in the past decade, zero, nada, none. Scientists who were told by Al Gore that the science is settled are stunned. Polar bears are not searching for ice. They swim distances of 30 miles and frolic on melting icebergs. The photo of two polar bears clinging to a melting iceberg was proof that man-made global warming exists and sure convinced the kids. In another time and space, that is also called summer.

My school district ordered new science books this past year. Usually, a chapter covers a scientific topic and then moves on to the next topic. The topic of man-made global warming is repeated throughout the entire book. Someone's agenda purposely wanted to drill this man-made global warming fact into our children who will be future voters. It is time for the public to ask, 'Why?' Why is man-made global warming being drilled into our children by our government and who is behind this? Is there a socialization agenda behind this? How much money is involved and who are the recipients? Most importantly, how is this agenda going to affect the future of my family?

Freebies vs. Freedom

February 11, 2012

People are giddy over all the possible Obama freebies. Tuition forgiveness? Free healthcare? Mortgage forgiveness? What else??? Now that the presidential campaign is shaping up, Obama is sending forth the gravy train. Even semi-reasonable people are salivating about the freebies that may come their way. What happened to the saying that nothing in life is free and that you have to work for what you want? The best way to describe what is happening to America is akin to a permanent parent/child relationship.

Children are dependent on the parents for home, food, cell phone, transportation, clean clothes, healthcare and every basic necessity to live. The catch is that the children live by the rules of the parents. As the children age, parents need to demand that children take on responsibilities, such as clean their own clothes, pay for their own entertainment or pay for an oil change. In these healthy parent/child relationships, the children are rewarded with a payoff. They become self-sufficient and get to live independently, making the best choices and decisions for themselves. The parent/child relationship develops into an adult/adult relationship.

In unhealthy parent/child relationships, the parents continue to take on all the responsibilities and the children never learn basic skills. Parents do this because it feels good to do things for our children and often is easier to get things done faster. Disciplining children takes a lot of time and effort. This feel good result ends in being a disservice to children who never learn the value or means of independence.

Obama is the epitome of the nice parent who continues to provide for the children. The scary part is that with government providing for you, the government can make demands of you as if you are a child. It is more than indebtedness and it is definitely not out of love. It results in the loss of control over your everyday freedoms that have been taken for granted. The Obama administration tells us what is good for us and then follows with mandates. The payoff for freebies is way too steep. The question must be asked, "Is all this really free?" and then leave Neverland behind.

43

It's Not about Obama's Skin Color

February 12, 2012

Conservatives think of Barack Obama (Barry Soetoro) the same way they think of Nancy Pelosi, Al Gore, John Kerry, Hillary Clinton, Barney Frank, Harry Reid, John Edwards, Howard Dean, Dick Durbin, Dennis Kucinich, Michael Dukakis, Barbara Boxer, Dianne Feinstein, Charles Schumer, and Christopher Dodd. These liberal, progressive, compassionate politicians have wreaked havoc in the United States and internationally with their policies and actions.

Weekend Furloughs for Lifers: Governor Dukakis vetoed a bill to ban furloughs for first degree murderers on the basis that this was rehabilitative and an experiment in JUSTICE. Willie Horton earned a 48-hour furlough and terrorized a young couple, committing armed robbery and rape. Over 80 convicted murderers, rapists and armed robbers walked away from their furloughs and back into civilized society.

Minimum Wage: Businesses were told they had to pay a minimum amount regardless of the work duties and employee experience. The black economist Thomas Sowell calls this a major social disaster. Businesses wanted to pay employees what they were worth, not what they were mandated to pay. They just did not hire employees to fill basic, entry level jobs.

Entry Jobs Testing: Businesses used tests on reading, writing and/or math to find employees that would be able to perform their duties. Government decided that too many blacks were failing entry tests, so businesses were ordered to simplify the tests. Businesses cancelled entry jobs tests all together. Instead, they required applicants to have a college degree. Qualified blacks who did not graduate with a college degree were kept out of the entry level jobs that would have been theirs.

Military Insults: Kerry quoted as 'you get stuck in Iraq' and testifying on stories that US soldiers 'personally raped, cut off ears, cut off heads.'

Cap and Trade: Al Gore almost brought America to its knees by promoting man-made global warming. Luckily, sensible Democrats refused to vote yes for the energy destroying Cap and Trade when all three branches of government were controlled by Democrats.

Housing Finance Program: During most of his congressional career, Barney Frank was the main advocate for ordering banks to lower underwriting standards for mortgages. In 1992, Frank was responsible for the affordable housing bill that forced Fannie and Freddie to meet quotas on securing mortgages from below median income-earners. By 2008, this quota resulted in Fannie and Freddie guaranteeing more than half of total US low quality loans. Result: poor people were pushed into homes they couldn't afford, ended up defaulting on their loans, and thrown out of their homes directly resulting in the financial housing bubble crisis.

Affirmative Action: Government forced mandates on racial quotas and preferences to promote diversity in schooling and work. The result has led to unqualified blacks being admitted to top-tier universities where they do poorly or are passed along without earning it. The blacks who do earn it have questionable qualifications. In the workplace, quotas determine who is hired. The quota hires and co-workers alike know that the position was not always earned, which is not good for work relationships or self-confidence. The result is the lowering of standards or being set up to fail. An individual can find himself being promoted to a position that he is utterly unqualified for based solely on his skin color. Now, one could reach this conclusion with Obama. He was voted in, but he definitely was promoted without credentials throughout his life. Maybe it is all about Obama's skin color, but it isn't the conservatives who feel this way.

What's wrong with Americans?

February 19, 2012

Americans have every opportunity to succeed yet do not take these opportunities; for many, it is easier to do nothing and complain. When Obama entered the political scene complaining how bad America and President Bush are, the liberals and independents jumped on board the complain train. In turn, they elected a con man who convinced them that some people have it better than them and that it was up to him to change that.

We all know that some people have been dealt an awful life. Government can only help so much. Then it becomes the responsibility of every person to improve his or her own life. Obama has made people believe that fairness is America's goal. It is not. Life is not fair. It's messy and wonderful at the same time. America's goal is to protect your freedoms. You even have the freedom to waste your time complaining but it's not going to get you much. A job and a hard day's work are where everyone can find self-worth and true value in his or her life.

Obama hasn't even begun the rhetoric of this campaign season. It will be more of the same claiming that the 99%ers are owed whatever from the 1%ers. The rich owe the poor. What exactly? To hand over what they worked for? Do the rich owe the poor jobs? Why does a mob like the Occupy Wall Street crowd think anyone owes them anything? We could ask the OWS what they have done for anyone lately. But, see, we really don't care. We just want them along with everyone else to go live their lives and do the best that they can. No one said it would be easy.

America is the land of the free, not the land of the free stuff. We have a free capitalistic society with an economic engine that grows as opposed to a country where our president takes hold of the wealth and divvies it up – unless you vote him in for four more years. This is exactly what we will all get in all aspects of our lives. Get your moral backbones in order and stop listening to empty rhetoric that will give you nothing in the end. The freebies may feel good for a while, but they will end, and Obama will have killed enough energy producers and businesses that you won't even be able to afford a little tattoo.

I'm offended!

February 22, 2012

If political correctness is about not offending others, then why does the Left get a free ride on offending others? Because I am unofficially a Tea Party member, I have been labeled a terrorist, racist, Hitler, dumbass, etc. Politicians and the media did not come to the defense of Tea Party members because they were the ones disparaging them. So, what really is behind political correctness?

Political correctness is a positive-sounding phrase to support Marxism and group think. Marxists hate Western Civilization with our individual thoughts and rights. PC has been so ingrained in the Millennial generation. PC dictates to us what is correct and safe to say. Cubans have also learned what is safe and correct to say to the point that if they do not say the correct things, they are imprisoned, killed or both. For Cubans, PC has become indoctrination which has become the law.

How far can PC lead us in the United States? Will there be a time when PC trumps our First Amendment and lands citizens in jail? Will a group similar to the Tea Party ever be banned? American citizens are being imprisoned for hate crimes which are derived from PC. If a group such as the Tea Party is designated as hateful, by, say liberal radicals in charge of government and the courts, members could be imprisoned. When conservatives claim that the Obama administration is taking away the rights of the individual, we are not saying the innocuous, seemingly funny remark, "I'm offended!" We actually mean that the Obama administration is taking away our individual rights as written in the Constitution!

Buying More Votes, by Kithy

March 4, 2012

So, President Obama tried to buy women's votes by making everyone pay for young women's contraceptives. How was that supposed to work? Yeah, yeah, lots of young women are getting freebies, and therefore should vote to keep the One who got them their freebies in office. I'm hoping that there are enough people out there who feel as I do. You don't buy votes in America! By buying votes of one group, he is taking money away from other groups, because we have to pay for the votes. Stop trying to buy votes! You can't pick and choose who gets the freebies, which are not free anyway. I do not want to pay for contraceptives, which are not medically necessary, when I am required to pay for transplant medication, which by the way, is medically necessary. Aside from the obvious, that I have other ways in which I would like to spend my own money, I really don't want to buy optional stuff for other people. The leader of the free world should not be so blatant in his desire to buy votes.

Rush Was Wrong

March 5, 2012

Sandra Fluke announced to the world that she's having so much sex during law school that she needs us to pay for her contraception that runs over $3,000. Me thinks she exaggerates. Isn't a monthly pack of birth control pills around $30 bringing a three-year total to a third of her claim? Rush Limbaugh, self-proclaimed America's Anchorman and Doctor of Democracy, called her out on her morals and called her a slut, which by definition is a female who has loose sexual morals or is sexually promiscuous. Now every guy at Georgetown knows the amount of Sandra's sexual exploits at her own expense. At least this is what Sandra Fluke presented to the world when she testified before Congress. Why then did Rush apologize? Why did Rush take it back?

Conservatives do not want our daughters and sons hearing Sandra discuss her sex life as though it is a perfectly acceptable lifestyle for a single lady. What Rush accomplished by calling her out as a slut was to defend conservatism. Rush Limbaugh caved to the liberal fake disdain and phony PC talk. Liberals are proud to be a part of this sexually free lifestyle. A slut in their world goes hand in hand with promoting sexual mores, promoting contraception, and then promoting abortion. In the end, it hurts the security of the traditional family.

I'm not so naïve to think that college students are keeping their legs closed, even with aspirin as a certain politician claimed. But to demand that the taxpayers fund her choice of sextracurricular activity is way out of line. This is her time to learn that if you cannot afford it, you cut back. You don't go ordering the taxpayer to fund your sex life through a mandate. Free contraceptives are already available through Family Planning Program Title X, if you need the assistance. Does Sandra realize how expensive free birth control for everyone will eventually cost?

Sandra made it a point that she is receiving financial aid for law school. The tuition at Georgetown averages $30,000 after aid, plus room and board. Was this supposed to drum up sympathy? Most people would be thrilled to receive financial aid to cover college tuition. She also claimed to work in the summer for extra expenses that wouldn't even cover all the contraception she needs. Someone needs to follow Sandra around and find out how often she walks into Starbucks for her expensive spiced mocha non-fat lattes. The sympathy level just might not be the same.

The Sandra Flukes of the world could have come to realize that, outside of their collegiate cocoon, lives a large segment of the civilized world that looks at sleeping around differently. Obama told Sandra that her parents should be proud of her. As a parent, I wouldn't feel that way if my daughter discussed her sex life out in the open and asked for us to pay for it. Rush did not disparage her. I don't think it is a coincidence that her last name pronounced as fluck rhymes with a certain sex word. He called her out and also brought in the absurd that if we are paying for it, why not get to watch. Rush has a wicked sense of humor.

All in all, the Sandra Fluke debacle is a political game based on lies, freebies and exaggeration to gear up the young and poor voting bases. This birth control mandate on the American people is being marketed to hate evil white Republican men like Romney because he obviously hates women. How dare you, President Obama, the Democrat party and the complicit media.

It's Not about Contraception, by Tbird

March 8, 2012

The contraception mandate is to Obamacare as the tea tax was to the American Revolution. It is just one manifestation of the problems with government having total control of health care. Obamacare gives the Secretary of Health and Human Services the sole discretion to decide what shall be covered, who will provide it, how much it will cost, and whether exemptions will be allowed.

Right now, the emphasis is on contraception; health insurance will cover birth control, sterilization, and the abortion pill at no cost. You are supposed to think these are now free. Well, nothing is free. The insurance companies are not allowed to charge any co-pays, making the price zero. However, price, when

48

decided on by the Secretary, is unrelated to cost. Obama, who obviously never took an economics class or ever had to pay for anything he couldn't afford on his own, thinks that if his administration mandates that something will be provided for a certain price, that is what it costs. People who run insurance companies know better. They know that if they don't charge anything for services, they will lose money, and if they lose money for long enough, they will go out of business. Therefore, they will raise the price of insurance to cover those costs, and we end up paying for it anyway, whether or not we want that coverage, or need it, or are morally opposed to it.

Then again, another little nugget inside Obamacare's 2000+ pages says that insurance companies will not be allowed to spend over a certain percentage of their revenues on the administrative cost of providing care, and they won't be allowed to raise their prices to reflect the cost of care mandated by the government. If you are forced to provide more things that cost you money, but you can't charge your customers enough to pay for it, you will lose money. There is no point to being in business to lose money, so insurance companies will go out of business. Who will be left? Why, the government, of course. Someone has to step in to provide health insurance, after all (few people can afford to pay out of pocket for expensive healthcare, which is why we give some money to insurance companies with the promise that they will pay for the expensive procedures should we end up needing them). The government, in charge of paying for healthcare, will drive up the costs of healthcare, and will have to charge a price to cover the costs or cut back on the care it can pay for. Either way, we lose.

The contraception mandate gives us a glance at what will happen to healthcare when the government is in charge. We will have no choices left, and we will have to pay for it anyway. We must get rid of Obamacare and put ourselves back in charge.

Obamacare's Next Step, Taxpayer-Funded Abortions

March 8, 2012

If we the taxpayers provide free contraceptives, the next move will be taxpayer-funded abortions. Abortions as safe, legal and rare is the Obama talking point. However, a $1 billion industry with over one million abortions performed annually in the United States cannot be defined as rare.

Back in the 1970's before abortion was legalized nationally, the pro-abortion crowd claimed that 5,000-10,000 women died every year from botched abortions. The real number was 200-300. It was also claimed that abortion would be safer with legalization. Ending a growing life inside a woman is neither a minor nor guaranteed safe surgery. With lies and exaggeration, the

49

public was conditioned into believing that abortion was morally acceptable and Roe v. Wade passed on January 22, 1973. I do remember that my parents were disheartened at this announcement.

Abortion was marketed as the Right to Choose and as Pro-Choice. Again, the public was conditioned into believing that a woman should be free to have an abortion. In the book *Unplanned*, the author describes watching the ultrasound images of an abortion. As the doctor prodded inside the uterus, the baby tried to get away from the probe. Then the whirling began, and the baby was sucked up with the spine being the last bit to go down because of its size. It wasn't a choice inside the woman; it was a baby whose growing body was dismembered and sucked away forever. Ironically to the idea of choice, studies show that women often feel forced or pressured to end their babies' lives. In China, women are physically forced to have abortions due to the one child policy that continues today, unbelievable immoral government policy and overreach.

Planned Parenthood has become the number one abortion provider in the United States. PP has received taxpayer funds close to $370 million annually, one third of its total revenue. Despite making an additional $630 million annually, PP has a nonprofit status. This taxpayer-funded, nonprofit company donates to Democrat candidates and, of course, to President Obama who vowed not to cut its funding. He's going to be getting millions returned to him from PP for his reelection.

Horton on Abortion

March 12, 2012

Everything you need to know about abortion is found in Dr. Seuss' *Horton Hears a Who!* "A person's a person no matter how small." Pregnancy is a gift from God no matter how it occurs, although it may not feel that way at the time. Up until the day of birth, the growing life inside is a baby, it's just very small. The mainstream media can regurgitate that the growing life is a woman's choice, that it is just a fetus, that it is just a mass of tissues. But that won't change the fact that it is a growing baby and that it all started at conception. It is a small person from the beginning. It doesn't miraculously turn into a baby at 6 months, 7 months or 8 months or when it can survive outside of the womb. We all know that a baby cannot survive on its' own for years.

In Illinois, the Born Alive Infant Protection Act was introduced to give medical care to babies born alive, sickening that the lack of human decency required a law to deal with live babies. Aborted babies were surviving but were left on metal counters and trash heaps to die IN AMERICAN HOSPITALS. One senator, in particular, voted no to medical care. He debated that this bill was just a way of getting around Roe v. Wade. Can you imagine anyone so callous as voting against medical care to living, breathing babies? That would be our president, Barack Obama as an Illinois senator. Unless Americans vote him out, he and his like-minded minions will have control over all of our medical care.

Another quote in Horton Hears a Who is, 'I meant what I said, and I said what I meant." We all need to grow a backbone like the Horton character. A person's a person no matter how small. Abortion has no place in America. It is a scourge on our nation.

Welcome an Open Republican Convention

March 30, 2012

Conservatives want a strong conservative candidate who can defeat Obama. Santorum is on a recent high but became un-presidential with his BS comment with a New York Times reporter. 'Quit distorting my words. It's bull----." Of course Santorum was correct in stating that Romney's insurance plan was too similar to Obamacare but that's not what always counts in a political race. Independents will not be supportive of his vocal social conservatism either. Romney is getting closer to the magical delegate count with the help of blue states that will go to Obama come November. His Florida and Arizona delegates are questionable being that both states violated national GOP rules with early primaries. Conservatives are feeling quite pessimistic about ever getting a true conservative candidate.

Just when conservatives were feeling comfortable with Romney's conservatism, his strategist blurts out an Etch-a-Sketch comment. When asked if Romney was forced to adopt conservative positions for the primaries, his advisor said they will reset for the general election like shaking away the Etch-a-Sketch. It leaves a strong smell of a RINO (Republican In Name Only.) Obama seems likely to run his campaign on taxing the wealthy, rousing the 99 percenters and railing against Wall Street. We'll be hearing the following Romney gaffes and quotes to drive this insane hatred against the wealthy that independents fall for:

- My wife drives a couple of Cadillacs
- $10,000 bet
- Not concerned with the very poor
- Speaker fees of $374,000 amount to not very much
- I like being able to fire people

If Romney is the Republican candidate, I hope that he can overcome the Obama barrage of his own quotes. However, a brokered convention is a possible outcome of this exciting primary season with one last opportunity to send Newt up against Obama. Newt's 21st Century Contract with America describes how America will be great again despite Obama's destruction of America. Newt is

51

ready with his experience as Speaker of the House to make necessary legislative changes, issue Executive Orders and balance the federal budget.

Conservatives should welcome a brokered, open Republican convention come August where the voting for delegates begins again. The GOP establishment wants Romney and will be calling Newt to drop out. Newt needs our support to keep Romney from reaching the 1,144 delegate-count. Otherwise, the end result, Romney will have become our Republican candidate with his steady 30% supporters.

APRIL 2012

So, capitalism is a failure? by Kithy

April 3, 2012

So, one of the candidates thinks capitalism is a failure that has never worked and why would we keep trying it over and over, it's insanity, etc, etc, etc. Doesn't he know that the only reason the economy hasn't totally collapsed despite his efforts is capitalism is working? That despite his efforts to raise the price of the energy that runs our economy, we keep on ticking. The overregulation has slowed the economy, but it keeps going. The ridiculous efforts to run certain companies (General Motors) and entire industries (health insurance), individuals keep working. When the costs became too high in Russia, the entire economy failed, and they had to let go of government run everything. Individuals had to stand up and take care of themselves. We are used to having the individual in charge, not government. That's how we roll.

And another thing. The Supreme Court, by discarding a law that is against the Constitution, is upholding the Constitution, which is its job. The justices are not being activists. The activists make new laws that have no basis in the Constitution. Will someone please tell him the difference?

I'm Voting for the Pro-American, Pro-Freedom, and Pro-Capitalism Candidate, by Kithy

April 7, 2012

So, it appears that our choice this year will be between the anti-American, anti-freedom and anti-capitalism candidate versus the pro-American, pro-freedom and pro-capitalism candidate Mitt Romney. Of course, Democrats are calling us names, like racist and greedy. They have to call us names because they have no record to run on. Their candidate apologizes for America all the time, tells us we are no longer great, we are greedy, etc. Their candidate wants to run 1/6 of the economy (medical) and run every other segment of the economy through extensive regulations. They are on their way to destroying the energy sector, wasting millions on green companies that go bankrupt, and a goal to bankrupt coal manufacturers with new regulations every day, and forbidding oil companies from drilling. The Democrat candidate said capitalism has never worked. I don't know why anyone would choose to vote for that kind of record.

Obama Supporters

April 10, 2012

Conservatives are not swayed into voting by a famous face. However, Obama surely recruits celebrities to showcase his likability and to fund his campaign. We conservatives need to let these celebrities know how we feel by hitting them in their pocketbooks. We may have to forego some nice eye-candy, some exciting films or a concert here or there. It is time to let leftists know that we do not agree with them and we're not going to pay them to tell us the wonders of Obama. If they feel comfortable proclaiming how great Obama is or providing $40,000 a-plate fundraisers, we need to let them know how uncomfortable that makes us.

Star-studded list of celebrities for Obama:

George Clooney	Will Ferrell	Matt Damon
Brad Pitt	Tom Hanks	Jennifer Aniston
Oprah	Gwyneth Paltrow	Jonas Brothers
De Niro	Eddie Murphy	Scarlett Johansson
Chris Rock	Steven Spielberg	Fergie
Samuel Jackson	Ben Affleck	Kate Walsh

Two-Year Anniversary of Obamacare

April 10, 2012

All of the Republican presidential candidates have vowed to repeal Obamacare, named the Patient Protection and Affordable Care Act. Obamacare's two-year anniversary on March 21 was an opportune time for Obama to showcase the greatness of this law. Why the silence?

Most people do not know what this 2700-page law entails. We know that 26-year-old children are welcome on their parent's policy but not much else. Here are the three promises of Obamacare: provide health-insurance coverage for all, reduce insurance costs, and increase quality of health care. In 2014, Americans will be required to buy government-approved private health insurance or pay a penalty. This will become a huge new entitlement, free to some, very costly to others.

Under Obamacare, 20 million more Americans out of the total 310 million Americans are to receive insurance coverage. The real cost in ten years is estimated to be $2-3 trillion. These trillions do not include the $4 plus trillion in costs for state governments, businesses and individuals. Obama promised that not one dime would be added to the debt. You know the joke; it won't cost one dime; it will cost lots of dimes. Real funny.

Half a billion dollars has been transferred to the IRS to hire 4,000 IRS agents to help all Americans acquire health insurance. This is truly ingenuous as we know what these agents are for: to enforce the mandate (collect the new tax). Obama has not promoted Obamacare because he can't. The truth is that this is a terrible law with its constitutionality now in the hands of the Supreme Court.

Obama will start campaigning full-time. When he shows Republicans throwing granny off a cliff, keep in mind his 4,000 IRS agents enforcing his government healthcare takeover with the sole responsibility to collect taxes. Republicans have specific solutions to solve the ever-increasing cost of healthcare.

Guaranteed Free Obama Money

April 11, 2012

Some very lucky Americans are paying themselves salaries of $500,000 and bonuses in the six figures. Many of these lucky people have already quit their jobs. Here is the simple formula to pay yourselves more than you ever imagined:

FOO + DOE + Green Company Name = Millions of $

Become a Friend of Obama, receive a loan guarantee from the Department of Energy, and start up a green company with good intentions and a cool name, preferably with Solar in it. There is work involved because you have to try and make it seem successful and that you are working. But you get to name your salary and bonuses. These company names have already been taken: Solyndra, Evergreen Solar, BrightSource, Sun Power, Solar Trust, Abound Solar, First Solar, Beacon Power and Ener1. Obama promised us that he would continue investing in green companies. How kind of him to hand our tax dollars over to his buddies.

The energy department's loan program has approved close to $35 billion in loans. If you just get a small piece of this pie, you could have half a billion dollars like Solyndra. Several of its executives paid themselves close to half a million yearly and awarded themselves nice bonuses prior to filing bankruptcy.

They did have to work for a while before closing their doors. The guarantee in the loan meant that they were not accountable for the money. This is true for all of the above-mentioned companies; they tried and failed but got paid. Why not pay themselves handsomely? When these companies failed and the money ran dry, all they had to do was close the doors. How easy was that? Taxpayers could be angry, but, really, didn't they do it all for us and the environment?

My Crystal Ball, by Tbird

April 11, 2012

Well, Rick Santorum has just suspended his campaign for Republican candidate for president. I have a lot of respect for the man, the only one who really understands how important it is to get rid of Obamacare's complicated, convoluted, unconstitutional government takeover of our health care. He hung in there longer than I really expected him to.

Gingrich and Paul don't have a chance, so we are stuck with Mitt Romney, another RINO (Republican In Name Only). That worked so well for us last time, didn't it? The national Republicans have been pushing for him all this time and they just got their man. I hope that running against a committed conservative during this primary season has sharpened Romney's views and toughened up his timid approach to the issues. Let's see whom he picks for his VP; that will tell us a lot.

My crystal ball says Romney will win in a landslide against Obama in November, as none of what Obama has done in his three plus years in office has been good for anybody who isn't one of his big moneybags' supporters.

GSA: Green Services Administration

April 17, 2012

GSA, otherwise known as General Services Administration, has been in the news lately for its extravagant vacation conferences. The GSA was established in 1949 to streamline the administrative work of the federal government. It has evolved into the nation's federal acquisition and procurement agency with over 12,000 employees, but that is not all. The GSA current website states that it oversees the business of the Federal government by promoting efficient government operations. The gsa.gov extensively detailed website contains very interesting information starting with the GSA vision of a government that works better for the American people. The values listed are: Integrity, Accountability and Transparency, Effective Leadership, and Responsible Decision-making. Ok, great values, so far, so good.

GSA's three strategic goals listed are: 1) Innovation - green proving ground, 2) Customer intimacy - lead with our expertise to drive market for high-performance green products, and 3) Operational excellence - commitment to a zero environmental footprint to support decisions that wring out inefficiencies in operations.

The very first initiative listed is Green Government. Under Green Events and Training are mundane things such as Earth Day events, Recycle Days and Eco-friendly Solutions. Under Training on Using Charge Cards, the GSA trains on using mandated travel cards and SmartPay integrated cards and how to protect your card from fraud and abuse. GSA's Agency Policy Statement signed by the GSA Administrator and Senior Sustainability Officer states that the GSA is committed to achieving President Obama's sustainability agenda and that it will achieve ZEF, a Zero Environmental Footprint. The GSA has a 67-page Strategic Sustainability Performance Plan. The words sustainability/sustainable are written 21 times on just one page, such as in Sustainability Councils, sustainable asset management, sustainability initiatives, Sustainability Steering Committee, sustainable acquisition, sustainable goals, sustainability plans, sustainable information, sustainable policies, etc, etc., a lot of wordy nothingness.

Under the heading Climate Change Risks is the Climate Adaptation Plan in which the GSA will consider climate change impacts. The Senior Climate Adaptation Official is responsible for implementing all aspects of the Climate Change Adaptation Policy which include: Develop and Maintain Agency Comprehensive Greenhouse Gas Inventory, Reduce Energy Intensity for Energy Efficiency of Buildings, and a Comprehensive Vehicle Allocation Methodology for internal fleet. The use of the GSA Carbon Footprint and Green Procurement Tool will be used to estimate emissions from employee commuting.

The GSA will follow the Guiding Principles for Federal Leadership in High Performance Sustainable Design and Green Buildings. The GSA will adhere to the GreenGov Supply Chain Partnership Program with the use of the Sustainability and Energy Scorecard. One goal is to reduce energy consumption per gross square feet of space by 30%. GSA does admit to some challenges: GSA lacks certain emissions data which will be costly to obtain. GSA will have difficulty calculating tenant energy consumption. When green and challenges are in the same report, the greenies are admitting that this is just a fabricated mess that doesn't even make sense to them.

Steps already taken to manage the effects of climate change include the following Building Operation Plans: turn off lights, control of shading and close doors. GSA's existing project delivery process can address design solutions related to potential impacts and couple with an investment strategy to implement those changes over time. Who wrote this stuff and has anybody really read this garbage? Page after page of evasive wording defines what a bureaucratic mess this one government agency has become. The bureaucracy grows: The Chief

Greening Officer of the Public Buildings Service has six regional sustainability managers and anticipates hiring more so that each of the GSA regions has a full-time position dedicated to sustainability buildings.

Green Services Agency is a more appropriate name than General Services Agency. A million-dollar vacation conference has put GSA in the limelight, but this should not be the focus. As funding taxpayers, we really should be concerned with the entire agency as a whole. The one thing I agree with of all these pronouncements and nonsense is ZEF. For the GSA to reach a Zero Environmental Footprint, GSA should do its job of making government more efficient by disbanding itself in its entirety.

Obama is calling for more taxes to continue to fund this type of green garbage already costing the taxpayers billions of dollars. This is our Government. A capitalistic investor would never put up with this waste of money and resources. Then again, neither should taxpayers. Oh, yeah, and like my parents said repeatedly - remember to turn the lights off when you leave a room and close the back door; you're letting the AC out. My parents were way ahead of the times.

Fleas

April 18, 2012

Liberals, progressives or communists, whatever you want to call them, cannot stand listening to Rush Limbaugh, conservative radio personality, because he is right in more ways than one. When you listen to Rush, you hear a totally different viewpoint on the talking points of the day. His flea comment sticks in my head from a few years ago.

Obama gave a speech to 9,000 graduates of Arizona State University telling them not to look for jobs in the private sector but encouraged them to go into public service. They should give back to their communities. Obama and Michelle continued to give speeches on the campaign trail exclaiming that people shouldn't be focused on earning money. Leave corporate America in favor of community service. Don't look for work in law firms and Wall Street firms. Look for work in the healthcare field.

Community service sounds all fine and dandy and Obama received huge rounds of applause. But not from Rush. His view is that college students should go out into the private sector, earn money and then use their own money for charity, if they so choose. The alternative encouraged by the Obama's would turn these college students into fleas. As we all know, fleas live off their hosts, sucking their blood and lives out of them.

About this same time, the New Orleans Jefferson family members were embroiled in their own nonprofit scandals. The nonprofit Care Unlimited received charitable and educational grants to provide educational support services to pregnant teenagers. Despite submitting reports of services provided, Care Unlimited performed no work. The reports were totally fictional. What fleas pocketed this money? Betty Jefferson pled guilty yet claimed that she really didn't steal the money because it was given to her.

Note to college graduates: public service workers are not Betty Jefferson fleas. However, government does NOT fund itself. It IS the private, successful capitalists who fund every single nonprofit. Profitable companies should be thanked, not vilified. Prior to the Obama's telling you not to focus on earning a living, Michelle Obama was paid a salary of $340,000 per year to perform her community service in the healthcare field, a job so necessary it was cancelled after she moved on.

Stop Celebrating and Sponsoring Earth Day

April 20, 2012

Just had to share information in an excellent article by Kevin DeAnna titled 'Do you know why Earth Day is April 22?' April 22 is the birthday of the founder of the Soviet Union, Communist leader Vladimir Lenin. His agenda focused on solving the problem of overpopulation. Communist dictators were very successful in solving this problem by starving and murdering millions of their own people.

In Lenin's case, he immediately enforced decrees to control the people. He declared a decree that ALL forests, waters and minerals were property of the state, as in the highly centralized government, not an individual state such as Louisiana. This decree led to a decree on hunting which led to taking away the right to possess hunting weapons. Lenin enforced a decree on nature conservancy in which natural resources were beyond human reach. Within a year, Lenin was in control of all activities of his people. Greenies, reread the above.

Similar to Lenin was Hitler. Kitty Werthmann described how Hitler came to rule Austria in 1938. Austrians voted him in on promises that everyone would have jobs, businesses would get help and farmers would get their farms back. Within four weeks, everyone had jobs, education was nationalized, and Hitler's picture replaced the crucifix in the classrooms. Hitler declared that women were equal to men and forced them all to work outside the home. They were threatened that if they didn't work, they would not receive their food ration cards. Children were required to attend National Youth Days and listen to political indoctrination. Parents were fined and then jailed if their children did not attend. They lost their freedom to raise their own children.

Anyone paying attention will see the similarities with Lenin and Hitler to Obama. Obama is pushing communist policies that will bankrupt the middle class. Obama can claim to be pro-business but that doesn't make him so. He is pushing the green agenda that will control how we live. He has promised to bankrupt the coal industry and has already hurt our oil producers. The middle class is hanging on for now. But if gas goes past $5 per gallon to the $10 per gallon that Obama's Energy Czar has stated as his goal, the middle class will disappear. The cost of food and everything we purchase will become unaffordable.

Responsible Americans who have jobs will be required to fund free healthcare, free college tuition and free mortgages. Obama also wants control of retirement accounts by phasing out private plans and converting to government annuities. Obama constantly disparages millionaires and billionaires and threatens to increase their taxes. Now his stated number for rich income is $250,000 and I have heard $200,000. Obama is quoted as wanting to soak anyone making over $250,000. That won't be enough money for Obama, especially with his friends' exemptions.

Many in the middle class live paycheck to paycheck and are already paying high taxes. When the middle class can't afford their property taxes, their properties will belong to the owner of banks. Obama is already on the track to government-ownership of banks claiming they are too big to fail. The gracious and generous Obama will send money their way should they make any major mistakes and go broke. I encourage all businesses and people to stop supporting Earth Day. It is not an event about keeping our environment clean and beautiful and saving Earth. Sure, they include a few bits of good information and common-sense ideas like turning off lights. But beyond this is a sinister agenda that has been followed by Marxists, communists, progressives and statists. None of these dictators came to office by claiming their true ideology. They lied and Obama continues to lie to us.

What's wrong with rich people?

April 25, 2012

What's wrong with rich people? The only answer I can come up with is that I'm not one, yet. I recently had a discussion with a woman who will not vote for Obama but did say that she agreed with him that some people are too rich. The only rich that should be disparaged are those who made money by fraud, theft or other illegal means. Other than that, you have bought into class envy and broken the 10th Commandment.

If you believe that people are too rich, you have to determine a specific number. And for people that have passed this number in earnings, how would you solve this problem? If you tax a person's earnings 100% past a certain dollar amount, where is the incentive to continue making the products or provide the services in demand? Should government have the power to take over anyone's business in order to share the wealth with someone needier?

Who is anyone to tell Donald Trump that he makes too much money? Should he be forced to stop investing his own money and stop building another high rise? Do you stop Apple from producing iPhones and iPads that people continue to purchase? Should Apple be forced to give away the products once the Apple executives make a certain amount of money? Should companies be forced to pay higher wages to all its employees? Who should determine the worth of each employee? Do you think executives become non-entities once they earn a certain amount? How much should an actor make for remembering his lines? What should the cap be for quarterback Drew Brees for throwing a football?

Big oil companies make a lot of money. Should oil executives be told that they can only make so much? How much should that be? Because of oil executives, we have the freedom to drive cars and fly in airplanes to anywhere in the world. We can and expect to turn on the air conditioner when hot and the furnace when cold. Oil companies provide income avenues to scientists, engineers, equipment producers, operating crews, shipping, storage, transportation, refineries, lease owners, gas store employees and so on. How much should the chemical engineers, drilling operators, and the manufacturers of drilling equipment be allowed to earn? What's the number???

The answer to all of these questions is either no or that it is none of your business, unless you own the business. America was built on capitalism and it is working extremely well. The harder you work and the more marketable your skills, the more money you will make. No one in this world is poor because the rich are rich. A great source of knowledge on how to get wealthy is the rich like Trump's *Art of the Deal*.

MAY 2012

History Will Describe Ignorant Americans

May 6, 2012

Prior to being elected president, this coke head, community organizer said that he would fundamentally transform the United States of America. And while campaigning without a teleprompter, he spoke of redistribution of wealth as a good thing. You take from one person and give to another. He once disparaged our Constitution as a charter of negative liberties and then takes an oath to defend it. He blatantly ignores the rule of law, chides the Supreme Court justices and advises them on how to rule, and bypasses Congress with his czars.

History will not be kind in describing the ignorant Americans who elected this man president. Historians will have to question how independent, hard-working, honest Americans were outnumbered by the whiny entitlement-minded crowds that helped get Obama elected. Many people, me included, are already banging their heads questioning how this happened in our lifetime and how to reverse it. A big part of Obama's success is due to the liberal media and the oh so intelligent celebrities.

There is no doubt that liberal policies discourage marriage and have resulted in the destruction of intact family units. Young, single women who have babies are rewarded with their own apartments, previously drug-infested tenement projects. As long as income stays below a certain level, plenty of entitlements flow their way. This is the way of life that they were taught to want. Why work and get married to lose all the freebies? It is easy to see why they have learned to ignore the American dream of a nice house filled with a husband and children, supported by an honest day's work.

This is just a small piece of the puzzle. Our media failed to vet Obama. A media that doesn't do its job loses its title. Most every company vet their employees – companies want to know college records, work history, job accomplishments, personal references and may even collect information on financial history. Yet for the most important position in the world, we knew nothing of importance about Obama but a fictitious autobiography and the color of his skin. The ultimate shame of American citizens is that they didn't care to know.

History will determine that Americans picked Obama based on his smile and his diversity. Really, could he have been elected as a half-white Barry? In general, Americans care about American Idol, reality shows, late-night comedians and fish face selfies (please disappear). Information on current events and politics is at their fingertips but many are too ignorant, lazy or just apathetic about the real world. Or they already feel so smart, no need to ask a parent or research the facts.

One positive about the Occupy Wall Street people is that they are involved. However, the following mindset shows their ignorance. They parrot the anti-capitalist and anti-bank rhetoric, but they like their cell phones. They should be told that if they reelect Obama, they should get used to owning nothing from a private company. Are these mindless people Obama's national civilian security force more powerful than our military?

I Know How the Republicans Can Win the Women's Vote, by Kithy

May 8, 2012

Just remind us how much the price of chocolate has gone up. That's it. Just keep reminding us, until November. Every time I look at the price of chocolate bars or chocolate chips, it gets me hot under the collar. That is definitely something we can all identify with except for my niece who has never liked chocolate. If a president doesn't care about the price of chocolate, or doesn't have a plan to bring it down, then he's going to be voted out! There are quite a few other reasons he needs to be gone, but this one is easily identifiable and easily understood. Who's with me?

Could Obama be a communist?

May 13, 2012

Obama's past is fictionalized in his book *Dreams from My Father*. Beyond that, most of his true past was (and is) hidden, including his college transcripts, birth certificate, writings, friendships, girlfriends, fellow students, relatives, co-workers and past work history. There is only one good reason to hide Obama's past. And that is to hide what his future may hold.

Obama's past includes the communist Frank Marshall Davis who served as his mentor during childhood. The high school years are a time of growth and finding one's self-identity. Obama grew up without a father and researchers have said that Frank was like a father to Obama. What impact did Frank have on Obama's life? Conservatives are quite sure that the answer to this is a tremendous impact. Some liberals deny that Obama has a communist bent even though his Green Czar was a self-proclaimed communist. Others I have spoken to reconcile that socialism is good and that spreading the wealth (commie talk) is a good thing.

Obama's chances of being reelected are not looking very promising. If Obama is a true communist, and come November 6, whether or not he is reelected, America is in serious danger. He will still have two months to sign away our sovereignty by way of treaties. He will still have two months to further devalue the dollar. He will continue to bypass Congress with business-killing regulations. However, we must chance these two months to get rid of this communist/fascist who is destroying the American way of life.

Do celebrities really want to pay higher taxes?

May 13, 2012

New York Governor Paterson raised taxes on the super rich and Rush Limbaugh moved to Florida. Obama wants to raise taxes on the super rich 1%. Will they move out of the United States? You can bet more will because almost 1800 already have renounced their citizenship. One of the co-founders of Facebook denounced his citizenship prior to publicly selling Facebook stock and he will save on taxes.

George Clooney and 150 Hollywood friends still support Obama by raising $15 million. $6 million came from the Hollywood crowd and close to $9 million came from small donors for a raffle to attend the $40,000 dinner event. It's kind of ironic that 99%ers donated to the candidate who is critical of the 1%ers to dine with the 1%ers. Obama rails against his friends and himself for your vote and you find this appealing? You think this Hollywood crowd really wants to pay more in taxes to the government or they are going to share their money with you? Get a brain.

Billionaire Streisand attended the George Clooney dinner. She avoided paying higher property taxes by transferring five of her properties to her husband. Warren Buffet has promoted Obama's Buffet tax while one of his subsidiaries owes a billion in taxes. Al Sharpton rabble rouses about the rich not paying their fair share. According to the New York Post, he owes Federal and State taxes of $3.5 million. Sharpton lists a profitable $250,000 income from his nonprofit. Combine this with his cable network salary and his income is close to half a million dollars.

This support by the Hollywood elite of taxing themselves more is not only hypocrisy. The millions and public support of Obama are more like protection money. In the end, the more people are taxed, the more loopholes they will find and the less they will pay. You see, people who earn money want to keep their money and do with it what they desire.

It's Time to Get Our Budget in Line

May 13, 2012

June ends my fourth and final year as PTA (Parent Teacher Association) president of a junior high. The executive board is to leave a balance of $1,500 in the account for the incoming board. While looking over the budget, I became concerned that the balance was lower than I expected. We still have a couple of pricey events, so I asked the committee members to watch their expenses. It looks like we'll come in just at the $1,500. PTA budgets depend on the generosity of parents and community support. Thank goodness they have always come through for our school. Our students have enjoyed the benefits of a well-run PTA. What if I overlooked the budget, miscalculated, or overspent by more than the $1,500? I suppose I would just leave debts and problems for the incoming board to deal with.

Budget overruns are happening all over the world. The spending continues while the money is not there. California's budget has a shortfall of $16 billion. Revenue collections are "disappointing." Taxes cannot support the state's spending. The same scenario is playing out across the globe for the entire country of Greece, for retirement accounts across the United States, and for the United States. Three ways to reduce this debt is to reduce spending, raise revenues through higher taxes, and grow the economy. Obviously, Obama likes spending money. He added $6 trillion to the national debt in less than four years. He is campaigning on raising taxes for the 1% and people will vote for him. Obama claims this will bring in $700 billion over the next decade. Wow, $70 billion annual additional tax revenue while the United States has $16 trillion in debt!

Our best option is to grow the economy. One has to know business and grow business. That's what candidate Romney knows. To help businesses, he streamlined them, got them through reorganization, bankruptcy when required, and, in turn, grew the economy. In all this talk about fairness and equality, Obama leaves out an important fact. Some people have business smarts, and some don't. People are not equal and never will be. People have different strengths, skills, motivation and intelligence; these can never be equalized through government mandates.

In spending time at school, I talk to a lot of teachers and parents. They are busy with their lives. I continue to hear them state that all politicians are bad or that there really isn't a big difference in them. Totally not true - their economic policies are night and day. Obama will spend the United States into oblivion. Romney has the smarts to turn our path into prosperity; that's what he knows. It's time to get our budget in line.

Stop the Stop Saverin Bill, by Kithy

May 17, 2012

I saw a report that some senators are getting together to propose a Stop Saverin bill – to prevent Eduardo Saverin (Facebook cofounder) from renouncing his citizenship and saving $67 million dollars in taxes. Anyway, I have a proposal. Lower the tax rate, so he doesn't want to renounce his citizenship. The bill that's being proposed is a "let's punish the guy and never let him come back" bill. Didn't he produce something worthwhile here? Isn't there a chance that he still has talent? Don't we want to keep the producers and intelligence in America? Who are these idiots proposing punishment?

America is the land of the free. Eduardo is free to leave America as he wishes. If he feels the tax rate is too high and another country won't gouge him as much (Singapore's capital gains rate is zero), we cannot and should not force him to stay. If a lower tax rate would give Saverin incentive to keep his citizenship, the US government would be wise to collect *some* taxes instead of scaring our citizens off to another country and end up with *none*.

The US capital gains rate of 15% is scheduled to rise to at least 20%. And if local sales tax, state, federal, and capital gains taxes aren't enough, everything you have worked and saved for will be additionally taxed at nearly 50% upon your death. How do you say 'Hello' in Singapore? I think all the tax evaders say 'Hello'.

Obama's Hope and Change

May 22, 2012

Bet you didn't know Obama meant 'Hope for opportunity, Change your citizenship' back in the Hope and Change campaigning days. I knew back when Obama told Joe the Plumber that spreading the wealth is a good thing. Joe the Plumber should have told Obama to his face that he created a company and hands out paychecks to his employees for jobs well done. That's the kind of spread the wealth true Americans like.

Obama WANTS more American citizens on welfare via wealth distribution. Once these citizens are used to government hand-outs as a way of life, the Democrats own them for life. When this number surpasses 50% of the population and this 50% plus continue to vote for their hand-outs, there will not be another Republican administration, ever. Until the money runs out.

The nearly 1,800 Americans who have given up their citizenship include the rich, the successful and the intelligent who have the foresight of what America is transforming into. America will not remain a superpower with this type of brain drain. Welcome to Obama's Hope and Change that YOU voted for.

Obama, like Zima Gold, is unbelievable!

June 3, 2012

Remember the clear malt beverage Zima? In the 90's, Zima was marketed as 'Zomething different' and 'a truly unique alcohol beverage.' Zima won over a small consumer base of women who liked the citrusy taste, for a while. The beer guzzling base of men avoided this girly drink like the plague. Coors came up with Zima Gold with the goal of attracting beer-swilling men to the brand. The problem with the product was that it looked like beer but didn't taste like beer.

My fun job at this time was promoting beer with a distributor in New Orleans. I brought Zima Gold to the happy hour hotspot off St. Charles Avenue called *Que Sera*. Such great memories, Kelly girl. Free samples of alcoholic beverages to a happy hour crowd are usually greeted exceptionally well. Not so with Zima Gold. To encourage consumption, I told people that the taste was unbelievable. They sampled and spit it out. This beverage was beyond awful but who could resist a sample when told that it is unbelievable? Zima Gold disappeared within the year, never to be seen or heard from again. I really liked my job.

As Zima Gold tasted unbelievable, Obama's first and hopefully only term has also been unbelievable. He ran an exceptional campaign in 2008 claiming that he would bring everyone together. Obama was something different and hip with the use of social media resulting in his followers fainting all over his campaign trail. Not much was known about Obama, with the exception of how he looked and how he could read a teleprompter. After the Greek Styrofoam columns from his acceptance speech came tumbling down, Obama started his term publicly criticizing everyone and anything for his own personal reasons and to gain points with various crowds. We know how this ends; we all end up being the brunt of this sooner or later.

Americans are coming to their senses that they not only want a leader who looks and sounds good, they want a true leader. When a foreign minister of an ally of ours proclaims that the Obama administration is ignorant and incompetent, unbelievable is an apt description of Obama. Americans got it wrong this time but have the opportunity to correct it November 2012.

Social Justice, by Tbird

June 5, 2012

Social justice is one of those vague terms that means different things to different people, but it sounds innocuous. Generally, we are social beings and we all want justice, don't we? It is difficult to discuss something when we don't agree on a single definition. I tried to find out what is considered social justice.

In the 1850's, an Italian Jesuit, Fr. Taparelli, coined the phrase "social justice". His thoughts were shaped by the Italian unification movement, the drive towards government centralization at home and throughout Europe. European societies used to be agrarian, and small groups of people fed, housed, and clothed themselves; they were relatively self-sufficient. The wisest and strongest person in a group was the ruler and made the important decisions for the group. When European societies shifted to crowded commercial towns and people worked for wages, they were no longer independent and self-sufficient but rather depended on wages paid by their employers. A middleman would buy products from different sources (such as fish from fishermen and grain from farmers) and resell them in towns. They "bought cheap and sold dear."

Progressives see the middlemen getting rich and the wage-slaves working sunup to sundown and remaining poor, forgetting that when they lived on farms, they also worked sunup to sundown and barely subsisted. Anyone else would see the middlemen working to buy stuff from sources farther away and bringing them to market where wage earners could buy them conveniently to be a good thing (my dad tells a story of a woman in Russia who bought meat from a farm, brought it home to the city where she re-packaged it into smaller, family-sized units, sold it, and got arrested for making money when other people didn't; her family lost her income, and other people lost their source of good, relatively cheap meat).

In Taparelli's ideas on social justice, the social habit of association and cooperation for attending to public needs leads people to form small bands of brothers outside the family who, for certain purposes, volunteer time and effort to accomplish something. They organized themselves for the good of the neighborhood, the town, state and country. This encouraged personal relationships and local responsibility, resulting in freedom and respect for human beings and small institutions through which they pursued basic needs. Social justice entailed a social order in which government doesn't overrun or crowd out institutions of civil society such as family, church, and local organizations, but rather respected, protected, and allowed them to flourish. Taparelli said that the centralization of government resulted in threats to local administrative structures. He defended local guilds and charitable associations against inappropriate government interference.

Centralized government tends to push local organizations from roles of public relevance. When we ignore, crowd out, or weaken local nongovernmental institutions in the name of social justice, we hurt those institutions and the larger society as well. In our own time, Illinois made gay civil unions legal and forbad Catholic Charities from turning away same sex couples when placing wards of the state for adoption; foster parents working with Catholic Charities dropped out of the program, and Catholic Charities dropped adoption and foster care in some dioceses rather than be forced to place children with unmarried, gay couples.

Pope Leo XIII wrote an encyclical in 1891 called "Rerum Novarum" to address new times where people were living in towns rather than on farms. He addressed the "evils of equality". Civil societies were centers of safety, commerce, craftsmanship, and prosperity, leading to the highest freedom. He said people are different with different skills, talents, health, and capacities. Unequal fortune follows. Social and public life can only be maintained by means of various kinds of capacity for business, and the playing of many parts. Each man chooses what part suits his own peculiar domestic condition. Leo praised the diversity of human gifts and human vocations and callings. He also predicted that under socialism, or total control by the state, that equality forces uniformity, killing off creativity and originality, resulting in breakdown of the entire system. Socialists want to reduce society to one dead level.

Contemporary social justice is the redistribution of resources from those who unjustly gained them to those who justly deserve them. It is creating and ensuring the processes of truly democratic participation in decision-making. Only a decisive redistribution of resources and decision-making power can ensure social justice and authentic democracy. If you can translate this into something that makes sense, tell me. It seems to assume that everyone who has more than someone else took it from the other person and must give it back, and if enough people vote to force others to give them their stuff, then it should happen, thus creating equality of result, or social justice.

Karl Marx said that man once existed in a simple, primitive state with happiness and tranquility (I don't know what world he is talking about, but I don't think it is Earth). He deplored the rise of economic classes where one oppressed the other, which ruined the imaginary utopia. The exploited will rise up and throw off their capitalist oppressors and replace capitalist societies with a harmonious society with equality for all. Very few countries still stick with Marxism, such as China (although somewhat modified with some capitalist ideas) and North Korea. A famous satellite picture taken at night shows lights covering South Korea and darkness covering North Korea, which shows us the results of capitalism versus Marxism. What he intended to replace the evil capitalist system with we don't really know, except that it was to be "perfect". Hmmm.

Liberation theology of Latin America from the late 1960's said that all theology is biased and reflects the economic and social class of those that developed it. The predominate theology of Europe and North America supports democratic capitalism, which is responsible for exploiting and impoverishing the third world. Sin is not individual and private, but rather social and economic; it would be sin for poor people to not resist and overthrow their oppressors with violence, if necessary. Salvation is not about life after death, but rather a new social order with equality for all. However, after eastern Europe threw off Marxism, Latin

American theologians became less hopeful of social structures and more concerned with issues of spirituality; they still don't like capitalism, think socialism seems to be bankrupt, and realize that bloodshed isn't so good when it is real. Evangelicals came in and preached salvation through individual change, and churches acted more like job and housing referrals, helping people develop skills so they could become more upwardly mobile.

Black liberation theology, like Barack Obama's former pastor Jeremiah Wright espoused, said that society was developed by white people and arranged so that the whites stay in charge and the blacks stay kept down. Blacks can't get ahead because whites won't let them. Blacks must have community organizers to get them all riled up so they can throw off their white oppressors. Those white people sure are powerful; too bad we'll never have a black president or black secretary of state or black attorney general. Oh wait. We already do!

Social justice went from local people helping one another to government getting rid of groups that help and replacing them with distant bureaucrats who don't know what is wrong or how to help without wasting all the money confiscated from the rich and making things worse for the people being helped and the society at large. Maybe social injustice is a better term.

Fundamental Transformation

June 7, 2012

I'm starting to believe that Obama will be responsible for America's fundamental transformation. His liberal overreach could be for our benefit. Conservatives feared (still do) that Obama's goal is to transform America from capitalism to communism. We overlooked what really needed changing and can thank Wisconsin Governor Scott Walker for showing us the way. Last night the unions forced a recall election of Governor Walker. The results are in and the referendums are for Governor Walker and for the end of public service unions. This will be the beginning of US's transformation from one of indebtedness to one of balanced budgets.

Public service employees work for the taxpayers. Without taxes from the private sector, these employees do not get paid. In the present form of public service unions, the power lies with the union bosses who help elect politicians who become indebted to the union bosses – not with the taxpayers. The result has been nearly bankrupt states. Democrats can complain upside down that Republicans want to take away their pensions and benefits. The truth is that the money is no longer there to pay for the overly generous pensions and benefits. How much longer can states continue these payouts before they truly become bankrupt? What happens when this time comes? Wisconsin showed us last night that they do not want to find out.

Thanks to Governor Walker and Wisconsinites who elected him, public service employees no longer are forced to hand over a chunk of their paychecks to the unions. Many have already opted out on this payment. Without money, the unions lose power. Like private sector workers, these employees will now contribute to their own pensions and benefits. Obama's mantra is fairness, but I doubt that he likes this type of fairness. His union boss supporters will no longer have these guaranteed, ginormous pots of money to donate for his reelection campaign. The money stays in the hands of the workers who earned it. Imagine that!

Obama's 100 Rounds of Golf

June 8, 2012

Hard workers often reward themselves with rounds of golf. With the presidency of the United States being the most important job in the world, presidents need the occasional break from the stresses of the position. No one would begrudge the president for the occasional round of golf. However, Obama has played 100 rounds in the first three years of his presidency. I believe he plays because he doesn't know what hard work is and most likely twiddles his thumbs at the White House. I imagine he sits at his desk waiting to be told what's next. Golf is a time-filler for Obama; he doesn't know what to do as president.

Being the president entails a huge learning curve, especially for one so inexperienced as Obama. The history and research alone to excel as president would take hours into the night. How much time has he spent looking into the Fast and Furious scandal which happened on his watch? Bad example, he was in on it. How much time is he devoting to the economic crisis which forecasters say is looming ahead? He should be meeting with business leaders for their input on how to create jobs for the millions of Americans who have given up looking for work. But that's not his focus.

Our figurehead of a president is not the smartest man ever to hold this office as the mainstream media reports trying to convince us. We know Obama lies to promote himself – his literary agent published promotional booklets stating that he was born in Kenya. This lasted for 16 years up until 2007. We know that he spent his time at Occidental College in a drug-induced haze – his own words. We know that he did not produce any writings while serving as president of the Harvard Law Review. He ascended the political career ladder by destroying his opponents, not by winning on his merits. In the 1996 Illinois Senate race, all four of his competitors had their petitions invalidated. In the 2004 US Senate race, the leading Democrat candidate withdrew due to a sex scandal followed by the Republican candidate also withdrawing due to a sex scandal. Too bad they didn't know to play the same game.

It is not unexpected that Obama's second term campaign is in shambles. The truth that is coming out and results of his efforts are hard to fight and defend. But here comes Republican candidate Mitt Romney who did not follow in his father's footsteps or dreams but follow his own path. He not only led as Governor; he has earned the reputation as having a sterling business career. I wouldn't doubt for a minute that Romney has earned 100 rounds of golf.

Obama Just Ignored Wisconsin

June 10, 2012

I'll bet Obama's handlers wished they had sent Obama to the golf course yesterday instead of having him comment on the economy. On addressing the issue of the economy, Obama said that the private sector is fine and that the weakness lies in our governors and mayors making cuts to the public sector. Then he added the obligatory blame of the economy on the Republicans in Congress. Obama back-tracked afterwards and said that he didn't mean to say that the private sector is fine.

Obama DOES believe that the private sector is fine and that is why he is pushing higher taxes. More taxes are needed to pay for government workers' pensions and benefits. Obama correctly expects to be rewarded by their votes. Private sector workers are tired of fully funding government workers' retirement and benefits at the expense of their own. Did Obama not pay attention to what just happened in Wisconsin? The rest of the world found out on June 5, 2012, that the staged fighting in Madison was the unions, not the majority of Wisconsin citizens. A liberal state just voted to stop the insanity of public worker unions, or at the very least, the forced funding of these unions.

Government workers used to be known as low-paid, public servants. Their wages were balanced out by pensions and benefits. They sacrificed generous private sector pay for the good of their city, state and country. This is no longer the case. The private sector is hurting. The jobs are not there, salaries and benefits have been cut, and many are underemployed and facing joblessness. Governors and mayors across America do not want a Detroit – a major city on the eve of bankruptcy. Without the strength of government unions, pensions and benefits can be pared down to that of the private sector. The unions have less power to hold over politicians. State budgets can be balanced. The Wisconsin recall ended up being a vote for the future of Wisconsin.

Austerity of the New Orleans Times-Picayune

June 15, 2012

The New Orleans Times-Picayune newspaper will no longer print a daily edition but will be following austerity for future growth and survival. The future is online and will soon be reduced to three times a week printing. The readers have been voicing their opposition calling the owners of the paper selfish, inconsiderate, arrogant and disrespectful. They have even begun to agree with the Occupy movement. Evidently, the reporters of the Times-Picayune have failed to inform their readers of truth and what has been happening in the world.

I am a daily reader who truly enjoys reading the paper each morning with my cup of coffee. A game I enjoy with the paper is reading the propaganda articles about global warming and climate change. They became weekly and nearly daily. These articles have lacked any questioning, research and facts but were written by the expert taxpayer-funded research scientists. Times-Picayune readers have read articles that the main culprit of global warming is power plants. I know if I want true journalistic articles on this topic that I have to search online. The global warming articles were wasted space that could have been devoted to good, journalistic stories on the reality in our lives. But online I found the Drudge Report, American Thinker and writers from all over the world. Austerity is coming on all levels. And it's best to be prepared. The pro-liberal mindset of getting what we want without regard to cost has to go.

Greece is one example of foregoing austerity. The country cannot sustain itself and has been bailed out by Germany. Yet the Greeks recently voted against the austerity candidate for the candidate who made unrealistic promises. Greece had an opportunity to get its house in order and stop depending on others to support its way of life. The Times-Picayune could cave to its readers and continue the daily paper. But with unstable gas prices, falling readership and falling ad revenue, it would eventually run out of money. Contrary to our current president, this is not called greed. Profit is a good thing because along with profits, workers continue to have jobs. The Times-Picayune, along with many failing companies, cannot plan on bailouts. If the government bails out these companies, they become indebted to the government and not their customers.

Could the Times-Picayune have prevented this future? Doubtful, the digital age is here. Could it have better informed its readers of reality and prepared them for the future? Yes. Look back at the Occupy and Tea Party stories and what was reported on their protests and beliefs. Your readers still are ill informed about these two major stories. Are Occupiers truly peacefully protesting against the rich or are they pooping on police cars yelling eff the police? Are Tea Party members really to blame for terrorist attacks or are they peaceful protesters and forming the silent majority?

The Obama Experiment

June 15, 2012

Obama is a test case of diversity and of propping up someone to such a level that he could only fail. The media and the Democrat party are at fault for pushing Obama on the American people by suppressing information. Now that the American people have experienced three and a half long years of Obama, we can proclaim that the Obama Experiment has failed.

Those who have followed the real news know what Obama is about and many more are soon to find out. The books that have recently come out and books that are about to be released are devastating. To misuse taxpayer funding to the extent that his administration has should be found and prosecuted as criminal. He spent a trillion dollars of hard-earned taxpayer money that didn't create any jobs while talking about the need to pay down our long-term debt. Our economy is in worse shape than ever. We've heard the hot mic with the Russian president. Just how flexible will Obama be with our missile defense after his last election? On a video, Obama is chuckling with his buddies that there never were shovel-ready jobs. Obama just had to have his trillion dollars for all those shovel-ready jobs. The fact is that Obama lacks character and is a fraud and a liar. But he and his buddies sure are raking in the dough.

The campaign season has just begun and it is painful to watch. Obama continues to blame George Bush for the state of the economy four years later. Shouldn't he be able to brag how much he has helped the economy? He likes using the line of failed policies from the past. True failed policies were followed by Jimmy Carter which led to long gas lines and mortgage rates in the teens. Obama is going to be the poster president for following failed policies from the past.

America will survive this experiment but by the grace of God. God has blessed us and will continue to do so. Obama has been an extremely risky experiment with resonating effects. Damage has been done and will take sterling experience and character from our next leader to begin repairs. God bless America and God bless Romney.

Why Romney Must Win

June 19, 2012

The United States is a country of justice by following the rule of law. Our Constitution is fundamental law and the nine Supreme Court justices ascertain its meaning. The president has the awesome responsibility of nominating ordinary humans to this lifetime tenured position. We can only hope that our president nominates the best and brightest legal minds that our country has to offer.

The most recent photo of the Supreme Court justices shows a tiny, 80-year-old Ginsburg looking like she belongs more in a nursing home than on the most respected judicial bench. From her comments about our Constitution, I hope she is rather senile than someone who doesn't respect and love our Constitution. During her February visit to Egypt, she suggested that the revolutionaries look to South Africa's constitution and not use the United States Constitution as a model. She must believe her 2005 comment that the United States Constitution is just a document frozen in time. It is unbelievable that one of our justices visits a foreign land and rebukes our Constitution and remains seated. Three more justices Breyer, Scalia and Kennedy are 75 years and older and some of the younger justices have health issues. The next president will likely be responsible for shaping this court for decades. Obama's presidency has already given us the disappointing Kagan and Sotomayor, two seemingly hand-stamped liberal votes.

Obama himself is finding it difficult to follow the rule of law. He has taken it upon himself to change immigration law on the grounds that it is the right thing to do. Are states to follow our immigration laws on the books or follow Dictator Obama? If Obama gets reelected, nothing will stop him from changing our laws of how he sees fit. He circumvents Congress. A Supreme Court shaped by Obama will give credence to his actions, whatever they may be. Within a week, the Supreme Court will present its decision on the Obamacare mandate, whether citizens should be forced to purchase health insurance. Had Obama replaced one of the constitutional conservative justices with his choice, Obamacare would definitely become the law of the land. Here's praying that Obamacare is repealed and that our healthcare remains between us and our doctors. Government bureaucrats not welcome.

Dig a Little Deeper, Nuns

June 20, 2012

Two Associated Press (AP) articles caught my eye in yesterday's paper, 'Nuns tour nation to fight budget cuts" and "Pension shortfall balloons for states." Activist Catholic nuns are touring the nation to show how Republican policies are negatively affecting low-income families. Nuns still have this unfounded notion that only Democrats help the poor while the mean, white Republicans want to hurt the poor. Democrat bills that are marketed as helping poor children have most of the money funding their own pay and pensions. Those darn Republicans object because they want a bill to fund the children only.

The nuns need to educate themselves on why Republicans and Democrats alike are now in the position of proposing budget cuts. Public sector unions have

74

worked in tandem with the Democrat politicians on generous retirement benefits, resulting in busted state budgets. 22.5 million public workers nationwide are counting on their retirement pensions and healthcare benefits for years to come. 34 states' pensions are underfunded – the money will run out if the status quo is followed. If the nuns would dig a little deeper, they would find that Republican policies will help EVERYONE in the long run.

Thievery during the Last Five Months of the Obama Administration

June 22, 2012

Anyone interested in the thievery of taxpayer dollars by the Obama administration need only look as far as how the Stimulus dollars were spent. This trillion-dollar fund was granted in the name of stimulating jobs for the American people. For a trillion dollars, Americans should be so excited about all the job opportunities Obama created. Instead, America is a country in decline with a reduced credit rating, downgraded banks, expanded welfare rolls and special interest bailouts. How many of the trillion dollars were redistributed to the 320 million Americans?

I have a theory that when the Obama administration is voted out of office on November 6, the administration will be laughing all the way to the bank. Their pockets, their friends' pockets, and friends of friends' pockets will all have been lined with taxpayer money. Another example is the measly $2 million grant from the Department of Energy recently awarded to the green company Solar Mosaic. Solar Mosaic has a website and describes in three steps how Solar Mosaic works. 1) People invest in solar projects through Solar Mosaic. 2) The solar is installed. 3) The Crowd is repaid from project revenues. Note: All of the current projects operate under a zero-interest loan model. This company does not deserve $2 million dollars of hard-earned taxpayer money. But, hey, Van Jones, ex-green czar to Obama, is listed as an advisor to Solar Mosaic.

I wrote earlier that if you put Solar in a company name, you can line up for your free cash. Who in Congress can stop this? It is sickening that it is legal for the Obama administration to hand out taxpayer dollars with zero accountability. How much more thievery is going to occur in the next five months when Obama realizes that he is going to be shown the door? Obama will continue to call this stimulus money, but it's just a giant Obama slush fund to play with.

Chief Justice Roberts on Obamacare

June 29, 2012

Chief Justice John Roberts sided with the liberal court justices in upholding Obamacare as the law of the land. He found the individual mandate to order people to buy health insurance unconstitutional and could have struck down the law on this basis alone. But to uphold the law, he wrote that the federal government can impose a tax on those without health insurance. He took it upon himself to change the mandate to a tax. He placated the liberals. The reputation of his court as being non-partisan was more important to him than the rule of law. Was he possibly threatened to comply?

Obama drummed up support for Obamacare on the basis that this was not a tax. Watch the video of the Stephanopoulos interview where Obama laughs off the idea that this is a tax. He knew it was and lied to the American people. I wonder how Obamacare supporters will feel when they realize that this law is one big tax. The poor won't care because they expect it for free. That leaves anyone with an income paying more. And now the government gets to butt into your doctor's appointments and determine if you are worthy of the treatment that your doctor recommends.

Obamacare mandates greater insurance benefits while at the same time can deny insurers' rate increases. This obliterates the free market and will eventually turn the world's greatest healthcare into socialized medicine. Chief Justice Robert's rule also turned Obamacare into the main issue of the November election. No matter what names the Tea Party has been called – homophobe, dead, terrorist, and racist – this is a faithful, grass roots party that likes freedom. Freedom from Obamacare is its number one goal.

Obama Wants to Help You with Your School Loans, by Tbird

June 29, 2012

President Barry Obama says Republicans want to raise your school loan interest rates. Bad Republicans! If you vote for him, he'll lower your interest rates! What a bargain! Only a stupid person would disagree with him, and you aren't stupid! Actually, the interest rate for subsidized Stafford loans is scheduled to double from 3.4% to 6.8% for next school year 2012-13. During 2007, President George Bush passed the College Cost Reduction and Access Act of 2007 (remember who was in charge of Congress, which writes the laws, after 2006?), which gradually lowered Stafford loan interest on new loans from 6.8% to 3.4% last year, returning to 6.8% in 2012-13. There are at least two sets of federal school loans, those in the students' names (Stafford loans) and those in the parents' names (PLUS loans). The Stafford loans are divided into two groups, subsidized, for which interest is paid by the government during the time a student is in school, and unsubsidized, in which interest accrues from the time the loan is disbursed. The Staffords are limited in amount (total for unsubsidized and subsidized is currently $5500). Parents can take out PLUS loans to cover what the Staffords (and scholarships and grants) don't cover. The lower interest rate of 3.4% applies only to subsidized Stafford loans. While our kids were in school, we made interest payments on all the other loans so that the interest wouldn't be capitalized and added onto the loan amounts.

In 2010, Obama passed the Health Care and Education Reconciliation Act of 2010, which means Direct Lending does all federal school loans starting in 2010, and PLUS loans went from varying rates dependent on T-Bill rates up to 8.5% to a fixed rate of 7.9%. When my oldest child started college, I was told that although we (meaning my husband, the money-maker of the family) took out the PLUS loans each year, our son would be consolidating his school loans and paying the money back to the government once he graduated. They did not tell us that the PLUS loans stay in the parent's name until they are paid off, including the consolidation of the PLUS loans, which they also don't tell you, roll subsequent consolidation loans of subsequent children all together.

Our son graduated, got his degree, and almost a year later got his job, which is a great job in his field. His school loans went into repayment six months after he left school, each on a ten year repayment schedule, and we actually made the payments on his five PLUS loans until we got them consolidated, by which time he had started his job and was also making payments on his five Stafford loans, which are held by two separate agencies. We could afford to carry the loans for a few months. By the time we started the consolidation process, those five loans had been passed around from agency to agency while our son was still in school, not together, and one of them was mislabeled "in repayment" unbeknownst to us, who didn't make any payments because we had placed all the loans in forbearance so that we wouldn't have to make payments while he was in school. We didn't know until several months later when we started getting nasty letters claiming we were in default and we better pay up NOW. I called every agency that ever had anything to do with the PLUS loans, including the state agency that had originated this loan, but nobody knew nuthin. The agency that had notified the credit reporting companies that we had defaulted on a federal loan said they couldn't do anything, because they had no records anymore that the loan was ever in default. Voila, credit ruined. Luckily, at consolidation, the suspect loan was paid off and although it is still on the credit report, it is no longer wreaking havoc (we replaced an old car with a new one two years ago and couldn't get a loan based on my husband's credit score, so we used my perfect score, perfect although I made $00.00, go figure).

The consolidation loan came in at 7.25%, much higher than any interest rate for anything else we could have bought, other than credit card rates (which skyrocketed due to another law Congress passed and the president signed).

Because the amount was high (over $30,000), it was automatically set for thirty years (thirty years for a school loan!!), and the payment was about $250 a month, most of which goes to interest, which compounds daily. After a year of payments, some a little more than required, he had paid down $1000, and most of that was due to payments we made before consolidation but credited to the new consolidated loan.

When our daughter graduated a year later, we did the same thing. She had four PLUS loans, which we wanted to consolidate into one loan so she wouldn't have to make four separate payments, each on a ten-year payment schedule. Her consolidation loan came in at 8.25% for thirty years (!!), even worse than her brother's. And the government put both those consolidation loans into one loan, still in two parts with two interest rates, and although we can tell them how to apportion them, we would have to do so in writing each month after the payment was made.

The kids cannot make separate payments with any assurance they will be sent to the right part of the loan, as we found out when they made payments (one made a bigger payment than the other) to the agency that held the loans until it sent them to another agency. The single payment coupon even had a section for "specific instructions", but when we checked online, they had split them randomly anyway. Record keeping is nearly impossible. We are taking out a cash-out refinance mortgage loan to pay off the consolidated consolidation multi-interest rate, multi-principal, multi-payment at less than 3% and the kids will pay us directly, and we will be able to track how much each owes. Plus, the loan is a fifteen year, and the payments will be about the same or less than the current payment on the thirty-year loan. When our other children eventually graduate with degrees and loans, mortgage loans will be a lot higher than 3.0%, and we won't be able to refinance their loans like we can with our first two kids' loans.

I just heard on the radio that there is a new agreement to keep the subsidized Stafford loan rate at 3.4% for now, but I don't know any details. In addition to interest rates that don't make economic sense, PLUS loan interest cannot be deducted on one's income taxes. PLUS loans, by definition, are in the parent's name. If the child pays back the PLUS loans, he cannot deduct the interest because it is not his name on the loan, and the parent cannot deduct the interest because he is not making the payments. Remember, the interest rate is so high that most of the first several years' worth of payments is interest. Also, student loans cannot be discharged in bankruptcy (because they would be the most likely cause of a recent student's bankruptcy, especially when the economy is as bad as it is now).

School loans sound like a good idea if a student goes to a school with relatively low tuition or he gets lots of scholarships and picks a major that will get him a good job that will provide him an income high enough to support himself and pay off his loans. Obama should never have signed a law that messes with the market interest rate. He did, and students get stuck with a much higher interest rate than they would otherwise. After all, someone has to pay for Obamacare, and student loans now top one trillion dollars. Government should not mess with the market, period. They make decisions based on politics, not common sense and realistic markets. How else would interest rates for student loans be over 7 or 8 percent, and home loans be around 3 percent? And Obama wants us to thank him for fixing student loans.

I'm Sick Now, by Kithy

June 29, 2012

Wow. I have such a sick feeling in my stomach because of the Supreme Court's ruling today on Obamacare. I feel so sad for our lost liberties. I could have been fined and then jailed when I failed to pay for health insurance in the recent past because I was laid off. So, instead of being able to decide what was best for me, which was to pay for health insurance on my husband only and a discount plan for me and the kids, I would have had to spend all our grocery money; that is about all I had left, on health insurance. So, at least when the kids started passing out from lack of food, a doctor could have charged me an arm and a leg to tell me to feed my kids. He would have charged me, because the only insurance I could afford had a huge deductible that paid nothing for regular visits. So, not only would I be forced to pay for insurance, it wouldn't cover anything. At least, had I saved money from not paying for insurance, I may have been able to afford an occasional doctor visit. Can the government really be expected to take all of this into consideration when it's choosing for me to pay for expensive insurance (there really isn't any other choice- there aren't any inexpensive policies for individuals/families)? I know that not having insurance was a crapshoot, but for me the choice was how to spend a limited budget on the most important items. I have six kids. I know that one of them could have had an accident. But they are kids and are generally healthy. I hadn't brought them to the doctor for anything but an occasional visit in the most recent years. But my husband has health issues. Should I spend more on him, who is likely to use the coverage? Should I spend so much on insurance for the whole family that we can't afford groceries and his medicine? Well, if Obamacare was already in place, I wouldn't have been able to make that decision. It would have been a fine and a jail cell.

Bigger Picture of Obamacare, by Kithy

July 1, 2012

Here is the big picture: the government has taken over 1/6 of the economy. The government dictates to insurance companies what they are to provide and how much money they need to spend. And the government dictates to doctors how much they can earn and how many patients they can treat and how they can treat those patients. This is America! The government doesn't get to tell anyone how to run his company! The government should not be running an entire industry! The government should butt out of private enterprise! The government does not have the ability to take into consideration all the ins and outs of running someone else's privately owned business, much less everyone's medical business. When the government takes over direction of corporations or other business telling them how to conduct business that is fascism. It would be socialism if the government seized or owned the businesses and directed them how to conduct business. Obama medicine is fascism.

This is about LIBERTY! If I were a doctor, I'd quit now. If I were a medical student, I'd quit school now, before running up additional student loans, knowing that the government will tell me how much I can make, and knowing that amount will not be enough to pay my loans. Hmmm, so if doctors will quit, who will take care of us?

The Church vs. Obamacare, by Kithy

July 1, 2012

Archbishop Carlson declares in a recent video that "you can fine me, we won't pay. You can throw me in jail, and I don't care." He is talking about the fines or jail time for hospitals and employers who won't provide abortions just because the government tells them to. Yesterday, I saw a commercial of an abortionist, who said a bunch of old white men are going to lose all the parishioners who don't agree with a religious debate over what is a medical issue, and the Church is going to be declared dead over this. Well, I'm with my old white guy. He is awesome!

He is 100% correct that this is a religious liberty issue. If the government can trample our religious rights, what other rights can they trample? Can our government tell automobile CEO's and bankers how much money they can make? Yes, already happening in America. Our government allows unlawful search and seizure every day at every airport. Since when did buying an airplane ticket automatically make you a suspected terrorist? Do some detective work and target the potential terrorists!

Back to the Church. Religious liberty is guaranteed in America. How can it be constitutional to force someone to do something against the core of his religion? Getting rid of the abortion mandate really won't solve the problem. The law hasn't been completely written – there will be thousands, or hundreds of thousands of pages of laws to spell out what the first 2700 pages say in general.

Our Constitution fits into a pocket size book of 39 pages, and that is to run the entire country for over 200 years. We do not need 2700 pages plus many more to tell us how to run 1/6 of the economy. I learned in grade school that planned economies don't work. I remember the planned economy in the Soviet Union. How did that work out? A couple of guys, or even a couple hundred guys, cannot come up with all the details needed to tell us how to run the entire medical field. Government bureaucrats are not the experts here.

We HAVE world-class medical care in America! It comes from the freedom of Americans, the freedom of doctors to run their practices how they want to, and the freedom of patients to choose their healthcare and their insurance. Don't make me pay for anyone's abortion!

The Truth About O's Free Colonoscopies, by Kithy

July 3, 2012

Go get your free colonoscopy, and hurry before they are no longer free. Oops, maybe you should know the truth about the free colonoscopies. First of all, insurance companies don't all of a sudden want to foot the bill for a very expensive test that supposedly all the aging boomers should be getting now. Second, if there is a way around a law, the insurance companies will find it. Third, if they can do it with this law, they'll do it with the rest of the required coverages.

Here's how it works: I schedule a screening test, because that is what is covered. Here's the catch. If the doctor finds something, it is no longer a screening, and I am stuck with the entire bill. Wow, what a bargain. A free test that ends up costing me $800 because the doctor clipped a polyp. I suppose I should be happy that we only have to pay $800 and no longer have the threat of colon cancer to worry about. But, good grief, it was supposed to be free and I don't have an extra $800 lying around. Speaking with the billing department, I realized this is common practice, and the insurance companies are not paying for very many tests. Prior to the "free" colonoscopy mandate, these were covered within the normal parameters of insurance. Now, they are effectively, NOT

COVERED!!!!! So much for free medical care. I believe these unintended consequences will happen to all the government mandated coverages.

Bias in St. Louis Newspaper, by Kithy

July 9, 2012

I hate the St. Louis Post Dispatch, and I don't know why I bother reading it. Here is the headline, "Debate reveals few differences." The point of the article is that the Republican candidates are carbon copies of each other and they trash the Dems. The first paragraph recites the Dem's talking points about the Republican candidates, down to the "fact" that they trashed McCaskill and Obama. The article complains about familiar issues with familiar responses. The last half of the article is verbatim Claire McCaskill's talking points. The paper obviously wants Claire to win. How this article came to be front page news instead of opinion journalism, I do not know.

Obama's Katrina, by CWK

July 9, 2012

The Washington DC power outage should be Obama's Katrina. He goes on a bus tour to the Midwest or a fund-raising tour to Europe where the tab is $20,000 for individuals and $30,000 for couples. DC electrical power is cut off by natural causes while his EPA plans to make electricity too expensive when it comes back on.

Why do we care about where Mitt's money is? by Kithy

July 9, 2012

The President wants us to believe that Mitt Romney is unpatriotic because he has money in foreign accounts. He wants to punish bad people like Mitt. Remember Eduardo, with Facebook, who changed his citizenship prior to the IPO? The President wanted to punish him, too. Why isn't he asking Mitt what we need to do to keep his money in America? Why isn't he asking what we can do to keep jobs in America? Surely, Mitt Romney knows what policies are not working, and he has an idea what policies would persuade him to keep money and jobs in the USA. We do have a choice. Punish these people who would dare to make a decision that benefits them or ask them what we need to do to fix the problem that causes them to make decisions we don't like.

82

Brad Pitt, what's a good liberal to do?

July 11, 2012

Brad Pitt hasn't defended his mother, yet. As a superstar liberal, what is he going to do? His Hollywood liberal friends are defaming his mother with hatred-filled, nasty vitriol for speaking her conservative mind. He could call the celebrity President and remind Obama of his urging to "help usher in more civility in our public discourse." Brad could put in a good word and urge Obama to call his mother. That's not going to happen because Jane Pitt is conservative. What I would like Brad Pitt to do is to stand by his mother and tell the liberal crowd to go to hell. In honor of his mother, he should also want to revisit his good old, Midwestern values and get back to his conservative roots. The alternative is to keep his mouth shut and kowtow to the close-minded liberals. Is blood thicker than his Hollywood lifestyle?

Chief Justice John Roberts' Silver Lining Isn't, by Tbird

July 12, 2012

After the Supreme Court's ruling upholding the Obamacare mandate thanks to John Roberts' tie-breaking vote, a lot of conservative pundits tried to find a silver lining. They said that the ruling prevents Congress from using the Commerce Clause of the Constitution to force people into doing what they don't want to do. Unfortunately, they are wrong. Congress may be limited in using the Commerce Clause (actually, I read that Roberts was writing as himself individually, not as a member of the majority, in which case the Commerce Clause ruling is not really a precedent future Supreme Courts must honor), under which it can regulate interstate commerce, but it doesn't end there. All Congress has to do is tax inactivity to force action. I pay tax when I buy a candy bar, fine; I want the candy bar and I am willing to pay a few cents tax. When I don't want to buy an item, I don't, and I don't pay tax. Now, Congress can decide what I should buy and make me pay a tax when I don't buy it.

People make fun of the broccoli tax example because they can't see Congress passing a law to make them buy something they don't want, but that is exactly what John Roberts said was constitutional. But it's not a tax when you make me pay for something I didn't buy, you might say, it's a punitive penalty! You are thinking like a regular person. John Roberts is not a regular person. He is the Supreme Court Chief Justice. He claimed that the Court should uphold a law passed by Congress by any means possible using any reasoning possible, even going so far as to rewrite the law to redefine a word into something it wasn't written to mean. I don't understand why he declared unconstitutional an Arizona state law regarding illegal immigration that exactly mirrored a federal law the

President doesn't feel like enforcing if he believes that; I personally think he caved to pressure from the liberal media and the liberal President.

When Congress passes a law using the Commerce Clause, shouldn't the Court make its ruling based on that clause? If it is unconstitutional to mandate that individuals and businesses buy a product (health insurance) under the Commerce Clause, shouldn't a penalty, or even a penalty tax, that enforces the unconstitutional mandate itself be considered unconstitutional? It doesn't look that way. We conservatives have learned a hard lesson: if we allow Congress to pass a bad law, we cannot look to a conservative Supreme Court to bail us out. There is no such thing as a conservative Supreme Court that does its constitutional duty of determining the constitutionality of a law under our Constitution, the defining document of our country. We must do everything we can to vote for a president and congress people and senators who do follow the Constitution. Otherwise, Obama will run our country into the ground if he is reelected, along with a Democrat Senate, and we will have no one to blame but ourselves.

Your Taxpaying Contribution to Obama's Campaign

July 13, 2012

Have you heard Margie's secret to looking amazing? She's on food stamps! The US Department of Agriculture is spending between 2.5 and 3 million hard-earned taxpayer dollars on advertising food stamps to increase enrollment. Agriculture Secretary Tom Vilsack said that several large states have underperformed in signing up more people on food stamps. Shouldn't he be thrilled with this news that Americans are providing for themselves?

I know the liberal talking points that people are forced to depend on the government to feed their families in these tough economic times. Advertising is just a public service to help those in need. Well, who has been running the country into the ground for the past 3½ years and wants 4 more to continue what he has been doing? Our tax dollars are already paying food stamps for 1 in 7 Americans, approximately 46 million recipients. Yet the USDA advertises on Spanish soap operas and in CA, TX, NC, SC, OH and NY stating that "even if you have savings you may be eligible." The USDA also encourages food stamp offices to throw great parties to increase enrollment.

Talking about parties, I was in line at Walmart at the end of the month. Another customer asked the cashier why it felt like a party that day with so much energy. The cashier replied, "food stamps." We looked at each other realizing it's a party we're not invited to but are funding. These 46 million people have their food stamp debit cards credited at the end of every month and aren't just buying bread and milk for sustenance. Our President with less than four months to election day has the gall to spend taxpayer money to recruit more people that are not even seeking out assistance to receive government freebies, including cakes, soda and chips.

You Didn't Build It, by Kithy

July 22, 2012

If we keep repeating, "you didn't build it" and reminding people that is what our current president thinks, surely Mitt Romney can win the next election. "You didn't build it" describes the main division in our presidential candidates. Do you want the anti-American, anti-capitalist candidate or do you want the pro-capitalist, pro-American candidate? "You didn't build it" epitomizes the far, far, far left, and reminds us that our current president wants us to share the wealth. He doesn't like capitalism and wants it to go away. He wants something else, where we all contribute to the general welfare and we are utopianly sharing everything equally. (I know that I just made up a word, but it fits.) The government is the means to do that. Take away all individualism and independence and replace it with government mandates and taxes and dependency. Mitt Romney, on the other hand, celebrates Americanism and the American spirit by congratulating successful people, and acknowledging that America was built by entrepreneurs and individuals, not by government. He knows that in order to survive and prosper, we need to follow the founding fathers' guidance, and give people independence. Over-regulation stifles independence and entrepreneurship. Let's keep this front and center through November: "you didn't build it".

The Presidential Response to the Massacre, by Kithy

July 22, 2012

James Holmes, a mentally unstable psychiatric out-patient obsessed with killing, committed a mass shooting, murdering 12 and injuring 70 at a theater in Aurora, Colorado. Here's another person who should have been committed to a psych ward BEFORE he killed. Under our current law, he can't be committed UNTIL he kills. I heard a tidbit of President Obama's response to the massacre and I was extremely thankful that he was not our president during 9/11. I compared it to Mitt Romney's response, and I favored Romney's. His was more presidential. The president leads. He sets the tone for the nation. By telling us to go home and hug our kids, he sounded like a lost puppy. (me, me, me, I, I, I, poor me, how can I make myself feel better?) Mitt, on the other hand, gave us advice how to go on. To pray with and to mourn with the victims and their families. (what can I do to make others feel better?) I'm just saying one of them sounds more presidential than the other, and it's not the one we currently have in office. Let's vote Mitt in!

You Didn't Build That; Other People Made that Happen, by Tbird

July 24, 2012

Poor Obama. Every time he goes off teleprompter, he accidentally speaks the truth as he sees it. He shows us how he thinks, and it isn't pretty. He thinks that because government caused roads to be built and teachers hired to teach that you could not have made your own wealth (does Obama understand that government gets it money from private enterprises that are successful? I don't think he had made that connection). You have a business? You know what you did to start it, keep it, improve it. It cost you time, money, and effort. You are not his target voter because you are a person of action. His target voter is the person who wants someone else to take care of him because he doesn't think he is capable of taking care of himself. Clinton was pressured into signing the welfare bill in the 1990's; it included a work requirement. People who had been on welfare went out and got jobs; they didn't know they could take care of themselves until they were forced to, and the welfare rolls dropped by half.

Obama just decreed that a person on welfare doesn't have to even try to get a job; if he can get more people to see that they are incompetent and must depend on him, the more people who will vote for him so they can keep their benefits. You have a lot of money or stuff? You know how you got it, and it most likely wasn't due to inheritance or winning the lottery; you earned it. Your stuff is your private property, and no one can take it away from you just because he wants what you have, or so you thought. Obama has millions in the bank; he knows he didn't earn it by his own sweat when someone else with well-honed writing skills ghost-wrote his autobiography. Because he knows he didn't earn all his own riches, he doesn't think anyone else earned his, that "someone else" made that happen. If what you have is because of someone else, it isn't really yours, and Obama can take it and give it to his friends, who will give some of it back to him in campaign donations. See how easy that is if you accept his premise? If you believe someone else really did cause you to have what you have, go ahead and vote for Obama for president in November; he'll be only too happy to relieve you of all that money and stuff you didn't earn. Now, that really is an easy decision to make.

86

What "You didn't build it" Means for a Second Term of Obama

July 24, 2012

According to Obama, you didn't build it because the government did. You may think that your business is your business and that your hard work made it happen. But you have a president who truly believes that your success lies at the hand of the government. If your success really belongs to the government, who do you think the money that came from that success really belongs to? Our extreme radical leftist president believes that it belongs to the government. Your savings, house and property that was acquired by your success does not belong to you.

A second term with Obama will be the end of government of the people, by the people, for the people. It will become an all-powerful government that takes from the people. If anyone is still considering voting for Obama, linking three Obama off-teleprompter remarks gives a crystal-clear picture. First, his response to Joe the Plumber's question about taxes, "...I think when you spread the wealth around, it's good for everybody." Second, "We are five days away from fundamentally transforming the United States of America." And third, "If you've got a business, you didn't build that. Somebody else made that happen."

If the little workers of the world stopped receiving paychecks for their work, they would quit working. If business owners have to turn over their earnings to the government, they will close their businesses. During Obama's first term, business owners have been dealing with Obama's policies resulting in many closing their doors already. Anyone STILL considering voting for Obama has to realize the link between his policies and high unemployment. Imagine living in our beloved United States of America if Obama is unleashed with a second term. Obama's government is going to go after what it feels is rightfully its own.

AUGUST 2012

The Gold Goes to the Black American Gymnast

August 3, 2012

The gold goes to the black American gymnast for the all-around title, but did she earn the silver? The gold medal came down to the very last floor exercise by the ballerina-trained Russian gymnast Viktoria Komova. Her routine was flawless, beautiful, Olympian and my untrained eye thought she earned a very high score. She needed at least 15.36 to be granted the title of all-around female gymnast of the world. The judges gave her 15.1 and the all-around went to Gabby Douglas who had come very close to stepping out of bounds. Possibly out of bounds?

The viewers were not given a close look or replay to determine if she was in or out. That would have been a full one-point deduction.

Gabby Douglas is an amazing gymnast with an infectious smile. She is also black and in our present affirmative action climate, I question if that was the deciding factor in the all-around gold. Receiving the silver still would be a great American success story but it wasn't a good enough story for the judges at the Olympics. As it is, this story of gold belongs to the first black gymnast.

I tie affirmative action into Obama's success. On the Rush Limbaugh radio show, a Harvard classmate of Obama's claimed that Obama received the lowest grades that a Harvard graduate ever got and that professors gave him passing grades even when he didn't show up for class. Another Occidental student claimed that the school is extremely difficult to get in. Obama wrote about trying drugs enthusiastically in high school and that he was a goof off. We will never be able to prove that the Russian gymnast was deprived of the gold. However, Obama can provide his school transcripts so that Americans can see if a flunky who didn't earn his way is leading our country. Americans may be able to deduce why Obama doesn't think successful people earn their way.

The Trouble with Harry Reid, by CWK

August 7, 2012

When someone has knowledge that a crime has been committed and fails to report the crime to an appropriate prosecutor or police official, one is guilty of the crime of misprision of felony or misdemeanor. If the Leader of the Senate has such knowledge of a crime it is his obligation to report such crime. The Leader may be guilty of misprision of a felony if he knows that a presidential candidate has failed to pay taxes for 10 years but has failed to report that crime to a prosecutor. That is, unless his information is incorrect, such a report may be subject to monetary damages in that he has made this falsehood outside the Senate floor as he has to the Huffington Post.

We Are No Longer a Christian Nation

August 7, 2012

Of course this isn't true, but President Obama stated this as fact while he was in the Muslim country of Turkey. Obama stated that we do not consider ourselves a Christian nation or a Jewish nation or a Muslim nation. One can deduce that he was trying to put Islam on the same level as Christianity in the United States. According to the Pew Forum on Religion and Public Life – World Religion Database 2010, 79.5% Americans are Christians and less than 3% follow

Judaism and Islam combined. So, Mr. President, we ARE a Christian nation. My priest was asked why he is a Christian. He put it quite simply. He is on this earth for a very short while. Being human, he is a sinner and knows that he cannot save himself.

The Truth Tour, by Kithy

August 9, 2012

Herman Cain is going on a truth tour. The Republicans are horrible at campaign politics, but Herman has taken this opportunity to make sure that we don't get another four years of Obama presidency. Herman was so good at the debates, he is a great speaker, and he takes complex issues and makes them simple and easy to understand. Here's what he'll cover: he'll speak to employers and employees about political positions that affect "their company, job security, wages and benefits, and their families" from a business leader's perspective. I think we're lucky to have him on our side. We need a good speaker, speaking up for the lousy party leaders who don't know how to get the message out better than the opposition.

Olympic Winners, by Tbird

August 12, 2012

The Olympics always produces feats of marvelous physical excellence, and it also produces moments of wonderful athlete reactions. Many of the runners, including Allyson Felix and Aries Merritt, gave glory to God after their gold medal performances, as did little Gabby Douglas after her individual all-around gymnastics' competition. Jordyn Wieber, expecting to compete for a medal in the same all-around competition as gold medal Gabby, did not qualify, even though she came in fourth in the preliminaries and the top twenty four gymnasts are allowed to compete (the Olympics committees performed their own spreading the wealth shenanigans by limiting each country to only two competitors, meaning teams with too many excellent gymnasts, like the United States with three gymnasts in the top four spots, were penalized); she cheered on her teammates anyway. McKayla Maroney, acknowledged as the best vaulter in the world and heavily favored to earn the gold, fell on her hiney on her second vault—and still won the silver; she knew she didn't deserve the gold (a picture of her with a very unimpressed expression on her face has been photoshopped in front of very impressive sights, which just made her laugh). Sam Mikulik stuck one of the best vaults of his career, and the expression on his face was so joyful I grinned myself; afterwards, he was eager to watch the world's best male vaulter, and it didn't matter that Sam didn't win a medal. Blade runner Oscar Pistorius made it to semi-finals in his race, though he didn't get to the finals; he took the time to run with a little girl, also on blades, who will never forget the kindness of an Olympic athlete. And Jewish teenager Aly Raisman honored the Israeli athletes murdered forty years ago by Palestinian terrorists during the Munich games with her gold medal floor exercise routine set to Jewish folksong Hava Nagila; the Olympic officials weren't that brave. Good athletes all, and decent human beings.

The Romney/Ryan Ticket

August 14, 2012

Romney didn't pick 'an incredibly boring white guy' for VP as he was asked by NBC's Brian Williams. He picked the guy that is depicted in video clips physically dumping Granny off a cliff. Unfortunately for the Dems, Paul Ryan sure doesn't look like a guy who hates his grandmother or anyone else's for that matter. He could be described as Obama has: articulate with perfectly creased pants. We have found out that doesn't translate into a great leader. It just means that the words coming out of your mouth sound great and you're well-dressed.

The Republican ticket of Governor Mitt Romney and Representative Paul Ryan is a formidable opponent to the Obama machine. It will be a relief listening to the ideas and policies that these two men will present to us and to the world. Obama's hokey hope and change type speeches will not work in this economy and his empty, bullying threats will appear juvenile. Americans are ready to listen to solutions. Both Romney and Ryan are big solution guys. Let the debates begin!

Biden Unchained, by Tbird

August 20, 2012

Vice President Biden says to an audience of black people that Republicans "want to put y'all back in chains." President Obama says Biden just meant that "consumers would be worse off if Republicans succeeded in doing away with new restraints on financial institutions." Romney says the President "should take his campaign of division and hate back to Chicago." The mainstream media says Romney is a racist. Obama should put Biden in an attic and chain him up.

Obama's Accomplishments vs. Romney and Ryan

August 20, 2012

In the past four years, Obama passed a nearly trillion dollar stimulus that did not stimulate jobs, a Cash for Clunkers program that destroyed more than 675,000 affordable used cars, the GM Bailout in which the taxpayers own 500 million shares of undervalued stock, and government healthcare which raids Medicare of $718 billion. The Obama policies and programs have failed to improve the job situation of Americans and to get our economy growing. Obama has said that in a second term that he would like to bail out more industries similar to the GM bailout and to pass another stimulus. The American people have to ask, "Really, that's all you've got?!?" So, as the campaigning continues, Obama wants us to focus on anything but his economy. Instead, we are supposed to care about Romney's past ten years of taxes, how Romney cut someone's hair when he was seventeen, how Romney treated his dog on his travels, how Romney's wife never really worked, etc.

Romney is a successful businessman and served as Governor of Massachusetts. His company Bain Capital is an asset management and financial services firm and did outsource when it was advantageous to the clients. In addition to Romney's experience, the American people are given a treat, a vice-presidential candidate in Representative Paul Ryan, the Budget Committee Chair, who is well-versed on the budget and economy. It looks like this campaign has turned into a choice of more bailouts and stimulus vs. successful problem solvers by financial experts.

We Want Akin, by Kithy

August 22, 2012

We voted: we want Akin because he has a proven conservative record. So, he said something incredibly stupid. Who cares? Everyone gets to say something stupid at least once in their lives. Look at his voting record vs McCaskill's. She rubberstamped every Obama decision ever. Akin apologized, now he has to move on to remind everyone why we voted for him, and why we don't want McCaskill. He has consistently stood his ground and voted against Obama just about every time it counted. And if the darn RNC (National Republican Committee) would butt out, and if Romney would stop telling our man to step down, Missouri would appreciate it.

Get some backbone and stand up for conservative principles. Where was the outrage when Biden offended everyone about chains? Why wasn't he told to step down? That's much more offensive to more people: everyone that he just accused and the (he obviously believes) idiots he's talking to. I really don't think

91

the offended police need to come out as often as they do, but if they're going to be offended, they should be offended equally for Dems and Reps. If the RNC would stand up for their own people, we wouldn't have to start brand new grassroots groups to overcome their shortsightedness. Tea Party, anyone?

Oh, and by the way, I wish the DNC would continue running ads against Akin for us. They tell us why we want him better than any RNC ads would. Yes, we want to get rid of the Departments of Education and Energy, and we do want to privatize social security and we don't want to pay for everyone else's contraception (we'd rather pay for our own medical needs). Let's fire the RNC and let the DNC do our advertising for us.

Do we want four more years of this?

August 22, 2012

If you are feeling chilly, this Drudge Report headline will burn you up, $500,000 of stimulus cash spent to air ads during Olbermann, Maddow shows – half a million hard-earned taxpayer dollars given to a PR firm to tell the MSNBC bots how great the Obama green jobs programs are. I doubt the ads told the bots how much stimulus money was steered to the many now bankrupt green companies and how few jobs were created; crony capitalism at its best.

To waste taxpayer funds on these types of political games is sickening and close to outright thievery. 23 million Americans are out of work, the economy is stagnant, and food prices may soon go through the roof. We have been warned that the man-made global warming-induced drought has killed corn crops, yeah, right. But Obama's green policy of burning up what corn we have into ethanol gas continues.

Poor Obama does not realize that bloviating on his greatness does not compute into reality. He may realize exactly what he is doing to America. He then can truthfully say that America is not a superpower anymore. We'll be transformed into a country wallowing in debt unable to protect ourselves.

Fellow Squealing Pigs Who Are Purchasing Chains

August 22, 2012

Hello, fellow squealing pigs! If you are a Democrat, I apologize. Squealing pigs is reserved for Republicans by our VP who says that's how we sound when making objections. Chain manufacturers sure should be excited for a Republican win. According to Biden, we are going to put the black community back in chains.

92

Is he getting more ridiculous on purpose so that Obama can bring in a ringer at the last minute and save his election? Or is this who Biden is? Unfortunately, Biden is our vice president and these statements have passed his lips. Presidential candidates have a first major decision to make, choosing a VP candidate who becomes a heartbeat away from the presidency. Biden is Obama's pick. Ryan is Romney's pick. I hope Americans listen very closely when these two debate on October 11th. Also mark your calendars for the presidential debates: October 3rd, 16th and 22nd. We will learn more about Obama's decision-making consequences on our lives.

Who's cutting more billions? by Kithy

August 24, 2012

You always hear about Republicans wanting to cut entitlement programs. Then, along comes Obama, and he cuts $718 billion out of an entitlement program and people are in an uproar. Why? It sounds like he did what Republicans want to do. Here's the difference. Most of the people who benefit from Medicare paid into the program for years. They deserve to get the benefits that they paid for. He's cutting their benefits, because he wants to pay for other people who don't want or can't pay for their own insurance. He's moving the money around, because it's in such large amounts, he thinks he can play with taxpayer money. He thinks that he should pick who gets the money. He doesn't care that people expect and deserve benefits that they paid for. To him, it's a large amount of money that he can buy more votes with. I sure hope the people who paid into it realize this, and that he's stealing your benefits and that he's losing a lot more votes than he's buying.

Republican Convention 2012

August 26, 2012

Ann Romney was scheduled to speak Monday evening before the major TV networks announced that they would not cover Monday night. Those tricky Republicans rescheduled her speech for Tuesday evening. What you can expect at the convention if you listen to Democrat talking points:

- No women since the Republicans are in a war against women
- No blacks since Republicans chained them up back home on the plantations
- No Latinos because Republicans sent them all back to where they came from
- No elderly because Paul Ryan threw them off the cliff in wheelchairs
- No gays because Republicans just plain hate them
- No police, firemen or teachers because Republicans cut them out of the budgets

93

- No middle class because they have to work because the rich don't pay taxes
- No young voters because Republicans took away their school loans and now that they cannot afford tuition, they are stuck living in their parents' basements
- Tons of babies because Republicans banned contraceptives
- Military because Republicans are warmongers

Besides babies and military, that leaves rich, boring old white guys sitting around smoking cigars, counting their oodles of money and sipping tea (that's what happens at Tea Parties). Babies cannot vote and the military overseas ballots may not even count. What are those rich white guys thinking? If nothing else, we should tune in for the entertainment value. This could be enlightening.

The Akin vs. McCaskill Vote, by Kithy

August 26, 2012

They're on TV again today, saying Akin is unelectable. But here's our choice: if we abstain from voting for senator, that's a vote for McCaskill. If we vote for anyone but Akin, that's a vote for McCaskill. McCaskill is an Obamacare, big government, big taxes, anti-life senator. Is that really better than a proven conservative vote, who happened to have said something incredibly stupid? The Dems, CNN, CNBC, all the regulars who pound the Republican candidates had nothing to do with blowing Akin all out of proportion. The Republicans and conservative talk radio did it all on their own. With the constant barrage and constant debating of the Akin issue, we have kept this on the radar. Even Jaco ignored the original comment, he didn't follow up with anything when Akin first said it. Let it blow over, and let Missourians decide, would we rather have Obama's right-hand senator, or would we rather have a conservative vote in the Senate?

Akin's Legitimate Comment

August 27, 2012

The Todd Akin quote got blown out of proportion with Republicans as the number one basher. First of all, Akin should not have said what he said, or at least he should have worded it differently. That said, let's break it down. Is underage consensual sex rape? Is a sexual assault rape? Does anyone know the difference between first-degree and second-degree rape? Is an alleged rape a rape? Is criminal sexual abuse rape? Akin was talking about forcible rape, a much better term than 'legitimate.'

Akin said he read that the 'female body has ways to try to shut that whole thing down.' That would most likely be from "Assault Rape and Pregnancy", National Right to Life News, July 17, August 21 and October 9, 1986, three-part series written by John C. Wilke, former president of National Right to Life. The main body of the article is that assault rape pregnancies are rare and backs this up with facts and statistics.

One of the major statistics came from the Guttmacher Institute who undertook a study on understanding women's reason for having abortions. Rape was reported as 1% in "Reasons US Women Have Abortions: Quantitative and Qualitative Perspectives", Perspectives on Sexual and Reproductive Health, 2005, 37(3):110-118. The institute was named after Alan F. Guttmacher, former president of Planned Parenthood.

Before Republicans started reacting to Akin's comment and proclaiming that he will lose against the Obamanite McCaskill, they could have used these facts against Planned Parenthood and abortion. Their first reaction to abortion and pro-life comments is to tremble and start acting like liberal babies. They condemn it, disclaim it and discredit it, over and over until every young liberal takes it as gospel. One of pro-abortion's most popular stances is to support abortion because of rape. It just sounds mean to be against it. However, being that pregnancy is rare from rape and that abortion because of rape is extremely rare, has this become our excuse to go against our pro-life view that all life is valuable? Is the rape baby less of a person and not worthy of life?

SEPTEMBER 2012

Who's showing leadership in Louisiana? by Kithy

September 1, 2012

Who is in Louisiana after Hurricane Isaac hit? Is it our fearless president? No, he's out campaigning. He's going to lead from behind again, after the candidate Romney visits and shows leadership from the front. He's visiting the people and showing sympathy, he's visiting the first responders, who deserve appreciation and gratitude. Who do we want as president? The lead from behind - I mean follower, or the one who is presently showing leadership? Let's keep watching these two and comparing them in all aspects. I suspect that I know who will come out on top every time.

Mitt Romney's Republican Convention 2012

September 2, 2012

Mitt Romney has the demeanor, grace, capability, integrity and experience to be the President of the United States of America. For those who missed the Republican Convention 2012 and want a short synopsis, here it is:

- Mitt Romney is a self-made man who donated his entire inheritance to charity.
- Ann Romney is a gracious lady who raised five boys, battled breast cancer and depression, and has multiple sclerosis.
- As bishop of his church, Romney worked tirelessly for his congregation.
- As CEO of the 2002 Winter Olympics and governor of Massachusetts, he accepted no salary.
- Massachusetts was number one in education during Romney's leadership.

Speakers who vouched for Romney:

In 1979, fireman Mr. & Mrs. Oparowsky described how Romney befriended their dying 14-year-old son, helped write his will, arranged a fireworks' show for him and was asked to say his eulogy. "You cannot measure a man's character based on the words he utters before adoring crowds during times that are happy. The true measure of a man is revealed in his actions during times of trouble — the quiet hospital room of a dying boy, with no cameras and no reporters." Pam Finlayson had a very ill preemie and Romney visited to pray with her. When her daughter died a year and a half ago at age 26, Romney personally extended sympathy and love. "It seems to me, when it comes to loving our neighbor, we can talk about it or live it. The Romney's live it every single day."

Grant Bennett, who worked over 1000 hours as Romney's apprentice in the church, described those as the greatest of his life. "Mitt prayed with and counseled church members seeking spiritual direction, single mothers raising children, couples with marital problems, youth with addictions, immigrants separated from their families, and individuals whose heat had been shut off."

Campaign Chairman Bob White has worked with Romney for the past 30 years and describes Romney as a decisive leader, the calm in the storm who runs towards the problems. He told of how Romney closed the Bain office, mobilized an effort to find a partner's daughter who went to a Rave party in New York high on ecstasy, and found her. "I was there when Mitt turned around desperate situations, fixed big broken things and had a profoundly positive impact on people's lives."

96

Jane Edmonds, a black liberal Democrat, who Romney picked as his Secretary of Workforce, loved working for him. "He is the real thing, authentic." "One area where he made a positive difference is in improving the representation of women in senior positions in Massachusetts state government."

Speeches not to be missed, definitely look them up:
Clint Eastwood speaking to an empty chair that substitutes for Obama
Susana Martinez, Governor of New Mexico
Mia Love, Mayor of Saratoga Springs, Utah

It is a pity that the Dems and supporters will focus on the phony charge of not paying taxes for ten years and other idiotic claims to disparage a good man who would make a great president.

The Gluteus Maximus Posterior Equality Act

September 3, 2012

This is dedicated in honor of the Democrat convention this week and Obama's social justice, equality, fairness and you didn't do it on your own.

Observing from behind, I think we can all agree that there are skinny butts, perfect butts and fat butts. The American view is that we are all individuals living freely amongst ourselves. Skinny butt people can invent butt padding and/or eat more towards the perfect butt. Fat butt people can move more and/or eat less towards a perfect butt. And, if they are happy being who they are, they don't have to do anything. They don't even have to think about the size of their butts. Perfect butt people can continue doing what they do. If they want to share their secrets, they can write books on diet and exercise, produce videos, invent exercise equipment and maybe make a few bucks along the way. According to Obama, this viewpoint is old, worn out and doesn't work anymore.

Obama sees social injustice. It isn't fair that skinny butt people have pants that fall off and fat butt people have pants that are busting loose at the seams. Perfect butt people just flaunt their perfectly fitting pants and make the rest of us feel bad about ourselves. These perfect butt people didn't get perfect butts on their own. They didn't grow the food they eat that contributes to their fine buttocks. They didn't manufacture their shoes that help them run to stay in shape. They didn't pick the cotton that their socks are made of that keeps blisters from forming so they can continue to run. Some of these butts were inherited through great genes. They owe the rest of us mere mortals for their good fortunes.

President Obama will help us form a more equal solution to this posterior problem. Because it is so important. The goal is to have all equal butt size. No one's butt should be any better than anyone else's. First step is to form boards and commissions on how to track everyone's butt size and determine the best direction towards butt equality. This will be fairly easy through Obamacare with a requirement for doctors to report butt size – skinny, perfect or fat. Tracking butt perfection will be admittedly tricky but in the name of social justice, it will be done. More boards and commissions will be formed to determine solutions, waivers and mandates. The details will be presented in the Gluteus Maximus Posterior Equality Act which we can read once the act is passed.

A preview to these details may include free shoes and exercise equipment for fat butts. If this doesn't reduce butt size efficiently, fat butt people will be given schedules at the new government butt-reducing clinics. Skinny butts will be asked to eat more. Monitoring food levels of the food groups will be required by the food police. If doctor reports on butt sizes are deemed unacceptable, mandates kick in for everyone and automatically withdrawn from bank accounts already on file through Obamacare.

Obama will have to be prepared to stop the Tea Party patriots who will be expected to complain. They will say nasty things like individual responsibility and Obama shouldn't have his nose up our butts. This will be counteracted as racist (his nose would get browner) and homophobic (the whole butt thing.) Any other dissenters? Social justice, fairness, and the rich aren't paying their fair share, blah blah, blah. Just shut up and vote for Barack Hussein Obama 2012 who is doing this all for our own good.

Obama's Economy

September 6, 2012

Michelle painted the picture she wants us to have of her husband, loving and hard-working. What she ignored is what this loving and hard-working man has done to our country. He has a three-and-a-half-year record, a really bad one.

Unemployment   8.3%
Gasoline $3.80/gallon
National Debt $16 trillion

Obama wants to move forward and has said that he will continue doing what he has been doing: ignoring his Jobs Commission, halting energy production and spending more stimulus money. Clint Eastwood said it best. We have to let him go. Note: Must watch Clint Eastwood 2012 Republican Convention Speech.

The Communist National Convention, by Kithy

September 7, 2012

What an exciting Democrat convention. First, the only president to rival Obama as the worst president in history (Jimmy Carter). Second, a dead guy, who was accused of murder (Ted Kennedy). A bunch of former officials. A whole lot of 'level the playing the field' (commie lingo for "we're going to make it harder for everyone to succeed"). A whole lot of we need government, we need higher taxes for rich people, we need social justice programs (commie lingo for "let's redistribute your wealth"), we need free contraceptives and the worst nun in the world saying that preserving her social justice programs are more important than preserving the life of the unborn. We took your money and saved the auto industry – I think they forgot to mention that they took the money from bondholders, a lot of whom were retired people living on pensions and gave it to the unions. By the way, a bankruptcy would not have closed the auto plants, because they would have filed a reorganization, but it would have 'levelled the playing field' by making the auto plants compete in the same way that every other business does. The auto plants would have had to follow the rules that every business that gets in trouble has to, without using a bunch of taxpayer money as a speculation. Leveling the playing field only works for commies when they get to decide which players need leveling. It is a clear choice, all right:

Freedom from excessive government versus excessive intrusive government.

Impressions of the DNC, by Tbird

September 8, 2012

I DVR'd the Democrat National Convention on PBS this week since they were running three to four hours a night instead of just one prime time hour. When I started watching, my husband yelled from the living room, "Turn that down! I can still hear it, and my blood pressure is rising too fast already!" The other day, Glenn Beck on the radio said he'd pay someone $500 to listen to Michelle Obama's entire speech as he didn't think he could do it. I tried, I really did, but I couldn't do it either. I basically watched a few minutes of the speeches and commentary, using my fast-forward button liberally.

The convention was a pro-abortion rally, including even the word "abortion". Usually, they don't use that word because it reminds people what the choice is. I listened to bits of speeches, and the main ideas seemed to be that Mitt Romney will take away all our rights to kill our babies and thrust us all back into the dark ages, and he won't let us marry whomever we love. If the point of the convention was to snag the "undecided voters" I don't think it could possibly have succeeded, considering all the people who are so aggressively pro-abortion and pro-gay-marriage are already going to vote for Obama, for whom abortion is practically a sacrament and gay marriage something he recently evolved into supporting. At this point, is there a person who honestly can't decide between Romney and Obama?

One day, Obama realized the Democrat platform did not mention God or Jerusalem being the capital of Israel, and he told the committee to put it back in (he knows most of the country believes in God and Israel, and Republicans were beginning to publicize it). Changes in the platform must be approved by the delegates, so Mayor Antonio Villaraigosa, who was in charge, gamely held a voice vote. A voice vote must have 2/3 support, and after three obviously failed attempts at a 2/3 outcome, Villaraigosa gave up and passed it anyway, and the delegates booed. They booed God! I wonder if they realized that is how we feel every time Obama goes against Congress and does what he wants anyway. One speaker was an illegal immigrant who said Obama made her legal; Obama declared his illegal amnesty program for people brought here as children by their illegal immigrant parents after Congress refused to pass a law doing just that. Delegates clapped for her.

The (central time zone) 9:00 hour of each night was supposed to be speeches geared to the normal, America-loving, hard working person. Michelle told us that she and Barry grew up in loving households where the parents worked hard at low-wage jobs and couldn't get ahead because of discrimination but did their best to provide good educations for their children. Barack wants us all to succeed by playing by all the rules. Huh? She sure sounded good, but I didn't see how she could believe a word of what she was saying. Bill Clinton said no one could have fixed the economy after Bush destroyed it so thoroughly so we shouldn't hold it against Obama that he couldn't either, and he spoke so long that Sandra Fluke was still blithering on about how her right to free birth control from her Catholic law school would be destroyed by Mitt Romney right into the 9:00 hour. Mayor Julian Castro mentioned how people were pulling themselves up by the bootstraps but realized he wasn't supposed to be a proponent of self-reliance and then said it was only done in Texas. Caroline Kennedy said she was Catholic and then went on to denigrate laws limiting abortion (Democrat speakers can be Catholic but must repudiate Catholic teaching on abortion rights). Obama's speech was same old, same old, and if he said anything new, I fast-forwarded through it.

I didn't listen to the whole three-day affair, so these are just some of my impressions. If I were a Democrat, I don't think I'd be too excited about my chances this voting season after that convention.

Send Cardinal Dolan to Cuba, by CWK

September 9, 2012

Cardinal Dolan gave the same benediction to both the RNC and the DNC so apparently there is equality between a party platform which represents President Obama's approval of sucking the brains out of a partially born child or four repeated votes to deny a survivor of an unsuccessful abortion any survival medical treatment versus Mr. Romney's position. The President has even termed a new child as a fetus. The ethics professor of a major Ivy League University has said that until a "fetus" is a few years old it can still be aborted. Yet the Cardinal did not make any distinction between the party platforms. He should have never been given a Red Hat and should surrender it having given scandal to the position of the Vatican.

Tax the Catholic Church

September 9, 2012

It is clear for everyone to see that our Catholic Church leaders are beholden to the government. Our Bishops refuse to denounce the DNC's platform which is in direct conflict with Catholic doctrine. Materials titled "Forming Consciences for Faithful Citizenship" will soon be distributed to the Catholic community via the US Bishops Conference. We will be told to carefully reflect on the dignity of workers, solidarity with others to end division and an option for the poor before we vote for a candidate. Also included is the "life and dignity of the human person" – plenty of room for interpretation.

I am sick of my church playing around with this social justice nonsense. The goal of social justice is to take the money from the rich and give it to the poor through excessive taxation. The means have been through friendly sounding agencies such as Catholics in Alliance for the Common Good (CACG) and Catholic Campaign for Human Development (CCHD). The former has been funded by atheist George Soros to promote Catholic social teaching. One area that the CACG has been successful is in making abortion respectable to Catholics – at least to the gullible. The latter is an agency of US Catholic Bishops that has funded ACORN to the tune of over $7 million in the name of advocating justice for the poor.

A solution to stop our church from playing with this leftist speak is taxation for the church. If taxation is what the church is advocating for its members, it is only fair and just for the church to contribute in the same fashion. Perhaps taxing the church would break its bond with liberal politicians.

Discovering Mitt Romney's Self-Assuredness

September 12, 2012

In following Mitt Romney through the primaries, Mitt Romney appeared to coast along, emitting little emotion, and keeping a calm demeanor. He followed a quiet, self-assuredness that could be construed as smugness. Almost every Republican presidential candidate had his or her turn at the top. The primaries pulled in Romney's favor and he became the last one standing. I think we will soon discover that our presidential candidate has been keeping something from us that is the opposite of smugness.

I caught a snippet of Glenn Beck today on the radio and he was his teary-eyed self in describing Mitt Romney. There are stories to be told of this man that can only define him as selfless as any we have known. Most great men do fly under the radar because they are not braggarts, but instead are very humble. Get excited to find out more about this man who will become the 45th president of the United States. It will happen, if necessary, by divine intervention.

"Obama, we are all Osama now" by CWK

September 16, 2012

A caller to Rush Limbaugh pointed out that the Egyptian mobs were calling out "Obama, we are all Osama now" indicating that their reason for attacking US diplomatic facilities is President Obama's bragging about his killing of Osama Bin Laden rather than a relatively unknown movie about Mohammed. The President's spokesman repeats that his policy was not a cause of the deaths of the diplomatic personnel. Many years ago, I talked to an American-Italian lawyer who had gone to the Milan Opera House and talked to the Italian policeman at the Opera. While next to the lawyer's car seat was a loaded automatic firearm, the Police carried unloaded weapons. He was told it was better that the Police died rather than cause a political uproar by shooting a Communist protester. This is repeated by the US ambassador to Egypt refusing to allow Marine guards to have ammunition for their ceremonial guard rifles. I hope the President's Secretary of State is happy with the denial of ammunition to Marine Guards.

Teacher Tenure in America

September 16, 2012

When new school boards were voted in, they often fired all the teachers, whether they were excellent or not. Then they brought in their own people, whether they were excellent or not. Tenure became a necessity to keep our good teachers from going elsewhere and leaving the profession altogether. So how did this safety net lead to never being able to fire a horrible teacher and zero accountability to the students and failing schools?

The answer lies in the Chicago teacher strike. The mayor wanted performance evaluations of the teachers and to be able to fire bad teachers. For God's sake, only 14% of Chicago fourth graders can read proficiently. Teachers through their union are demanding a 30% pay raise and to forget about those other two items above – you know, accountability to the 86% of fourth graders that cannot read and to keep their jobs even though they fail at their jobs. It looks like they will receive only a 16% raise on their paltry salaries of $70 grand plus.

Can everyone see why conservatives want to revamp education? But Mayor Rahm Emanuel is a liberal, so what is going on? Has it become too crystal-clear that changes are needed and that the unions shouldn't have this much control over the education of our children? We WANT tenure for our good teachers. We also want to see bad teachers find a new profession. Is this too much to ask? Evidently, the Chicago strike this close to Obama's reelection campaign has to be resolved in favor of the unions. Who else is left to vote for Obama but the unions, his most loyal and generous supporters?

Who wants a two-ounce burger? by Kithy

September 17, 2012

Michelle Obama's newest food police regulations are not only ridiculous, they are discriminatory. On Monday, anyone eating USDA supplied food is limited to 10 ounces of protein per week for lunch and breakfast, unless he can pay for seconds. This applies to the kids with behavioral and mental problems at a residential treatment center. These kids mostly have no resources - no family, no money, no job opportunities. They are kids that have been abused, their foster parents don't want them anymore, etc. Picture one of these teenagers, getting his USDA provided lunch, and picture a 2-ounce burger. Disregard the fact that no one supplies 2-ounce burgers. Is a week 7 days, or is it 5 days? These kids are in residential treatment and are there during weekends. So, is 2 ounces too big? Maybe the center has to divide 10 ounces by 7, instead of by 5. So, if a teenager eats his 2-ounce (or less) burger at lunch, he won't be allowed protein for breakfast. If he's still hungry, he has no money to buy more protein. Have you ever seen a kid fill up on veggies and fruit? Protein is what keeps a kid from being hungry. No worries. The director is no dummy. She's going to give the kids a nickel before they eat, and then charge a nickel for seconds. Not only is the rule ridiculous, but anyone with a brain (and a heart) will find a way around it.

Auto Maker Bankruptcy, by CWK

September 17, 2012

Obama has made much of Mitt's comment that the GM and Chrysler auto makers should have gone into bankruptcy. In fact, both did go into Chapter 11 bankruptcy under Obama. The difference was that Obama effectively changed the procedures and shafted the secured creditors and shareholders and put the few remaining union auto workers in their position so the union and the United States now owns GM. GM bondholders were called parasites and were told by Obama agents that they would be subjected to the full weight of the Obama administration it they appealed the bankruptcy court ruling on diminishing their secured creditor status. Chrysler is now owned by an Italian corporation. Non-union employees were also shafted by eliminating their GM pensions and health care.

Why does the Republican presidential candidate not point out that both Obama and Romney did suggest the use of bankruptcy and that Obama did in fact use his own version of bankruptcy? Why does the Romney camp give up on Ohio and its voters?

Our Own Baghdad Bobs, by Tbird

September 18, 2012

During the 2003 invasion of Iraq, Saddam Hussein's Iraqi information minister broadcast daily press briefing reports for the Iraqi citizens. The reports got out to the rest of the world and became a source of amusement and enjoyment because they were patently ridiculous. Americans called the propaganda minister Baghdad Bob. Two days before Baghdad fell to US forces, Baghdad Bob stood in front of the Tigris River broadcasting that there were no American troops in Baghdad and that Americans were committing suicide by the hundreds at the city's gates. In the background, on the opposite bank of the Tigris, we could see two American army tanks. The next day, Baghdad Bob said Americans were going to surrender or be burned in their tanks, and Baghdad fell the following day.

Last Tuesday, the anniversary of 9/11, Muslims rioted and destroyed our consulates in Cairo, Egypt, where our Marines were not allowed to have real bullets in their guns, only rubber bullets, and Benghazi, Libya, where they killed four of our diplomats, including the Ambassador. The Secretary of State's office put out a statement deploring the violence, but that America had upset the rioters by allowing an obscure little filmmaker to produce an obscure little anti-Muslim film. She is in charge of embassy security, but she didn't allow Benghazi to even have Marines, just Libyan nationals with no ammunition hired by an American contractor. Jay Carney, the White House press secretary, said the violence was not a case of protests directed at the US writ large or at US policy, and Susan Rice, our UN ambassador, absolutely agreed and said the unrest was because of the very hateful, very offensive video. Obama is sticking with his claim that the attacks on our embassies were spontaneous acts that just spun out of control. Libya now says they were planned assaults, probably by al Qaeda, and that Obama's claim is completely unfounded and preposterous. I just heard on the radio that the administration says there isn't enough information to decide if the attacks on our embassies were terrorist attacks.

It is obvious to me, a regular person with no government power, that barbarians attacked our embassies not because they were upset by a YouTube video but because they hate us, our freedoms, and everything we stand for. It is really as simple as that. Obama's administration officials have become Baghdad Bobs, only instead of amusing us, they are scaring us with their absolute failure to understand anything about third world Muslims in the Middle East.

Obama Needs More Time to Hurt the Middle Class

September 18, 2012

Obama wants more time to help the middle class. When I fill up my car and shop for groceries, I see that prices are doubled. Many in the middle class live paycheck to paycheck and are having a difficult and stressful time making it in the Obama economy. The result is a decreasing middle class and an increase in the poverty class. This is Obama's track record.

Obama has proposed more stimulus, more printing of money, more taxes and not much else. Well, socially, he sure promotes abortion and gay marriage. Millennials love these while ignoring that four more years of Obama will push the middle class into poverty. What will America look like when the middle class is wiped out? Is everyone in the poverty class going to cheer that there is no middle class to strive for? Will fairness have been achieved in Obama's eyes?

His opponent Mitt Romney, a sterling businessman as described by Bill Clinton, has achieved the American dream and will shape America's future with his knowledge and expertise. When more jobs open up and the economy improves, everyone benefits. Obama is asking for more time. Having the most important job in the world, why did he squander more than half a year on the golf course, vacations and fundraisers? He sure wasn't helping the middle class. Meetings with his Jobs Council past six months: zero.

47% Pay No Federal Income Taxes, by CWK

September 19, 2012

Mr. Romney is correct that income taxes are avoided by 47% although they pay some FICA taxes. Consider that Republican President Nixon initiated the Earned Income Tax Credit after he ran to the Right before his election but functioned to the Left after he was elected, also reflected by his approach to Mao in Red China. Still fewer income taxpayers were the result of President Bush's tax cuts which the Democrat platform terms as a tax cut for plutocrats. Unless Congress acts before January, those paying less than 10% will start paying taxes. Plutocrats such as Mr. Buffett and Mr. Gates still will put billions in "charitable" trusts to avoid any taxes, income, capital gains, dividends or death taxes while his or Mr. Gate's family trustees take millions as trustees and pay out perhaps a minimum 5% or possible more generously to charities.

One Party Rule by Supporting Obama's Redistribution

September 19, 2012

A vote for Obama is a vote to support 100% of all Americans who choose not to work which is closing in at 50% of the United States population. That is what this election is all about. If you vote for Obama, you are giving him carte blanche to redistribute your income. Once this tipping point passes 50%, you can vote in the next election to reverse this, but it will be too late. Those people being taken care of by the government on your dime are not going to give it up. Their votes will continue to be Democrat. Welcome to one party rule.

Obama's 'Trick' to Redistribution

September 21, 2012

Redistribution is the same thing as welfare dependence on steroids. Obama understands this and that's why his ideal transformation of America into government dependence requires a trick – his exact wording at a speech at Loyola University in 1998. Obama's trick is how he can structure government systems to pool resources to hand out money. Obama is hellbent on separating you from your money and giving it to people who do not have money. When government kills motivation to succeed and get ahead, you're stuck with communism. In communist countries, who has the money? Have you ever heard communist leaders sharing their wealth with their citizens fairly?

106

The Scared 47%, by Tbird

September 27, 2012

I talked to a woman yesterday about the presidential race. She is in her 40's, single, no kids, and dependent on disability, Medicaid, and housing benefits. She was able to support herself for a few years until she was promoted beyond her ability and got fired for trying to cover up a mistake. She has tried and tried for years to get another job, but she just can't hold a job of any type, even simple, easy, and low stress. She finally gave up and applied for benefits. She doesn't do drugs, drinks little, and doesn't sleep around producing babies she can't raise. She is the kind of person government benefits were designed for, and no one resents it. When I asked her who she would vote for, she said, "There is no reason on earth I'd ever vote for Romney because he will take all my benefits away." She said that he kept saying he was going to cut spending and that benefits would be the first thing to go. I tried to tell her that no one was ever going to take her benefits away, but she is scared and won't chance it.

Romney needs to explain that benefits were meant to be a safety net for people who can't make it on their own and that welfare is for people in a bad spot who need help temporarily. He will never toss them out and hope for the best. Those people will continue to be taken care of. He wants to get more people off welfare who are capable of independence by putting in place policies that will allow and encourage businesses to create jobs. When he says he wants to get people off welfare, he means to grow the economy and produce jobs for the capable, not toss off the truly needy.

Romney's Next Press Conference

September 28, 2012

Romney recently had a press conference on the Mideast embassy attacks. The journalists were caught on an open mic discussing how to frame questions to ask Romney. Sure enough, out of seven questions on the Mideast embassy attacks, six were strictly on the 'appropriateness' of Romney's statement. Not one question was asked about the embassy attacks themselves. The mainstream media has discredited their profession. I propose that immediately following Romney's next press conference with the mainstream media, he should dismiss them and continue with a second press conference with true journalists. Compare both press conferences and put it out there. The American people deserve a media with integrity and honest reporting. Put the mainstream media on notice. Their primetime seating at our next president's press conferences will not be guaranteed. They should earn their seats.

It's Time to Change the Dialog, Mr. President

October 1, 2012

It is time to change the dialog of the United States and it should start with our next President Mitt Romney. The mainstream media need to be put in their places along with the liberal talk shows who consider discussing the president's preference of underwear as a national past-time. From this point on, the media needs to be called out for their biased questions. The liberal media should not be calling the shots on national discussions. On November 6, 2012, the media will learn how irrelevant they have become. We deserve better than a media that fawns over our president at the expense of informing the American people on reality. The media should have never had the power to overrun the airways to promote hatred of President George Bush for eight years. We are tired of the divisiveness that the media has perpetuated year after year. Why are they considered the mainstream media when they are truly the marketing division of the Democrat Party? Someone needs to stand up for the American people over the complicity of the media that sets the agenda rather than reports the news. The outright lies and the absence of truth from the media have put the safety of the United States in danger.

Legitimate Abortion, by Kithy

October 2, 2012

My friend and I were having a discussion the other day about Akin's unfortunate comment. He said "legitimate" instead of "forcible", and everyone automatically reiterated that abortion is acceptable if a woman gets pregnant from being raped. My friend, who adopted a child, doesn't believe that killing a baby solves the problem of a result of rape. Aside from the point that women rarely get pregnant from rape, stating that it is ok, or expected, to kill the baby, is disgusting. Becoming a murderer after a horrendous trauma adds trauma to the trauma. We can understand that a mother might not be able to keep her child if he reminds her of the circumstances in which he was conceived. But there are plenty of couples who cannot have their own children and would love and raise the baby. Why do we keep saying abortion, in case of rape, like it's a legitimate use of abortion? There is no legitimate use of abortion.

Unions in America

October 2, 2012

Something is very wrong with unions when the overriding reason to vote for Obama is that he's pro-union. Why are unions so afraid to work with Republicans? The lies Obama claims about big business are true for unions. The unions are the ones who have overstepped their bounds and have become so greedy that states are going bankrupt trying to meet their demands and pay their pensions.

Obama continues to be not only an embarrassment to the United States but also truly dangerous for our country. Obama's pronouncement that he leads from behind is ludicrous. It means that he isn't leading at all on the international stage. As the President of the United States, he proclaimed at the UN meeting that the future must not belong to those who slander the prophet of Islam. Union workers, did you hear what Obama holds dear? A second term for Obama could mean jail time for anyone who speaks against Islam. Union pensions trump protecting America from encroaching Islam?

Lawless Again, by Tbird

October 2, 2012

The WARN Act is a twenty-year-old federal law that stands for Worker Adjustment and Retraining Notification. It basically requires employers to warn employees at least sixty days in advance of mass layoffs to give them time to make other plans and find other jobs and compensate them with 60 days' pay. On January 1, mandatory automatic across-the-board budget cuts will take place due to sequestration, agreed on last year when the deficit supercommittee could not agree to budget cuts and tax increases to stay within budgetary limits (that happens when you don't bother drafting a budget for several years in a row). As a result, many federal contracts will be cancelled, and hundreds of thousands of jobs lost, because there won't be any money for them. Coincidentally, the sixty-day notification must be given November 1, just days before the vote, which would reflect poorly on President Obama and hurt his reelection chances.

Obama doesn't want to lose the election, so he has decided to violate the WARN Act. He has told contractors to ignore the law and not give notifications to their employees, claiming that the layoffs are "just speculative" so no notices are required. Anything that has not happened yet could be considered just speculative; obviously, the law is meaningless with that interpretation, so that interpretation is flat out wrong. When the contractors answered that they would be liable for employee compensation costs for WARN Act liability, Obama said, don't worry, the taxpayers will pay it for you as long as you follow the Department of Labor's guidance on the matter.

Obama already had his labor secretary issue a guidance saying not to send out layoff notices. On Friday, Lockheed Martin, which had been trying to decide whether or not to comply with the WARN Act, capitulated and will not notify their employees of the coming layoffs. We must vote Obama out of office. This is only the latest in a long line of laws Obama has ignored if they've been implemented or implemented if Congress did not pass them into law. He has no respect for this country's Constitution or laws.

Romney Is That Good

October 5, 2012

The debate on the economy went as expected for conservatives. Governor Romney cleaned Obama's clock. Romney understands the economy, the importance of small business and how to produce jobs. Obama has failed in the past four years in improving the economy because he follows big government tax and spend policies. They are job killers and the results are high unemployment and stagnant growth. Obama has nothing to defend. His stock answer is that he saved us from the financial cliff and has more work to do. Romney, on the other hand, explained how he worked with a Democrat majority in the Massachusetts legislature with terrific results and will lead the same as president.

Romney's history is that of a successful, caring leader of his own company, his church, the Olympics, his state and his family. At the Republican Convention, the people who stood up for Romney and vouched for his leadership and character had outstanding stories. The man portrayed by the Obama administration is a total fabrication and that is why Obama stood at his podium scratching his head. Obama believes the lies he constantly harps on about Romney: that he is a greedy capitalist vampire who sends jobs overseas, doesn't care about the middle class, and has a primary goal of cutting taxes for the rich. We also should not forget the attack ad that accuses Romney of causing cancer that kills a woman. Does Obama even know that Romney's wife Ann fought breast cancer?

Romney is an elegant man, highly intelligent, kind and steady. Obama was not expecting this and was shocked that Romney is everything Obama pretends to be. Obama's strategy to wear Romney down with false accusations failed miserably. Three times he claimed that Romney will cut taxes for the rich by $5 trillion. Romney responding pleasantly and knowledgeably each time, perfectly explaining his positions all the while treating Obama with utmost respect. In closing statements, Obama looked very small mentioning fair shot and fair share without passion. He didn't even seem to believe his own rhetoric. Romney is the real deal. He is presidential and will share his expertise in making everyone's life better.

Obama Conned Himself, by Tbird

October 6, 2012

Mitt Romney did so well in the debate Wednesday night against Barack Obama that even the mainstream media had to acknowledge it. The next day, the MSM came out with excuses for why their candidate failed so miserably to show himself to be presidential material. He was tired, he was too busy being president to bother studying up on the issues, his mock debate partner John Kerry didn't prepare him well, just to name a few. My personal favorite excuse came from Al Gore who blamed Obama's poor debate on the high altitude of Denver.

I think the real reason for Obama's pathetic performance was his own arrogance. Obama is a supremely arrogant man with nothing to be arrogant about. He conned over half the voting American public four years ago into perceiving that he was more qualified than first, Hillary Clinton, who apparently was actually working as a senator, and second, John McCain, war hero and long-time senator. Obama has such confidence in himself that he cannot listen to any views that contradict his own or admit to ever making mistakes and learning from them. During his first two years as president, he refused to have anything to do with the Republicans because he didn't need any of their votes to pass his pet pieces of legislation; after all, he won and had a Democrat Congress. During his second two years as president, he refused to have anything to do with Republicans because they didn't agree with him and his governing philosophy. He never learned to work with opponents, or discuss the issues, or compromise in any way with anyone. He avoided any challenges and never learned to deal with a challenger.

Once Romney became the probable and then official Republican nominee, Obama made up stories that Romney was a greedy, detached, uncaring, waffling man with no plans other than to cut taxes for the wealthy by $5,000,000,000,000 and raise taxes on the middle class to pay for it. He repeated it often enough that maybe even he believed it. With a worthless debate opponent like Romney, he saw no need to work at preparing himself for a debate. Besides, if he said anything stupid, which he knew he wouldn't, the MSM would cover for him like they always have. Romney challenged him on one issue after another, and he couldn't respond with any coherence. He conned himself into believing his innate superiority would carry the day.

111

Will Obama do better at the next debate, which will be held on the 16th? It will be in a town hall format with Candy Crowley moderating and undecided voters asking the questions. I am betting he will have a better command of facts (at least his own facts) but will just continue to repeat lies he has already told about Romney. I suspect there will be a lot of softball questions to Obama and harder ones to Romney, but we shall see. My crystal ball says Romney will win handily again.

Our Teleprompter President

October 8, 2012

The October 3, 2012, presidential debate was a much-anticipated event for Obama and Romney to convince the American people who should be president. President Obama lived up to Clint Eastwood's prop of an empty chair. Our president is unable to think and speak about his beliefs and policies off-the-cuff, even with debate preparation. Was it fair that Obama was not allowed to use a teleprompter at the debates when Romney eloquently speaks his thoughts and ideas?

Obama is known for his great oratory skills. Without teleprompters, he is a mess. Put a teleprompter in front of him, and he is an expert, pausing at just the right time, emphasizing just the right syllable and acting out the facial features to best effect. The teleprompter has become an extension of himself and he is lost without it. In observing his speeches, it is quite noticeable that his head moves back and forth like he's following a ping pong match. I know I am not the only one who cannot stand to hear his voice and watch his arrogance any longer. If you can find them, videos exist of Obama talking without teleprompters that are so painful to watch; he stutters, cannot express ideas or find the words he needs.

Obama Defending His Economic Policies in Debate

October 9, 2012

Obama could not defend 47 million Americans on food stamps. He could not defend 23 million Americans unemployed, underemployed or who stopped looking for work. He could not defend increasing our debt by $6 trillion to $16 trillion. He could not claim that his Affordable Care Act (Obamacare) reduces costs. What did he expect to run on after recruiting people to apply for food stamps, killing the Keystone pipeline and illegally enforcing a moratorium on Gulf Coast drilling, spending billions on now bankrupt green companies, and passing a healthcare mandate that adds a government bureaucrat into our medical decision-making?

Targeted marketing or breaking the law? by Kithy

October 12, 2012

Let's say a company wants to send out marketing materials to people who will respond, and not waste money sending it out to everyone. That sounds reasonable, right? Especially with today's data mining, where a company can sift through prior sales and marketing results and can separate customers by various profiles. That sounds downright smart to me. Well, the government won't allow banks to do that.

Someone decided that banks have to be fair, and therefore, either everyone gets the marketing materials, or no one does. Banks pretty much will break the law if they target their marketing, even if it will save them money and make more money for their shareholders. Apparently, if you are one of the people who didn't get the advertising, that is unfair. Because we all want more junk mail. Because we are too stupid to search for information for products we are looking for, especially with internet searching available to us. When the bank unfairly excludes groups, the government requires the banks to provide a certain amount of loans to the excluded group. The excluded group is usually not credit worthy. But that doesn't matter, because the government has legislated fairness. The Fair Credit Act is obsolete and needs to be repealed.

Let's say a company targets a group of people who generally respond and take advantage of the advertised product. In the name of fairness and equal credit opportunity, the government said the company didn't advertise all of its products, so the company owes a fine. Only someone in government would think that targeted marketing of subprime loans to poor people who qualify is unfair. Inherently, what they are presuming to be true is that poor people who watch advertising are too stupid to realize that they don't have to purchase a product just because it's advertised to them. Too stupid to realize that they can research on their own whether or not a product is good for them. Perhaps the government should start regulating the consumer. The consumer should take a test and be licensed to make purchases. He fails if he tells the government he will not comparison shop, or if he will purchase anything based solely on an advertisement. OR maybe we should repeal the Equal Credit Opportunity and the Consumer Financial Protection Act.

I Hated Martha Raddatz as Moderator, by Kithy

October 13, 2012

Wow – she was awful. I thought she set up the abortion questions to make Ryan look terrible and to offend all pro-life voters. He didn't take the bait, though, and his responses were appropriate. Life does start at conception, whether or not the

113

mother is happy with the circumstances. If that offends voters, so be it. If we don't defend innocent life, all the social justice programs in the world are worthless.

I thought the moderator relied heavily on the foreign affairs questions because she thought Ryan wouldn't be able to answer them; after all, he is the domestic affairs expert. He was well versed in foreign affairs; and really, Biden has absolutely nothing to say about his administration's lack of reaction and inaction to the Middle Eastern acts of war towards our embassies.

And the buffoon was a buffoon. Biden tried to scare the elder population away from Romney and Ryan, but Ryan called his bluff. It's true that he has absolutely no record to run on. His plan is to do nothing, except take money from Medicare – which was paid into it by everyone who is taking advantage of it – and put it into Obamacare, which will cover everyone who doesn't want to or can't pay. That's what I think.

You Can't Make Me Lose Weight, by Kithy

October 13, 2012

I am such a dangerous person. Oh my gosh. I weigh too much. Better legislate my weight away. Tell me how much soda I am allowed to drink. Then tell me how much chocolate I can eat. Then tell me how much (enter your own favorite food) I can eat. Do the Libs really think this is a good idea? I'm pretty sure there are more important things to defend the United States against. Weight is not one of the ones the government should be working on. Ask anyone who's ever lost weight why they did it. I'll bet it boils down to 1) I got sick, or 2) I felt like it and finally decided to do something about it.

Debate Style Mirrors Administration Style, by Tbird

October 14, 2012

So far this election season, we have seen two debates, one between the presidential candidates Mitt Romney and Barack Obama, and one between vice presidential candidates Paul Ryan and Joe Biden. Both debates reveal how Democrats view Republicans, if you didn't already know. Obama sleepwalked through his first debate; he couldn't be bothered to study up on the issues because Romney is not worth his time. Biden grinned manically, laughed, and interrupted repeatedly because he couldn't make himself act respectfully toward a young, well-prepared Ryan. That is pretty much how these men have run their administration. Their first two years, Obama and Biden had a fully Democrat congress and could have passed any bills they wanted; they wasted most of their time on health care, bribing and threatening any Democrat shirkers, and passed a 2000-page bill without any input at all from Republicans. They rarely even talked to the minority leaders and wasted no time talking to any Republicans about the issues. After all, Obama won. The last two years, with a Republican House, Obama and Biden accomplished very little. It's difficult to get things done when you need to communicate with people with whom you disagree and can't stand to even meet with them or delegate someone else to meet with them.

Romney governed Massachusetts with a vast majority of Democrat lawmakers. He talked to them and listened to them and got things done. Both Romney and Ryan tried, and succeeded, in keeping their cool during the debates. Romney did interrupt respectfully when Obama told his whoppers but didn't talk over him as Biden did to Ryan. Romney and Ryan will interact with Congress when they are inaugurated in January and use persuasion to bring Democrats around to their way of thinking on many issues. I don't trust Obama and Biden to change their personalities in order to persuade anyone who doesn't already agree with them. Hopefully, they will both be out of a job come January, and it won't matter.

Libya Is Obama's Swan Song

October 14, 2012

Four Americans were murdered during the embassy attack in Libya on 9/11 under Obama's watch. Ambassador Stevens requested security repeatedly, he was denied, and then he was murdered. That in itself is reason enough to realize that Obama does not have America's interests at heart. What continues to follow this terrorist attack is beyond believable. The American people were told that this was a spontaneous protest against an anti-Islam web video. The Obama administration went so far as to spend $70,000 in advertising on Pakistani TV to apologize for this video.

Our State Department admitted that it knew this was a terrorist attack. Two weeks after the attack, Obama spoke before the UN General Assembly and continued to blame the video. The Libyan president stated that the video that came out months prior to the attack had nothing to do with the 9/11 attack. Biden now claims that he did not know that the embassy required more security.

Obama has a history of refusing to call terrorism what it is. We cannot forget the Fort Hood 'Allahu Akbar' workplace incident. American history will tell otherwise. We will not accept being lied to for whatever reason Obama can contrive. Good-bye Obama, Biden and the rest of your lying, incompetent administration.

Class Action Lawsuit Against Federal Government for Weight, by Kithy

October 17, 2012

I was just thinking how fun it could be to start a class action lawsuit against the government for telling me all through my childhood that I should eat three squares a day. Now they're telling me they were wrong, and I should eat pyramid style. The government caused mass obesity, to the point that the government is now declaring war on obesity. So classy. Cause a major problem, and then tell the victims you're going to fix them because you know the right way to fix it now. Sorry, but I don't believe there is a one size fits all diet, and I don't think the government should be involved in any of these public service messages. Maybe Mitt will get rid of all public service messaging. I like that idea.

Is $250,000 rich? by Kithy

October 17, 2012

Here's how I look at the $250,000 arbitrary number to indicate whether someone is rich or not. The original income tax was targeted for the top 3% of income earners, and it was supposed to be the top 3% forever. It was not supposed to hit everyone. Maybe today $250,000 is a big number. But as a millionaire recently said, "One million dollars just doesn't go as far as it used to." We already know that $250,000 doesn't go very far on either coast. In five years, is $250,000 going to be the new average? Whatever number is chosen, it will be obsolete in a few years. Some of the richest people in America have already announced that they are considering becoming citizens of other countries. Do we want to run off all our income producers? Do we want to kill capitalism?

What He Meant to Say, by Kithy

October 17, 2012

Mr. Obama, what will you do for me if I reelect you for another four years? Here's what I'll do for you: higher gasoline costs, higher food costs, higher energy costs, more businesses going out of business, and higher taxes. I have a vision and I won't stop until I complete it. I won't let anyone get in my way. My vision is to use all those electric cars I ordered GM make. To use all the solar power that should be being produced by the Solyndra's of the US. I spent a lot on those, and I have Bernie printing a whole lot more money so that I can keep spending (oops, I meant to say investing because it sounds better) and we'll get this technology to work. Meanwhile, you may be a little empty in your pockets,

116

because you haven't seen $7/gal yet, and that's what I'm aiming for. When gasoline hits $7, you won't be able to drive your gasoline powered car. You'll have to buy an electric. Bernie's printing so many dollars, and you won't have any money left to buy one, so we'll probably have to give away those cars. It's ok, we can always print more dollars.

And, coal. You know I want the coal companies to go bankrupt. How are we going to switch technologies when we already have a cheap, efficient technology up and running? Price it out of the market. The coal miners already said they won't vote for me, so I'm definitely getting back at them, and in the meantime, accomplishing my vision of green energy. Someone once told me it takes more coal powered energy to produce and use ethanol than it's worth. Trust me, ethanol is better. Don't use it in your boat, though, because it will eat up the motor. Oops, that slipped out. Good things cost more, so get used to it.

Which brings us to food prices. I really have no idea why food prices went up. I think it is a Rightwing conspiracy. The businesses that will go out of business are too greedy anyway. Did you see what I did to the banks? I punished them over and over and they went ahead and had serious profits this quarter. It's ok, I'll find a way to steal their profits and put them into one of my visions. The businesses that I want to provide are good businesses. They won't be greedy businesses. Everything I want costs a little more. And you know what that means. Pay up.

Obama's Green Energy Policy

October 18, 2012

When you hear Obama touting his green energy policy on the campaign trail, take the following into account. Obama picked A123, a lithium-battery company, to receive $250 million in taxpayer stimulus. A123 had hired lobbyists with close ties to Obama at the cost of $1 million, a pretty darn good payoff. And to continue playing the free taxpayer money game, A123 donated to Obama's campaign. A123 produced batteries with defective cells and is now going through bankruptcy. In the meantime, salaries were paid courtesy of the "shovel ready jobs stimulus" American taxpayers.

Annual Salaries of A123:
$656,000 David Vieau, Chief Executive Officer, President and Director
$368,000 David Prystash, Chief Financial Officer and Secretary
$358,000 Eric Pyenson, VP and General Counsel
$414,000 Robert Johnson, VP and General Manager of Energy Solutions Group
$414,000 Jason Forcier, VP of Automotive Systems Group

Obama has told us that he will continue investing in green energy. To summarize his green energy policy, the American taxpayers will continue to fund this game. This is what the greenie global warming supporters support. You didn't get your fair share that these VP's got, did you? You really didn't think it was all about the environment, did you?

Romney Is Rich

October 19, 2012

Obama's basis for his reelection has been that Governor Romney is rich. With all that money, Romney obviously must be greedy and out of touch. Thank goodness Romney had a national stage with the debates to override this ignorant thinking. Romney created his own wealth. On the other hand, Obama has lived lavishly on our dime for the past four years as president. American taxpayers will continue to fund his lifestyle with his presidential pension of $200,000. The citizens of Illinois will also be contributing to his lifestyle through his Illinois Senate pension. Is this not rich to Obama?

Despite Obama living off taxpayers for years, he has contempt for private businesses that employ the tax base. His disdain for business and taxing them into oblivion does not make sense. Unless he thinks he is just shoring up his pension which kinda makes him sound greedy. Shouldn't Obama supporters worry about how rich Obama is? That's right. It doesn't matter.

Reasons to Vote for Obama

October 22, 2012

According to the millions of dollars spent in negative advertising by the Democrats, we should vote for Obama because:

- When Mitt was a teenager, he pranked a kid by cutting his hair.
- When Mitt went on vacation, he packed his dog in a crate on the top of his car.
- Mitt is rich and greedy.
- Mitt has investment income in foreign companies.
- Mitt fired a man who lost his health insurance and caused his wife to die of cancer.
- Mitt doesn't like women.
- Mitt hired women in his state cabinet by looking through their resumes in a binder.

118

Obama's infamous quote from the 2004 campaign is getting a lot of play these days, "If you don't have a record to run on, then you paint your opponent as someone people should run from." Well, Obama does have a record these past four years and it is terrible for the United States. The negativity about Romney being rich is one of the major reasons NOT to vote for Obama. Obama is worth $6 million. The rest of the 'dirt' is to divert us away from Obama's policies.

Obama will continue to denigrate the rich while he hangs out with them. Politics is a game to him, and it is all about the money. No rich person I know looks down on the middle class and poor and strategizes how to control and hurt them, except for one person – Obama. The rich I know are charitable and very giving individuals and want the best for everyone. Obama does not see this. Wonder how much Obama will be worth in a few years. You can bet that he's not going to be sharing his wealth with you.

Obama's Alternate Universe, by Tbird

October 24, 2012

I watched the foreign policy debate between President Obama and Governor Romney last night. I learned some things from Obama I hadn't known before:

Libya is better off now than it was four years ago. Obama's foreign policy is keeping Americans safe. America is stronger now than ever. Navy ships are as obsolete as horses and bayonets. Obama considers Israel our greatest ally. Obama did not go around apologizing to dictators around the world for our bossy superiority. Obama saved GM and Romney wanted to liquidate GM. Romney is a warmonger. Romney wants to spend $7 trillion we don't have and take it from the middle class. War is over and we need to start nation-building at home. Obama will bring manufacturing back to the United States.

Come January, Obama can go live in a nice, big house in Hawaii and dwell in his own alternate universe. I'll still be in the home of the brave and the land of the free with a President Romney who understands the greatness of our country.

Do Not Vote for Obama

October 29, 2012

Obama promised jobs and independence from Middle East oil. Obama refused to build the Keystone pipeline to bring oil to Texas refineries from Canada. He invested our taxpayer money in Brazil to produce oil. He gave Al Gore 'green energy stimulus' money to build the Fisker car in another country. He promised to bankrupt the coal industry. He promised that energy prices would necessarily

119

skyrocket under his cap and trade plan. Cap and Trade is on his second term agenda.

Christians should not even consider voting for Obama. At the National Democrat Convention, Democrats put forth a vote to restore God in their platform. God had been taken out of the Democrat platform PURPOSELY. They had to vote three times because it was obvious that the nays outnumbered the ayes. It was deemed passed. Wisconsin Bishop David Ricker has claimed that voting pro-choice and for same-sex marriage will put your soul in jeopardy. It is the Republicans that stand up for the weakest and smallest of us all – not the Democrats who claim to be for the little guy.

Obama promised to reduce the deficit in half. He added $6 trillion to the deficit in four years. The Obama administration has run our country without a budget for three years. Obama presented his budget to Congress and received zero votes by Democrats and Republicans – I suppose this can be claimed as a bi-partisan victory. Obama's policies go directly against what he promises the American taxpayer with the exception of skyrocketing energy policies. One can describe Obama as a liar or just a typical, disgraceful politician. I have wondered if a white man with a common name like Barry campaigning on Obama's policies would receive any votes. Does Obama deserve your vote?

NOVEMBER 2012

Deficits, Good and Bad, by Kithy

November 2, 2012

The only deficit that counts is your bank account. My employer runs a deficit with me. It pays me more than it gets back from me. I don't pay my employer anything. Is that bad? No, my employer gets my services, and I get a paycheck. This deficit is win/win. I run a deficit at the grocery store. I pay them and they never pay me back. I get groceries, and they get money to keep their business running, and so that I can come back and get more groceries next week. I put money into my personal bank account, and if I take more out than I put in, then I'm in trouble. Then I have a deficit that counts. I'm not giving the bank my money; I'm letting them hold my money in my account.

I wonder how this works with government and with China. Romney's plan to even the playing field doesn't sound right to me. I'm not a fan of "even the playing field", because it never takes into account all that goes into the field. We all like a bargain, and if China can provide a bargain for us, that sounds good to me. Now, if they're stealing our patents, and selling fake products as genuine products, that's a problem. I'm just not sure that currency manipulation is a horrible thing. Sure, we have less manufacturing because of that. But that makes

120

us provide more servicing. It's a tradeoff, and I'm not sure that is bad. If China is getting dollars for its products, and then making more products, what's wrong with that? If we are borrowing money, we can't pay back to buy things we can't afford- that is where the problem lies. By itself, if China hoards dollars and then the dollar drops in value, they are losing their shirts. They don't want our economy to collapse, because theirs would, too. So, the real problem is not deficit spending, it's borrowing money we know we can't pay back and the Chinese stealing patents and making copycat products that are sold as the originals.

Why You Should Vote Republican, by Kithy

November 5, 2012

Social Justice: The people who vote for Obama because of his social justice views might be interested to know that capitalists are better for social justice than government. The United States has the highest standard of living in the world. It's because success brings everyone up. Successful people are able to share their wealth. Unsuccessful people are not able to share wealth because they don't have any to share. Obama wants us all to be equal, and all success should be redistributed until there are no more successful people. Romney supports success, and his policies will be aimed at allowing more people to succeed without extreme government interference.

Right to Life: There is another really important issue connected to social justice. If you are not given the right to life, you have no need of social justice. All the social justice policies in the world will not help the lives of people who were never allowed to live in the first place. The right to life is the first social justice issue that needs to be addressed. Only Romney is pro-life.

Jobs: People who want jobs know that they need to vote for Romney. Obama, who claims to be the savior of Detroit, did nothing to save Detroit. GM did file bankruptcy, which it should have done in the first place, before receiving millions of tax dollars and before the president could decide who got the shaft according to who he wanted to reward, instead of like every other company that has filed bankruptcy and played by the rules. Talk about an uneven playing field. I guess that argument only stands when it suits them. Romney supports policies that encourage small businesses and job creation. Obamacare is the biggest obstacle to job creation right now.

Energy and personal budgets: Obama wants energy prices to go up even further than they have, so in his grandiose head, he can be the savior of the environment. All it does to us is hit our pocketbooks. Gas, beef, bread, milk, etc, all the things we buy on a daily or weekly basis have become outrageously expensive. Do you remember when gasoline was $1.89/gallon? Or milk was less than $2/gallon? We need these days back, and Obama wants the opposite. Romney will encourage energy production. Obama likes to say he does the same, however his record on withholding permits tells the opposite story.

Cheap Healthcare: Obama wants universal healthcare at a cost of the biggest tax increase in US history. Already, mine went up 10% in ANTICIPATION of Obamacare passing. That's right, before it ever got passed, I got a 10% increase. (The same thing happened with my credit card interest rate, in ANTICIPATION of Dodd-Frank, but that's another story.) Obamacare is the program in which I get to pay for everyone else's colonoscopy, AND I have to pay a huge deductible to cover my husband's required lab tests (not for preventive screening, but for an actual health issue). I'd rather have Romney repeal it and provide incentives for health care to become less expensive. Ever hear of capitalism? Got any idea why pharmaceuticals have decreased so much?

There are a lot more reasons to vote Republican, but I can't keep writing and writing and no one would read that much anyway. Trust me, the list goes on and on.

Musings on Macroeconomics and China, by Kithy

November 5, 2012

Does currency manipulation matter? Sometimes, I feel like we are selling America for baubles, kind of like the Indians did in Manhattan Island. They sold the island for beads (this might not be true, but it makes a good legend). We buy baubles from China, and they hoard our dollars. If they hoard enough, can they buy America?

It's true that if you can print the money that you borrow, you will never go broke. Third world countries borrow in dollars and pay back in dollars. Since they can't print dollars, sometimes they get in big debt trouble. We borrow in dollars, and if we get into trouble we can print more. We are at the point that if we print enough to get out of debt, we will cause hyperinflation. It also means that China, who has lots of dollars, doesn't want us to print more, because their dollars will become worth less. Money is power. The one holding the money can pull the strings, but only if the one printing the money plays along with them.

Is China really hoarding our dollars? We run a deficit with them. I wrote about running deficits in a previous article. Do they use our dollars to manufacture, package, market, ship new items? Are they hoarding, or are they recycling? They do not keep every dollar they collect, because they need to keep their businesses running. They do want to make a profit. They do need to keep dollars in order to do business because dollars are still the universal exchange. Are we in jeopardy of keeping the dollar universal? They made noises about changing the universal currency of trade, but then it seemed like no other country or group of countries even comes close to having the stability or the massive amount of capital that it takes to be a universal currency.

Really, four more years of this?

November 7, 2012

How ignorant are our fellow Americans? What the hell is wrong with them that they 'think Obama is doing a good job' and that he just needs more time to 'help the middle class'. Are you not doing crappy enough that you want more of the same? Is the right to kill your baby your defining passion? Please don't tell me it's all about the $30 per month birth control pills you want everyone to pay for. This $360 per year is the basis for government control Obamacare. How stupid are you?

Obama bowed his way through the Mideast apologizing for American strength. He accuses the police of acting stupidly. He accuses doctors of needlessly cutting off limbs to make more money. At a Town Hall meeting, he recommended that old people should take pills instead of having life-saving surgeries. People should have told Obama that if a surgery would relieve their parents' pain, they would like the option of surgery. He cheered on the loser Occupy Wall Street crowds who are most likely his very own paid agitators. Obama's job killing policies are the major causes of these loser Occupoopers living in their parents' basements. Obama hates business and shows it. How could our fellow Americans continue to buy into Obama's blathering on about the rich not doing their fair share when his campaign raises $1 billion from them? Why do you think the rich owe you a dime? Did you notice the lavish vacations and lifestyle the Obama's were living during the past four years? You didn't see that as hypocritical to the Nth degree? The Democrats took God out of their platform. Why not? Obama doesn't consider the US a Christian nation.

Everything Obama is selling has been sold before. Just read the Communist Manifesto and Saul Alynski's Rules for Radicals. He's doing a play by play towards communism. I suggest to all you Obama-heads to go live in a communist country or Obama's beloved Mideast where a 14-year-old girl was nearly murdered because she wanted an education. Go live in North Korea where everyone gets their fair share of nothing. Find out how it is to live in violent Zimbabwe. Please go and leave. Go live in China and tweet all you want about the unfairness of whatever. Oh, wait, you can't – Twitter isn't legal in China. Maybe it's time for your dream vacation in the socialist utopia Venezuela. Please go and leave before you help turn America into a hellhole.

Guess what? You don't have to move to find out. You have just reelected the jerk that promised a fundamental transformation of America and gave him four more years to complete the job. I'm going to bed, saying my prayers and hoping this is a bad dream. Obama's waking up laughing because he can't believe he fooled you again.

Why Missouri's Akin Lost, by Kithy

November 8, 2012

Really, his comment one week after winning the primary should have been nonconsequential. The ad that Claire put out a couple days before the election put the nail in the coffin. It featured Republicans condemning him, including Mitt Romney. McCain is featured, stating, "he will not be welcome in the Senate". The Republican Party destroyed him. The Dems didn't have to do anything but feature his own party ostracizing him publicly.

Let's take that to heart. Let's feature them in their own words saying really offensive (to conservatives) things. We should have featured Obama in ads in his own words. We could have featured the open mic gaffe to Putin, "just wait til after the election, then I can be more flexible". Or talking to Joe the Plumber, "we need to share the wealth" (long time ago, but so blatant and still what he believes) and of course "you didn't build that". There was so much material to choose from, let's remember this for next time. Not that Obama will be running, but it is his party. And let's bombard the airwaves with his or their own words over and over so that voters can't mistake their meaning or look the other way. Wait, maybe the Republicans aren't really trying to win.

Living the Green Dream in New York

November 10, 2012

Don't buy the despair and anger of the New Yorkers living the post-Sandy life. It's obviously an act because finally they get to live the true green life. First of all, they blame Sandy on global warming due to man's use of our fossil fuels. Secondly, because of Sandy, they are forced to go without energy to heat their homes, gas for their cars and all-around electrical use such as for refrigeration of food. Thirdly, due to the forced way of life post-Sandy, they again prove man-made global warming. Within a week, the weather got colder and even snowed!

The greenies have harped on us for years about man-made global warming and our greed for dependence on fossil fuels. Now that they get to live how they speak; they should be overjoyed and proud to be living without electricity and gas. The way they are acting, it's as if they appreciate our fossil fuels. We global warming deniers have always appreciated big oil and gas companies for allowing us to live a comfortable life because we know the alternative. We also know that the liberal's solution to man-made global warming is to tax big oil and gas out of existence.

What's next for the Republican Party? by Kithy

November 10, 2012

Here's what I've heard so far: The only way Obama won is because the electorate is now more takers than givers, we'll never win it back. George Soros owns the company that provides the voter counting machines, which leaves the counting open for fraud. We need to cater to the Hispanics, women, gays, etc by appeasing every one of them, by changing our platform to mimic the Democrat platform (that's from one of the top Republican party strategists - let's fire her). Some are saying that the House has to do whatever Obama wants now, because he won. I say, the House better darn well do what we elected them to do, and that's stop Obama.

Many companies announced layoffs immediately following the election because of Obamacare. They were holding off announcing, in case Romney won and Obamacare would be repealed. The House needs to put forth a bill to repeal Obamacare anyway and the Senate needs to convince several Democrats that it's in the people's interest to repeal it. Dems say they're for job creation, and for getting the economy working again. If they remain supporters of Obamacare, and all their constituents get laid off, don't you think we can convince some of them?

57% Death Tax Has Unintended Consequence

November 11, 2012

Most comforting is that God works in mysterious ways and loves us unconditionally and we will survive another Obama term. A photo taken from Obama's thank you speech to his campaign workers shows him crying real human tears. Why cry? Is it because he knows that he will reach his destiny of destroying America, or that he sees the goodness in Americans and may have to rethink his ideology?

Here on earth, two major subjects of concern arise for the second term, Obamacare and Benghazi. Businesses have started announcing layoffs and reduction in labor hours in anticipation of Obamacare taxes. Obama has to know that he can only raise taxes so much before the economy free falls. Benghazi is getting worse with the resignation of CIA Director General Petraeus. The need to suppress information on an al Qaeda attack prior to the election led to the idiotic lie about a video. No one believes that al Qaeda died with Bin Laden. So why lie to pretend there is no danger from al Qaeda? Was this 'pretending' the reason for inaction that led to four American's deaths? Obama could likely go the way of Nixon.

Take note, on the positive side, the 57% death tax will motivate people to live past these four years. Yay for the sick and elderly!

Obama's Second Term Circumventing the House

November 13, 2012

Obama's first term started with an 'I won' statement. It's similar to the birthday brat who says that it's his birthday and he can do whatever he wants. Obama neglects the fact that John Boehner and the Republicans still hold majority of the House with the major powers of passing federal legislation and initiating revenue bills.

Conservatives talked about constitutional freedom and liberty during the election and how Obama is taking our freedoms away. Obama accomplishes this primarily by circumventing the House with the use of his czars and regulatory agencies. The Regulatory Flexibility Act mandates the release every April and October of a description of all rules and regulations likely to have a significant economic impact. This basically calls for a notice of upcoming regulatory actions in which Congress can engage in oversight and businesses can plan ahead. In the Fall of 2011, the administration released 2,676 regulations. In the Spring and Fall of 2012, agenda deadlines were ignored, and none were released. Sixty departments, agencies and commissions including the EPA, Health and Human Services, Department of Labor and Departments of Energy and Transportation, did not publicize their regulatory agendas as required by law.

With the election over, Obama is free to unload his regulatory agenda on us. Those who voted for Obama have no room to complain when government takes over their lives. Then again, the only liberties important to Obama voters appear to be the rights to free birth control and abortions. If the economy is destroyed, you get neither. Has it every occurred to the younger generations to ask the older generations about politics and their views? I know why they don't. Millennials are so waking and smarter than other generations.

Incompetent or outright fraudulent? by Kithy

November 15, 2012

Susan Rice was either ridiculously stupid or purposely misleading when she stated that Benghazi was caused by a movie. Either way, she has no business being in charge of anything. You have to be outright stupid to believe a line about a movie, when there was a calculated, planned attack with mortars. You have to be purposely misleading to say I was just repeating the intelligence. If your intelligence agency tells you something that stupid, you have to question whether your intelligence officers have any brains in their heads. You're a yes-man, proceeding with a coverup. We don't need an idiot or a yes-man in a position of power. I didn't have to besmirch her reputation, she did it herself.

Go After Me

November 15, 2012

Obama told Senators Lindsey Graham and John McCain to go after him, not Susan Rice who had nothing to do with Benghazi. Senator Graham has said, "Mr. President, don't think for one minute I don't hold you ultimately responsible for Benghazi. I think you failed as commander-in-chief before, during and after the attack." Obama is mad that Susan Rice's name has been besmirched for saying what the White House told her to say on five Sunday morning talk shows prior to the election. The senators are mad that four Americans are dead from a terrorist attack. Obama can count on the senators to continue their inquiry of Benghazi that will lead back to his coverup for his lack of leadership.

Capitalism 101

November 16, 2012

Capitalism is an economic system with the freedom to exchange money for goods and services that you desire. It is starting a business. It is being an employee. And it is being a customer. The opposite is socialism in which the government is in charge of the economic system and gets to make all the decisions. In capitalism, companies thrive or fail on their own merits. In socialism, all companies fail.

Schools have been invaded by liberals who have been teaching anti-capitalism for a long time. They have been teaching that everyone is equal, and that the successful, big businesses are greedy. This is what Obama ran on and got reelected. However, I have not heard one Obama voter tell McDonald's that the

$1 McDouble is gouging them. Not one Obama voter has told Apple to stop inventing fabulous technology such as the iPhone or iPad. True anti-capitalists would tell Apple that they cannot develop another product because it makes Apple too rich. True anti-capitalists would tell the owners of Apple and McDonald's that the workers should take over the business or that Apple and McDonald's should share their wealth with them.

When you put a face or a name of a company into the rhetoric anti-capitalists make, it sounds superbly idiotic. Capitalists support capitalism. You see, a capitalist is not just the successful businessperson. It is the ordinary citizen who dreams of making more money, getting a promotion or moving on to a better paying job elsewhere. You make money, spend money and help make the economic engine roar. When the socialists destroy the capitalists, the dreamers have nowhere to go.

Please Help Me Understand Unions, by SH

November 16, 2012

Please help me to understand why 30% of the Hostess work force that is union can cause everyone at that company to lose their jobs (18,000 total jobs). The news is reporting that Hostess will begin liquidating the company because of union strikers. I have heard no details on the union demands but it's usually the same thing – guaranteed pension, low cost health benefits, etc. Well, I'm sorry, but there are only so many Ding Dongs and Twinkies that can be sold and therefore, limited profits to pay for everything. My dad always told my sisters and me that we could do anything we want. My outlook on a job is if you don't like it, get a new one. I love the occasional Ding Dong or other Hostess product, but I can guarantee you that I won't buy any of them if the prices keep going up. (As it is already, I won't pay $5 for a box; I'll wait for a sale or go to the outlet store.) So, yes, if you are a Hostess employee that is fine with the company closing down because you didn't get what you wanted, find another job that gets you what you want...without affecting other employees or consumers!!!!

P.S. I am not totally anti-union. I have friends in the plumbing and electrical unions where I think the unions are a good thing. However, I also worked with a union call center where we had a problem with a client, proposed a solution along with the recommendation that a certain supervisor head it up but was told that he could not be offered the job until two other people who knew nothing about the client were offered the position...hence, my outlook on unions is not always favorable.

Unions and Their Job Killing Demands

November 16, 2012

It is difficult not to think of the Hostess union workers as fleas who picked at their host until it died. Union workers continue their demands of pensions, healthcare and increased pay. Compare this to non-union workers who would also like just one of these. If they ask for it and the company tells them that the money isn't there, they accept the news and continue working or look elsewhere for a job. Not true for unions – they keep demanding. Ask the 18,500 Hostess workers who lost their jobs today. The strikers were told that the money was not there for their demands and to get back to work at the end of the day or the entire company closes down for good.

The union killed Hostess. The workers may have been the best bakers in the world, but that doesn't mean they get to make the rules for the company or that the company owes them anything – despite what your president tells you. It will be interesting finding out exactly what the demands were that caused Hostess to close. The owners of Hostess did build their company and they alone decided its future. Now, if Hostess was a friend of Obama, it could have received free grant money to keep going. Obama might have had to raise taxes to get the money to give to Hostess, but he's already doing that to his favored people in the billions.

What if the GOP targeted the wrong groups in the election? by Kithy

November 17, 2012

For Dems, women were the major target, then Hispanics, then you name the race. What if the GOP should be separating groups by government employees, on welfare and wanting freebies, on Medicare, on Medicaid, none of the above? That seems to make more sense. We could have explained to government employees that some of their jobs will be cut with budget costs, or that we were targeting attrition and would move people to other positions, or whatever the plan was for them. And we could have explained what will happen if nothing changes, that instead of some people getting the ax, all will when we fall apart in chaos without a plan.

I don't know how you target the people who want more freebies, give them GOP phones instead of Obama phones? Maybe we could have paid them with pizza to vote for us (wait, aren't those ideas bribery, and not legal?) I think the Dem's line about the GOP cutting Medicare was repeated so often, that the seniors believed them. We didn't get the message out more than the Dems that Obamacare is stealing the money they put into their healthcare and giving it to people who did not pay into the system.

129

Surely, the none of the above group understood the message. This makes way more sense than picking people based on a common thread that has nothing to do with the way they vote.

States Should Fight Against Obamacare, by Tbird

November 20, 2012

States have two big decisions to make regarding Obamacare. They must decide if they will implement state healthcare exchanges and expand Medicaid. If a state has any sense of self-preservation, it must decide against both.

In June, the Supreme Court ruled in favor of plaintiffs on the Medicaid mandate which they claimed commandeered state authority. As a result, states do not have to expand their Medicaid enrollment. Medicaid would add millions of people to be covered by states already stretched to the breaking point. Here in Missouri, Medicaid already takes up a third of our budget, crowding out education and roads spending. Even though the federal government would subsidize Medicaid expansion for the first three years and 90% after that, Missouri would have to spend an extra $100 million starting in 2017 and $150 million by 2020. Last I heard, the federal government is already running $1 trillion plus yearly deficits; where is the money to come from for the subsidized Medicaid expansion? In addition, by expanding Medicaid rolls and accepting federal subsidies, the states are not allowed to reform their own systems because of Obamacare's "maintenance of effort" requirements. The feds are threatening to take away money they currently give states for hospitals that serve a high proportion of poor people; they will continue to shift more costs to the states. Instead of expanding an already bankrupt and inefficient system that distorts the private healthcare insurance market, states should demand that Washington give them block grants for non-disabled and non-elderly poor with state discretion over eligibility and benefits, turning Medicaid into a premium-assistance program to help people enroll in mainstream insurance plans.

States should also say no thanks to setting up their own exchanges. The whole idea of state-controlled exchanges is just an illusion, as everything will be controlled by federal law. States would just be doing the federal government's dirty work at their own expense; they would have to follow the HHS Secretary's mandates with little or no room for independent judgment. We've already seen Sebelius's birth control mandate, which takes away our religious liberty (that wasn't even part of Obamacare, but separate). States were given until November 16 to tell the federal government if they will institute state healthcare exchanges in accordance with Obamacare. A lot of states said no, they would not, and Obama decided to give them another month during which they will be pressured to change their minds. The law was written without requiring states to form their own exchanges (probably by mistake), and only state exchanges may distribute credits and subsidies for healthcare insurance. If a state defaults to a federal exchange, that state's employers are exempt from the employer mandate of $2000 per employee per year. Running the exchanges would be a nightmare states would be better off without.

Obamacare made a complicated set of rules, mandates, databases and interfaces to establish eligibility, funnel subsidies, and facilitate purchases, all under broad and often incoherent statutory requirements and federal regulations that haven't even been written yet. If states just say no, they pass the burdens and costs of these exchanges back to the administration that foisted Obamacare on us. Congress didn't allocate money to administer federal exchanges, and the law prohibits federal exchanges from providing subsidies to individuals.

The feds are already trying to rewrite Obamacare law when provisions prove inconvenient. Obama decided to funnel credits and subsidies through federal exchanges, which is clearly illegal, and the IRS agreed through a final rule. Oklahoma sued in US District Court for the Eastern District of Oklahoma saying it exercised its right not to establish an exchange, which Obamacare law permitted, and created a mechanism by which Oklahoma can put its decision into effect (Oklahoma passed a constitutional amendment prohibiting any rule or law forcing a person, employer, or healthcare provider to participate in any healthcare system). The state's reasoning was the same as the Supreme Court's ruling on the Obamacare Medicaid expansion, that the federal government commandeered state authority.

We still need to fight tooth and nail against Obamacare through the states. Refuse to set up state exchanges and refuse to expand Medicaid. Obamacare will collapse on its own.

Sources
Wall Street Journal, Capretta and Levin: Why Obamacare is Still No Sure Thing
National Review, Obamacare is Still Vulnerable by Michael Cannon

Stop Tearing Down Romney, by Tbird

November 21, 2012

Everybody is bashing Mitt Romney these days, and the worst are the Republicans. I don't get it. I didn't want Romney as the Republican nominee because I thought he was too moderate, had flip-flopped on issues, didn't really believe much of the conservative things he said, and had enacted Romneycare in Massachusetts when he was governor. The national Republicans decided he was their guy because he was a moderate and the mushy middle would go for him making him electable, and they pushed him hard. When the conservatives in the race were ridiculed and pushed out for being too extreme, I reluctantly accepted that Romney was our nominee. I was glad to see he was sounding more positively conservative on the economy, at least, and I really liked his vice-presidential pick Paul Ryan, and it seemed that the bruising primary fight had sharpened him up. He still wasn't really standing up to the lies Obama spewed about him (vulture capitalism, wanted to prevent women from access to birth control, hated the poor and wanted to leave them to fend for themselves) until that first debate with Obama when he actually called Obama on many of his lies. Unfortunately, that was the only time he really did so.

Recently, Romney said Obama gave presents to his victim groups, and the media jumped all over him. Romney wasn't wrong. What would you call free birth control, Obama's declaration that he would legalize young illegals even though Congress had voted against the Dream Act, Obamaphones, and relaxed requirements for food stamps? Romney is a moderate who ran a mostly moderate campaign, just like the national Republicans wanted, and he lost. Stop blaming him now.

Romney Should Have Won

November 22, 2012

Last thoughts on the election: Romney would have made an excellent president and deserved to win. He is correct in that Obama divided our United States into separate groups granting them specific freebies that were enough to garner their votes. He was also correct in that 47% would never vote for him based on lowering taxes. The major fault of Romney is a good one. He is too kind and decent of a human being. He overestimated the ignorance of the electorate. I think Romney thought he had it locked up after the first debate, as well he should have given Obama's performance. He should have gone on attack mode on the third debate, looking Obama in the eye calling him out as the radical that he is and listing the damage he can inflict on us with a second term. Romney would have won.

If our economy fails, it will be because of Obama. Plenty of Democrats were warned that Obama is a radical communist, but they just failed to care or believe it. Others were happy to get their free stuff, not realizing or caring about anything else. Luckily, Republicans are in places of power to hold back Obama's agenda. Obama helped lose 1,000 Democrat seats across the board since 2008. Republicans hold 30 governorships and the majority of the House and will have to work overtime to keep America safe.

Susan Estrich and Bleeding-Heart Liberals Bleeding Us Dry

November 25, 2012

Susan Estrich is a professor of law and a political talking head who supported Obama. Susan's finding out what it means to be a bleeding-heart liberal under a radical liberal agenda – her money will be taxed away and given to someone else. Bleeding-heart liberals voted for Obama for a host of reasons without any consideration for the most important – his economic agenda. Susan claims in her 11/14/12 article 'The Mandate to Raise Taxes on the Rich' that Obama did not get a mandate to raise taxes on the rich such as small businesses and herself. She also states that we are not a society divided by economic castes. Obama has successfully been reelected by specifically marketing divisions in the United States, most prominently the poor against the rich. Obama has not been secretive about redistributing wealth. This includes the wealth of small businesses, gays, women, blacks, Latinos, environmentalists, middle class, liberals and the anti-war crowd – basically anyone with wealth. This redistribution of wealth is legal theft of money through taxation and does not discriminate.

Susan is just now concerned that the middle class will be priced out of housing. She is now just concerned with charities' inability to raise funds. She is now just concerned with small business owners being unable to afford college for their kids and to help their aging parents. The time to be concerned with this was prior to the election. It is the conservative Republicans who are concerned with EVERYONE'S ability to keep what they worked for – especially property and savings. With all the pain ahead, radical liberals will have redefined what the bleeding-heart label stands for – bleeding us dry.

Voting for Legal Theft

November 29, 2012

That's what just happened on November 6, 2012. Obama had to win so people who think they are liberal will get to learn what it really means to be liberal. If Romney had won, the liberals would have gotten more violent and accusatory and would have continued fighting for their so-called social justice. Now that Obama has won, they get to sit back and experience liberal policies.

Republicans in the House should be fighting against this liberal onslaught, but they know that they will be blamed for whatever is ahead. Obama will go around the legislative branch with his czars and faux agencies to push his agenda forward. Liberals will be taught what legal theft is all about through taxes, EPA, Obamacare and all the forthcoming regulations. Until the policies truly start affecting their bank accounts and way of life, they can go on enjoying their 'win' of reelecting Obama, a radical liberal who told his followers that he would transform America and change our traditions. They don't realize that they gave up a decade of their lives to stagnation.

DECEMBER 2012

Checkmate! by Kithy

December 2, 2012

So, a lot of states decided not to play Obamacare, and are not going to build exchanges. That should be it. The end. Instead, a committee (who knows who's in it) produced a new regulation. If the federal government has to build a state's exchange, then everyone in that state has to pay an extra premium on top of their already outrageous premiums and taxes that they are already required to pay! What a bargain we're getting in this Obamacare. Not only do we have to pay for our insurance, we get to pay for everyone who doesn't want to pay, and we get to pay for labs that we don't want, and we get to pay another federal tax on top of that. Seems to me like we were better off before Obamacare.

A Return to the Clinton Tax Rates, by Tbird

December 2, 2012

President Obama claims he wants to raise the tax rates on "the rich" to the levels they were during President Clinton's two terms in office because when Clinton did it, the economy boomed. Clinton did raise rates, and the economy did boom during his second term, but the two are not related. If Obama gets his way and raises our current rates, the economy will go into recession.

When Clinton took office, the top tax rate was 31%. He raised it to 36% and 39.6%. The rich were those who made $250,000 and up, the equivalent of $400,000 today. He also raised the corporate rate from 34 to 35%, increased the taxable portion of Social Security benefits, and raised the gas tax 4.3 cents per gallon. The voters rewarded Clinton's tax increases with Democrat historic losses in 1994.

NAFTA (North Atlantic Free Trade Agreement), passed in 1993, reduced tariffs among us, Mexico, and Canada and increased trade. In 1995, Clinton was forced to sign the welfare reform bill after Congress presented it to him for the third time, resulting in a cut in the welfare rolls of over half, because they got jobs and took care of their own families. Average GDP dropped a half percent, but it was still a relatively healthy 3.2%, and employment grew a modest 2,000,000 per year. Average hourly wages stagnated. Federal government tax receipts increased $90 billion per year, while spending increased just $45 billion per year. Clinton's spending averaged 19.4% of GDP. The deficit came down to $107 billion by 1996.

During his second term, Clinton cut the capital gains tax from 28% to 20%, increased the death tax exemption, and kept spending increases to 3%, about $57 billion per year. Economic growth then averaged 4.2%, average hourly earnings increased, and unemployment dropped from 5.4% to 4.0%. Revenue growth went up 59%, or $143 billion per year, resulting in a surplus of $198 billion in 2000. Clinton was still riding Reagan's economic boom, and raising taxes slowed down the economy somewhat. Welfare reform, free trade agreements, and lowering the capital gains tax helped offset the higher income tax. Just as important, though, is that Clinton kept spending increases lower than tax receipts. Obama claims that President George W. Bush's tax cuts gave away too much to the rich, exploded the deficit, increased income inequality, and didn't spur economic growth, and therefore, he wants to let the tax rates expire and raise taxes on those evil rich. He is wrong.

When Bush became president, the economy was coming back from the dot-com tech bust. During two rounds of tax cuts, Bush cut income taxes, with the lowest rate at 10% and the highest at 33 and 35%, doubled the child tax credit, and reduced the marriage penalty on two-earner families. The top 1% paid $84 billion more, not less; their share of taxes paid rose from 37 to 40%. Meanwhile, the bottom half paid $6 billion less, and their total share dropped from 3.9 to 2.9%. The CBO projected surpluses by 2002, which of course went out the window with 9/11 and the subsequent war on terror. Deficits did shrink down to $160 billion by 2007, with surpluses again forecasted by 2012 (that didn't happen because the economy went into tailspin during the mortgage and financial crisis at the end of Bush's second term; Bush had been unsuccessful in getting Congress to reform those sectors). Unemployment averaged 5.3%. Also, by 2007, federal revenues as a share of GDP rose to 18.5%, higher than the 60-year average of 17.8%. Bush's tax cuts did not starve the government of revenues. Bush's spending averaged 20.5% of GDP, the highest being his last two years under a Democrat Congress.

Obama's economy grew at 2.2% his first three years, about 1.5% his fourth. His tax receipts have gone down 2.45% per year, but unlike Clinton, he spent way more than he collected in taxes, about 60% more. Obama's spending has averaged 24.1% of GDP. Would he be willing to couple Clinton's tax rates with Clinton's spending rates? Just kidding, I know he wouldn't. Social Security has run a deficit each of the last few years, and last year $165 billion had to be taken out of general revenues to make up the shortfall; Obama does not want to touch Social Security or other entitlements. Obama has not had an actual budget yet, and his annual deficits have been over $1 trillion, adding about $5 trillion to the national debt. He has collected less revenue than during Bush's or Clinton's years, but he didn't even try to keep spending to a reasonable level.

135

Unemployment did decrease from a high of 10.1% and is now at about 7.9%, but instead of doing anything to lower it, he considers that rate to be the new normal. It is not normal and should not be considered so. He doesn't collect too little in taxes, he spends too much. Obama could collect more in taxes only if the economy grows at a greater clip. Raising taxes will not raise more revenue. Clinton's tax hikes plus higher spending will not help our economy; Obama has already said he wants more stimulus spending, not to mention spending on Obamacare. If Obama takes more money out of the economy through higher taxes, the economy will fall into a far worse recession than what he inherited. Republicans must fight against higher taxes and for lower spending. I wish I had confidence in them, but I don't. I think that if Obama and the Republicans do come to an agreement, it will be a poor one with higher taxes and no actual spending cuts. If they don't come to an agreement, the United States will go off the fiscal cliff, but at least that way, spending will be cut. I just hope conservatives will be there to pick up the pieces.

Why You Should Fear the Obama Administration

December 4, 2012

The Obama administration is comprised of fascists, Marxists, and communists, otherwise known as radical, liberal progressives. I have heard people say how that's not really a bad thing because Obama just wants social justice and fairness. And, ya know, he believes in gay marriage and abortion and cares for the little guy and for women. My friend's smart college-age son didn't vote because politicians are all the same and he's disenfranchised with the system. It is time to wise up and stop believing this nonsense. Because of his ignorance and people like him, the United States' system will continue to be run by a dangerous group of individuals who enjoy power for power's sake and not for the good of the citizens. Most people cannot fathom anyone, let alone our present administration, of pursuing the following:

- Internet activities should be monitored and closed down if deemed unacceptable by a government bureaucrat (just another citizen with an opposing viewpoint).
- Individuals should not have the right to own a gun.
- Your bank account and all monetary transactions should be monitored by the government.
- Government should decide your medical care based on statistics such as age and weight instead of your own personal decision.
- IRAs should be converted to government bonds.
- Separation of church and state is meant for Christians and not Muslims.
- The disabled should not be allowed to live.
- Abortion up to the day of birth
- People should not own property, including land, homes and cars.

- Ethanol gas should be increased up to 30% which would damage engines.
- People should not use fossil fuels (coal, gas, oil) because they are bad.
- Government should have population-control powers.
- Meat should be banned.
- Anything from the oceans should be shared globally, including offshore drilling royalties.
- Our military should not have bullets in their guns.
- NASA should focus on Muslim outreach.

The above is not crazy talk. These are all ideas and beliefs of the progressives that are in play. If you missed this prior to the election, you weren't looking. Social justice equals communism. The United States government system is not the problem. The communists trying to take over our system are the problem. They are getting away with it because they wrap it up with a bow and say they are doing it for you. To add to the confusion, the Republican elite or Republican establishment sides too often with Democrats.

Obama's Economic Plan Hits the Marx

December 5, 2012

Obama's economic plan is to tax the rich, as if this is the answer to reducing his trillion dollars over spending per year. To make it sound more believable, he adds that he can afford to pay a little more, like he really wants to pay a little more. Yeah, right. He has the opportunity to do that every April 15 and doubtful he ever told his accountant, "Hey, pay a little more!" Here's what he really is saying: There's wealth in America that I don't have access to. I'll start with taxing the rich, which for now is $250,000, or maybe even $200,000. I know this will hit the top small businesses who employ the middle class so this will really hurt the middle class.

Central to the Marxist agenda is destruction of the middle class and to end up with exactly what he claims to despise – the ultra rich (he and his buddies) and then everyone else living on their scraps. There is no one out there who would not like to be rich, including our president. Obama is living like a king getting ready to take off on his $4 million, 21-day vacation to Hawaii. He needs our money to continue this charade. When are people going to wake up and realize that they appreciate successful, rich businesspeople, they like cool things and services, they like having a job to get to buy these cool things and they love dreaming of being rich one day themselves? An over-taxing government will eventually kill our businesses, and with it, our dreams. Does it kinda seem like Obama is getting more than his fair share? Now you're understanding Marxism.

So, what's the next step for Repubs? by Kithy

December 6, 2012

Ok, we all know Obama's plan is to blame the chaos of 2013 on Republicans. Republicans must cave to all of his demands because he won, or else. How about at the last minute, House Republicans pass a bill to permanently extend the Bush tax cuts for everyone, and then when the Senate Democrats vote it down, we can blame it on the Democrats? Either way, Republicans want to lower taxes, and Obama wants to raise taxes. How come our message won't get heard?

Senator Resigns, by Kithy

December 10, 2012

So, what does it say that a senator, one of the most powerful people in America, says he is resigning because he can be more influential on the outside? Being a senator doesn't much matter anymore? Lobbyists have more influence than the elected Congress? I understand that liberal, progressive think tanks have so much power with this president, that conservatives need to strengthen their think tanks. But, to resign as senator? Something's not right in America.

New Horror Story, by Kithy

December 10, 2012

I'm reading a new true-life horror story, and I just got started, but I'm already horrified by what I've read. It's called, *Fool Me Twice* by Aaron Klein and Brenda Elliott. It's about Obama's plans for his second term. It is very well researched, and explains what Obama meant by his Holy Grail, "I want to fundamentally transform America." "We need to share the wealth, spread it around." "You didn't build that." So far, and I haven't read much, I've been reminded that the best way to transform a country is to get rid of its money. Sound familiar? We are on the brink of a financial calamity like we haven't seen, and everyone on Obama's side says they want to go over the cliff. Geitner said it, Obama said it, Howard Dean said it. They really do want to destroy the dollar and start over with their own system that has nothing to do with private enterprise, private property rights, ambition, freedom of opportunity. Marco Rubio is right, the Republicans have to repeat over and over again that it is the party of opportunity, the party of private property rights, the party of freedom of speech and freedom of religion. The Constitution has stood for two hundred years, and we can't let someone fundamentally change the greatest nation on earth.

138

Taxes Are Going Up, by Tbird

December 11, 2012

Taxes will go up regardless of what the Republicans do or don't do. And they will get blamed for it. I think they should stand their ground and not give up Republican principles of lower taxes and higher growth. They should stand on the rooftops and shout that lower income taxes, lower corporate taxes, and lower capital gains taxes will promote growth, leading to more jobs for the poor and middle class. They should pass their own bill extending the Bush tax rates, all of them, including income taxes and capital gains taxes, and lowering the corporate tax, which is the highest in the world. Harry of the Senate will not let it even go to a vote, but it doesn't matter. The Republicans will have stood on principle. The fiscal cliff will happen, and all the tax rates will increase, and spending will decrease a little. Obama's administration will run out of money soon and need the Republicans' vote to raise the debt ceiling (Republicans won't have the nerve to say no). That's when the Republicans will have all the leverage. They can insist on lower taxes and entitlement reform, and they may even get some of it. They have to try, because the life of our country depends on it. We can only pay down our massive debt by growing the economy.

High Taxes Equal No Taxes

December 11, 2012

France's Socialist President Hollande has pledged to tax the top income-earners at 75%. He has stated that he doesn't like rich people. France's leading actor Gerard Depardieu is responding by moving across the border to reside in Belgium. New York did this back in 2009. When Governor Paterson told Rush Limbaugh that he would be paying a lot more in taxes, Rush moved to Florida. Californians are leaving to avoid the ever-expanding government. It has been proven over and over that higher taxes will result in no taxes because people will leave. This is all Obama has – tax the rich. He throws in a few bones like free contraceptives and his idiotic followers ignore the reality of the Obama economy. Republicans know this will kill jobs and hurt Americans. This is the heart of socialism, liberalism and the present Democrat Party. They love their power and want to keep spending, spending, and spending. The only way they can keep spending is to find more money and if they can squeeze more out of the rich, then so be it. All they have to do to correct these over-blown budgets is to stop spending. Are there any sane politicians out there that can convince the loonies on how to be responsible servants to the people? Or are they having too much fun with all this free money?

Why Sandy Hook?

December 16, 2012

Sandy Hook is too painful to contemplate. Still, we ask why. Huckabee has responded eloquently. God has been taken out of our schools and this killer was obviously not a God-fearing man. My priest asked why mourn these twenty babies when millions of babies are voluntarily killed in utero every year. Obama even shed human tears for these white babies. Maybe he will learn that white and black are just colors and that humanity connects us all. Maybe he will learn that his ideology of fundamental transformation is evil because it does include taking God out of our lives. God is involved in Sandy Hook as He is involved in our lives every day. This doesn't make this tragedy any less painful and we do mourn for these parents and families whose children will never come home from school.

$5 Gallon of Milk

December 18, 2012

A few years ago, I hated paying over $4 for a gallon of milk. Today, I did a double take at my grocery store when I saw $5 a gallon. The thought crosses my mind that hyper-inflation may hit soon and then what? Am I going to be wishing for the days when milk was only $5 a gallon? Hyper-inflation doesn't just happen to an economy. The government manipulates the currency by printing way too much knowing that the value of a dollar will go way down. It was such a relief knowing that Obama's four years were coming to an end and that we survived his term pretty much intact. These next four years are going to be brutal if Obama's main goal continues to be wealth redistribution. How does one prepare for hyper-inflation? I don't have any answers except to stock our pantries. I have some research ahead of me.

Obama Was Asked a Real Question Today

December 20, 2012

At a press conference, a reporter asked Obama where he has been on violence. Obama didn't like this at all. His response was filled with excuses and all too familiar rhetoric, "I've been President of the United States dealing with the worst economic crisis since the Great Depression, an auto industry on the verge of collapse, two wars. I don't think I've been on vacation." The facts are the facts. He hasn't done a thing to curb violence and was just called out on it. And he has taken six months of vacation and about to jet off to Hawaii for three weeks. Obama reacted petulantly in the essence of a spoiled child.

$56 Toilet Paper and Contact Solution

December 22, 2012

I went to a large wholesale club today and bought contact solution and two large packs of toilet paper and the checker rang up $56. I laughed and said that that's a lot for toilet paper. My checker said that she is noticing prices are going up, but her wages are staying the same. She asked about what happens when the toilet paper costs three times as much. I just shook my head. But the honest answer is that we pay a ton more or we go without. We conservatives remember exactly what the Obama's have said. It includes Obama's version of a fundamental transformation and Michelle's "we're going to have to change our traditions, our history; we're going to have to move into a different place as a nation." Instead of questioning this fundamental transformation or what traditions and history need changing, the Obama's were applauded. This should have scared the crap out of all Americans, but it didn't. It got us four more years of being scared for what comes next from the Obama administration.

JANUARY 2013

Ignorance of the Smart, Liberal Educated Young Adults

January 3, 2013

These students seem to ground their beliefs in stupidity. They voted for Obama because of the social issues such as gay marriage and abortion. They fight for gay marriage, but for themselves, marriage is rejected as nothing but a piece of paper. It is ironic that it is the gay community that yearns for the stability and the legal and financial benefits that beget marriage. Young adults reject what their parents taught them and choose to believe in nothing. They reject God and formal religion although they were brought up in religious homes. For me, civil unions are fine for gay couples, but marriage is reserved for a man and a woman like the Bible says so.

When Obama told us that we have to change our traditions and history, these smart, young adults were too ignorant to care or ask the simple question, "Change to what?" The change to what is actually how they are living, hedonism. What else can you call the rejection of the traditional family unit, the sanctity of marriage, and the value of human life to a life of atheism, hookups, and abortions? If their way of life continues, they will find themselves living in a country with no churches or traditions to celebrate and a history of lies. That's what changing history means – lying about the past. Liberals have convinced generations of Americans that our country is arrogant and greedy. Our history tells a different story. America is the greatest country on earth due to hard work, perseverance and patriotism. But it won't be if the younger generations reject

141

what made it great. And in Catholicism, they are free to start living their lives without guilt. A benevolent God forgives all sin. Go enjoy your lives.

Economic Reality of the United States

January 7, 2013

The United States is in debt over 16 trillion dollars. The result of this latest economic crisis that Obama and the mainstream media kept marketing to us did not solve nor reduce any of our debt. People only heard that Obama wanted to increase taxes on the rich. What happened is that everyone who works will pay more in taxes and that Obama will spend more. The deal the Republican House signed prevented us from paying tons more in taxes. No entitlements or spending were cut. That's Obama's balanced approach. I'm tired of hearing how Obama saved us from the fiscal cliff, the auto industry, out of control healthcare costs and a second Great Depression. He accomplished none of these. Americans will start feeling the pain of Obama's economy and one day will come to the realization that Obama is in it just for himself.

Why is Congress wasting its time with gun control? by Kithy

January 7, 2013

Isn't Congress allowed to determine how it will spend its time? I guess wasting it on a lengthy gun control battle that has no chance of winning is acceptable to me, because nothing will get done and that is what this Congress needs to do – not let anything radical get done. I'm afraid, however, that since Obamacare won, maybe gun control has a chance. Here is my problem with it: Adam Lanza, the most notorious killer, didn't own any guns. He stole them from a legal gun owner. His problem was that he should have been institutionalized as a threat to humanity prior to committing his crime.

There are a lot of issues about institutionalization that need to be discussed and resolved, and that will have more effect on the safety of the citizens of the United States than any discussion about gun control. Maybe we should remember why the Founders were fond of guns. Was it because they hunted? No, it was because it is the only way to keep a check on a forever more power-hungry government, so that it will not take away citizen's rights. It's all about checks and balances. How do we get Congress to address the real issue of keeping Americans safe by institutionalizing sociopaths before they injure us?

Millennial Liberals Should Be in a State of Flux

January 10, 2013

Al Gore, the almost Godfather of man-made global warming, just sold his Current TV station to Big Oil Al-Jazeera and nets a cool $100 million. If we are all taught by Al to hate Big Oil companies, you would think Al would stand up for his beliefs and pass on this dirty money. People consider being green so important that they have changed their way of living. For God's sake, people are driving next to 18-wheelers in miniature mobiles – nothing Smart about this. Al Gore scared the bejesus out of people screaming like Chicken Little that the ice caps are melting, and polar bears are dying. You know now that the melting ice caps floating aimlessly about in his propaganda film were made of Styrofoam, right? As dire as the situation is, you would think Al could have found real ones floating all over our oceans.

Not only should greenies be in a state of flux about their feelings toward oil, liberals in general should be wondering why Al Gore wants $100 million. Liberals believe in social justice. When there are poor blacks, it's not fair to have rich whites, right? Weren't they supposed to hate Romney because he is a rich white guy? Misinformed people who think it is cool to be liberal were just taught what true liberalism is – a big fat lie. Al Gore never wanted to do without his cars, his air-conditioned mansion and his private jet rides. He never expected to ignore money and profits. That's what work is all about. The more money you make, the more freedom you have to do with your money as you please. The irony here is that liberal administrations tax away middle-class income so they can spend our money as if they are generous benefactors. And we become less free, pretty similar to a third-world dictatorship.

What's really behind the undeserved awards?

January 12, 2013

Obama received the Nobel Peace Prize before he did anything deserving, and everyone knew he didn't do anything. He also received two Grammy Awards for Best Spoken Word Albums for his audio books. Rapist Bill Clinton recently won Father of the Year award. We haven't forgotten how this married man fooled around with another man's young daughter in the Oval Office. Hillary Clinton won the MAW again for the 18th time – Most Admired Woman award. This is beyond undeserving. She not only stood by her man when he used and abused women on a regular basis, she was the point person for the cover-ups. This MAW will be testifying in a couple of weeks on another cover-up she took part in by lying about a video as the cause of our ambassador's death on September 11, 2012, two months before the presidential election. She is sure to leave out the part where she denied our ambassador security protection.

143

Organizations prop individuals up to be in the good graces of the politically powerful, if the individuals are not the organization themselves. In Obama's case, the propping up gave him the presidency and a second term. For the Clinton's, it is just plain ludicrous. Then again, Hillary got very close to the office of the presidency and may still be after the job. Gotta keep her in the public eye reminding us how great she is and in our good graces with a little prodding. It is our duty to admire the Most Admired Woman, right, and then vote for her, right? What a great country we could have if the truly deserving men and women could rise to their rightful political offices. Was there truly not another woman more admirable than Hillary for the past two decades?

A Very Painful Inauguration Day for Conservatives

January 16, 2013

Soon Obama will be taking the oath for the office of the presidency to preserve, protect and defend the Constitution of the United States for the second time. Our Constitution is a set of principles that state how our nation will be governed. The three specific branches of government were written to prevent the government from abusing its power. Conservatives know that Obama is a fraud and will not mean a word of his oath. The Constitution has a second amendment that states, 'The right of the people to keep and bear arms shall not be infringed.' Today, Obama is to announce the 23 or so Executive Orders infringing the rights of gun owners.

As a rule of law, Obama should send his gun control bills through Congress to be voted on by our representatives. He knows gun control will not pass. To Obama, the rule of law does not apply to him and he will continue to disregard the Constitution during the next four years. Is there a different inauguration for dictators? For this dictator, his reasoning to disregard the law is that it's the right thing to do. For Conservatives, we expect that if our representatives do not agree with the president, the law does not pass. Almost all of the mass killings could have been prevented with sane psychiatric care laws. Guess which politician introduced advertising gun-free zones on school buildings to the Senate? That would be your current VP Joe Biden.

Will gun control prevent evil? by Kithy

January 16, 2013

I hope that all the congressmen voting on gun control will ask themselves if this would this have prevented Newtown. If the answer is no, then their votes should be no. Also ask, what are the unintended consequences that we can anticipate? Would banning legal weapons have stopped Newtown? Would banning buying bullets have stopped it? Would banning automatic weapons have stopped it? No, no and no. He was a criminal who stole weapons from a legal owner. He used illegal weapons. The only way to have stopped this criminal would have been to remove all weapons from America, of every type. That's not going to happen.

What will happen if we ban buying bullets? Only criminals and organized criminals will have bullets. What will happen if we ban automatic weapons? The weapon makers will adjust something so that they can get around the ban, criminals will start making bombs or other weapons, something other than what is intended will happen. Enforce the rules we have, evil will happen, and each neighborhood and each school can decide for itself what precautions they need to take, can afford to take and are willing to take.

Could the mothers of insane, violent children be sued?

January 18, 2013

Adam Lanza shot and killed his mother, then shot and killed 26 at Sandy Hook Elementary School. I wonder if the mother of the Sandy Hook shooter Lanza was alive today could be sued. She knew her child was violent. She taught him how to shoot the guns that legally belonged to her and kept them in her house where Adam lived. Supposedly, Adam reacted to news that his mother was in the process of committing him to an institution. At the murder scene, Adam had his mother's rifle and two pistols. It looks like a case of negligence on the part of his mother in not securing her guns from her insane, violent child. Also, prior to the shooting, one woman had overheard Lanza saying that he planned this shooting at Sandy Hook and then contacted the police. She was told that Lanza did not own the guns so there's nothing they can do. This is another mass shooting that could have been prevented.

Details are still very sketchy about his psychiatric care and possible prescription medicine he was taking. We don't know what actions his mother had taken for his medical care and may never know due to privacy laws. Mental health laws in dealing with institutionalizing insane children and relatives need to be addressed to reduce the violence. Bring back the politically incorrect nut houses and send them there. The police should have been able to bring Adam to a nut house and have him evaluated the minute he was reported. Adam's mother should not have had to jump through hoops to have him institutionalized. Even Obama stated that his 23 Executive Order gun restrictions would not have prevented Adam from committing this horrific act. But that's all he did besides shed a tear.

Obama Vows Action on Climate Change

January 21, 2013

Obama vows action in the name of climate change. Not only will we get bankrupt coal companies, out of control EPA regulations and $10 per gallon gas, we may get a complete bankrupt America with the destruction of the dollar. And there will still be climate change – storms, hurricanes, freezing weather and hot weather. Obama does not have power over the sun and never will no matter how many tax dollars he spends or gives to his cronies.

The Irony of Obama's Inauguration on MLK Day

January 21, 2013

Obama has been a racially divisive president pitting the poor blacks against the rich whites, not surprising for someone who sought out a Black Liberation Theology pastor who railed against evil whites. Martin Luther King, Jr. stood up for civil rights on the basis of love and hope. MLK's *I Have a Dream* speech is clearly the opposite of Black Liberation Theology. Conservatives do not treat the black community as a separate group of people needing special treatment, precisely what Martin Luther King, Jr. talked about in the 1960's Civil Rights era. "I have a dream that my four little children will one day live in a nation where they will not be judged by the color of their skin but by the content of their character."

Intact, black middle-class families were growing in numbers since the day slavery was rescinded with the 13th Amendment in 1865. The focus of black culture was family, church and education up to the 1960's. Educated black men served as great role models to black children as teachers improving the overall state of blacks. So, what happened from then to now that decimated black family structure? Fathers have become basically non-existent to families: 67% black families live without a dad. Democrat's expanded welfare policies are what happened. Black women were rewarded with government benefits IF the fathers were not around. Money for free food, housing and medical care won out over black fathers and intact homes. Good-bye fathers as role models and hello to black children being raised by only their moms or grandmas.

Conservative policies are geared to raise the poor into middle-class status. Liberals are known to be members of the compassionate party with noble goals of helping the poor. Their policies have unintended consequences. Four more years of Obama's liberal policies will result in more people, black and white, losing their middle-class status, having to depend on the government, similar to that of slaves. The train wreck of Democrat policies on welfare could and should be diverted by our first black president. Unfortunately for all Americans,

Obama's focus is division by skin color. Imagine his legacy if he chose to follow in Martin Luther King's footsteps.

Crawfishing Phil, PGA

January 22, 2013

Top PGA Golf Professional Phil Mickelson publicly stated that he will definitely be making changes due to his 63% tax rate while living in California. And then the next day he apologized for upsetting and insulting others. The rich are playing into the communists' hands by agreeing that they should not speak up for themselves and stand up for what they believe. Soon the rich will also be completely indoctrinated into the belief that they should be grateful for what the government determines how much of their income they should keep. It is neither greedy nor insulting to want to keep what you have worked for. If the rich will not speak up for themselves, no one else will. Phil could have explained that he hones his craft, practices so many hours per day, studies up on all things golf and whatever he feels helps him become a PGA professional golfer. And then he could have said that the opportunity was there for him, and if people continue to mimic this communist lingo of the rich not paying their fair share, the opportunity will no longer be there for the next generation. And then he should say hello to Texas or Florida.

Happy National Squirrel Day! by Tbird

January 22, 2013

Today is Inauguration Day, but I just am not in the mood to celebrate the second inauguration of a president dead set on destroying this country. Instead, I am celebrating National Squirrel Day by watching squirrels in my backyard. Squirrels know they must plan for the cold winter when their food does not grow by gathering their nuts ahead of time; they know they can't just conjure nuts out of the air. I am finding more value in a squirrel's instinct for self-preservation than in our human president's penchant for bankrupting us into oblivion. Happy National Squirrel Day!

Is the Constitution obsolete? by Kithy

January 30, 2013

Why are we discussing immigration? What happened to the fight over gun control? Oh yeah, there were 32 presidential executive orders, case closed. Can't we do something to stop the train wreck of Obama's policies? Can't the

147

legislators stand up for themselves and their duty to uphold the Constitution? When the president does something clearly unconstitutional, he should be held responsible. Remember the right to bear arms? Just because the Founding Fathers lived over 200 years ago, doesn't mean they didn't think things through. Changing the conversation to rural versus city folks does nothing. Why do you want guns? Hunting. Ok, you can keep your hunting weapons. But there's no reason to have anything more. Oh, really? If we think back to why the Fathers thought it was important to have the right to bear arms, maybe then we'll realize we can't take this right away. (yes, take it away, Obama doesn't believe anyone needs a gun) Anyone remember why the American Revolution occurred? Does tyranny ring a bell? The government can force anything on an unarmed population. We already feel like the government is forcing ridiculous policies on us. We only have to make it four more years under this repressive government, and we can vote out a bad experience. But, what if, in the meantime, we have a conversation about why the Constitution is irrelevant because a couple guys a couple hundred years ago didn't know what it would be like now, and it's a living breathing…nonsense. Let's herd a bunch of apathetic Americans over the cliff believing this nonsense and end up in tyranny. We wouldn't need another election, because we'd have our king.

Truth Matters, Hillary

January 30, 2013

Here is Hillary's newly infamous remark about Benghazi, "What difference at this point does it make?" It doesn't make any difference if we accept our government lying to us. For most, the truth matters. During his reelection campaign, Obama repeated that al Qaeda was on the run. Obama presented himself as a foreign policy expert and that we no longer had to worry about Islamic terrorism. When al Qaeda killed four Americans in Libya including our ambassador on 9/11, Obama, with Hillary's assist, lied to preserve his story line. Secretary of State Hillary had the responsibility to keep Ambassador Stevens safe. He's dead and when Congress questioned her on his death, Hillary belligerently answered that it doesn't matter.

Now that Hillary is no longer a member of Obama's administration, perhaps we will get to hear the truth that promotes her agenda. Obama better beware of the woman he crossed eight plus years ago. Americans should be told by their government that Islamic terrorism is alive and well. If the government won't do it, maybe Hillary will. Nah, that won't happen.

Work on the Budget, Drop Immigration and Gun Control Now, by Kithy

February 1, 2013

So, the House put off the debt ceiling and budget talks for three months, and the Senate just now got around to putting it off. Now they only have two and a half months to come up with a budget. Shouldn't every minute of their time be spent working on an acceptable budget for both Houses to pass? Shouldn't that be the number one priority? Shouldn't they be debating this and compromising in a public forum, instead of waiting until the last second to pass something no one has read? Or is spending $3 trillion of taxpayer money just a simple formality?

Obama's Tent

February 2, 2013

Obama's tent can be labeled as socialist, Marxist, fascist, and radical but all that really needs to be said is that his policies are making us broke. He claimed he is for cutting the deficit, but the truth is that he grew it more than all the former presidents combined.

He claimed that our insurance premiums would go down, but they are reaching unaffordable levels that many are starting to drop their health insurance. He claimed that al Qaeda is on the run and that the wars are ending, completely false with a terrorist attack on another American embassy. In Obama's LaLa land, if you stop fighting the enemy and reduce our military to bare bones, wars are over. He claimed that our economy is improving although it is stagnant with high unemployment. It has not improved for the 8.5 million Americans who have left the labor force during Obama's first term.

Obama's tent of gays, blacks, Latinos, students, poor, union workers, and the good-hearted liberals may want to find out what the Republican tent is all about. Not one of these groups will be coddled but each one will be treated equally with low taxes, less regulations, constitutional rights, and free markets. All these conservative values add up to the freedom of opportunity for upward mobility without the interference of government bureaucrats. You can continue to listen to your ring master barking out how great things are going while ignoring your dwindling bank accounts. Or you can seek out and listen to whom Obama fears as he noted in his last press conference: FOX News and Rush Limbaugh.

Obamacare's Biggest Supporters Exempt from Obamacare

February 4, 2013

A bill's biggest supporters tell us all we need to know about a bill. Obamacare's biggest supporters are exempt from the bill: Obama, House Speaker Nancy Pelosi, Senate Majority Leader Harry Reid and the unions. Shouldn't the loudest cheerleaders for this Affordable Care Act be rushing to the front of the line thrilled to join rather than demand exemptions? Maybe they knew about the latest requirement. Under Obamacare, doctors are to report all your private medical news to the government. If you like your privacy, too bad.

What more is there to learn About Hitler?

February 4, 2013

So, Obama has been compared to Hitler among other dictators, blah, blah, blah and still gets elected a second term. I happened upon a documentary on Hitler's propaganda machine. Hitler's propaganda minister Joseph Goebbels took a well-known event, lied about it and blamed Nazi opposition. He commissioned a movie to be made called *Titanic*. In his version, Titanic starts with the parent company stocks plunging and the greedy need to increase stock prices. The British capitalist owner brags that the Titanic will make him richer with its record-breaking voyage. A German Nazi Officer serves as the hero who advises against the speed, concerned about the lack of lifeboats, and saves an abandoned child before the ship sinks.

Standard maritime practice was to maintain normal speed in waters with icebergs. The Titanic, considered to be unsinkable due to its fine construction, hit an iceberg and sank. Survivors describe how the men, rich and poor, tried to save as many women and children, also rich and poor, as possible. Obama has mastered Hitler's propaganda in twisting facts and lying about the truth to destroy his opposition – conservatives. One of Obama's successful propaganda is that the rich are greedy (only Republican rich) and don't care about the poor. What would have been the result of this last election if the poor were repeatedly told that the Christian rich are very charitable and giving of their riches? If you want the truth, take the opposite of what Obama says.

150

Obama and the Lethal Operation, by Tbird

February 7, 2013

The Department of Justice gave a sixteen-page "white paper" to members of Senate Intelligence and Judiciary committees last year. It was obtained by Michael Isikoff of NBC. The white paper is entitled "Lawfulness of a Lethal Operation Directed Against a US Citizen Who is a Senior Operational Leader of al Qaeda or an Associated Force" and summarizes the Obama administration's killing by unmanned drone strikes in 2011 of American Anwar al-Awlaki and his sixteen-year-old American son, among others, in Yemen. The paper says that three conditions must be met in order for an American to be killed outside the United States without having been indicted by the US government or charged with any crimes.

First, an informed, high-level official determines that the target poses an imminent threat of violent attack against the US. Who is the informed high-level official and how is he picked? We don't know. "Imminent threat" here does not mean about to happen right now or even the existence of any actual intelligence about any ongoing plot against the US. The suspect may have been associated with such things in the past and hasn't renounced his associations. It is not defined but just a broad concept.

Second, capture of the target is infeasible. The paper's example of infeasibility is that an attempted capture of the suspect would pose undue risk to US personnel or be due to time, capabilities of the place, or whatever. Does use of an unmanned drone automatically assume that no attempt to arrest a suspect is feasible? Again, infeasible is just a vague concept.

Third, the strike must be conducted according to the law of war principles, which are necessity, distinction, proportionality (no excessive civilian casualties), and humanity (avoidance of unnecessary suffering). The paper doesn't say much else about these terms.

What is a senior operational leader of al Qaeda? What is an associated force? Is a sixteen-year-old boy ever a senior operational leader of anything? Who decides who is a target? How can that person decide on the basis of a target's past associations without any ongoing plot to harm the US? At what point do you draw the line between "knowing" an American is a bad guy who has something to do with terrorism and deciding he has no right to due process other than having an anonymous high-level official decide he must die and giving the president the final say-so? That is way too much power in the hands of way too few people with no checks or balances. Obama has made a point of rewarding his friends and punishing his enemies; I don't trust him with life and death decisions. Do you?

Where will Governor Christie be in 2016? by Kithy

February 8, 2013

Slam! The prison door shut firmly behind his corpulent body. A murderer came up to him and asked, "What are you in for?" Governor Christie answered, "I bought a Big Gulp in New York City and then brought it to an elementary school. It's a banned substance, you know. The Queen had me thrown in jail for life." The murderer killed him on the spot, as he shouted, "You're the reason our food is so terrible now!" Christie didn't even have a chance to explain that it's not his fault that the Queen decreed what we can and cannot eat.

Obama Has to Go and He Will

February 9, 2013

I wrote earlier that Benghazi would be Obama's downfall. Back then, Benghazi was a cover-up for Ambassador Stevens' death. Secretary of Defense Panetta's Benghazi hearing leaves us believing that Obama should be charged with dereliction of duty. Obama was informed of the terrorist attack on our Libyan consulate within the first hour. Seven hours later, four Americans were killed. Obama was not engaged after being informed of the attack, he never called for any action, he never gave any orders except for possibly a stand down order, and he never contacted anyone about the attack. He did fly off to Las Vegas the next morning to campaign.

Obama's administration lied about it afterwards while he arrogantly campaigned on killing Osama and forcing al Qaeda on the run. Obama claims no help could have arrived in time to make a difference. The Ambassador's Deputy reported that Special Forces in Tripoli were on their way to board fighter jets but were told to stand down. The flight would have taken one hour. Besides being a consummate liar, Obama has a much deeper fault, putting his ideology ahead of everything, including American lives. This isn't surprising being that Obama's belief in America is that she is too strong, too powerful, too rich and too successful and that she needs to be brought down to her knees. After all, these faults are the cause of other countries' lack of being strong, powerful, rich and successful. It is truly moronic thinking and a danger to America's future, our lives included. Each day he continues as our president, Obama is getting closer to his goal.

Ben Carson Isn't Fair

February 14, 2013

That's Dr. Ben Carson, Director of Pediatric Neurosurgery at John Hopkins, brought up in Detroit by a poor black, single mother. He's rich and successful and to Obama, that isn't fair. According to Obama, he isn't to be admired. Instead, Dr. Carson is one of the greedy rich, not paying his fair share, and got this way by living like a white man. What is unforgivable to Obama is that Dr. Carson is a self-made black man who was taught by his third-grade level educated mother that welfare keeps the poor down. She cleaned homes for rich people and noticed on their shelves were lots of books, something lacking in her home. Little Ben was ordered by his mother to read two books a week and turn in book reports to her. Little Ben wasn't a slacker and did as he was told. In school, the combination of reading and education clicked for this angry young black child and he worked his way to a noble profession.

Dr. Carson is the antithesis to Obama. If Dr. Carson's story and conservative values spread, the fraud that is Obama will be exposed. Obama's Marxist rhetoric of equality for all will be rejected. Obama knows that his time to transform America into a communist utopia is limited. If he fails, Dr. Carson could be elected president in 2016 and become the transformational president Obama yearns to be. If he doesn't fail, the election in 2016 will already be fixed, communist style.

President of All or Just the Middle Class, by Kithy

February 14, 2013

Once again, Dr. Ben Carson distilled Mr. Obama's speech with clarity of thought. Is the President for some of us only, or for all of us? Obviously, he's a picker and chooser. Some classes are the chosen ones, while the others are vilified. We are never all chosen by Mr. Obama. Last night's chosen ones were the middle class. Until he decides he needs the fat cats from Wall Street to guide him. Then, they will be taken care of, although never in a public way. (Right, all the money printing might have something to do with the stock market rebound, and who profits from that?) The problem, of course, is that the President should be for all of us. The laws that are passed should be applied equally to everyone, including the lawmakers. We need to get back to the basics: government of the people, for the people and by the people. It's not for the middle class, or for the rich class or for the poor class. It's for all of us.

Rubio's Watergate, by Tbird

February 15, 2013

Marco Rubio, Florida's new senator, made the Republican rebuttal to President Obama's State of the Union address Tuesday night. During the middle of his speech, he reached for a bottle of water and took a sip. The mainstream media could talk of little else afterwards but how terrible that moment was, and that Rubio might have just ruined any future political career. Say what?

Obama's SOTU was a rehash of his old ideas with some whoppers thrown in. He claimed the economy is strong and then gave many plans for new government programs that won't cost us a single dime to fix. He said he will eradicate global poverty. He also omitted some big events. He didn't mention the loss by murder of our people in Benghazi or the murders resulting from Fast and Furious.

Rubio responded to Obama's economic plans and pronouncements. He said Obama doesn't understand our free enterprise economy. Obama thinks the economic downturn happened because the federal government didn't tax, spend, or control enough, which explains why his solution is always to tax, borrow, and spend, even though that's an old idea that's failed every time it's been tried. Any time people raise valid concerns about Obama's plans to grow government, Obama falsely attacks their motives. According to Obama, Republicans want dirty water and air and to let the elderly and disabled fend for themselves. Obama criticized Republicans for being willing to allowing cuts to defense in the sequester he himself insisted on a year and a half ago.

Economic growth, Rubio said, even just 4% growth, would create millions of middle-class jobs and reduce the deficit by $4 million. He suggested opening up federal lands for oil and gas exploration and basing reasonable energy regulations on common sense; simplifying the tax code to make it easier for small business to hire and grow; securing the borders and enforcing the laws before dealing with illegals; and passing a balanced budget amendment so government can't spend $1 trillion more in a single year than it takes in.

I liked Rubio's speech and wish Obama could act for the good of our country and enact some of his ideas to get our economy back on track. The mainstream media ignored everything Marco Rubio said. They instead focused on his sip of water. The producers had placed a heat lamp right near his head and the bottle of water out of his reach, and not surprisingly, Rubio sweated and got thirsty, so he leaned over (a boardinghouse reach, my dad would call it) to get a bottle of water and take a drink before continuing on with his speech. It did look a little awkward, but I dismissed it as irrelevant. Van Jones, Obama's former White House advisor, spoke with CNN's Carol Costello afterwards. When she made fun of Rubio's drink of water, Jones warned her that Rubio is dangerous for

154

Democrats because he can connect emotionally with people and that "he is to the heart what Ryan is to the head." I thought this was quite interesting because I realized that the Democrats and their media are trying to destroy Rubio, who is a rising star in the Republican party because he is a conservative who can reach regular people emotionally, something most Republicans don't do well, and that Ryan scares them because he has ideas that can work to improve things so that those same regular people will become less dependent on the Democrats. Rubio scares them, so they must destroy him.

$1.84 Gallon of Gas

February 18, 2013

$1.84 was the cost of a gallon of gas at the beginning of Obama's first term. Every time we fill up our tanks and see the price of gas, we should reflect on some of our president's energy policies: prohibit new offshore drilling, prohibit drilling on millions of acres of federal lands, prohibit pipeline of Canadian oil, and moratorium on Gulf Coast drilling.

Obama handpicked Steven Chu as his Energy Secretary who had previously said that we have to figure out how to boost the price of gasoline to levels in Europe. Europeans pay around $10 per gallon. Obama's energy strategy during the 2008 campaign called for us to inflate our tires. I am not kidding. When gas prices started to rise during his presidency, Obama said that if we can't afford high gas prices, we ought to buy more efficient cars. What makes Obama think that if we cannot afford $3, $4 or $5 gallon of gas that we can afford an expensive, government-mandated specialty car? When my car battery died, I bought a new one for $100. The batteries in these efficient cars are $10,000, again, not kidding. My tires are full, and the price of gas keeps rising.

USDA's Cultural Transformation Program

February 18, 2013

The US Department of Agriculture hired speaker Samuel Betances to conduct cultural sensitivity training sessions as part of a cultural transformation program. He describes himself as a citizen of the world. A video of his three-hour session was released to Judicial Watch through the Freedom of Information Act. In it, his audience of government workers chants, as asked, "Pilgrims were illegal aliens. The pilgrims never gave their passports to the Indians." "Thank you, white males." No history on whose heads the Indians scalped to settle the land.

NASA, the agency for exploration and science of aeronautics and space, is ordered by Obama to make Muslim outreach its priority to help them feel good

155

about their contribution to science, math and engineering. Through a whistle-blower, we learn that the USDA, the agency for food safety, is teaching fellow Americans new racist history. Wonder how else Obama is corrupting our government agencies. Note: A citizen of the world cannot have allegiance to his own country AND believe that we should live in a world without borders. All this globalism talk and Obama's apology for America go hand in hand in diminishing the United States of America.

Obama on Sequestration Simplified

February 20, 2013

Obama has overspent a trillion dollars each year of his presidency. US debt was $9 trillion in 2008 and is now $16 trillion, both ridiculous numbers. He ran his reelection on higher taxes on the rich which he knew would have infinitesimal effect on the trillions of debt. It sounded good to the poor. In the debt ceiling crisis of 2011, the Bush tax cuts were set to expire. If they expired, taxes would have increased on everyone. Obama would have let the tax cuts expire if Republicans would not have agreed to his demands of tax increases on the rich and sequestration, automatic spending cuts of $1.2 trillion beginning March 1. Obama put the sequestration in the Budget Control Act of 2011 and pledged not to put the sequestration into effect. Sure, Obama.

Obama now threatens that defense, border agents, police, firemen, etc. will have devastating across the board cuts if Republicans let the sequestration occur. The details call for the $1.2 trillion cuts over 10 years and not completely in defense. Obama, once again, is scaring the American people to get his tax policies enacted. If it were true that defense would be gutted $1.2 trillion, why would Obama have put America's safety on the line? It's close to suicide to cut our defense this drastically during these turbulent times. Why is he intent on taking money from business owners at a time when millions of Americans cannot find employment? Obama is purposely leading America to her demise. It is his ideology that guides him.

Climate Change Threat Will Heighten

February 21, 2013

Climate change defined is the change of weather. When I was growing up in the Midwest, a snowstorm meant fun and excitement, snow angels, snowball fights, sled riding down Suicide Hill and a chance to make money clearing neighbors' sidewalks. A PGA tournament in Arizona had to be temporarily postponed due to snow. How exciting must that be for Arizonians to experience? My family recently drove one-and-a-half hours to Hattiesburg, MS, to play in the snow. We

156

have also walked around uptown New Orleans with snow falling all around us. Absolutely beautiful! Now, instead of deriving sheer pleasure and wonder from the beauty and magnificence of weather events, the greenie sheeple act like Chicken Little. Before the greenies labeled weather events as climate change, this very same group with the very same solutions to this non-problem labeled the weather as global warming and before that, global cooling. Believe it or not, winter weather is happening because of the warm weather. Yeah, right.

Al Gore often scheduled his conventions in New York in late winter. One of his global warming conventions had to be cancelled because of winter weather. On another, he had to convince his fellow greenies that the earth was burning while they froze their tushies outside. It helped to turn up the heater in the convention room; who could deny global warming while sweating profusely? I'm sure it has been scrubbed from the internet, but there is a photo of a temperature station for measuring global warming. It shows a box with a thermometer and a lightbulb (the kind that produces warmth, not the newer LED type). Al Gore wrote a book labeling the internal combustion engine as deadlier than any military enemy. That's right – cars are more deadly than radical Islamists with atomic bombs. The liberal media made what has become of global warming and climate change. Without the media's blessing, changes in weather would be a non-issue as far as fixing it.

Obama's media will be bombarding us with any and all weather and non-weather events as evil climate change. People need to be scared so that their solution of sky-high taxes can be imposed upon us. Solutions range from: ban oil and gas, ban cars, become vegetarians, reduce population, ban light bulbs, hefty tax on businesses, reduce sunlight reaching the planet, tax cow flatulence (farts), install smart meters to regulate our home usage, ban coal, reduce family size, tax miles driven, and (slip this one in) end capitalism. What is the end game for these destructive ideas? It's about destroying America and forming a one world government. That can't happen unless the citizens are controlled.

We really need to be strong and ignore these Chicken Little warnings if America is to survive. Weather just is. Sometimes it's too cold, sometimes it's too hot and sometimes it's just right. But maybe someone will get a job measuring and regulating cow farts.

Obama's Sequester Threats, by Tbird

February 21, 2013

Obama has been saying that the coming sequester will destroy our economy and jobs and that Republicans must agree to hike taxes in order to avoid it. This is strange, considering he proposed the sequester and insisted he would veto any attempt to repeal it. In 2011, Obama got his debt ceiling raised $2.1 trillion. He wanted to avoid any debate about specific prioritization of government spending before he came up for reelection, so his Budget Control Act of 2011 created a supercommittee to come up with $1.2 trillion in spending cuts and tax hikes, something he knew would never happen, as Republicans swore they would not raise taxes and Democrats swore they would not cut spending. If the supercommittee couldn't agree, the sequester would automatically cut spending by $85 billion in the year 2013, half in discretionary defense and half in discretionary domestic spending across the board (a meat cleaver approach, Obama claims now). Obama figured Republicans would rather hike taxes than cut defense spending, which would get him off the hook for cutting programs his supporters like. The Republican House twice sent spending bills that made careful cuts to the Democrat Senate, which Obama refused to even look at them. Obama never had any intention of cutting any spending.

Sequestration does mean actual cuts in defense, but it is not as bad as Obama is pretending. Defense spending baselines are currently $491 billion, as opposed to 2012's $554 billion, and will grow with inflation. Defense will be able to shift funds to maintain critical military readiness. Cuts will exempt military personnel and veterans' affairs. General Service personnel will be cut through attrition and furloughs, and service contractors will be hardest hit. It works out to about a 9.4% cut for Defense. Obama, of course, wants to gut defense, but this is the closest he will get. The Pentagon will still be spending more in 2013 than it spent in 2006 at the height of the Iraq War. Obama is not concerned with cuts to defense spending.

The world will not end with sequestration. According to the Congressional Budget Office, discretionary outlays will drop by $35 billion and mandatory spending by $9 billion, for a grand total in 2013 of $44 billion; additional reductions in outlays attributable to cuts in 2013 funding will occur in later years. This year's spending will be cut by less than 1.5% compared to what it was going to be. Federal spending in 2012 was $3.538 trillion with a T; spending in 2013 will be $3.553 trillion, which basic math says is an increase of $15 billion. Discretionary spending in 2012 was $1.285 trillion, in 2013, $1.213 trillion, for a cut of $72 billion from last year. Of that $72 billion, $29 billion is being cut in discretionary domestic spending, which Obama says is coming from teachers, first responders, food inspectors, and Head Start, among others, and will destroy the economy. Put in perspective, the federal government spends $29 billion every 72 hours. This year is not a leap year, so there is one fewer day, so over a third of the $72 billion would have been cut by the calendar. Obama is saying that 72 hours' worth of cuts in domestic discretionary spending will destroy the economy and result in the loss of 750,000 jobs. He sounds like the Boy Who Cried Wolf. He has cried Wolf (economic crisis!) so many times that I cannot take him seriously. When will other people start realizing that? His poor supporters will hear that those mean Republicans cut their programs.

From Failure to Success: Ben Affleck, by Tbird

February 26, 2013

Last night, Ben Affleck won an Oscar for directing the best picture of 2012, Argo, a movie about a hostage rescue in Tehran in 1979. His career had been declared over and left for dead many times before then. He never gave up, and now he is an undisputed winner.

Affleck and his best boyhood friend, Matt Damon, burst on the scene in 1998, winning a screenwriting Oscar for Good Will Hunting, which was about a genius from a blue collar background who, with the help of a professor, leaves his comfort place for the unknown world of knowledge. Unfortunately, after winning instant fame, Affleck became wildly over-exposed and, according to critic Ross Douthat last November, starred in bad action movies, mediocre dramas, lousy comedies and bloated Titanic wannabes. He and his relationship with actress Jennifer Lopez became tabloid fodder, and their movie Gigli was so bad it made in revenues less than a tenth of its production costs. Affleck's reputation was so poor that his name on any project almost guaranteed near certain box-office death.

Ben Affleck started focusing on directing, rather than acting. He directed Gone Baby Gone in 2007, starring his younger brother Casey, following it with The Town, both of which received critical praise. In December, Barbara Walters interviewed Affleck and asked him how would he advise his younger self (if he could go back in time) about navigating stardom, assuming he would say to avoid the errors he'd made by steering himself away from bad scripts and embarrassing tabloid covers. To her surprise, he said he wouldn't change much of anything because his failures made him—failure ultimately was the best teacher of all. At the Oscars last night, he said it doesn't matter if you get knocked down, what matters is you've got to get back up.

I have to respect a man who slowly worked his way up from box-office death after writing an Oscar-winning screenplay to winning the Oscar for directing the Best Picture. He knows his many failures really taught him important lessons that he used in honing his craft. No one bailed him out or soothed his shattered ego. He learned from his mistakes. Boy, did he learn. More people, such as Barack Obama, need to learn that people must be allowed to fail before they can learn how to succeed.

Our Children Are Being Acclimated to Islam

February 27, 2013

Remember Michelle Obama's famous line about changing our history and traditions? And she received hearty applause. Here is just a sampling of what liberal progressives do with our children when we are not paying attention. In a Texas high school, a teacher had the female children don burkas during a world geography lesson and described the 9/11 bombers as freedom fighters. The teacher said that the goal was to change the way Islam is perceived. In Massachusetts, students took a field trip to a mega mosque for social studies class. The guide taught the students that jihad is not a holy war but a personal spiritual struggle. The students were lectured on Muhammad. While the girls were separated from the boys and taught that Islam is pro-women, the boys prayed to Allah with Muslim members.

In Ohio, a teacher was fired for having a Bible in her classroom. It is the liberal progressives who took Christianity out of our classrooms and are openly promoting the religion of Islam. Liberal progressive ideas and values are pervasive throughout public education. The goal is a fundamental transformation of America. Those were the exact words Obama campaigned on and received wide applause.

One of my bleeding-heart liberal Obama supporters said that she didn't believe this was happening. There are photos to prove it. But what Obama supporters would believe their own stinking eyes over a smooth-talking charlatan?

Did 34 bankrupt green companies cool our planet too much?

February 27, 2013

These winter blizzards sure are proof of global warming, I mean climate change, at least that is what we are told by government-sponsored scientists. It is so cold that it feels like hell has frozen over. You would think Obama would give it up. Our country was having a mild winter which was also marketed constantly as due to global warming. We can thank Obama for spending billions of our tax dollars on green companies that have obviously worked too well. It is surprising to hear, despite over 34 of these green companies having gone bankrupt, how efficiently our planet has cooled. Obama has also cooled our planet by reaching just 5% of his goal of selling one million electric cars – and that was by spending our tax dollars on fleet sales of Volts.

Tea Partiers can frivolously claim that the cold winter weather has set in and is naturally colder, ignoring Obama's green policies. Although I love the color green, I hate that liberal progressives have taken it over. I hate seeing green labels and green info on consumer products. I hate seeing it all over our schools – Green Zone signs, green stickers on every single light switch reminding us to Turn Off the Light, green clubs, green contests, green recyclables, green tips and throughout my children's schoolbooks. You would almost think it is being drilled into our children.

Thankfully, the Obama administration was smart to rename global warming as climate change. It can be confusing to connect blizzards to global warming. Where do we go from here? The solution would be for Obama to make spending cuts to his green energy agenda and call it a success. Personally, I would appreciate this gesture because my Bambusa oldhamii froze a few years ago down here in the south and I have replanted with 15 degrees freezing point bamboo.

Obama's Tactic May Fail This Time

February 28, 2013

Will Obama hurt Americans intentionally or make smart cuts? Obama has been holding rallies to warn us about doomsday when the 2% spending cuts automatically happen on March 1. The cuts of $1.2 trillion are to happen over 10 years which make them close to 2% of a $3.7 trillion annual budget. Obama promised us that he would review the federal budget page by page and line by line to eliminate programs to cut spending effectively. This is his chance to make good on just one of his promises. We've seen pictures of the lavish conventions and heard about the ridiculous pork projects of the many government agencies.

Obama decides what spending cuts to make and yet he falsely states that children's programs and security will be drastically cut. He has the power to cut these programs with sequestration and truly hurt Americans in order to assign the blame on Republicans. But will he? The word is getting out that Obama did sign this very sequestration into law and of his ability to direct which cuts to make. His actions will determine his true intentions - hurt Americans intentionally or make smart spending cuts.

MARCH 2013

Our Community Organizer President on Display

March 1, 2013

If you were on an Obama or Democrat email list, you most likely received the following scare on the sequestration cuts:

161

- Cuts to education: Sequester cuts will hurt kids of all ages.70,000 young children would be kicked off Head Start, 10,000 teacher jobs would be threatened, and funding for up to 7,200 special education teachers, aides, and staff could be cut.
- Cuts to small business: Small businesses create two-thirds of all new jobs in America. Instead of helping small businesses expand and hire, the sequester cuts would reduce loan guarantees to small businesses by up to $540 million.
- Cuts to public safety: Federal funding to programs that help local fire departments meet staffing and equipment needs would be cut by an estimated amount of more than $35 million. The sequester also includes cuts to the Federal Aviation Administration and the Transportation Security Administration, meaning more delayed flights, longer wait times at the airports, and less security monitoring our nation's flight systems.
- Cuts to food safety: Outbreaks of food borne illness are a serious threat to families and public health. The sequester cuts could mean up to 2,100 fewer food inspections, putting families at risk and costing billions in lost food production.
- Cuts to research and innovation: The impending sequester cuts would delay progress toward cures for many diseases and several thousand researchers could lose their jobs. Up to 12,000 scientists and students would also be affected.
- Cuts to mental health: The sequester cuts could mean that up to 373,000 seriously mentally ill adults and emotionally disturbed children go untreated.

The above is from an Organizing for Action email. It ends by asking to chip in $25 or more for the cause. It continues:

"Sequester cuts already hurting small businesses"
CBS News – February 28th, 2013

Friend,

Before the sequester officially starts tomorrow, before airport control towers start shutting down and construction projects grind to a halt, let's remember why this is happening in the first place:

The sequester was created because, without it, Republicans threatened to destroy the world economy by forcing America into default. It's time to hold Republican state legislators accountable for the damage they're doing to our economy – can you contribute $10 or more to the DLCC by tonight's deadline? This constant Republican cycle of hostage-taking and manufactured crisis has been a disaster for our economy, and it needs to end.

The Democratic Legislative Campaign Committee sent the above email. Drumming up hatred for Republicans is an Obama specialty as he jets his family off for another $1 million taxpayer funded vacation. The threats, scares, and doomsday predictions were all orchestrated by our community organizer president. If he scared the American people enough, he would get his tax increases. He even went so far as to release illegal immigrant prisoners a day ahead of sequestration. If he didn't scare enough politicians into voting for tax increases, he also got his way. He would lay the blame for our economic woes on Republicans for not stopping sequestration cuts. Fortunately for us, Obama ran into a small speed bump with his version of sequestration. A prominent journalist from the Watergate scandal Bob Woodward reported that Obama was responsible for sequestration, and, fortunately, Republicans held firm on no more taxes. Republicans presented sensible, alternative cuts to the across the board cuts in the $3.7 trillion budget. Obama refused any change to sequestration unless he got higher taxes. Obama counts on his constituents to believe him when he claims future economic pain will be the Republican's fault. This community organizer president hasn't learned yet that the buck stops with him. The economy belongs to Obama. Now, we just need more media to come forward and begin reporting the truth.

Sequester, by Tbird

March 1, 2013

Whoops! The sky is still there!

Mitt Romney, The Man Who Should Be President

March 3, 2013

Mitt Romney, the businessman and past governor who should be president, will soon be explaining to newsman Chris Wallace how he would have handled sequestration. This will be very painful for some of us to hear because we will hear common sense towards bringing the United States to economic stability. Obama's scare tactics on sequestration has the end goal of blaming Republicans for any and all ill-effects to the economy. What kind of man is Obama that he claims that he would have to choose to close funding on the poor kid or the disabled kid?

In two years, Obama wants control of the House of Representatives so that he can complete a final transformation of our beloved country into the United Socialist States. This can only happen if Obama destroys capitalism and everything great about America. Republicans have the most important job ever which is to hold back Obama's agenda at every junction, however minor it may be. Our media has not reported the truth or facts about Obama's policies and agendas. Let's pray that more mainstream media, elected Democrats and minority leaders begin to report how Obama's agenda is hurting everyone, the wealthy, the middle class, and the poor. It is time to live up to our country's name, the United States of America.

A Dangerous President, Marketing the United States as Weak

March 5, 2013

Obama is marketing the United States to the world as a weak country. Obama is displaying unconscionable behavior of putting Americans at risk, all for the effect of blaming Republicans. According to Obama, a 1% cut to his $3.7 trillion budget is causing a reduction in the security of our country. Obama and his administration have announced that cuts have been made to ports of entry, security checkpoints, and borders. They have also announced that they have no choice but to release thousands of illegal immigrants. Obama has also delayed fueling and cancelled maintenance of navy aircraft carriers. He even delayed deployment of a carrier to the Mideast due to the budget cuts. A loyal and true United States president would never ever consider doing this to our country.

Austerity Has Hit the White House

March 5, 2013

Austerity has hit the White House. The White House has cancelled public tours due to sequestration budget cuts. Either the United States is so broke that tour volunteers cannot be paid, which is strange since volunteers are unpaid, or we Americans are being played for fools. The irony is that if Obama successfully implements his fundamental transformation, real austerity will befall us all. Austerity just is not happening at the moment.

Obama has put us on a path to economic collapse. What else can account for nearly doubling our deficit after Obama promised to cut it in half? When an agreement is finally reached to enact spending cuts, Obama puts on a show for the world that doomsday is here. What will Obama's next act include? My guess is that he may lie low for a while and when the 2014 elections close in, he'll ramp up the global warming scare. Or he will finally pass the Keystone Pipeline to claim that he is for oil independence, if Republicans pass Cap and Trade. If that's the case, the global warming scare will be ramped up as soon as the freezing weather and blizzards die down.

Challenge for Believers of Man-Made Global Warming

March 7, 2013

If you believe in global warming, here is a challenge to your beliefs:

From all the information you gathered to back up the theory of man-made global warming, name one that originates from sources other than government subsidized scientists, scientists from the Intergovernmental Panel Climate Change, and universities funded by government grants.

Can you name any article or study from a government subsidized scientist with an opposing view?

A US Department of Energy graph shows carbon dioxide as 99.438% of total greenhouse gases, omitting water vapor. With water vapor included in greenhouse gases, what is the percentage of man-made carbon dioxide? Answer: 0.117%

Have you read the 2008 US Senate Minority Report that quotes international scientists that dissent over man-made global warming? More than 700 international scientists dissent.

Have you researched Climategate in which emails of leading climate scientists discussed 'how best to squeeze dissenting scientists out of the peer review process' and 'that we can't account for the lack of warming at the moment and it is a travesty that we can't'?

Do you think taxes will change the temperatures of the world? Obama's solution to global warming is taxation on carbon, something we can't live without and something that can't be seen.

How do you feel about a top global warmist, UN IPCC official Ottmar Edenhofer, calling the 2010 Climate Conference as an economic conference, not a climate conference? Or that climate policy is the means to redistribute wealth globally?

With a Cap and Trade energy policy, will you be able to afford energy for your home?

A congressional global warming hearing was scheduled for March 6 but was canceled due to the threat of a DC snowstorm. Irony is that the meteorologists were wrong in predicting the weather one day out; snow only accumulated one inch. One more point, Al Gore is neither a scientist nor a meteorologist but is an opportunistic politician. With all the hot air coming out of his mouth, the global warming scare has made him a very rich man. If Cap and Trade taxation is passed, what will it make us? Very poor.

Gun Design Contest

March 11, 2013

Our kids are getting punished in our public schools for anything gun-related and it has gotten out of control. The latest is a child who has been suspended for chewing a pop-tart into a gun and saying, "Bang, bang." This all ties into socializing our children on how dangerous guns are and ignoring that guns also keep us safe. These children will be voting within two to three elections. How do you think they will vote on gun control if they are conditioned by being punished for anything gun-related?

To honor the kid whose cupcakes were confiscated because they were topped with miniature toy WWII soldiers, to honor the kid who was punished for pointing his finger like a gun, and to honor the kid who was punished for nibbling his Pop-Tart into a gun shape, I would like to suggest a contest on gun design. Guns must be created out of everyday items. Creativity wins. The prize is pride in being an American. Good luck and may the best gun design win.

Bill O'Reilly Finally Gets It

March 12, 2013

Obama entered office vowing to cut the $9 trillion budget in half and chastised Bush for bringing up the debt as unpatriotic. So far, so good, except that I know where Obama is coming from - a communist upbringing, hanging with his choom gang, seeking radicals throughout his college years and starting his political career at 1960's communist bomber Bill Ayer's house. He said the right things to get elected but does the exact opposite. Four years later, the debt jumps up to $16 trillion. Obama focuses on increasing the welfare state and taxes. If Obama stays on track, he'll add another $4 trillion before he leaves office.

Bill O'Reilly, political commentator and cable TV host on the most popular Fox News Channel show *No Spin News*, is finally mad that our economy is a mess and that Obama has zero intention of cutting any entitlements. He had a shout-out with Obama talking head Alan Combs who could not state one plan that Obama has to cut this debt. Discussing this outburst with Glenn Beck, O'Reilly stated that he is surprised that people do not see the facts and are in denial about the debt. A stunned Beck summarized O'Reilly's questioning as how do you tell people of a danger or something that's in the future that you can't really prove. BEFORE Obama was elected president, Glenn Beck tried to warn O'Reilly

166

about Obama's communist leanings. O'Reilly didn't listen to his own friend and colleague back then and still has not called out Obama as a communist.

It is difficult to consider that our president is a communist. Okay, how about agreeing that Obama says and does the same things communists do? The main component of communism is to label capitalism as bad and encourage workers to rise up against the greedy business owners. If people would stop to ask the question, "Then where the #!@k would I work to provide for my family?", no one would buy this nonsense. Expanding the debt with entitlements is all geared towards collapsing our capitalist economy. I'm glad Bill O'Reilly finally gets it.

Obama's Charm Offensive

March 13, 2013

The media has been reporting on Obama's Charm Offensive. Obama may be feeling the need to prop up his poll numbers. He actually dined with a dozen Republicans and met with the House Budget Committee Chairman Paul Ryan for more than two minutes. Obama must really be serious about a budget – he had his first ever conversation with Ryan. In Obama's less than charming moments, he sat with congressional leaders in 2009 listening to their concerns about a spending bill. Obama responded, "I won." Right, and you are supposed to lead as president, not as a bratty child. After meeting with Ryan, Obama had another less charming and a more idiotic comment on the budget. He won't balance the budget just for the sake of balance. If any CEO heard this from a budget director, that person would be fired. The point of a budget is to balance to stay within your means. Companies that are not fiscally sound go broke, bankrupt and out of business. This is how Obama is running the American economy. Charm isn't going to change the economy. Then again, his main voting base doesn't care and isn't listening.

Comparing Pope Francis I to Obama and My Pope Hope

March 15, 2013

Jorge Bergoglio, an Argentinian of Italian descent, was ordained a Catholic priest in 1969 and elected pope in 2013. Barack Hussein Obama II, an American of African American/English descent, was elected United States president in 2008. Pope Francis I speaks Spanish, Latin, Italian, German, French and English. Obama speaks and writes English poorly – corpsmen for corpsmen, numerous subject/predicate mis-agreements, and the educated-sounding I after a preposition 'for Michelle and I' when it should be me. Pope Francis has a reputation for humility and lives a simple lifestyle. Obama talks of humility but has a reputation for arrogance, living an ostentatious lifestyle. Pope Francis is against contraception and calls the pro-choice movement a culture of death. Obama voted twice as an Illinois senator to deny medical help to babies who survived an abortion and is forcing Americans to pay for contraception through Obamacare. Pope Francis believes that same-sex marriage deprives children of a father and mother willed by God. Obama has instructed our justice department to stop defending the Defense of Marriage Act and promotes same-sex marriage. Pope Francis helps the poor through charitable works. Obama promotes helping the poor through wealth redistribution, though cancels a successful school voucher program that benefitted black children in our capital Washington, DC; teacher unions trump even poor black kids. My pope hope is that he is a defender of all the people, rich and poor, and that he leads as many people to lead spiritual lives. May Obama and the most spiritual needy listen to the pope.

Something Sinister about Obama's Policies

March 17, 2013

A recent caller to Rush Limbaugh described himself as a low information voter and a die-hard Democrat. He has noticed that Obama doesn't take responsibility for anything and that there's something sinister about him. The caller has started listening to Rush, Sean Hannity, Mark Levin and Glenn Beck and realizing that they speak the truth.

Obama recently stated with a straight face that our $17 trillion debt is on a sustainable path and that our economy is strong. So, our country on the brink of financial insolvency is nothing to worry about. And adding $8 trillion in new debt isn't his fault because the economy was worse than he thought. Obama's favorite phrase during his presidency is that he inherited the worst economic crisis since the Great Depression. Completely false but he repeated this ad nauseam to help justify his social programs and spending. He gets a tiny cut to his spending plan and closes tours to the White House. Obama isn't straight with Americans and even low information voters are smelling his garbage.

What is happening in politics is not the usual Democrat versus Republican. Obama is spending our future into oblivion and Republicans are trying to stop him. I compare Obama to a manic-depressive in the mania phase spending profligately without a care to the consequences. However, he does have an agenda and it is sinister. He wants the consequences to be a breakdown of America. Obama's ideology is all about fairness - if you have wealth, you didn't earn it; you stole it and he is going to punish you. He directs his ideology at our citizens, but he also directs his ideology at our entire country. His fairness means taking money from the United States and handing it to his favored countries. If you cannot relate to this, take one hour and listen to someone who loves America. I suggest Mark Levin.

How far will our government go with our bank accounts?

March 18, 2013

A small country near Greece called Cyprus is bankrupt and needs money. The government announced that it will impose a tax of 10% on all bank accounts. At least the Cyprus government is honest and calling it a tax. Obama prefers the terms income redistribution, an investment in the people, increasing revenue or paying a fair share. The fact is that people's private property is being stolen by the government. Could this ever happen to us in the United States? During Obama's reign of terror, absolutely. During the Clinton presidency, Hillary wanted a one-time 20% tax on IRA's. Then again, she also wanted the profits from oil companies. She got neither; people were informed and paying attention. Obama wants us to buy government debt with our retirement accounts. First, he will offer to convert 401K'S and IRA's into annuities backed by the US Treasury for our own security. Then he will demand it through regulation for the good of the country. Once you die, the money stays with the government.

You Can't Be Anti-Abortion

March 18, 2013

You can't be against a naturally and spontaneously occurring abortion. Abortions happen, whether due to abnormalities, stress or accidents. What you should be against is man-made abortions. Liberal greenies, isn't your religion against man-made things? Our rights end when someone else's begins. And we all began the same way, no matter how small. God taught us that we were already someone to Him before we were even conceived. **I knew you before I formed you in your mother's womb. Jeremiah 1:5**

Man-made abortions go against humanity. No reason is great enough to kill the innocent child forming in the womb. However, Margaret Sanger, the founder of Planned Parenthood, had plenty of reasons. One was her Negro Project to sterilize black women. A second reason was to limit a woman to one child. A third reason was the wickedness of creating large families. The majority of people have never heard about this evil woman. Her vision is flourishing today.

Liberals love using the unwanted baby from rape as justification for abortion. Alan Guttmacher, a former president of Planned Parenthood, formed the Guttmacher Institute that promotes abortion worldwide. His study titled *Reasons U.S. Women Have Abortions: Quantitative & Qualitative Perspectives*, found that less than 1% state rape as the reason for abortion. The most common reasons were that the baby would dramatically change their lives and that they can't afford a baby.

169

My personal viewpoint is that humans conceived by rape are as much human as anyone else. Man-made abortions should be criminalized. Ask liberals to abort their dogs' puppies and they will scream bloody murder.

How many Smart cars would it take to clear the snow?

March 25, 2013

None, they wouldn't be found until the snow melts. A humongous snowstorm is continuing its path across the United States dumping a foot of snow along the way. I'm glad my daughter does not think that she is saving the planet by driving a tiny Smart car. If she could find her micro-mobile in this snow, I wouldn't allow her on the snowy, icy streets anyway. Global warming fools continue to have difficulty promoting a cause that just isn't there. And yet, as highlighted on the Drudge Report recently, Al Gore is pushing a carbon tax. Anyone believing in the man-made global warming apocalypse is also pushing an energy and business-killing carbon tax. This is the agenda of the global warming leaders. Read my lips: a lot of money is going to be made trading carbon credits and I'll bet multi-millionaire Al Gore is on the receiving end.

And he isn't a Republican, he is a die-hard Democrat. I know it is hard to believe that the Democrat Party has a lot of rich, old white men. But, then again, it is the Democrat Party that has many convinced that it just isn't so. How many times have we heard that the Republican Party is the party of rich, old white men? This humongous snowstorm almost makes the global warming sheeple questioning if they have been snookered. But, no, they will hear that a warm spot caused the cold spot so the cold happened because of the warm...and continue to believe. We'll be punished with a carbon tax, and winter, spring, summer and fall will proceed with the same unpredictable, yet predictable, weather.

Obama and His Fake Sequestration and Fake Austerity

March 26, 2013

Obama promised us lots of scary cutbacks if sequestration passed into law. Austerity cutbacks include suspending tours to the White House and tuition assistance for active duty service men and women. 149 airport towers are scheduled to close starting April 7. The IRS will be unable to process tax refunds in a timely manner. I suppose if we raised our taxes, would we receive our tax refunds sooner than later? A 6-minute video recently released showed our IRS employees as Star Trekkies in a comedy routine costing $60,000 to produce. That's a good waste of money, but even worse, the studio it was produced in is owned by the IRS costing $4 million a year. In the Star Trek

170

routine, the IRS agents fist-bump to becoming rich and famous as public servants, more public servants enjoying the lifestyle of the rich and famous travel extravagantly on the taxpayer dime. Obama took an entourage of 600 to travel with him to Israel. Our Catholic, abortion-supporting VP Biden took a 2-day trip to Paris and London after attending Pope Francis's installation. Hotel cost $1 million. Limousine cost $300,000. Priceless.

Why Obama Can Blatantly Destroy the United States

March 27, 2013

Obama can and is destroying the traditions and the economy of the United States because he has a loyal voting bloc and our congressmen and women refuse to challenge a black man. Obama gets away with telling us that a $17 trillion debt is nothing to worry about and that our economy is fine. The people who understand what Obama is doing can rant and scream all day that our economy is on the verge of collapse. Obama puts on a thinly veiled front that he cares, but he knows that his voting bloc isn't listening, doesn't care and will believe whatever he wants them to believe. The majority of his voting bloc are the ignorant, the uninformed, and the misinformed. His loyal voting bloc includes those dependent on government handouts to smart, liberal women.

Hope exists that more and more people will understand the conservative principles that made our country so great. One of those principles is traditional marriage between a man and a woman. If this definition of marriage gets perverted on the basis that people should get to love whoever they want, it will eventually allow any type of marriage. This includes the ever-growing Muslim population to marry as they do abroad, many wives, including very young girls. Who could deny a grown Muslim man the love of a young virgin? I think Obama would be just fine with that.

Loved Reading Killing Lincoln and Killing Kennedy

March 29, 2013

Most people live self-centered lives and believe that they live in the most momentous of times. Reading these two books puts this in perspective. Lincoln dealt with a raging Civil War to end slavery and bring our country together. Kennedy dealt with the Cuban Missile Crisis, the volatile civil rights movement in the 60's and the start of the Vietnam War. These books allow us to relive our history which brings us to the present with Obama. How will history define the Obama years?

171

As the American citizens during the Lincoln and Kennedy years lived in tumultuous times, so do we. We are fortunate to also live in the most prosperous and technologically advanced times. Obama's focus should be our security, but his ideology leaves us more vulnerable than ever. 911 during Bush's term left us no doubt that radical Muslims want to kill us. Obama claimed that al Qaeda was on the run all because one lonely, has-been in a Pakistani compound was killed. He seems intent on minimizing our impact in the world by gutting our defense. He claimed that our borders are more secure than ever. Ironically, as our committee members on immigration were standing by the Mexican border, a woman scaled the 18-foot fence a few yards away.

History will show that his first term focused on his idea of what kind of healthcare we should have. It should be noted that every congress member who voted for it is exempt from Obamacare along with their families. It should also be noted that many of his union supporters are exempt. Obama and the Democrat congress are solely responsible for subjecting us to a massive bill that had to be passed for us to find out what's in it. Hopefully it dies in its own quagmire without destroying our healthcare industry. His other focus continues to be green energy and harming our oil and gas industry.

Obama's second term is his for the making. He seems intent on amnesty of 11 million illegals and for expanding entitlements that will surely destroy our economy. His major aim is wealth redistribution which goes against everything our country was founded on - hard work, independence and a government for the people by the people of the people. May God bless America.

Whoever Has Control of Your Money Can Control You

March 29, 2013

Children learn really fast that debt is bad. Financially struggling adult children who ask their parents for funds know that they are beholden to the parents. The responsible adult relationship shifts into a needy relationship. When the debt is paid off, there comes a sense of relief and ownership over their lives. The majority of college-age voters voted for Obama and they own his policies foisted upon them. A student loan bill was tied into the phony named healthcare bill, the Affordable Care Act, that disposed of the competition of private lenders. They will still believe that Obama did it because he was trying to help them. Because he said so. Over and over. The government promised more reliability and affordability and to offset expenses in the Affordable Care Act. Student loan interest rates are doubling come July. Parents will be depleting their bank accounts, or the students are going to be saddled with expensive debt to pay for college.

172

Adults learn really fast that US debt is bad, especially that China owns a large portion. Drudge Report's main headline is that North Korea is set to bomb DC, Los Angeles and Austin. Crazy Kim could blackmail China with a bomb or assist him in destroying the US. I don't feel very secure knowing that we are indebted to communist China. However dependent we are on China correlates to however much less control we have over our own lives.

APRIL 2013

Better Pass Those Global Warming Tax Hikes Quickly

April 1, 2013

Famed United Nation climatologists and every other scientist on the tax-funded grant receiving end have harped on how hot we are. But now we are told that global surface temperatures have not followed the expected global warming model patterns. "The mismatch between rising greenhouse-gas emissions and not rising temperatures is among the biggest puzzles in climate science just now," The Economist said.

Climate scientists are puzzled by the twenty-year hiatus in rising temperatures. Twenty years! It isn't puzzling why this may be the first time the global warmist greenies are hearing about this. The believers are absolutely needed to keep the pressure on this non-issue so our trusted politicians will pass life-saving tax hikes. Politicians who want tax hikes will always exist. Politicians who want massive, life-changing tax policies that control our lives are extremely dangerous. Citizens who love the freedom their cars bring and love the electricity that keeps our air conditioners humming and our furnaces burning have the duty to speak out against dangerous politicians and their policies.

Obama's April Fools' Joke

April 2, 2013

On April 1, 2013, Obama stated that he wants to help prepare young people to tackle financial challenges and to budget responsibly. Such a commonsense statement is welcoming. Coming from Obama who may have already destroyed our economy, it's a sick joke. Our President submitted previous budgets for our country that received zero votes from the US Congress. Not one Democrat approved his budget. Our ridiculous debt of $9 trillion could have been significantly reduced if Obama strengthened our oil and gas industry. Instead, he sicced the Environmental Protection Agency (EPA) on the industry to hinder it and he wasted billions of dollars on the green industry. Instead of pricey, business-killing Obamacare, we could have been given the opportunity to

173

purchase the same health insurance that congress members have and subsidize the truly needy. They like their choices and the system is all in place. US debt is nearly $17 trillion. The future of our country is in the hands of someone who makes a mockery of our very own security and economic freedom.

Obama's economic policy is to keep printing more money, borrow more money and spend more money. David Stockman, former Budget Director for President Reagan, is expecting the US economy to collapse within a few years. He says that Wall Street is being propped up with this phony money and the resulting bubble will pop. Young people should learn to budget responsibly. But this will not change the direction of our economy. It is up to Obama and his economic policies to avoid Stockman's prediction. Have we been taken for the fools?

What Obama's 2 for 22 Basketball Shots Tell Us

April 2, 2013

The Obama family was introduced to the crowd attending the White House Easter Egg Roll. Michelle Obama welcomed everyone and told the kids to celebrate nutrition, health and activity. Some of the kids were playing basketball with Washington Wizard pros. It must have been exciting to have the president join them for a game, or rather watch Obama try to make a free throw over and over and over again until he made it. Most adults would have taken a few shots and then let the kids show off a little. Obama is no adult. He tried 22 times. No one does this but a very self-focused, selfish man without regard to others around him. It also takes arrogance to keep control of the ball among a crowd until he was satisfied with his skill. Kids do not want to watch an adult take over the basketball court. They want to take part in it. After Obama made the free throw on his 22nd time, he sauntered off happy with himself. It didn't occur to him to stay around and watch the children enjoy themselves. Adults know when to step aside, a lesson Obama never learned. And, yes, we realize that you are the president of the United States. Please act accordingly. It's really not about you.

Most Americans Agree with Obama Because He Says We Do

April 3, 2013

Obama often begins statements with 'Most Americans agree with me that...' Obama says these words on almost every issue, and I know I have never been asked my opinion. On gay marriage - California voters voted against it. Gun control - Americans like their guns and demand their second amendment. Immigration reform - is not good for the middle class. We know that these newly acquired citizens will be funded with our tax dollars and will most likely

174

vote Democrat to continue being funded with tax dollars. The food stamp program is even advertised in Mexico! All his talk about a balanced budget is hot air. The only time I agree with Obama is when he lies about his agenda. He made a statement that we shouldn't have to decide whether to fund a poor kid or a disabled kid. A few weeks later, he sent his girls on a spring break trip to the Bahamas and then to Idaho for skiing. The travel and security costs are all on the American taxpayers. He has scheduled a Memphis Soul Concert at the White House featuring Justin Timberlake and Queen Latifah. Yet without those tax increases, he may have to defund the poor kid and the disabled kid. Obama is a very disingenuous person. His policies have resulted in poverty for one in six Americans. All Americans agree that poverty should be minimalized in America. Obama has already given us lip service that most Americans agree with him that it is time to focus on jobs and the economy. It has been since he came to office. But he did tell us that his goal was to fundamentally transform our country and that has been his focus. Are you now kinda noticing what he meant? I'll bet most Americans would not agree with this transformation if they were paying attention.

Where Obamacare Stands April 2013

April 4, 2013

The Affordable Care Act, or Obamacare, was signed into law three years ago and was scheduled to go into full effect 2014. People have been thrown a few bones – the raised age limit to 26 for adult children and a credit by insurers due to the 85% rule. Obamacare requires that 85% of premiums be spent on care. A family with a policy of $7200 with a $5000 deductible may receive a rebate of $75 with an accompanying letter praising the benefits of Obamacare. The letter itself is regulated by Obamacare. The Obamacare legislation is 2700 pages with the phrase throughout "as the secretary shall determine." Regulations for Obamacare now pass 10,000 pages.

Seventeen states are setting up their own online exchanges where people will go to purchase insurance with subsidies, the lower your income, the bigger the subsidy. Thirty-three states have left it up to the federal government which has no allotted funds to proceed. The exchanges will either not be ready for 2014 or will be set up with a policy of one choice. If your income is greater than expected, one of the new 16,000 IRS agents will deduct the difference from your tax return. Anyone who got the impression that national healthcare is free is misinformed. The exchanges are designed to have one, all-inclusive policy with different levels of deductibles. If you still cannot afford the insurance with subsidies and do not purchase any insurance, you will be fined by the IRS. At a certain maximum of income, you cannot purchase Obamacare but are instead directed to apply for Medicaid. Not many doctors accept Medicaid patients because the government limits payments to doctors.

The goal of Obamacare as declared by Kathleen Sebelius, Secretary of Health and Human Services, is to move everyone into a fully insured product for the first time. Naturally, a fully insured product will cost more and now will be mandatory. If this was such great healthcare, why would it be mandatory to purchase? Just a thought. The regulations are unclear for the 11 million illegal immigrants, but if reform goes through, I imagine that they will be subsidized, a nice word to say paid courtesy of your taxes. The government does not have the money for subsidies. A copy of your policy will be required with your tax return. If you are lucky enough to find a policy that you feel better suits you and that costs less, you will owe the taxman for not purchasing the Obamacare policy.

Obamacare is national fascist health care. Government already runs a healthcare program for the VA serving over 8 million veterans. Has healthcare for 8 million been perfected? Course not, it is a disgrace with long wait times for our veterans. Now the government is in the process to control healthcare for over 300 million citizens. Note to Americans: You should never want your government to have that much control over your lives. If this concerns you, vote conservative in the 2014 election.

Obama's Feelings toward the United States of America

April 8, 2013

The United States is made up of land and people. Land cannot be arrogant so Obama must be talking about we the people. I'm fairly sure that no one reading this believes that he or she has been arrogant or knows anyone who has been arrogant towards other countries. The United States has become a rich and most powerful, economically sound country and, to Obama, this is our weakness, not a strength. In Obama's world, it is the United States' fault that other countries are not as successful and powerful as we are. What has been Obama's solution? Look around. Our economy is on the brink of collapse, high unemployment, lots of closed businesses and no job growth in our future.

Our healthcare system was looked upon as the best in the world. Ground-breaking surgeries and technological advances from our citizens have made impact all over the world. Doctors are now on the brink of bankruptcy due to many things but primarily regulations and malpractice insurance. We were sold a bill of goods with Obamacare such as everyone will have access to healthcare, and everyone will be insured. How's our healthcare going to be when there are no doctors? The White House is now stating that Obamacare is having operational difficulties. In other words, the administration has no idea how to implement this monster it is creating.

176

We once had a president that reminded us that the United States is a shining city upon a hill whose beacon light guides freedom-loving people everywhere.

Hannity Subjects Himself to a Room of Angry Blacks

April 9, 2013

Fox News works hard to keep its ratings up for all their white racist viewers. Sean Hannity did his part by subjecting himself to a room of angry blacks on April 8, 2013. These blacks rail to Hannity for an hour on all the injustices directed to the black community. Hannity even brings a black woman sitting in the front row to tears. Not one of them when asked would reveal which African tribe they came from or evolved. They claim that they have been called ugly names unfit to repeat and how they have specifically been treated by the elite whites for being black. I give my kudos to Hannity, but really, were you just placating your ignorant, racist viewers?

You get to see how Fox News has gotten its reputation as a conservative news outlet and why Obama has told his brothers not to watch. These particular Americans are black, proud conservatives and dare to state their unhappiness with Obama who is helping to keep blacks uninformed and broke.

Hannity's ratings are two to five times that of the other cable news shows. What does this tell us about the state of our citizens? I wouldn't be surprised if his ratings increase after more people watch this particular show. Hopefully, you can watch it on a rerun or internet before it is scrubbed. The idea of conservative blacks does not jive with the Democrat Party; blacks are not allowed to step out of line with Democrat leadership.

Gosnell's Abortions Are Your Abortions

April 10, 2013

The Kermit Gosnell trial began with opening statements on March 18, 2013 and is expected to last 6-8 weeks. But you won't hear a word of this trial from the media; the truth about abortions and babies is too ugly. He is accused of murdering a woman and seven infants in his abortion practice. He allegedly snipped the spinal cords of living, breathing infants which is the procedure in the "Live-Birth Abortion Process." Bags and bottles of dead babies and baby parts were found throughout his clinic named the Women's Medical Society. Gosnell was known as the doctor to go to for cheap abortions and late-term abortions. With the reputation as an urban physician helping minorities and poor women, he allegedly was making around $1 million per year.

177

Gosnell graduated from Thomas Jefferson University's Jefferson Medical College in 1966 and set up shop in Philadelphia, PA, in 1972. He also is associated with clinics in Louisiana and Delaware. The 1973 landmark abortion case Roe v. Wade legalized abortion until viability which is 24-28 weeks. Pennsylvania law allows abortions through 24 weeks. Gosnell's defense is challenging the gestational age of the aborted babies calling the age inexact estimates. Is Gosnell only guilty in the babies' deaths if one of them was a minute older than 24 weeks? Maybe he should be given a week or two leeway since the ages are inexact estimates. The babies were breathing, and some were crying out, but they aren't really viable for years. Imagine your own crying babies. The first year of their lives all they do is cry when they are hungry. It's not like they can help themselves to a buffet.

What difference at this point does it make? Wasn't the point of the abortions to end up with dead babies? So what if he had to break their necks to ensure that they were dead? The death of the babies is the intended consequence of abortion. At least the investigations and trial will bring the pesky truth and facts to life. If you are for abortion, be proud. Gosnell's abortions are your abortions.

Liberals' Plans for Your Children

April 11, 2013

A Tulane University professor Melissa Harris-Perry recently hired by MSNBC spoke the following for a promo for her new show:

"We have never invested as much in public education as we should have. We haven't had a very collective notion of, these are our children. We have to break through our private idea that children belong to their parents, or children belong to their families, and recognize that children belong to whole communities. Once it's everybody's responsibility and not just the household's, we start making better investments."

Treating everyone as a whole community is communism, mandatory government control over people's lives. It is not a cutesy, neighborly situation where we all watch out for each other. Liberal talk about the collectiveness of equality, fairness and the best interests of society as a whole is communism, the end of individual freedom. Liberalism is not about being more caring, carefree or hip. Sure, grooving to Timberlake in the White House adds a bit of 'hipness' to the image of liberalism. But if liberals used the word communism, too many Americans would be alarmed and have nothing to do with them. Ironically, this soul concert in the White House gives us a taste of communism. The little people are not even welcome to tour the White House, but the celebrity and political elite treat themselves to a great party.

178

Obama said about his budget, "America needs to start enrolling four-year-olds to make sure the children are better prepared for the demands of the global economy and to help parents save on childcare costs." Obama wants to make it mandatory that our four-year-olds leave our homes and into the hands of the public schools. Remember Michelle Obama's words about the need to change our history and traditions? They can't change people like me. Public school children are a different story. They are already being subjected to Common Core that is filled with liberal thought of collectiveness. They will have never experienced saying the Pledge of Allegiance, will never have learned the true founding of our country and will never have experienced the freedom of being an individual. If you like your family, your children and being responsible for them, please repeat the following, "I didn't leave the Democratic Party. The party left me."

Liberals Want to Tax the Air We Breathe. Why not rain?

April 12, 2013

That would be crazy except that starting July 1, 2013, residents in the ten biggest counties of Maryland will have to pay the Storm Management Fee, also known as the Rain Tax. Obama's EPA is demanding $14.8 billion from Maryland to manage a problem of too much rain. It has become obvious to the EPA that the nitrogen and phosphorous levels need to be reduced 22% and 15% in Chesapeake Bay. Obama's EPA has determined that the culprit is surface area that prevents rain seeping directly into the ground. No lie, not making this up. The surface area that residents of Maryland own includes their roofs and driveways. Thanks to drones, the residents won't be expecting federal employees to come knocking on their doors to measure their private properties. Government employees will measure your surface area in the comfort of their rain tax exempt properties from satellite imagery. Think liberals will feel good paying this tax for the better good of society? Those silly conservatives will consider this an excessive regulation and government overreach. They sure have earned that Right Wingnut nickname.

Boston Marathon. Boston Tea Party. Patriot Day. Tax Day.

April 16, 2013

Add these together and it looks like the bombing of the Boston marathon was the work of a Tea Party member mad about paying taxes. At least this is the narrative the Obama administration and his lying media would like you to believe. Obama campaigned on the fact that Osama is dead, and al Qaeda is on the run. So that rules out Islamic radicals attached to al Qaeda and obviously leaves a radical racist, right wingnut Tea Party member to blame for the

179

bombing. No worries about decimating our defense budget or closing our borders.

This narrative of dangerous Tea Party members is pushed with absolutely no basis. New York City liberal mayor Bloomberg accused the conservative Tea Party of attempting to bomb Times Square because of the healthcare bill. The press blamed the shooting of Democrat US Representative Gabrielle Giffords on the rhetoric of the Tea Party. The press reported that a Tea Party member Jim Holmes may be the Colorado movie theatre shooter as he did have the same name of the actual killer. To be sure, Obama's media will suggest that a Tea Party member bombed innocent children and families at the end of the Boston marathon.

Obama rhetoric is rubbish, amateurish and will be proven to be utterly false, again. Islamist radicals will continue to threaten Americans for the rest of our lives. Al Qaeda is not on the run. It came to the run.

Must Find Tea Partier with Pressure Cooker Fetish

April 17, 2013

Find a Tea Partier with a pressure cooker fetish and all will be well in Obama's world. In Obama's world, Islamic radicalism was cured by bowing to the Saudi King and by killing OBL. In Obama's world, American citizens do not need guns to protect themselves. In Obama's world, every illegal immigrant is welcome to become an American citizen with voting rights. Hell, every one of the 6.5 billion poor is welcome to cross our borders.

The Boston massacre at the Boston Marathon has reignited our fear of international terrorism and focus on the intrinsic need for national security. Not one of the nineteen men who boarded our planes on 911 was a Tea Party member. Not one of the terrorist acts and plots can be in anyway tied to a Tea Party member. Not one radical, extreme act can be tied to a Tea Party member. The only way this will ever happen is if an imposter poses as a Tea Party killer and instead of yelling, "Allah Akbar!" would yell, "God is great!"

Tea Party members believe in less government and less taxes. That's it. People who consider themselves Tea Party members are primarily Christian, peaceful, law-abiding citizens. No specifications are required such as race, skin color, gender or sexual preference. When they gathered on Capitol Hill protesting the healthcare law, Nancy Pelosi and her liberal cohorts marched through the Tea Party crowd antagonizing them by carrying an oversized gavel with cameras and video focused on them. News commentators reported that lawmakers alleged that Tea Party members yelled out the epithets 'ni--er' and 'fa--ot.' Thus, the

Tea Party was labeled racist and homophobic. Breitbart offered $100,000 to anyone with proof of the alleged epithets. No one came forward to collect.

It's Time to Answer Hillary's Question.

April 22, 2013

During hearings questioning the details of the deaths of our Libyan Ambassador Chris Stevens and three Americans, Hillary's shocking, nasty response was the question, "What difference at this point does it make?" The answer is that it has to do with terrorism and the people of the United States would like to know what we are facing. Secretary of State Hillary, President Obama, Vice-President Biden and Ambassador Susan Rice told the world that the Benghazi al Qaeda terrorist attack wasn't that at all. It was just a spontaneous reaction to a video made by an American, their best convenient lie before reelection. The Obama administration has a difficult time accepting the truth about terrorism and radical Muslims. If they can't call a spade a spade, then they can't treat terrorism as the threat that it is.

Forward six months from the Benghazi terrorist act, and we have a terrorist act in the American city of Boston. This would have been avoided had the Obama administration taken the warning from Russia seriously - in 2011, the Boston bomber Tamerlan Tsarnaev was involved with Chechen terrorism. Even more incriminating, Tsarnaev should have been deported in 2009 on a domestic violence assault if immigration laws were enforced.

Now that we have come face to face with terrorism on our soil once again, what difference at this point does it make? It should make a huge difference when considering an amnesty immigration policy. Obama should focus on our security and treating terrorism seriously. A good start would be to adhere to our current immigration laws.

Obama and the Gracious Ex-President George W. Bush

April 26, 2013

The five living presidents met at the dedication ceremony for George W. Bush's presidential library, including the current one who has bashed Bush for the past five years. Bush sat through Obama's speech and heard that to know him (Bush) is to like him as absolutely true. This should be news to the Left who has been nudged to virulently hate him for all his 'failed' policies that are being followed today. It also leads one to believe that 'the failed polices of G.W. Bush' was just a successful campaign lie. Obama continued his speech on how honored he was to be there (he absolutely should feel honored) and then he went into the need to

181

repair the broken immigration system and how long it is taking. He called on congress members, senators and Speaker John Boehner to come together so that 'we can bring it home.' Obama tied up his immigration spiel in thanks to the hard work of George W. Bush.

There is class and there is classless. The most redeeming part of Obama's speech is that he spoke of *his* successor. Unfortunately, we just don't know when this time will come. Amnesty leading to citizenship is being touted as a civil and human right by the Obama administration. If unlimited millions of these new citizens vote Democrat, Obama's presidency may last longer than a couple of terms. The speech at the ceremony ended with what we need to hear from an admirable man, "...I will always believe our nation's best days lie ahead." The words came from a choked-up President Bush, not Obama.

MAY 2013

While You Were Working

May 5, 2013

While you were working, the Obama administration has been very busy. Hard-working Americans may want to know what they are funding with their taxes, from terrorists to the incredulous to the downright disgraceful.

Immigration Bill: *welfare for all* added to the soon to be named bill

The number of illegals is no longer 11 million but closer to 35 million and growing. Taxpayers would be on the hook to fund our new citizens. Heck, we already have funded the Boston Bomber family with cash, Section 8, food stamps and I'm guessing free healthcare which has added up to $100,000. Shouldn't that have made them love us?

STOCK Act: a bill that makes insider trading illegal for members of Congress

Pelosi and members of Congress have access to insider information and purchase/sell stocks accordingly. This is incredulous – we're paying our public servants who have made it legal for themselves to pad their own pockets with insider trading. They are citizens first just like the rest of us who would be jailed for doing exactly what they are doing. Obama just signed a minor change to the STOCK bill that exempts top federal officials including him from disclosing their financial holdings, a nice loophole to exempt themselves from the STOCK Act. Is this how Obama and friends get their fair share of Wall Street, or rather, more than their fair share?

182

Benghazi-Gate: the manufactured stories about the cause and death of our Libyan ambassador and three Americans due to an anti-Muslim video

At the last Benghazi hearing, Hillary answered questions with her own question. "What at this point does it matter?" It's nice to get answers and we're about to find out. More hearings are scheduled. Hopefully, we will get to hear from the survivors of the attack from September 2012, eight months ago. CIA and State Department employees have been threatened by Obama administration officials to keep quiet or lose their careers. At least four are retaining lawyers and appear ready to talk.

New York's Dignity for All Students Act: anti-bullying workshops are required which states that instruction in civility, citizenship and character would include concepts of tolerance, respect for others and dignity

That sounds so nice but here are the actual workshop details. Two middle school female students had to stand in front of class pretending they were lesbians. One had to ask if she could kiss the other. Our dear children learned about pansexual and gender queer. College students were invited to speak before the class and encouraged the students to be sexually active.

Planned Parenthood and the Gosnell Trial: Planned Parenthood, a more apt name Planned Non-Parenthood, receives approximately $500 million in taxpayer funding and aborts approximately 333,000 babies per year.

CEO Dayle Steinberg of the Southeastern Pennsylvania Planned Parenthood knew about the problems at Gosnell's abortion clinic and did nothing. Gosnell's clinic was the place to go for late-term illegal abortions. To ensure the deaths of the babies making noises and movement, Gosnell took scissors to their necks. We will soon find out if the law considers beheading babies to insure deaths as murder.

The Unaffordable Affordable Care Act: Obamacare

Congressional staffers cannot afford the thousands of dollars for healthcare premiums from the future healthcare exchanges. And Harry Reid has denied that there are any talks about exempting them from Obamacare and that no legislative fix is necessary. So, what will the fix be, Harry? The word is that the exchanges are affordable for the middle class and that the younger crowd is needed to fund Obamacare. Huh? The magic income level to not receive subsidies is $90,000. So a husband and wife who make $40-50,000 each will pay full price for Obamacare – around $2000 per month. During a routine budget hearing, Senate Finance Committee Chairman Max Baucus who helped write Obamacare said, "I just see a huge train wreck coming down." Max Baucus recently announced that he will not run for reelection for senator of Montana 2014, pretty smart to take his pension and run.

183

Waterboarding Terrorists, Wrong. Drowning Babies in Toilets, So What.

May 6, 2013

This headline describes what is wrong with today's media. The media hammered us with the news of how terrible the USA is to torture terrorists. 'The poor little freedom fighters need to be released from GITMO. The USA is just a big bully and that's why the terrorists hate us.' In reality, this safe procedure of waterboarding gave us invaluable intelligence on terrorist activity. NO ONE died in this drowning simulation.

The media is absent in telling the news about the most horrific abortion doctor and all the information coming forward from his trial. The abortion doctor had his patients sit on toilets to expel the babies. Testimony stated that the babies were alive, taken out of the toilet if they were too big to flush and placed in a final solution. ALL the babies died. Recapping the values of our liberal media:

Waterboarding terrorists is torture and is bad (the waterboarding, not the terrorists); security information gathered is irrelevant. Drowning babies is not torture and is just a medical procedure; information gathered from trial is irrelevant. There is a scourge on our nation and it ain't dealing with terrorists. The scourge is that we allow our babies by law to be tortured and legally murdered. Liberals aren't winning the terrorist narrative and are losing ground with the abortion narrative. Abortion has nothing to do with reproductive rights or a choice. The medical procedures happening across our nation include drowning babies, beheading our babies, breaking their spinal column, chopping our babies into small pieces, sucking our babies to pieces and chemically burning our babies to death. These are neither rare nor safe, and definitely bad choices for our babies. Thank goodness we no longer depend on the liberal media for our news and thank goodness for cable and internet. I look forward to the day when the majority sees abortion for what it is and begs to ban it.

Hillary Gets Screwed by Obama a Second Time

May 7, 2013

The first time Hillary got screwed by Obama was the 2008 presidential election. It was hers until Obama came along and stole it. She was to be the first female president and earn her place in history. Instead, a young, affirmative action candidate entered the race and his race was the determining factor. His skin color trumped her gender. And in helping Obama win reelection in 2012 and by being a loyal warrior, her 2016 candidacy is dead in the water. As Secretary of State, Hillary had the responsibility of keeping her state employees safe and she didn't. When Ambassador Stephens asked for more security, none came. When the Benghazi consulate in Libya was attacked by al Qaeda, Hillary followed

184

Obama's request to do nothing. In doing nothing, she did something very wrong. Was military help from Tripoli told to stand down?

If the terrorist attack came and went two months prior to Obama's reelection with no deaths, this Benghazi episode would have ended. Instead, our ambassador and three Americans were tortured and murdered. Plenty of senior administration officials lied about the Benghazi attack and had their own motives. Obama ran and was reelected on decimating al Qaeda, General Petraeus was dealing with his own peccadilloes, and Hillary didn't want a dereliction of her duty to become public.

The Obama administration chose lies instead of truths about the attack and suppressed the facts. This is so childish in a way because Obama voters would not have blamed him for an attack across the world and would have still voted for him. Yet, the lies kept coming: a video upset Muslims so they held a protest demonstration, help couldn't have gotten there in time, the Libyan president lied about it being a terrorist attack, etc. These lies also paint a picture of Obama's thinking towards terrorism. If a radical Islamist attack happens, try to ignore it and blame something other than a Muslim. It is time for Obama to step down. And, Hillary, your chance for presidency has come to an end with Benghazi-gate.

Hillary and Obama: Disgusting, Offensive, Reprehensible, Crude . . .

May 8, 2013

These two characters feigned outrage at an anti-Muslim video that was posted on YouTube July 2012, using all of these adjectives. How and why they came up with the idea of this video as the cause of the terrorist attack on our consulate in Benghazi on September 2012 are, well, all of the above: disgusting, offensive, reprehensible, crude and hateful. Obama also used the words blasphemy, bigotry and slander. He and Hillary used all these adjectives attempting to convey to us how upset they were over this old video. They even ran advertisements on Pakistani TV condemning this video and "absolutely reject its content and message." A real president would have condemned the attack itself and call out terrorism as unacceptable for any reason.

Benghazi congressional hearings have begun, and whistleblowers are coming forward. There were, after all, survivors and other witnesses to present the facts of the attacks. First of all, the threat of a terrorist attack was ignored. Secondly, the attack was ignored while it was happening. Obama went to sleep during the attack and hopped onto Air Force One to a Las Vegas fundraiser the next morning. Thirdly, the Obama administration lied about it. During this time, a major fluctuation in the Gallup polls of Obama's handling of terrorism and foreign affairs could have hurt his reelection chances. When Obama's opponent

Mitt Romney brought up Benghazi, Romney was accused of politicizing the attacks. In retrospect and according to recent allegations, Obama and Hillary neglected their duties to the security of our citizens. Four Americans died because the Obama administration politicized the Benghazi attacks. Reprehensible is an excellent word to describe these two, and Mitt Romney absolutely should have politicized this attack.

Castro the Kidnapper Just Performed Abortions

May 9, 2013

I believe I have that right. Isn't killing babies inside the womb called abortion? Ariel Castro kidnapped, raped and brutally assaulted the women, especially when pregnant with the objective of a dead baby. According to the definition of abortion of what we have learned from the Gosnell trial, if the babies were inside the womb when they died, there is nothing illegal about that. Gosnell's crime was that he failed at the inside the womb killing so he resorted to breaking the babies' necks while on the outside of the womb. Castro the Kidnapper didn't wait until the babies were outside the womb. He resorted to beating the crap out of the women so that the babies died **inside** the womb.

Supposedly that's the difference on the definition of legal baby killing - inside or outside the womb. Liberals, such as our President, don't even make that distinction. If abortion fails to kill the baby, the baby should be left to die on its own. Castro's method should be celebrated by liberals for creativity and for his success. Liberals didn't support Gosnell during his trial, and he was, after all, the well-known abortion provider to poor minority women. We'll have to follow Castro's trial and see if liberals support this pro-abortion, registered Democrat, and definitely not a Tea Party member.

Republicans were excoriated by liberal Democrats for being in a War on Women. Their grievous fault was that they did not want to pay for other people's contraception and abortions. The true War on Women is abortion and all that it entails. It degrades women and their essence of carrying life inside them. Abortion literally and physically sucks the life out of women. Then people like Castro and Gosnell come along and have zero conscience about degrading women and zero respect for life. Burn in hell, Castro and Gosnell.

Is Amanda Berry's child a punishment?

May 10, 2013

Amanda Berry escaped with her six-year-old child May 6, 2012, from ten years of hell in the hands of Ariel Castro. I imagine that Amanda Berry's child is her greatest blessing who kept her sane during her heinous ordeal and will continue to do so. During the 'Republican' War on Women days, Obama said that he wouldn't want his daughters to be punished with a baby. That is the mindset of a liberal progressive that has permeated into Republican territory. RINOs, Republicans In Name Only, claim to be for abortion in the cases of rape. They are stating that a child of rape is not worthy to live. I am sure that Amanda Berry would say otherwise. The only people who fight for children's rights to exist in all instances are conservatives, including radical right wingnuts.

Every baby should be protected in utero. It doesn't matter how ill or deformed the baby may be. It doesn't matter if the mommy isn't ready for a child. It doesn't discriminate on how the baby was conceived. There is no magical moment during development that should determine when its rights begin. The mother's rights end when the baby's rights begin. It is the smallest of the small and helpless that needs its rights protected. Amanda Berry and her child should be celebrated for the rest of their lives and beyond. This child should not have to grow up hearing that she is a punishment and should have been aborted.

There's No There

May 13, 2013

That's our President's answer to Benghazi-gate. Hillary's answer to four dead Americans in Benghazi is, "What difference at this point does it make?" Our President's answer to the tyranny of the IRS is that he just found out the news on TV like the rest of us. No special briefings, no daily memos, no assistants updating him on real-time, no cabinet members apprising him of events, no reports from the summer of 2011 by IRS officials. Obama had no knowledge of conservatives and Tea Party organizations being targeted and hindered by the government IRS agency prior to the 2012 elections. Obama did proclaim that the IRS should operate in a neutral and nonpartisan way. Shouldn't this apply to his administration? Likening the Tea Party to terrorists is neither neutral nor nonpartisan. He spoke to the graduating class of Ohio State University on May 5, 2013, warning them not to listen to anyone voicing the opinion that his administration is tyrannical.

A week later and the liberal media is talking about the tyranny of the IRS. Should we all pretend that there's no there there, also? Obama spoke at a news conference May 13 and had a tear streaming down his face. The Not Just Fox press asked Obama about Benghazi and the IRS. Is the tear a sign that Obama knows the jig is up? These are two impeachable offenses that cannot be blamed on George W. Bush, the Tea Party or Republicans. It appears that Obama didn't trust his no and low information voters to put him in the White House for a second term. He is his own worst enemy and treated his presidency without the reverence it deserved.

Why Obama and Democrats Feel the Need to Lie

May 16, 2013

Obama feels the need to lie to us because this isn't your daddy's Democrat Party anymore. If Obama's ideology is so terrific that he stands by it no matter how it affects our security and economy, why is there a need to lie about it? Look at all the major things he lies about.

Calling Islamic-radical terrorism as workplace violence, a spontaneous protest, or the work of lone wolf criminals doesn't make it so. Why not admit that he believes that if he ignores terrorism, there is no terrorism? In a sense, he did. In answering about Benghazi terrorist attack, he said that there is no there there.

Why didn't he push for gun control legislation without operating a gunrunning operation to Mexico named Fast and Furious that resulted in deaths? Was it the need to falsely claim that the majority of guns recovered in Mexico come from the bad, gunslinging USA?

Democrats defend abortion as safe, legal and rare. Why don't they celebrate the third of a million babies aborted in 2012? Why didn't the liberal media cheer on Dr. Gosnell during his murder trial of babies born alive during abortions? Obama did not comment on Dr. Gosnell, but he did thank and God blessed Gosnell's accomplice Planned Parenthood during the trial. Obama could have bragged that he voted in the Illinois Senate that babies born alive during abortions should be left to die.

Democrats have convinced millions that global warming is our biggest threat. The goal of greenies in this administration is social justice, to ultimately transfer America's wealth to third world countries. Instead of admitting that this is the objective, we have been subjected to the threat of global warming for decades. Obama nearly got his Cap and Trade bill pushed through Congress. In no shape or form would this tax scheme have lowered the world's temperature. These liberal Democrats are very patient. Our next generation is being well-groomed and tested in school on their knowledge of global warming. Liberal Democrats expect them to be obedient voters in time to complete the cause.

And lastly, the IRS has admitted that conservative groups were targeted prior to the 2012 election. Leading the investigation is Democrat Senator Max Baucus who once wrote a letter asking the IRS to target nonprofit conservative groups. Obama stated how he is mad and that the conduct of the IRS is inexcusable. He acted tough by firing the acting IRS commissioner May 16 whose assignment ran from November 2012 to early June 2013. Obama has engaged in Chicago-style politics in Illinois in which his opponent's private information was divulged. Is it really that far-fetched to deduce that he was involved in the same nationally? This IRS scandal is an opportunity for the Democrats to proclaim how the Tea Party's conservative movement is their enemy.

Would Americans have voted for Obama and this Democrat Party if they had the truth and facts about the above? Sadly, I think the answer is yes because truth and facts haven't had any bearing in our politics for a long time. And Obama sure is hip, hanging with Beyoncé and Justin Timberlake.

Dems HAVE to Win the House 2014 for Last Chance to Transform U.S.

May 20, 2013

Yes, HAVE in capital letters at any cost. The election of 2014 determines if the US becomes a third world dictatorship. This sounds far-fetched but is exactly what will happen with complete amnesty and the ruin of our energy sector with Cap and Trade. Judgeships, regulatory agencies and policies are lined up to execute this transformation. With control of the presidency and the Senate, the only missing link is the House. The progressive liberal dreams are closer than they may have ever imagined. All that is needed is information suppression and donor intimidation for a little more than a year, plus enough fraud.

The IRS scandal highlights the major deterrent: the conservative movement and the Tea Party. The Obama administration went full panic after losing the House in 2010 to conservative Republicans. Democrats should have fought back with promoting their policies. Instead, Obama brought a gun to the knife fight as he threatened to do. His administration sicced the IRS on any and all conservative sounding nonprofits to suppress their viability. Approval for nonprofit status for Tea Party entities continued for over two years. Time, money and energy were spent dealing with the IRS rather than promoting conservatism. Donor lists, social media and prayer information were requested.

Donors supporting conservative nonprofits know fully well that audits and the intrusiveness of the IRS may follow. Although the law is on conservative's side, Obama's attorney general Eric Holder will never prosecute against Obama. The ends justify the means in the Obama administration. Voters will have to outnumber the fraud that will surely happen this coming election. An easy way for extra votes is to not require Voter ID. That's crazy. I'm sure the Dems haven't considered that.

189

The Obama's Advice to Graduates: Do What We Say, Not What We Do

May 20, 2013

In a nutshell, the Obama's are telling graduates to go into service and freeload off the large, successful corporations who fund service projects. Rush Limbaugh once compared this as telling graduates to become the fleas of a host. Service isn't free and generally doesn't pay well. If our graduates do not make any money, they will become fleas to their parents for life. And once they are kicked out by the parents, the service-oriented children will become dependent on the government dole, which is still actually living off their parents' money.

Here's the truth that our graduates need to hear: Go out and make something of your lives and preferably make a lot of money doing it. If you have dreams of buying a beautiful house one day, drive around in a new automobile, buy grown-up toys and provide for your family, you need to make lots of money. Go for it if you want to live the American dream. Just know, it is not going to be easy. In Obama's world, you are welcome and advised to remain the flea; it's just not for him. The Obamas have a dream of ruling the fleas, the more, the merrier for them. And they are being very successful at their dream.

Legal Justice in the Obama Administration

May 22, 2013

There isn't any for conservatives. Obama has illegally targeted and used government agencies to punish them throughout his presidency. The IRS has admitted to targeting conservatives including the Tea Party. It has used its regulatory powers to financially ruin businesses and individuals. In this scandal, the voice of the Tea Party was suppressed to the point that the liberal media reported that the Tea Party was dead. Obama knew this wasn't true but if he can suppress the conservative viewpoint, the sheeple will continue to believe him. The only plausible objectives are the reelection of Obama and election of Democrats in 2014.

Other conservative targeting is the focus of congressional questioning and hearings including auto dealerships in the 2009 auto bailout. The truth will come out on the number of the nearly 2000 auto dealerships ordered to close by Obama's task force to be conservative. Freedom of the conservative press is being attacked. News agencies are being monitored by this administration and an individual reporter is being charged with a crime.

Americans with opposite views from Obama can no longer expect legal justice during the Obama presidency. Congressional hearings are being held attempting to get to the truth. Obama's response to these claims is that he is just finding out

190

about these like the rest of us. Obama is admitting that he is not involved in running the United States or lying. The leader of our country in essence is claiming that his task force, his regulatory agencies and his Cabinet members are keeping him out of the loop. This could be true if Obama is just an acting figurehead allowing a shadow government to rule over the United States.

The Cost of Obama's Dictatorship: Free Contraceptives

May 22, 2013

With the Obama administration free to target political opponents and silence the press, Obama is that much closer to a dictatorship. All it took was a black man promising free birth control to the hip Millennial crowd. All it takes to cinch the deal is winning the House back in the 2014 election. Is there any doubt how far this administration will go to see this through? For anyone paying attention to the news channel that Obama has urged to ignore, we have learned that an ambassador's life wasn't worth risking his reelection. We have learned that a Border Agent's life was a sacrifice during the Fast and Furious operation with the objective of gun confiscation legislation. Don't think for a moment that something as inane as an election will stop Obama from his ultimate goal of dictatorship. The Obama administration, including his shadow people (Valerie Jarrett) calling the shots, will have rigged whatever takes rigging to win this next election. If the media fails to nail Obama on the scandals within the next year, the loss of our freedoms that we take for granted as Americans will be on their backs. Obama has only succeeded in his goal with the complicity of the liberal media. Can the media be tried for treason?

Obama Should Cancel the Internet if He Believes What He Says

May 24, 2013

Our smartest president ever gave a speech abroad blaming the internet for domestic terrorism. If he truly believes this, it is his duty to cancel the threat by cancelling the internet. He also blames Islamic terrorism on our failure to reach out to the Muslim communities. This almost sounds like a warning to the American people from Obama to expect Islamic terrorism on our shores and that we will be to blame.

Americans remember who bombed the Boston marathon, two Muslim brothers who were given every opportunity America had to give. It was and is the job of our government to do everything to prevent attacks such as these. Our government was warned about the Boston bomber, questioned him, let him go and dropped his case. The government left him free to travel to the Mideast for six months and enter back into the US without any follow up. Obama does not want to see terrorism as the dangerous threat of its own making. He puts the blame on American citizens and now the internet. Americans are less secure with Obama at the helm of our country. Can anyone imagine our information flow about terrorist threats if there was no internet?

Obama Thought Conservatives Would Win

May 25, 2013

It is the scandals that prove to us how truly worried Obama was about losing to Romney. First is the Benghazi scandal which occurred in September 2012. Stand down orders were given to prevent Special Forces from saving our Libyan ambassador. Whoever gave the stand down orders is irrelevant – the buck stops with Obama. Obama lied to the American people about Benghazi to present himself as strong on defense and as an expert in foreign affairs.

Second is the IRS scandal which had been occurring ever since Republicans had gained over 700 offices nationwide with the 2010 midterm elections. The IRS director of exempt organizations was briefed in June 2011 of the targeting of conservative organizations. Letters with intrusive questionnaires were signed by the director in March 2012. By holding up the exempt status on hundreds of these organizations, their fundraising and voices were suppressed.

Third is the Associated Press scandal in which Obama's Department of Justice spied on reporters and editors. The DOJ stated that a grave national security leak was the basis for months of spying. But this leak wasn't so grave as to notify Obama. At least Obama claimed he knew nothing about the DOJ's actions, again claiming to learn about it on TV like the rest of us. The bottom line is that the relationship between reporters and their sources is sacred, but not if the government is spying on them, especially a government that punishes political enemies.

Obama used the big arm of government to punish his opposition instead of trusting the American people to find his policies more favorable than conservative policies. But Obama did fire his rogue DOJ for spying. Just kidding.

192

Obama's Loyal Lying Benghazi Lapdog Gets Rewarded

June 6, 2013

Less than two months prior to the November 2012 election, US Ambassador to the United Nations Susan Rice lied to the American people with a straight face about the Benghazi terrorist attack. Five days after the attack, Rice went on the talk show circuit posturing the narrative that an anti-Muslim video caused a spontaneous protest. Her talking points did not include reporting on the deaths of four US diplomats including the US ambassador to Libya by Islamist extremists. On the very same day, the Libyan president went on the talk circuit proclaiming that the attack on the US consulate was preplanned months ahead and that talk of a video was preposterous. Within two hours of the attack, an al Qaeda group had claimed responsibility.

Rice's lies may have boosted Obama's foreign policy poll ratings to help his reelection. Obama nominated Rice as his new Secretary of State which required congressional approval. Her responsibilities would have included advising the president on ambassador appointments and diplomatic representatives, principal advisor on foreign policy, ensuring protection to American diplomats, and provide information to the American citizens regarding political conditions in foreign countries. Rice withdrew her nomination after realizing that she would not receive congressional approval. How arrogant and disrespectful of Obama to have considered this woman. Or should I parrot the Dems – if not for those obstructionist Republicans!

Obama once said that he would punish his enemies and reward his friends. We already know through the IRS scandal who Obama considers his enemy. Now we know just how important among his friends is Rice, the loyal lying lapdog. Obama announced Rice as his new national security advisor which is a promotion for the known liar about al Qaeda terrorism.

How do you like being spied on?

June 9, 2013

A whistleblower who worked for the National Security Agency (NSA) for the past 10 years has handed over documents to journalists on the all-consuming surveillance activities of our government. News came out that every phone conversation of cell phone companies Verizon, T-Mobile and AT&T users has been collected by our government. Our government has complete access to internet servers and has been looking into our emails, videos, online chats, photos and search queries. A judge approved a secret court order for this internet intrusion with the code name PRISM.

The NSA response to this information is that it "at times mistakenly intercepted the private email messages and phone calls of Americans who had no link to terrorism..." According to our government, this monitoring of every conversation known to them is for our own protection against terrorism. What kind of government has this much intrusion into the lives of its citizens? The only ones I can think of are Cuba, China, the Soviet Union and other totalitarian countries. The information gathered on their citizens is ultimately used to control the communication flow – not to protect them.

For those citizens who claim that they have nothing to hide are missing the point. A government may want to silence the opposing political party and gain total control; now they know who you are and what side you are on. I can hear the Dems – but I'm on the good side. Yeah, right.

Why a Communist Style Regime Needs the Tea Party Silenced

June 9, 2013

The Obama administration used the IRS, the most powerful non-political government agency, to help silence its political opponents. The IRS has admitted that it used its powers to target conservative nonprofits associated with the Tea Party, patriots, education of the Constitution and Bill of Rights, and government spending. When the Tea Party started gathering strength in numbers, Betsy Rosses, Paul Reveres and Abe Lincolns strutted around in red, white and blue spouting off about freedom and could be rightfully described as buffoonish. I'm sure many younger generations couldn't see through the costumes and slogans to consider the Tea Party as a strong political entity. But Obama did. In the 2010 election, over 700 offices nationwide went to strong conservatives and turned the House to Republican majority. He blamed the Tea Party and he was right.

The media is starting to report on the IRS scandal and congressional hearings are underway. Scandal isn't the right word to describe what has been transpiring for the past few years with the IRS. A scandal to Obama would be getting caught in bed with another man or caught smoking with his choom gang. IRS targeting is a communist tactic to deliberately silence opposition. The loss of freedom of speech as stated in the first Bill of Rights, among others, is exactly what the Tea Party warned us about. The Constitution of the United States and the Bill of Rights are the basis of our freedoms and hinder the Obama administration from turning the United States into a communist style country in which government control is the norm. It is the Tea Party, the silent majority, that stands in the way of Obama's fundamental transformation.

194

Scandals Prove That Obama Doesn't Have to Answer to Anyone

June 12, 2013

The Obama scandals prove that this administration is more than dangerous and doesn't have to answer to anyone. The administration's reactions to the exposure of the scandals prove that they know we can't do anything about them. Obama and his attorney general Holder are at the center of the scandals and neither will react other than giving the standard verbiage of holding people accountable. They have no intention of resolving the scandals that promote the progressive ideology. In fact, officials who aid in the scandals are being promoted. The woman in charge of the IRS during the targeting of conservatives has been promoted to the IRS position in charge of healthcare enforcement instead of facing criminal prosecution.

The danger of this unaccountable administration is that they are shredding the Constitution in front of our eyes and getting away with it. Our government who is responsible for upholding the laws is committing the crimes. It is not difficult to imagine Obama putting in place enough poll workers, voting machine attendants and fraud to steal the 2014 election. A voting scandal may erupt, but it will be too late for anyone to change the results.

If Obama has the Senate and the House during his last two years of office, the laws that will be passed will devastate our country. We'll have amnesty with open borders, a halt to our energy production, an expensive cap and tax energy policy, gun control and a transfer of wealth to pay for more entitlements. Capitalism, which has made our country the most prosperous of any, will be destroyed and replaced by socialism. People who think they can vote this out in another two years if they don't like it do not understand what is going on. We'll be living in a fascist/communist state that doesn't rule by the Constitution. For the younger generation to relate to communism, all your social media like texting and Facebook would be monitored and restricted. Like that would really happen.

Vote Democrat in 2014 If

June 12, 2013

You are happy with the economy and job prospects.
You believe that business owners should be told how much to pay their employees.
You want more people on welfare than working.
You want the government ordering us what we can and cannot eat or drink.
You truly believe that the automobile is ruining our country.
You want to pay $10 per gallon of gas.

195

You believe that an organic rock made up of carbon (coal) should be banned.
You believe that a mother and a father are not important in raising children.
You believe that the opposing political party should be silenced.
You believe that reproductive right is another word for abortion.
You want tax dollars funding Planned Parenthood to perform 300,000 abortions yearly.
You believe that since you are not doing well that no one else should either.
You believe that if you became successful that you wouldn't deserve it.
You believe that equal outcome is more important than hard work and effort.
You want your government to have complete access to your social media.
You want the United States to open its borders to 6.5 billion poor.
You like our space program NASA being a Muslim outreach agency.
You like the IRS targeting Americans that disagree with the present administration.
You believe your privacy is overrated.
You want a government bureaucrat deciding your healthcare.
You want the EPA to regulate and fine people out of business.
You are pleased with the improvements made in the black community.
You want the rights of Muslims to encroach on your way of life.
You believe that socialism and government control will solve your problems.
You believe that the cell phone and the internet would have been invented without capitalism.
You believe it is either too cold or too hot outside due to our fault and taxing would fix the temperature.
You have a better idea for running an economy without banks.
You think competition is a bad thing and that is isn't fair for someone to win.
You believe that guns should be banned.
You believe that it is our fault that terrorists want to kill us.
You also believe that terrorism is not a threat to our way of life.
You believe that if we disarm our country that the enemy will do the same.

IF you want this stupidity out of your life, vote conservative.
Bring common sense, law and order back.

Thanks to Obama, There's No Justification for Abortion

June 14, 2013

The Gosnell Trial showed the world what abortion has become in America: a money-making machine with a total disregard for women's lives and their babies. During the trial, Obama God Blessed Planned Parenthood, possibly as a thank you for its $4.1 million donation for his 2012 reelection. Obama has unwittingly accomplished something the Pro-Life groups have not. He has made the issue of rape a non-issue in the abortion debate. He legalized the morning after pill to be available over the counter to anyone of any age. Parents of young

196

girls are appalled by this, but this is an avenue for abortion to go the way of the dinosaur.

The major justification for abortion has been the rights of rape victims. I personally think that rape babies are just as human as non-rape babies. However, the Left has been very persuasive in convincing the general public that rape victims should abort their babies. Now, thanks to Obama, rape victims can head to the nearest pharmacy and purchase a pill. Future Gosnells and Planned Parenthood should be put out of business. The need for an abortion past one day of pregnancy has been eliminated. Democrats should be thrilled that their platform of safe, legal and rare abortions may become a reality.

The Truth about Obama and Wars

June 23, 2013

Before Obama was elected, I asked a Generation Xer why he was voting for Obama. His answer was that he didn't like war and Obama doesn't like war. He apparently got the impression that Bush and conservatives like war. When asked how he would have responded to 3,000 dead on American soil from 911, he had no answer. The marketing of Obama took on a life of its own and as far as my friend knew, Obama didn't like the 'blood for oil' Iraq War.

The intelligent Charles Krauthammer wrote the article *America sidelined, barely relevant* that describes the debacle of Obama's foreign policy. Bush's war in Iraq was over prior to Obama's election with Iraqis participating in free, democratic elections and al Qaeda actually on the run. The US received no oil in return. The departure of US troops was negotiated in 2008 through the status of forces agreement between US and Iraqi officials. When troops started departing in 2011, Obama spoke of this dumb war (the blood for oil war) and how special America is by bringing democracy to the Middle East. Obama sounds dumb. A dumb war does not bring democracy to the Middle East. Obama's Iraq War policy led to complete evacuation of Iraq instead of strategically leaving a powerful stabilizing force of American soldiers behind.

Obama now faces the civil war of Syria with a mounting body count. Obama's foreign policy appears to have not considered enemies. Russia and Shiite Iran must be ecstatic that the United States president doesn't like war. They are now free to take over the entire Middle East including the Sunni countries of Syria, Turkey and Jordan - except that Obama has begun to send F-16s, Patriot missiles and the 1st Armored Division headquarters unit to Jordan.

Democracy in the Middle East with a strong, stabilizing presence of the United States isn't sounding so dumb after all. And to all Generation Xers, every sane person hates war, but an American president better be aware of what a stronger

197

enemy can do, especially a nuclear Iran. Even a president who hates war engages when the enemy does.

Michelle Imprisoned and the Obama's African Trip

July 7, 2013

The first lady arrived in a $1,295 dress to begin her family's taxpayer-funded estimated $100 million African summer get away. The Obamas visited a prison cell where Nelson Mandela spent part of his nearly 30 years imprisoned for violently opposing the racist and segregationist policy of apartheid. A few days later, Michelle Obama compared her role as First Lady to that of a state prisoner. She continued to ungraciously comment at the African summit of female leaders that her job is liberating in some respects but confining in others. Her stay at the White House with chefs and twenty or so personal assistants is comparable to a prison – but at least a 'nice' prison.

Barack and Michelle Obama were photographed looking out from the Door of No Return while touring the House of Slaves. It was most probably a very poignant experience believing that millions of slaves walked the plank from that door to the slave ships. He called the trip a reminder that "we have to remain vigilant when it comes to the defense of human rights." However, historians have noted that the door was not used to transfer slaves but was physically a non-eco garbage dump site – garbage was chucked right out into the ocean. The Obamas could have acknowledged the history of the slave trade to help reduce racism. African Kings raided rival tribes of people who were then traded or sold for barter and or money. Slavery continued in African Kingdoms after slavery was officially abolished in the United States in 1865. Blacks sold blacks. Period.

President Obama addressed the energy situation in sub-Saharan Africa where two thirds do not have electricity. He could have talked about affordable and potable energy in the form of organic substances that comes from Mother Earth such as coal, oil and gas. Instead, Africans heard the following from Obama, "Ultimately, if you think about all the youth that everybody has mentioned here in Africa, if everybody is raising living standards to the point where everybody has got a car and everybody has got air conditioning, and everybody has got a big house, well, the planet will boil over unless we find new ways of producing energy." He seriously told impoverished Africans that they should not strive to raise their standards of living or have energy unless they get it in his ideological green form. He basically told them to stay in their huts and live in poverty for the good of the temperature! In the same speech, Obama blamed primarily whites for Africa's poverty, "…countries that are very wealthy are expected to do more, and countries that are still developing, obviously they shouldn't be resigned to poverty simply because the West and Europe and America got there first. That wouldn't be fair."

Obama missed the chance to visit his half-brother George who lives in a Kenyan hut on less than one dollar a day. They could have had an interesting dialogue on race. From an interview with the filmmaker Dinesh D'Souza of *2016: Obama's America,* George said that he believes Kenyans would have been better off if the British weren't removed from rule so abruptly. He also said that Kenya would've been better if the white men stayed in order to help develop the country. Poverty-stricken Kenya has been independent from British rule since 1964, meanwhile South Africa today is much better off, even with Apartheid coming to an end in 1994.

What a hundred million can buy – a little eye-opening into the Obama's world and how they feel about it.

Hispanics Have Learned All They Need to about Democrats from the Zimmerman Trial

July 16, 2013

Somehow liberals in America have built a reputation for caring about the poor and the working man. The truth is that liberals have taken over the Democrat Party and care about no one, but their own power, all the while ignoring our laws and Constitution. How did they care for Hispanic George Zimmerman? He was painted as a white racist and charged with second degree murder subject to life in prison. Luckily for him, our legal system worked. His case was heard by a jury of peers who determined that he killed Trayvon Martin in self-defense.

America is the greatest country on earth and every president has called for the unity of our nation. The difference between Obama and every prior president is that Obama wants the opposite. His background is a community agitator who now relishes dividing our country by race. One could ask what his motive is, but it doesn't matter. He showed his love to all Latinos during his push for immigration. The love is gone. All Hispanics need to know is that liberals have cornered the black vote for years. In certain urban areas, the majorities of blacks live in poverty with up to 90% of black children living without fathers. Blacks have been dumbed down by disgraceful public schools and have been conditioned to accept welfare as a way of life.

Blacks in America have come a long way despite liberal policies, and many are successful beyond their dreams. Many are working their way into the middle class and enjoying life. But the blacks that liberals love are the poor and ignorant. The Zimmerman trial has given liberals a platform to race-bait and it will continue until another crisis takes its place. Instead of helping the black community, liberals are infusing hate into them for the non-black man. If Zimmerman was white enough, so are all Hispanics. Democrats expect the Latino vote for life if amnesty is granted. In the Zimmerman case, blacks trumped Latinos. Latinos can expect to be used in the future by the Democrats as blacks have been used for decades.

Democrats paint Republicans as greedy white corporations. Here in America, everyone is given the opportunity to be successful. And the successful can be any color, imagine that. Successful businesses can turn into successful corporations that grow jobs and the economy. Conservatives love jobs and the independence that work brings. Compare that to the welfare state where the voting bloc is given just enough to think that they are doing OK. It takes strength and a leap of faith to believe that America offers something greater than a monthly welfare check. The race-baiting happening right now is just that. True Americans will ignore the race-baiting call of liberals and instead continue dreaming and living their lives in our melting pot of immigrants.

ANY Man Would Be Followed in a Shopping Mall

July 22, 2013

Obama continues to whip up the racism war claiming that he had been followed in a shopping mall when he was a teenager, presumably by a white racist. Here's news to Obama – guys don't go shopping in shopping malls. Guys don't hang out and search for the perfect blouse or sniff all the products at Bath & Body Works in shopping malls. They go to Walmart for clothes and pick up the first item they find. They spend their time at Lowes or Home Depot looking for whatever will look good hanging up in their garage or some item to make their lawn look better than their neighbors. Then they go home and mow the lawn.

For Obama to nationally state that he hung out at the shopping malls and was followed do not jive with his pot smoking choom gang days as written in his book *Dreams of My Father: A Story of Race and Inheritance*. And if they did hang out at the mall smelling like choom, they would appear suspicious no matter what color their skin. Get over the racism war, Obama. His history of whipping up hatred of blacks for whites started with his father's dreams, continued in his community organizing in Chicago and somehow found himself in the White House continuing his race baiting. It is bad for the black community and it is bad for America. One would expect him to focus on helping the black community and the Ahlittia North's of this world instead of telling the gullible black teens that the white man hates them. If they were reminded by Obama that America is the land of freedom and opportunity, they just might believe it and step up and become real men. Obama is wasting his time in the White House.

200

Why was six-year-old Ahlittia's body found in a trash bin?

July 24, 2013

Six-year-old Ahlittia North of greater New Orleans was murdered and found stuffed into a trash bin. Similar stories are happening in communities throughout the United States over and over. Young single moms, in this case now married, entrust their young children to unemployed loser drug addicts who end up taking their frustrations out on the children. For Ahlittia, her babysitter was her stepfather's 20-year-old nephew who ending up stabbing her to death. Matthew Flugence has pleaded guilty to murdering her and has been charged with first degree murder and sexual battery.

Why does this continue to happen? First blame goes to the liberal Democrat policies that encourage and reward bad behavior. Second blame goes to the mothers that aren't doing their most important job of shaping and protecting their families. Mothers are ultimately responsible for the children's welfare. Fathers are important but mothers are the ones that kiss a scraped knee, do the laundry, cook the meals and oversee the children's time. It's called mothering. The mothers that have children out of wedlock and then work while their young children are growing up have set up repeating cycles for their own children. Ultimately, no father or mother is around to raise the children and they are physically put into a stranger's hands or elder relatives such as great grandparents. In Ahlittia's case, the mother entrusted her child with a distant relative whose parents most probably weren't around for him when he was growing up. Now Ahlittia will be buried at age six and Matthew will become another statistic of a young black man spending the rest of his life in prison.

So, where are you, mothers? Your children need you when they are young. Ahlittia's mother was thirteen years old when she got pregnant. Where was her mother during her early teen years? Where was Matthew's mother when he was in his teens? Ahlittia also died because her parents did not see any danger with Matthew. At twenty, his personality and character were on full display. Did he have a drug problem or anger issues? Matthew should never have been granted access to Ahlittia.

To prevent farming out their children to whomever is available, young ladies have the power to shape their destinies. If they want a good spouse and father, they need to civilize the young men. They know how. It's as old-fashioned as crossing one's legs. This baby daddy thing is one of the main causes of why young children are put in the position that leads to their deaths. Finding a good man that will provide for and protect his family is the responsibility of young ladies that want to raise children. Children get lost in the liberal village mentality in which everyone but no one is truly responsible for the children. Too many have ended up stuffed in a trash bin like the heart-wrenching death of Ahlittia North.

201

Third World Has Come to the United States in Detroit

July 30, 2013

President Obama has called Republicans deadbeats. These deadbeats have not ruled Detroit for 50 years; the Democrats have, specifically, Democrat politicians indebted to the public sector unions and the United Auto Workers (UAW). City leaders overspent $100 million annually and acquired $14 billion in retirement liabilities and unfunded pensions. Back in the fall of 2010 right before the midterm elections, Obama proclaimed that he saved Detroit with his $77 billion auto bailout bankruptcy. Obama screwed the bondholders and shareholders who fall first in line in a bankruptcy and handed the tax dollars over to the UAW. Despite Obama's proclamation, Detroit declared bankruptcy on July 18, 2013.

Union demands helped kill the competitiveness of the Big Three car manufacturers in Detroit by driving up costs. The demand for cars never stopped but the competition grew. The unions gouged their golden geese instead of being flexible with the times and allowed foreign auto companies to thrive. Detroit's so-called greedy capitalists with their corporations and businesses left or closed down along with the jobs, tax revenues and 65% of the population.

Republicans can't blame Obama for Detroit BUT the liberal policies Obama is promoting nationwide WILL turn the United States into Detroit. They are the same policies that killed Detroit - high taxes, overspending, unfunded pensions, environmental regulations, safety regulations, welfare entitlements, race-baiting civil rights laws, CAFE standards (Corporate Average Fuel Economy) and union thuggery. Detroit has become the entitlement welfare city with no one to support them. More cities run by Democrats will collapse into third world status, not by the deadbeat Republicans who tell Obama 'no' and call for fiscal sanity.

AUGUST 2013

The Marketing of President Hillary

August 1, 2013

The marketing of a President Hillary for 2016 is gearing up to full speed. Hillary has been named the Most Admired Woman, now twenty times, by someone or some group who really admires Hillary. Maybe Hillary herself? Hillary's term as Secretary of State was heralded by Obama, "…I think Hillary will go down as one of the finest Secretaries of State we've had." Nice prop by the President but she left Benghazi burning with one dead ambassador and three dead diplomats. A liberal media spokesperson had this to say about Hil, "…the smartest, sharpest, savviest lady in captivity…so brilliant and focused…so far, ain't nobody smarter to come down the pike." Yet her most common response to questionings on her responsibilities and actions is, "I don't recall."

Speed bumps can cause great damage to a marketing campaign when in full speed. Republicans continue to look into Benghazi inquiring about gunrunning to terrorists through the consulate. Patricia Smith continues to ask why her son Sean died in Benghazi. Monica Lewinsky's sex tape has resurfaced reminding us that Fathers of the Year do not have sex with 22-year-old interns in the Oval Office. Both Hillary and Bill are sucked into Weiner-gate. Hillary is phony marketing. America will survive the fraud that is presently in the White House and surely deserves better than a second go around of the Clinton fraud taking up residence.

Al Qaeda Is on the Run . . . to Kill Us

August 6, 2013

Remember Obama and Biden campaigning to adoring crowds on how Osama bin Laden is dead and al Qaeda is decimated? Anyone paying attention to the campaign leading up to the November 2012 election knew that al Qaeda had just attacked the Benghazi consulate and killed Americans. After bin Laden's death, Biden publicly announced SEAL Team Six involvement. Within three months, two dozen Team members were shuttled on a twin rotor Chinook and shot down by the Taliban with a rocket propelled grenade. Did Obama consider SEAL Team Six deaths a quid pro quo to bin Laden's death? Questions have been raised if an inside job tipped off the Taliban. Why were they shuttled into hostile territory on a cargo airship rather than a special ops helicopter? To get a clearer picture of how our military heroes were treated even in death, a Muslim cleric resided over their funeral in Arabic.

Less than a year after Obama told us that al Qaeda was on the run, the United States is on the run from al Qaeda. Nineteen US consulates and embassies are closed due to al Qaeda threats. Obama purposely led us to believe that the threat was over to get reelected and to decimate our military. Obama knows that the international terrorist network, al Qaeda, has underground cells all over the world.

The definition of al Qaeda is the Base and that its focus is Jihad. Jihad is the religious duty of all Muslims to defeat non-Muslims. Ask your kids what they have learned about Jihad with Common Core Standards. The correct answer for the definition of Jihad is spiritual freedom fighting. Obama talked about transforming our country and changing our traditions and rewriting our history. Americans either weren't paying attention to his words or they don't appreciate what we have in the United States of America. They better start paying attention to his actions, or in some cases, his inactions.

Politics 101 on Why Obama Should Never Have Been Elected

August 8, 2013

The importance of who is elected president of the United States cannot be downplayed, but it is the president's beliefs that decide how to shape our military, healthcare and energy policies that affect our lives. It is important to know the difference between what a candidate says and what the candidate believes. Actions always trump words in the political world.

War on Terror: This will never be over in our lifetimes. Muslims take their religion seriously and they are taught to support Jihad, a holy war against non-Muslims. This religion does not win over new members by kindness but by force. If the younger generations do not support Christianity and the power of our churches, Christianity will die as a deterrent to our safety. Obama is ruling, on purpose, as if terrorism does not exist. He's like the monkey who sees no evil, hears no evil and speaks no evil. Obama is slashing our military defense budgets.

Health Insurance - Affordable Care Act nicknamed Obamacare: Obama's goal is single-payer, fascist government-run healthcare; government would collect all medical fees and then pay for all medical services while making demands on doctors and hospitals. He would first have to destroy our medical system of insurance companies, and he started with Obamacare. His $2000 fine per employee for businesses with 50 or more full-time employees caused the unintended consequence of replacing full-time employees with more part-time employees. Part-time employees are now on their own to purchase Obamacare insurance or be fined starting October 2013 which is now extended past the 2014 elections. In Obamacare, an amendment required federal employees to purchase health insurance through the exchanges. Obama exempted federal employees August 2013 because the premiums are too expensive. Obama gave the impression to younger voters that everyone would have free healthcare – you and I are not exempt. Medical care is not free and never will be. If you want free healthcare for yourself, you can stop working and become dependent on the government. Prior to Obamacare, you could purchase a cheap major medical policy to cover catastrophic illness; Obamacare made this coverage ILLEGAL. Government care is giving us one choice policy and you are going to pay for it.

Included in Obamacare is the cost-cutting board IPAB. In the original bill, end of life planning was encouraged with recommended care rationing. Obamacare now prevents this...by reducing provider reimbursements. If you, your mom or grandpa needs a heart-saving procedure, the government would not only have the power to approve or disapprove, it controls the funds to pay for it. If doctors don't get paid, you ain't getting the surgery.

Green Energy: Billions of taxpayer dollars have been spent on green companies run by FOO (Friends Of Obama.) Many of the companies have gone bankrupt while leaving big bucks in the bank accounts of the FOOs. When you hear Obama critics accusing him of picking winners and losers and crony capitalism, this is what they are talking about. Obama has been critical of successful companies turning profits, making too much money, fairness, equality, and more of the same crap. Profit is what business is all about and the FOO are given taxpayer-funded opportunities to make profit. In a free market, businesses use their own money and investments and consumers decide if businesses thrive. In Obamaland, Obama decides who gets the opportunity to thrive (who gets your tax dollars) and, as in health insurance, who the consumer pays. You can decide for yourself where the greed really is.

What is the difference between Obama and an empty suit?

August 10, 2013

At least the empty suit shows up at important meetings. Sixteen senior officials met on Saturday, August 3, 2013, to discuss the biggest terrorist threat since 911. Our Commander in Chief went golfing with his buddies and then headed to Camp David to continue celebrating his birthday. He didn't feel the need to pretend that his attendance at the meeting mattered. Nineteen embassies and consulates were closed due to this terrorist threat. Obama made the time to appear on a late-night comedy show with Jay Leno during this difficult week and then reopened the embassies and consulates.

If Obama's attendance is inconsequential, then who really is taking care of the details of running our country? In whose hands has Obama left our fate and the direction of our country? This is a legitimate question. Obama's first coup as president was to pass a $1 trillion stimulus bill to help poor and working Americans. Obama left Pelosi and Reid to write the bill. The self-proclaimed communist Green Jobs Czar Van Jones helped dole out the money that neither helped the poor nor working Americans. The money went to Obama donors in the name of green companies. As to the importance of green energy and global warming, Van Jones stated that green energy is really all about social justice and redistribution of wealth. A trillion dollars were basically stolen from taxpayers and remain mostly unaccounted for.

Obama's major coup was signing Obamacare into law. Obama did not write the thousands of pages of healthcare rules and regulations. That would be Robert Creamer who, while in jail, wrote how the government can get its hands on 1/6 of the American economy. Creamer even stated that universal healthcare was not about the policy but about distribution of wealth and power. Here's a man who defrauded banks out of $2.3 million in connection with his nonprofit organization. He now runs a nonprofit organization called Americans United for

Change with the help of his multi-million-dollar backers: MoveOn.org, Occupy Wall Street, SEIU, Teamsters and other unions. The website reads that conservatives for too long have been mistaken for mainstream American values. Creamer wants us to believe that Occupy Wall Street is more in line with mainstream America.

One more coup for Obama that will destroy America is amnesty. Conservative mainstream America will be inundated with new Democrat voters that will end our two-party vote. Whatever amnesty is agreed upon by the Republicans will not end up in the law. It has already been written by Obama's communist radical friends in high places.

Why shouldn't Obama enjoy himself and stop being the empty suit in the room? He's got everyone in place to do all the work for him. He keeps the media pacified with the occasional press conference and reads teleprompter speeches pretending that he has the same values as us, continues parroting that he is trying hard to fix everything. America is so close to being fundamentally changed as he promised. However, liberals are ignorant of the silent majority.

Bono and Kutcher Surprising Speeches

August 16, 2013

The famous Bono of the U2 band and actor Ashton Kutcher delivered speeches about capitalism and hard work. These speeches should be required YouTube viewing for our younger generations who have been taught that life is about social justice and equality. Social justice is a catch phrase of communism. Everyone must stay equal in all areas – pay, housing, food, and healthcare. Life in a communist society is nearly incomprehensible to Americans except those dependent on welfare. Plus, it would be extremely boring if we were all the same.

Bono gets capitalism which is the alternative economic system to communism. He said that capitalism takes more people out of poverty than aid. Aid is just a stop gap. Capitalism is commerce that provides opportunities to improve everyone's life. Kutcher said that the harder he worked, the luckier he got and that he never had a job that was better than him. He also said that opportunity looks a lot like hard work.

The tombstone of communist Karl Marx reads, 'Workers of all lands unite.' For an equal society, workers are prodded into believing that companies should belong to the workers and not to the owners who invested and created them. Under communist rule, no one has the right to grow a company and profit from it. The Occupy group which stands against successful business owners is supported and encouraged by President Obama. Common sense tells us that the

United States without successful companies would turn us into a typical communist hellhole.

Politically, the government of the United States is a Constitutional Republic with two parties, the Democrats and the Republicans. One party has been taken over by communist sympathizers and the other party believes in the traditional conservative values of hard work and capitalism. Most other rights and issues should be left to the states to vote on. Anyone disenfranchised with our government or not sure which party to vote for deserves the government he or she gets.

August 2013 Town Hall Meetings

August 23, 2013

The plants were in for amnesty. The first meeting I attended had over two dozen alleged illegals with a translator all wearing matching t-shirts promoting themselves. Two of the illegals spoke through the translator on how these are the faces of amnesty and that they are afraid of being deported. Then five different people in the audience including a nun spoke for amnesty, reasons ranging from the Christian thing to do, parents separated from their children and payback for helping rebuild the area (from Hurricane Katrina 2005). The second meeting I attended had a nun stand up for amnesty and, again, that it is the Christian thing to do. My representative defended immigration policies of solving the specific problems of immigration rather than blanket amnesty without border control. He told us that the United States follows the rule of law. Four million immigrants have been waiting in the legal immigration line and that one million are granted citizenship annually. Forty percent included in the 1986 amnesty did not want citizenship. They just overstayed their visas and wanted to come and work and head back home.

Blanket amnesty would be a disastrous law for the United States. The poor in the world numbers 6.5 billion. Mexican illegals are generally uneducated and would be (are) an easy target for the welfare promoters. Obama's Department of Agriculture (USDA) has advertised in the Spanish market encouraging them to sign up for food stamps. How upside down is that? Our tax dollars are used to sign up illegals to use more of our tax dollars to feed them. On the online news website Drudge Report is another ridiculous CA law; the California Legislature has passed a bill that would let non-citizens who are "lawful permanent residents who meet all the other requirements for being eligible to vote except for citizenship" work at the polls. Sounds like straight out corruption of election integrity with English-speaking and ID not required. Most importantly, amnesty would increase the chance of legalizing future terrorists.

Back to the town hall meetings, not one person asked for the funding of Obamacare. They asked for the defunding of this bill. Other topics raised were the NSA snooping, the targeting of the IRS, Benghazi, and the Muslim Brotherhood invited into the White House who are now slaughtering Egypt's Christian population. A major discouragement of the constituents is the lack of accountability of the Obama administration. As soon as the committees of Congress find egregious acts of this government, the administration lies about it, admits fault followed by apologies and then nothing. No one in the administration is feeling any repercussions from the actions themselves to the lying to the cover-ups. The government is no longer working for the people but against the people. Of all these concerns, the one directly under the Republican's control is the defunding of Obamacare.

Democrats Need to Save Two-Party System to Save America

August 27, 2013

Our politicians know better than us plebeians how corrupt and lawless the Obama administration truly is. It is much more than stealing our tax dollars or even using federal agencies for its benefit. The ideology, policies and laws are destructive to the world. Obama made a promise to reward his friends and punish his enemies and this is one promise this politician has kept. I understand politicians sticking with their party and not rocking the boat. The path of least resistance is the easiest to take. But America deserves better and our politicians know it deep down in their souls. I have not heard a word from any Democrat speaking against this presidency.

Republicans are not strong enough to fight against this administration. We can wait another year praying that Republicans take the Senate and keep the House and change the course of our country. But the power now lies in the Democrat-controlled Senate. Harry Reid is in too deep and needs to be bypassed; he is a despicable person. He throws any decent Republican bill into committee never to be voted on. If Democrats are truthfully too fearful to act out in the open in our best interests, a majority needs to secretly take charge of voting blocs. The funding should stop for Obamacare. Impeachment proceedings should begin on grounds of lawlessness. How can a lawless administration including the attorney general be held accountable?

Americans need to know that true partisanship will act in our country's preservation as a Constitutional Republic. Trust, at this point in time, August 2013, does not exist for either party. If enough Democrats can pull this off, we the people will be able to trust Congress's two-party system of checks and balances. Future generations will have the same opportunities that we had: life, liberty and the pursuit of happiness. The only negative is that the Greatest Generation may lose their title. Godspeed.

You Are Next under the Liberal Progressives

August 28, 2013

In his own words, President Obama has been looking for whose ass to kick. Oh so tough as seen in his bike riding photo in mom jeans and a helmet, often compared to a photo of bare-chested Putin riding a horse. He asked us to vote for revenge and he has stated that he would reward his friends and punish his enemies. It's getting obvious that we the people are his enemies. Obama may not personally go after us, but he has set up our federal agencies and his minions to do his dirty work. Liberal progressives progress away from the Constitution towards a power grab for themselves. The United States has been built upon the greatest equalizer to all, our Constitution. It stands for all citizens, not just some and not just for the elite politicians in power. We are all equal by this one document. It is not the job of our government to dictate how we should live our lives.

Government has determined what size soda we can drink, how much water should flush our toilets, banned affordable lightbulbs for expensive eco-bulbs, that we should fund abortions to who should have a voice by targeting conservative groups. Whether or not you support the Tea Party, this citizen group has been targeted by the IRS in order to silence them. Guns came very close to being confiscated. The auto bailout took the rights of the bondholders away and handed over to the unions. Louisiana Governor Jindal's school voucher program is being targeted right now by attorney general Holder. Holder's objective is to keep the money with the campaign-donating teacher unions while blocking the opportunity to a better education for children in failing schools.

Obama's healthcare law will not apply to the politicians and their families or the unions that supported the bill. The freedom of healthcare choice will be diminished for the rest of us. Michelle Obama envisioned thin children and dictated what schools should serve for lunch. The kids don't want what she's serving and are not eating it. Yay for push-back from our kids.

Obama's dictatorship administration will force you to live how it envisions your life. You are next and you will soon undeniably understand the difference between a government who works for the people and a government who dictates to the people. It could be strict monitoring of your energy usage. It might be the banning of medicinal herbs and natural remedies or it might be laws about who can attend med school, or it might be $10 gallon of gas – on purpose. But whatever it is, it will be government intrusion into your life, and you won't like it. It is time for push-back from the adults while the kids yell out "resist".

Are enough people fed up with Obama?

August 30, 2013

Unless he is impeached, it really doesn't matter. He was reelected on November 2012 to lead our great country. He gets to continue disregarding the Constitution and destroying our country for three more years. I told a 20-something five years ago that Obama was a communist and he just laughed like that was the funniest thing in the world. And then he voted for Obama twice. He also said how stupid Sarah Palin was when she mentioned death panels. Again, I asked him what he would call it if the government told him that his mom had to take a pain pill instead of a necessary surgery. He found that funny, also. Obama said this at a Town Hall meeting. That's how you save money. It's not quite a death panel but a pretty good name for a government who has taken over the health industry saying they won't pay for a surgery.

I understand him. Why would ordinary citizens who live in the greatest country in the world blessed with the freedoms we have, ever think that a communist would be elected president and infiltrate every federal agency we have? It truly is inconceivable to think that one of our own, or one who passes as one of our own, would have the ideology that calls for the destruction of our country. The media and the Hollywood celebrities promoted him. The Democrat Party stood behind him. Are they all super intelligent, plain ignorant or communists? They may also just plain be power-hungry and like their cushy positions.

Here's an example of how Obama is leading by ignoring our laws. He wants WiFi in all our public schools with a program called ConnectEd. That's admirable but it isn't free to do this. The cost is estimated to be six billion dollars. More taxes are necessary because Obama really doesn't have a stash of Obama dollars. Normal legal procedure is to go through Congress for any and all tax increases. Instead, Obama called on the Federal Communications Commission (FCC) to take the necessary steps to get the WiFi in the schools. This five-member commission filled with Obama nominees has been asked to tack on new fees, liberal speak for taxes, to all cell phone users.

Another example is gun control. Obama went through Congress who voted against his gun control legislation. But Obama wants gun control. He assigned a new director to the Bureau of Alcohol, Tobacco, Firearms and Explosives. We can expect some legislative fixes through this bureau to solve gun violence. Connected to the gun violence are young black men who commit crimes and are inordinately jailed more so than Asians, blonde-haired girls, honor students, housewives, and basically every other group of low crime-committing people. The liberal response is to release the young black men from jail. Problem solved of too many young black males in jail. Obama's gun control will take guns away from law-abiding citizens who want to protect their families. Who will have the guns?

If you are fed up with Obama, too bad; liberals don't sleep. They are in constant attack mode on our way of life. If amnesty passes through Executive Order or by convincing Republicans that it is the right thing to do, conservative votes will forever be outnumbered.

To Honor Londyn, Arabian and Ahlittia, Young Ladies' #1 Job Should Be to Find a Good Husband

September 4, 2013

One-year-old Londyn Samuels was shot in the face while being pushed in a stroller on the sidewalk of New Orleans. Eleven-year-old Arabian Gayles was shot to death while sleeping inside her house. I already wrote about the stabbing death of Ahlittia North and then stuffed into a trash can. All three young innocent girls were killed by young black men. The pundits are calling us to action, but the average citizen cannot do a damn thing about cold-hearted killers. No rehabilitation, community program or gun control measure can transform enough of these young males into decent citizens. They have wasted their lives and should be removed from society.

The only lasting solution to prevent young black men from committing these atrocities is to tame them before they reach this point. Young ladies have the power to shape their families' destinies. If they continue to choose to jump in bed with whomever as young teens and end up single and pregnant, nothing will change. Their little girls may be the next Londyn, Arabian or Ahlittia and their little boys may turn to the streets. The same young ladies could choose to take on husband-hunting as their #1 job with the goal of providing intact homes for their future children.

Single parents make it in this world but the time, attention and activities that their children require are automatically limited. This almost sounds like a case for 100% welfare so that a parent can be available. However, young black men will continue to be starved of strong male role models called Dad and continue to find action on the streets. The lack of guidance and boredom attributes to the shaping of killers without conscience. If the deaths of these three sweet angels do not motivate young ladies for a better life, nothing will.

211

Maybe It Was the Rodeo Clown Who Set the Red Line

September 6, 2013

Who to blame this time? Obama set the red line and cannot blame this on the Tea Party or W. He is trying to blame it on Congress and all Americans, but he clearly set the red line. Hundreds of thousands of Syrians have died fighting their civil war since 2011. Syrian President Assad, or possibly the rebels fighting against Assad, killed 1400 Syrians with a weapon of mass destruction - chemical gas. Obama stated that he will launch missiles and specific targets to send Assad a warning and as punishment for the chemical weapons. He had his war-hating Secretary of State Kerry announce the urgency needed to punish Assad. Kerry's message mimicked his previous testimony against the US in Vietnam. As a counter follow-up, Obama announced that he may strike in a day, week or month and asked Congress to vote approval of the warning shots, allowing him to blame the Republican House for any fallout.

In rounding up support for the missile strikes, the Obama administration has stated that America will not send boots on the ground. Obama talking points also state that this will not be war, just a limited response - something he cannot promise. Iran has announced that there will be retaliatory strikes against Israel. US strikes Syria, Iran strikes Israel. Iranian communication intercepts also include retaliation against US embassies. Russia's Putin has also claimed support for Syria if the US strikes.

Obama is not punishing a rodeo clown. He is now playing with the big boys who can seriously harm us and possibly start World War III. Obama, who started his presidency apologizing for America's greatness and vowed to equalize us by diminishing our superpower status, threatens the world's stability by going rogue. What needs to happen is for Obama to announce that the US will stay out of Syria's civil war and then focus on rebuilding our military's strength that he has purposely dismantled. He can only save his presidency if he denounces his ideology of appeasement and mean it from now on.

Obama Succeeded – Putin Called America Weak

September 20, 2013

Putin just called out Obama's success. Obama's goal of the fundamental transformation of America from a superpower to a weak nation has come to fruition. Putin announced to the world that we are weak and unexceptional. Obama continues acting as a president who cares while not overtly concerned about being called weak. BECAUSE I HAVE MORE TO DO, another Obama saying we hear ad nauseam. Ask young, moronic Obama supporters why they support Obama and their answers are the same – Obama is trying really hard because he has more to do but the Republicans obstruct him.

Americans continue working and inventing and creating with their independent spirit in our capitalist economy. Obama's transformation is incomplete, but with three more years, he surely has the time to complete his agenda. For Obama to claim total success, our healthcare, education, banking and energy will be under government control.

If anyone is unclear about Obamacare, government has control over our healthcare. As Obama used the IRS to stop Tea Party and patriot nonprofits by holding up nonprofit status, he has set up the IRS to track our healthcare and healthcare insurance. Those not purchasing healthcare insurance will see a 'Shared Responsibility Payment' on their IRS forms. Pertaining to education, teachers and parents are finding out that Common Core is not only new standards but also curriculum changes that are indoctrinating our children. With banking, Obama has already declared the larger banks as too big to fail and require government bailouts as he sees fit. Risky loans? Don't worry, bankers!

Obama's biggest challenge is energy. His moratoriums on offshore drilling and ban on fracking government land should have hiked up our gas prices to his desired $10/gallon. He didn't plan for American ingenuity and the fracking on private land. Obama did have the support of UN's IPCC (International Panel on Climate Change) that has published ridiculous reports on global warming causes, including cow flatulence. So, if we kill off all cows, our world will get colder? Give up your cheeseburgers for civilization! Scientists from the Non-governmental International Panel on Climate Change (NIPCC) have published a 2013 report that rejects the IPCC's findings. Despite Obama's administration claiming CO_2 a poison, CO_2 remains a mild greenhouse gas that does not affect our temperatures. Solar cycles determine the temperature – that's right, the sun determines the temperature and humans have no control over the sun. With the end of the global warming scare in sight, Obama has no justification to spend billions of our tax dollars on his green policies. But he will continue to scare his uninformed supporters who will regurgitate the stupidity.

Republicans Should Hold Their Ground until Congress and Obama Agree to Sign Up for Obamacare WITHOUT Taxpayer Subsidies

September 30, 2013

Me thinks Nancy got her Talking Points messed up. She called us arsonists while Obama and Reid called us anarchists. Other talking heads are calling anyone against Obamacare a political terrorist. Cruz was elected senator of Texas to fight against Obamacare and he is keeping his promise. The House of Representatives used its control over funding to rightfully pass a budget

213

defunding Obamacare. The Senate voted against defunding so either the Republicans cave or the government shuts down.

Obama and Congress should agree to delay the individual mandate for a year as they have already delayed the employer mandate for a year. To exemplify how simple and affordable and how wonderful Obamacare really is, Obama and Congress and their families should refuse special tax subsidies and sign up for Obamacare starting October 1, 2013, as is expected of the rest of us. Sounds like tyranny for the political elite to pass a bill that they themselves are exempted. Until they agree that Obamacare is good enough for them, then Ted Cruz and the Republicans should hold their ground. All exemptions made to Obama supporters should be null and void, including the unions who are seeking exemptions.

Ted Cruz believes that Obamacare is bad for America. Ted Cruz is no slouch. He graduated high school as the valedictorian, Princeton cum laude and Harvard Law School magna cum laude. A law professor called Cruz off-the-charts brilliant. His father fled communist Cuba in the 50's. Hispanic, Southern Baptist Senator Cruz is a threat to progressive liberals. He knows that fighting against Obamacare is fighting for America's medical system. As the law stands, the people who do not sign up for $100 plus monthly health insurance will be taxed $95 for a year or two. Health insurance companies have been dropping out of the healthcare exchanges prior to opening day. The people who opt for the $95 tax may get sick, apply for insurance through the exchanges and the insurance companies must pay due to the pre-existing conditions law. This is great for the sick, but the insurance companies are based on reducing risk. They'll go out of business and we'll be left with a government, bureaucratic nightmare controlling our healthcare.

OCTOBER 2013

Obamacare is non-political? Here Are the Pushbacks

October 2, 2013

My newspaper quotes a gal with pre-existing health issues trying to sign up for Obamacare, "I just don't understand why there's so much pushback on it. It just seems like a non-political issue to me." To her, it's just going to be affordable health insurance. The pushbacks to Obamacare are that the government is sticking its nose into our doctor visits and so much more.

- The government has made it illegal to not buy health insurance.
- The IRS will impose a fine on anyone without insurance by taking it out of any tax refund and possibly directly from our bank accounts.

- The IRS will also impose a fine on anyone receiving a non-verified income subsidy and the income on a tax return is too high.
- The government has decided that everyone's health insurance policy covers the same stuff.
- The government option on the health exchanges is one size fits all with varied pricing due to deductible amounts.
- The government has mandated what health insurance companies should cover, pay out and charge. Fascism is when government dictates to industry, command and control.
- Catastrophic health insurance is not acceptable and will no longer be available.
- Having no insurance is not acceptable, even for people who want to pay cash for healthcare or for those who cannot afford it.
- The IRS will check all tax returns to determine if your health insurance is acceptable and fined if not.
- One person, the Secretary of Health and Human Services, has discretion to change the healthcare law.
- Every policy has a tax for abortion coverage.
- Every group, state and government health plan will have a monthly Transitional Reinsurance Assessment (fancy words for another tax).
- No health insurance company on the exchange can refuse anyone for any reason, including transgender surgeries – now a major benefit with the possible consequence of bankrupting the company.
- The government has mandated doctors to ask specific, personal questions of their patients, one being if you own a gun.
- Data from the private doctor/patient relationship is to be uploaded to a government database.
- Gold-plated health insurance will be taxed 40%.
- Businesses with 50 or more full-time employees are required to provide insurance or be charged $2000 per employee per year. An unintended consequence is that businesses are hiring more part-time employees.
- The 15 people who comprise the IPAB (Independent Payment Advisory Board) have the goal of reducing Medicare costs by lowering doctor's Medicare reimbursements. Palin was the first to call this the death panel. Ya really think doctors will agree to not getting paid?

Obamacare success depends on high enrollment to pay for it. The truly needy are expecting free insurance. But they already have Medicaid. The young Obama supporters are expecting nearly free insurance. Illegals will be getting free insurance. Obamacare has been described as a train wreck from the author of the bill itself – misinformation, business requirements, penalties, rules, regulations, complexity, expense and unintended consequences. It is a stepping-stone to single-payer, complete government-control over our healthcare by destroying private health insurance companies. A single-payer system is designed by control-freak people who were elected as our public servants who want to make decisions for us as a whole. Americans want the doctor/patient relationship to remain private and have individual control over their own healthcare choices. Obama lied about healthcare reform and there is nothing non-political about this. NOTHING non-political about Obamacare.

How IT Became Law of the Land – Obamacare

October 3, 2013

Any law that has a tax in it must be started and passed by the House of Representatives. At Obama's urging, the House passed a health care bill in November 2009 and forwarded to the Senate. The Senate had already been working on its own health care bill by completely revising an already passed House bill dealing with housing tax breaks for service members. Sixty votes were needed to pass the bill and Democrats only had 58. In April 2009, Specter switched to Democrat. Democrat Al Franken lost his election by 725 votes. After finding votes post-election, he won by 312 votes and sworn in July 2009. Yeah, a cheater who got away with it. In August 2009, Ted Kennedy died, and a temporary replacement was sworn in September 2009. Reid made deals to guarantee Democrat votes such as more Medicaid money for his state and Louisiana, deals nicknamed the Cornhusker Kickback and the Louisiana Purchase. He also had to address abortion funding for moderate Democrats. The Senate passed the bill on December 24, 2009.

Republican Scott Brown was elected in January 2010 to Ted Kennedy's Senate seat guaranteeing Republican filibuster. The House dropped its bill and took up the Senate bill. House Democrats expected to make changes to the Senate bill but knew it would not have passed with the election of Brown. A voting procedure used to make fiscal year budget changes called reconciliation does not require a supermajority. Changes to the major health care legislation would require a supermajority. Pelosi pushed the Senate to use reconciliation to pass the House amendment of budgetary changes to the bill. Moderate House Democrats opposed wording of federal funding for abortion in the Senate bill. Obama signed an unenforceable Executive Order to prohibit federal funding for abortion. The House passed the Senate and amendment bills on March 2010 with 34 Democrats voting against it, 219-212. The Senate passed the amendment bill 56-43. Obama signed the Affordable Care Act into law two days later to great fanfare.

Democrats shut out Republicans by avoiding the normal negotiation process between Houses to pass major legislation. Not one Republican in Congress voted for the now called Obamacare. Not one Republican had any input into this bill. Obama's claim of bipartisanship is a fabrication. The ongoing lie about Republicans is that they have no alternative to Obamacare. Health care pricing could have been brought down by simple tort reform to reduce skyrocketing

216

malpractice insurance. Obamacare is deluging our doctors and businesses in bureaucratic nightmare resulting in a shortage of both doctors and jobs.

Obama is on video stating that his goal is single payer in which the government pays for all health care costs primarily through taxation. You really don't mind having 70% taken from your paycheck to pay for this FREE healthcare, do you? Obamacare is a step towards total government control over our health care. The success of Obamacare or complete breakdown of our medical system is yet to be seen.

Obama's Fraud Is a Criminal Offense. Will anyone charge him?

October 4, 2013

I have always considered President Obama a fraud. Wayne Allyn Roots describes the fraud in his op-ed, Obama is 100% Red, White & Blue American Born. Obama laughed when people questioned if he was a foreigner and therefore ineligible to be president. We should have been laughing along with him. He is the one who posed as a foreigner to receive special admittance to Columbia University and Harvard Law School. A high school student with average grades and poor classroom attendance would not be considered entrance into these prestigious schools. But for sake of diversity, a Kenyan-born, Indonesian-raised student did. These universities would never charge him with the crime of fraud. The question now that the information on fraud is out there, can anyone else charge him with the crime of fraud? His rise to the presidency is based on fraud and this fraud is affecting every citizen of the United States.

You're Racist if You Think Obamacare Is Too Expensive

October 8, 2013

If you think Obamacare is too expensive, I hate to tell you, but you are Tea Party. You have the gall to criticize black president Obama's Affordable Care Act. Back in 2009, people could see what Obamacare really was designed to be – an oversized, expensive, bureaucratic nightmare for American citizens. Our present government wants complete control over the healthcare industry beginning with this legislation. The Tea Party is a grass-roots political effort to limit the size of government, get bureaucrats out of our lives, and uphold constitutional rights for every citizen. That's the Tea Party. That's all. The Tea Party is against Obama's goal of government control over our lives.

For this reason, the Tea Party has been disparaged as:

Racist	Extortionist
Terrorist	Dangerous
Arsonist	Propagandist
Anarchist	Anti-Government
Homophobe	Suicide Bombers
Fringe	Fanatic
Violent	Rightwing Nut Job
Tea Baggers	Hostage-taker
Traitor	Blackmailer
Jihadist	Cancer
Biggest terrorist threat to the US	Extremist

The Tea Party is patriotic and started with protests and rallies costumed up in the red, white and blue. Abe Lincolns roamed around. Paul Reveres, Lady Liberties, Uncle Sams and Betsy Rosses also attended. This turned off many people and gave leeway to poking fun at the 'fanaticism' of the members. When Libertarians such as Glenn Beck advised them to pack the costumes away, well, yeah, good advice. However, they have been standing up for our rights as written in the Constitution and have elected conservative candidates that are fighting for our constitutional rights.

We all have a choice. We can acquiesce and accept Obamacare as Obama and Sebelius see fit and the growing taxes that will accompany it. Or we can stand up against it as is the Tea Party. You better expect being called any of the above names. I personally consider the names a badge of honor. And, heck, wear whatever costume you want. It's a free country.

How many people signed up for Obamacare?

October 8, 2013

The American people have been bombarded about the greatness of Obamacare for three and a half years – in public relation campaigns, news talking points, celebrity endorsements, concerts, TV show series, schools, signage, mail-outs, award shows, advertisements, late-night talk shows, etc etc etc. To answer the question of how many signed up a week into the rollout of Obamacare, Obama's Press Secretary Jay Carney said that he doesn't know. When asked on Chris Wallace's weekend show, the Secretary of Treasury Jack Lew said that he does not have the exact number and that it is the wrong question. He also said that seven million people visited the Obamacare exchange/website. Secretary of Health and Human Services Kathleen Sebelius on the comedy show "The Daily Show" said that she can't tell us but that hundreds of thousands of accounts have been created but that 85% of people already have health insurance. Huh?

218

Obviously, Obamacare has horrible sales numbers. A website program that can tabulate how many people visited the site can also tabulate how many purchases were made. Enrollee reports on drudgereport.com have 12 for Louisiana, 326 for Maryland and zero for Kansas. After constantly selling us on the benefits and affordability of Obamacare, Obama expected people to be eager to sign up. They haven't, otherwise we would be hearing how successful enrollment is. Obama oversold his healthcare to the very low and misinformed voters as healthcare for all. These people expected free healthcare. People who truly deserve free healthcare are already signed up or qualified for Medicaid. Seniors have Medicare which is a low-cost insurance program of which they have paid into. Why would these groups sign up for Obamacare?

The only way for Obamacare to have any pretense of success is to gin up fake numbers. Just as Obama's and Michelle's twitter accounts have up to 55% million phony followers and just as the failure of the green car sales numbers were jacked up by having government agencies purchase Volt fleets, Obamacare enrollees will be non-existent or funded by taxpayers, as in the 75% subsidies for congressional employees. The future avenue to Obamacare success is to sabotage private insurance companies and employer-funded insurance to leave Obamacare as the only option.

Democrat Marketing Ploy of Being FOR Children Has Worked until Now

October 10, 2013

Democrats, up to this point, have gotten away with this simple marketing ploy. They have learned to lay claim to a group or idea and promote that Republicans are against the group or idea. In making the simplistic statement that Democrats are for children, women, blacks and gays, unthinking people have bought into the idea that Republicans are against children, women, blacks and gays. Republicans make up half of the country. How is it that Democrat supporters truly believe that Republicans hate their spouses, mothers, aunties, grandmas, sisters, cousins, and hate an entire race and sector of the community? It doesn't even make sense to think we have that much hate in ourselves.

It is kind of difficult to remain the party for children when its leaders can so brazenly respond in the following ways. Democrat Harry Reid, Majority Chair of the Senate, questioned a reporter on why would he fund a child with cancer. Obama's head of Health and Human Service Kathleen Sebelius refused an adult lung transplant for a dying child. Obama himself laughed at his bowling scores comparing them to the Special Olympics.

On the same week of the Gosnell Trial, Obama stood before a Planned Parenthood convention and God Blessed them. Obama has often inserted his opinions into legal trials but never once mentioned the Gosnell trial. Perfect

219

human babies, mostly black, were birthed and left to die or had their spines snapped. This should never happen, but this is what the abortion industry has become. If women were taught that their rights end when someone else's begins, they would not become victims of another Democrat marketing ploy of 'Choice' in dealing with their own flesh and blood.

Democrats have won over many younger voters by the pro-gay issue of gay marriage. They claim that adults should be able to marry whomever they love. Conservative Republicans do not want to change the definition of marriage as being between a man and a woman and therefore are labeled gay haters. Believe it or not, conservatives are not gay haters. Gays can receive all the legal rights they want through civil unions. Long ago, Liberace, Queen, and Elton John began their successful music careers with their own flamboyancy. There was no in your face shouting how gay they were; everyone just knew and loved them. My personal view is that marriage is about the family and the children. No child should purposely be denied a mother or a father. A gay couple cannot substitute for what is missing. Anyone who thinks otherwise, please explain which parent you would have picked to have never known, your mother or your father.

Sometimes marketing claims are true and sometimes they are just unfounded claims stated repeatedly that they become ingrained as fact. It doesn't take much to realize the truth from a marketing strategy.

Hating Sarah Palin or the Barry-Cades

October 14, 2013

Not many people heard of Sarah Palin prior to McCain's pick as vice-president in 2008. Her political opponents studied her and couldn't criticize her on her political achievements, her family, her looks or her past. Somehow, Obama and the Democrat machine were able to convince many Americans to hate her with their own War on a Woman. They bashed her, poked fun of her, lied about her and the hate grew. Briefly, Palin was a mayor of a small Alaskan town, rose to the governorship of Alaska, took on Big Oil in Alaska along with the political machine and won, had a son in the military, had a pregnant teenage daughter, has a special needs baby, loves her guns for food and protection, and has a supportive husband. She's American through and through.

She spoke with the veterans as they stormed the Barry-cades of the World War II Memorial. The difference between Palin standing with the veterans and Obama who set up the barricades to keep the veterans out is striking. One loves America without a doubt, and one shows disdain for America's bravest. Barry Obama's rhetoric is over. I hope Palin's is just beginning. She was cast out as a Tea Party rightwing nut job which should be worn as an honor against all that is Obama. As she helped many Tea Party candidates win their seats in 2010, she is about to perform an encore with the 2014 elections. Her political opponents hate her because she is formidable.

In feeling comfortable dissing our veterans in front of the world, our commander-in-chief finally went too far for the masses. Palin made a promise to our veterans, "Our war memorials remind us of the cost to keep us free. You paid the price. Rest now. We will pick up the mantle. We won't let you down. We now take up the fight for freedom." We will stand with Sarah Palin so we can uphold her promise. Checkmate, Obama, your hateful communist/Marxist game is over.

Obama's Social Justice Is Not Compassionate

October 15, 2013

I realize social justice sounds just. However, social justice is truly forcing one person to give up his or her property to someone else. Property is anything owned - money, house, land, personal belongings, business and your own body. The basis of social justice is jealousy, resentment, envy, and covetousness. No one is allowed to prosper or motivated to prosper with the exception of the ruling class who always take more than their fair share, including Obama. It is the opposite of capitalism which gives everyone the opportunity to thrive. It's hard work, but anything worthy is.

America has always been very charitable to the less fortunate. President Obama believes it is his duty as a politician to take away from the successful and give to the unsuccessful (and to his well-off buddies). The irony of this government policy/ideology is that the success of capitalism is required for the government to have anything to steal. Obama's solution is to tax away any property above the amount he thinks is enough for you. Our president has said that at some point, you've made enough money. What about Obama and his cronies? They could hand out their money and not force the government do it for them. Believe me, their money will be exempt.

A YouTube video (taken down) shows what happened when welfare recipients realize a glitch on their debit cards left off spending limits for a few hours. Police officers were called to a Walmart to maintain order when a spending spree got out of hand. Not one of the people on video realizes or cares where the money came from. It's on their government welfare cards and now it's theirs to spend. Many probably don't understand that the money is taken directly from other people's paychecks and basically handed over to them. Another video shows a woman in line for welfare and when asked what she is waiting for, the answer is Obama's stash of money and he's giving it to us. And that's why we love him and vote for him. These citizens have given up any idea of working for what they want. There is no justice in this, social or otherwise.

Another term for social justice is wealth redistribution. Obama has assigned management of wealth distribution in nearly every department of our government, including the agencies of science, medical, regulatory, DOJ, legal, education, defense, communications, energy, internet, and national security. In social classless utopia, government rules as an elite class over the rest of us 'class-less' people. The largest class in the United States is the middle class – can't have this class in a social justice world. It is no surprise that this class is shrinking under the Obama administration. To support Obama is to support the declining size of the middle class through taxation and job losses. Obama's rhetoric of equality, fairness and change is false talk to advance America away from its independent spirit and towards socialism. It is infuriating that many people do not realize this and fear this. I also fear that bored Millennials will be all good with trying socialism. Do they really not understand why people living in communist countries cannot just vote out communism?

Obama Learns How Business Really Works

October 23, 2013

It's not just about public relations and catchy marketing slogans that make a business work. The business itself has to work. Increased advertising through the Baltimore Ravens football team won't convince us that healthcare.gov is a good thing. An estimated half a billion websites take up residence on the internet. Obama had his signature healthcare plan Obamacare scheduled to be up and running October 1, 2013. Available to him were the best and brightest techies that America has to offer. He chose the Canadian firm CGI with the past failures of Canadian gun registry and healthcare database websites and paid it $94 million to build healthcare.gov. Three weeks later and the website does not work; it is a disaster. A techie during a Hannity interview said that he would be able to build a much better website and would be embarrassed to accept $1 million saying $500,000 is a reasonable price to build the entire website.

Health insurance is already sold online on websites such as online-health-insurance.com and ehealthinsurance.com. Various policies are listed, more details accessible with a click, and then you fill out an application to purchase. This is what Obama promised and sold to the American people – something we already had. Obama may not have known that you have to hire the best and brightest and pay them well to perform their work if you expect a great product. Or he had to hire a firm that he could trust to hide the truth.

Obama knew Obamacare and all its details had to be kept under wraps. Transparency would have killed it and maybe Obama knew he could count on CGI to be discreet. Had Obama brought in techies that he did not have relationships, healthcare.gov may never have made it this far. The pricing and high deductibles are product killers. Many laws bring unintended consequences.

Obamacare is meant to bring intended consequences such as insurance companies dropping individual enrollees, businesses dropping employees' health insurance and hospitals laying off employees. Obama must think that Americans will stand by and let him take complete control over their healthcare. He has not even begun to hear from the Tea Party that he tried to quiet and dismantle through the IRS.

Obama: The Very Best of Liars Has Jeopardized the Lives of Millions

October 29, 2013

A great liar can look a person straight in the face with a bald-faced lie without any conscience as to the consequences. The health of many Americans has been put into jeopardy due to Obama's big lies selling Obamacare. Millions of Americans are getting cancellation notices because their health insurance policies do not meet Obamacare standards. Obama has designed his affordable health care plan to push people who do not want nor can afford it onto his plan and signed off on this in 2010.

Americans are starting to realize the dangers of liberal utopian via Obamacare. Obama's liberal utopian healthcare plan is the catalyst for leaving previously insured millions of Americans without insurance unless they sign on to Obamacare by January 1, 2014. People hate losing their favorite doctors. The debacle of the healthcare.gov website has delayed the sign-up date to March. But what does the date matter when Americans cannot afford the monthly premiums? Young people who have stood by Obama and have been waiting for Obamacare to finally address some medical issues are dumbstruck. They cannot afford the monthly premiums along with the large deductibles. Many others will be left without insurance to help pay for life-sustaining drugs, surgeries and doctor care. The reality of Obamacare is that their lives have physically been put in danger.

Obama's goal of government-centered healthcare trumped any conscience to the predicament of Americans. It is odd that he didn't take up the Republican request to delay the health mandate past the 2014 elections. He had the perfect ruse to delay Obamacare details due to the messed-up website. His supporters would have stayed with him building up excitement for a big 2015 Obamacare roll-out. Obama's lies of keeping your doctor, keeping your plan and reducing costs by $2500 lead to questions:

- What has Obamacare taught us about Obama the man?
- Can someone who lies directly to our faces ever be trusted?
- What else has our President lied about?
- Has every time Obama told us that he was not aware, never knew, or not involved a lie?

- Would you trust your life and health to Obama to run a government single payer system?
- Will Americans be so desperate for medical care that they welcome single payer?
- Do supporters of our liar-in-chief deserve our votes in 2014?

Obama, Obamacare and Tea Party Forever Connected

October 30, 2013

The Tea Party protested against Obamacare in 2010 for its unconstitutionality, expense and government overreach. Obama sold a pack of lies which the Tea Party never bought and called him out. In Obamacare, the Tea Party knew what Obama's government healthcare insurance entailed:

- Individual mandate or tax for not buying health insurance with minimal essential coverage
  2014 = $95 per person per year or 1% of your income
  2015 = $325 per person per year or 2% of your income
  2016 = $695 per person per year or 2.5% of your income
  2017 = Tax penalty will increase by the rate of inflation or 2.5% of your income
- Maximum tax penalty is capped at the lowest cost Obamacare plan.
- Employee mandate to provide health insurance for 50 or more employees or $2000 fine per employee
- Free or subsidized insurance for millions to be paid by taxpayers
- Medicare cuts to Obamacare of $700 billion resulting in doctors leaving Medicare
- Minimal essential coverage defined by government for everyone includes pediatrics, maternity, abortion and behavioral health treatment such as transgender
- Price of health insurance has to rise to cover these essentials
- Private insurance companies have to charge more to cover/pay more or they go bankrupt
- Anyone without essential coverage will be fined and/or pushed onto Obamacare
- Government database on everyone's medical care, including if you own a gun

Millions of Americans have received notification that their health insurance policies are cancelled. They are directed to the government website that doesn't work. People that have gotten through have found out that the government insurance has costly premiums and deductibles. Where does this leave lower and middle-class Americans who cannot afford the premiums?

224

Obama's words on keeping your doctor and insurance have proven to be false. Worse yet is that he knew they were false each time he repeated this and boy did he repeat this. Obama is forever tied to the Tea Party. Obama's IRS targeting and disparagement of the Tea Party helped win his reelection. The Tea Party has been vindicated and will continue to fight until this law that hurts Americans is an asterisk in history.

NOVEMBER 2013

Why not universal healthcare to end the disaster of Obamacare?

November 4, 2013

Democrats are selling socialized healthcare on the basis that it would simplify our healthcare. My 20-something relative agrees. He has a health condition and thinks that letting the government take over is the answer to affordable healthcare. He is missing the obvious. Once government takes control, our individualized healthcare turns into a bureaucratic nightmare with budget overruns combined with endless fines, fees and tax hikes. Running healthcare is not a government specialty. Everything medical would be taken from the private market and given to the government for total control. Being that the health insurers, hospitals, doctor practices, pharmacies and laboratories already exist, they will be nationalized through a fascist takeover - the government will dictate to them how medical care goes forward.

Conservatives protested losing our freedoms and rights and Obamacare is the prime offender. The government budget and bureaucrats will dictate who gets what, when they get it, how much to charge patients and how much to pay medical care givers. Doctors are refusing to take more Medicaid and Medicare patients because the government pays minimal reimbursements to the doctors. Government wants to pass a law that doctors cannot refuse these patients. Obama declared healthcare as a right and doctors had better provide their services for people who request it. If you believe healthcare is a right, then you should be able to demand doctor and nurse services, right? You must believe that you can demand that a doctor see you and operate on you. It is easy to see how dictatorial this becomes and what it truly means to lose freedom and liberty. Where's the doctor's freedom? See, it's not always about you.

The United States government was designed for limited control over our lives and this is how America has flourished with the best healthcare system in the world. Liberal progressives sound like nice people who want to provide for the poor. Instead of charity, they want the political power over our lives and the legal right through socialized medicine. If government needs 70% of our paychecks to pay for this, well, that's the necessary tax. There is a limit.

225

Government can only tax, fine and regulate working Americans until they have nothing left to give.

Here's what to expect with government healthcare: I spoke with a back doctor about his stats on back recovery. He said it depends on if we are talking about his privately insured patients or his workers' compensation insured patients. You see, the latter rarely have good stats. If they did, they would have to go back to work earlier. And, hey, with worker's comp, a bad back keeps on giving. I can only imagine the fraud in government-run healthcare.

Our President, the Healthcare Huckster

November 6, 2013

Obama has been peddling his healthcare plan for over five years now. You would think he could finally stop now that it has become law. Despite his pleadings and promotions, Americans still hate the law and are experiencing the effects of his lies. People love their doctors, and many have been with their same doctors for decades. They are comfortable with their insurance policies that are often tied to their doctors. Obama marketed his reelection on people being able to keep their policies and doctors. Liar. Remember how Obama is all about equality and fairness? Now we find that the cost for everyone is not equal. The people that have earned money have to provide for those who do not have money. Many can no longer afford the premiums for policies accepted by their doctors.

People with private individual policies are receiving letters of cancellation or premium increases. Mine came today and to comply with Obama's law, my premium will increase $1900. I never believed Obama when he said that my premium would decrease $2500. To continue being insured, I have to decide in a month and a half if $1900 is in my budget. If not, I am directed to Obama's malfunctioning website where people are already finding out that the insurance premiums are still very high.

The Healthcare Huckster had the nerve to say that we can keep our policies and doctors, now adding IF your policy hasn't changed since the law passed (they were required to change). Our "substandard" policies in Obama's eyes are now "transitioning" to his better policy. This is a president who does not care one wit what the American people want or need. Then again, Americans knew that the main regulations to Obamacare didn't kick in until after the 2012 election with plenty of warning out there as to what to expect with Obamacare.

Obama Had to Win a Second Term

November 8, 2013

The 60s and 70s liberals can be pictured as pot smoking hippies sitting cross-legged in tie-dye t-shirts and bell bottom jeans. The radical liberals of the day protested the government and police through violence. The same people today as radical liberals are nicely dressed with pant creases and hold the offices of the presidency, administration and the legal courts. Their target is the American way of life.

Liberals have the reputation of being for the little guy although their true goal is power over the people. Their laws and regulations focus on taking from the rich, giving to the poor after first lining their own pockets. They rant against big corporations and the wealthy as taking away from the poor. The difference between corporations and the government is that corporations earn their money while employing lots of people to do it. Government steals the corporate earnings through over-taxation and fines and can then employ lots of people. Present day liberals are the closest they have ever been in the United States to completion of the wealth transfer and are not about to let go.

Obama was able to obtain and keep the office of presidency by stating obvious problems, presenting solutions and then doing the exact opposite. When his opponents complained about him doing the exact opposite, Obama turned the blame on the republicans for exacerbating the problems. Obamacare got support to insure the uninsured. His supreme mistake was lying to the American people about keeping doctors and insurance policies. Although he is trying to attach the blame for the millions losing their health insurance on the Tea Party or insurance agencies, it's not working. Obama has become the problem.

I have determined that Obama had to win a second term to teach Americans what liberalism truly is. Obama talked about getting burned from the Obamacare website and carefully reworded it that the American people have gotten burned. The truth is that the American people have gotten scorched by the ideals of liberalism and better get out of its clasp soon.

One Group Stood Up Against Obamacare

November 13, 2013

Not many people understand Obamacare and probably never will. Obamacare has become a fluid law that changes by the whims of our president, not by legal congressional means. What it is today may change tomorrow and what has been promoted about the law just isn't true. Much of the promotion was and is stealth. WebMD has a government contract of $4.8 million to pay for pro-Obamacare articles, videos and online quizzes. AARP has received millions to convince the elderly that it's good for them. Our tax dollars are paying Hollywood to insert Obamacare into TV shows and paying football and basketball teams to encourage Obamacare enrollment. Nonprofits including Planned Parenthood and ACORN offshoots as navigators have been handed millions of taxpayer dollars to help sign up enrollees and pad Democrat voter rolls.

One group stood up against Obamacare because it knew that our taxes would rise, our premiums would increase, and our liberty would dwindle under Obamacare. The group was mocked, derided as crazy and targeted by the IRS just for standing up against Obamacare. Of course, I am talking about the Tea Party that is made up of normal, everyday people who don't want Obama mandating our healthcare. One of its leaders Senator Ted Cruz had the guts to stand up against his own party to warn everyone about the disaster about to be unleashed on the American people. If you are realizing the dangers of nationalized healthcare, you might as well be considered, gasp, conservative and Tea Party. The Tea Party has one major goal, to stop Obamacare and its destruction of our medical care. The 2014 and 2016 elections are our opportunities to stand with Tea Party candidates.

Our Government Does Not Agree with Rapper Sir Mix-A-Lot

November 14, 2013

Well, well, Obamacare architects don't agree with Rapper Sir Mix-A-Lot at all. In their world, they see the disparities in life much clearer than ordinary Americans. The ideal genetic lottery winners just for having great genes (most likely with smaller butts), have been paying an artificially low price for healthcare. It's downright discriminatory for healthy people to pay less than sick people. Obamacare architects designed the new healthcare industry for these healthy people to pay their share for the sickness in our world.

According to the progressives in the Obama administration, those good-looking people out there are obviously healthier than their ugly cousins. The ugly cousins walking around with big butts or maybe sitting on them too long have been paying more for their medical care. The good-looking people may put up a fight claiming that they work out, they eat healthy and take good care of themselves, but they are already rewarded with looking good. Since they somehow avoided derrieres dented with cellulitis, Obama has decided to jack up their health insurance premiums to meet up with the undesirables.

If Obamacare seriously takes hold, this is the beginning of pitting the healthy versus the unhealthy. Whenever a genetic lottery loser stuffs a donut into his/her mouth or guzzles a Big Gulp, this becomes the business of everyone including the government. The government is now in the business to bring down

228

healthcare costs. The genetic lottery winners are already being punished with higher premiums. The genetic lottery losers are going to have to be monitored very closely. Perhaps the government will promote or force butt reduction and deem a TBA acceptable size of butt. See, progressive liberals don't like big butts and they cannot lie. They are equal in punishing everyone for all types of inequalities in life. Rapper Sir Mix-A-Lot really does like big butts and raps about it.

Millennials Aren't Really into Obama's Fairness and Equality After All

November 14, 2013

The Millennials that voted for Obama haven't enrolled in Obamacare. Obama needs them to start signing up and paying for Obamacare health insurance policies to help pay for the poor. After all, it isn't fair for the poor to go without health insurance. Isn't that why Millennials voted for Obama, that everyone should have health insurance? Millennials also fought and voted for the free birth control. Millennials never considered that the birth control would be free AFTER paying the monthly premiums and high deductibles. Obama told everyone prior to being elected that spreading the wealth is good for everyone. Were the Millennials expecting to be on the receiving end of the wealth redistribution? Was spreading the wealth OK only if the wealth didn't come from them?

Do they not understand that they are the young and healthy and should be working to support the liberalism ideals that they voted for? Did they really expect rich, old people to purchase and pay for their health insurance? Liberalism is government that makes big promises that require a lot of money. The young idealists that fall for liberalism do not consider where the money is coming from to pay for the promises. They might want to adopt the conservative ideal of working for what you want. That means whatever it takes. Obama is destroying the economy, but with a will, there is a way.

Unfortunately, Obama has expanded the welfare state that gives him a solid voting base. Any wealth that Millennials have will be taxed, regulated or fined just like the rest of the working Americans. Millennials have a choice. Join the welfare state and get the freebies while they last. Or they can work their butts off and start voting for responsible leadership for our country. See, no one wants their wealth forcibly redistributed by a lawless, runaway government. It doesn't seem fair or equal to take from one group who works for it to be given to another group who sits around waiting for it, especially if it's your money. Young idealists may ask what about the truly wealthy that can pay for everyone? They no more want to give up their wealth than anyone else. For protection, they donated huge amounts to Obama. You're on your own, Millennials.

229

Obama Knows Who He Needs to Call to Fix Obamacare

November 17, 2013

Obama knows sales and promotion. His business acumen lacks in all other aspects of business models – research, customer service, operations, finance, execution, and basic product and industry knowledge. And on this basis, he sold us a healthcare law that never went beyond the sales and promotion part. The name Affordable Care Act does not represent what he sold to the citizens of the United States. Millions of more citizens are losing their health insurance than are getting insured for the first time. Now we are left with an over-priced website that cannot get up and running and a product that nobody wants.

What Obama needs is an expert in turning around a flailing business, a consultant who can redirect Obamacare into a success. Is Obama aware of any self-made, successful business leader known for turning around failing companies? Of course he does. He ran against a proven business leader for president. We need Mitt Romney. Obama would only call on Romney if he seriously wanted to halt the destruction of our healthcare industry. Romney shouldn't be waiting for a call anytime soon. He could, however, work in his spare time on a business plan to save Obamacare by doing the actual work that we expect of our president. It just doesn't seem fair that the wrong person got elected by complaining about fairness and equality.

Would Obama have ever admitted that he chopped down a cherry tree?

November 19, 2013

Children love to hear the story about George Washington when he is confronted by his father about his favorite cherry tree. George replies, 'I cannot lie. I chopped down the cherry tree.' It endears us that our president was an honest man. George could have said, 'I didn't know about any cherry tree.' Or 'That cherry tree isn't chopped down.' Or 'What difference at this point does it make?' Or 'I plead the fifth.' Or 'A fanatical Tea Party member chopped that tree down.' Most likely Obama would have said, 'Let me be perfectly clear. If you like your tree, you can keep your tree.' That Obama destroyed the tree is irrelevant to him.

Let us be perfectly clear. A growing number of Americans realize how Obama lies. You can keep the tree except that it is dead. Just like we can keep our health insurance policies except that they don't exist anymore. Just like we can keep our doctors except that they are kicked off our policies. We expect politicians to make grand promises that they hope to uphold. Fine, but don't tell us outright lies to reach a socialist goal of government healthcare takeover. Now we're left figuring out how to stop Obama and his administration. Can a presidential election be recalled? If we had a do-over with the truth on Obamacare, and now fudged employment reports, could this disaster of an administration fade away from our lives never to rise again?

The Desperation of Obama and His Al Green Moment

November 20, 2013

"On a scale of 1 to 10, how awesome was it when the President started singing Let's Stay Together by Al Green? That was pretty awesome." And pretty desperate to send the president's wife to BET talking him up with Bow Wow and Keshia on his Al Green moment. Michelle also shared with Bow Wow that Obama has a little swag and sings all the time when he is in the bathroom.

For God's sake, Americans are desperate to find a solution to their interrupted healthcare through policy cancellations and unaffordable insurance. Obamacare has cut off millions of people from their doctors and hospitals while in the midst of trying to save their lives with necessary medical procedures, prescriptions and surgeries. The American people no longer care about Obama's singing ability. They already feel duped by falling for it the first time. They demand a leader who is in charge and knows how to help them.

Obama was given the greatest gift of a second term because Americans trusted that he had their best interests at heart. The lies and deception keep building, especially on Obamacare. 60-70% of the website including the payment system and accounting hasn't even been built. Herein lies the biggest racquet of liberalism: huge amounts of taxpayer dollars go unaccountable because, hey, it's not their money and the bureaucrats will continue to be paid for crappy work. Try that in a privately-owned company based on capitalism. Recalling Obama's human side including his bathroom habits won't change the reality that he is destroying lives.

Why did 60 Democrat Senators and 219 Democrat Representatives vote for Obamacare?

November 21, 2013

These 279 American citizens are responsible for destroying our healthcare. They were responsible to look out for the best interests of Americans and they failed. Why did they hoist this disastrous bill on us? Obama can't even be to blame. His former bodyguard describes him as an actor playing the part of our president. Without his teleprompter, he would have no lines to recite. He's just acting as the leader of the Democrat Party. But no matter who resides in the White House, our congressmen and women have the ultimate legislative responsibility of passing laws for the citizens to follow.

It appears that they were corralled like sheep to fall in line and offer a Yes vote for the Democrat Party. There was enough opposition to Obamacare for each one of these 279 American citizens to stop and reflect. Just maybe, something about this law needs more research before voting Yes. They should have taken the time to find out what they were voting for and what consequences would follow. In basic contract law, you never sign on the dotted line unless you know exactly what you are being obligated to and what the consequences will be. American's healthcare deserved these basic considerations.

Two possibilities for the Yes votes: they were either ignorant of the law or they were complicit with the law. They either had no clue that people would lose their health insurance, or they knew people would lose their health insurance. Neither is acceptable because Americans were deceived. Did any of these 279 people question how government bureaucrats could run the entire American healthcare system? Did any of these Democrats over the past three years look into the state of Obamacare? Did not one person ask how Obamacare was coming along? It looks like the only responsibility these 279 people had was to hold a seat to vote Yes. Now it's time to do their jobs and make it right for the American people.

Medicaid Enrollees Should Get Their Assets out of Their Names Now

November 27, 2013

What if an unworkable website was part of a diversion to the meat of Obamacare coming in 2014? Senator Ted Cruz begged us to look closer to what the law truly contains through his 21-hour Obamacare filibuster. Shortly after, the October 1 website rollout date came and went with what can be labeled as utter incompetence. Incompetent or planned, progressives keep marching on with their plan to state control or social justice control. The majority of sign-ups are to Medicaid – free healthcare. We are now one month away from being under the law of Obamacare.

Free healthcare means somebody else is paying. While alive, Medicaid is paid by the taxpayers. When dead, states have the right to go after the Medicaid patient's assets, including jointly held assets. A grieving spouse can be kicked out of the house so the government can recover the free funds. Granted, Medicaid patients should not own many assets. But for those who do own a home and are not in optimal health, the assets should be transferred to someone else such as a spouse. The laws keep changing but one states that assets that have been in the patient's name in the last three years are recoverable.

As for the meat of Obamacare, Medicaid fund recovery is just a small part. The law was designed to put the insurance companies into precarious positions. Come December 15, the insurance companies are required by law to sell only one unaffordable, Obama approved standard policy. Who goes broke first is yet to be seen – anyone who falls ill or the insurance companies themselves who fall to bankruptcy. There remains a very short window to at least purchase a catastrophic plan for the year 2014. The application period is to be approved and set up prior to the December 15 deadline. Good luck to all. We are going to need it.

DECEMBER 2013

What do Catholics do about a Marxist Pope?

December 3, 2013

Pope Francis just said that the American way is wrong. Our way of life with the freedoms we enjoy, the freedom to succeed and invent, the freedoms of opportunity that have lifted so many people up from poverty and the free markets that determine the costs of business is wrong in the pope's eyes. We do have a questionable pop culture and liberal policies that go against the Bible but he's not addressing these. He has bought into the liberation theology that is against Catholic teachings and that the rich are too rich and the poor are too poor. The rich must give to the poor via all-knowing, virtuous government bureaucrats, not via charity. Liberation theology does not consider that the rich were previously poor and worked their way up through our free market. Liberation theology totally ignores the middle class that also were previously poor and worked their way out of poverty. It also ignores the status of American poor compared to third world poor.

All liberals claim to see is the very poor who need help. We have come to a crossroad of powerful forces against conservatism and capitalism. The Pope and our President see the world differently than more than half of Americans. We can either empower the government to help the poor or we can empower the people to help themselves and, in turn, have the ability and means to help others. The United States was founded by people who wanted another way of life other than an all-powerful government directing every area of their lives. The theory of Marxism is based on the success of capitalism. After the success of free enterprise and the expansion of money, Marxists want to come in and take over. The money has been made and they want to be in charge of that money. Without the title of government behind them, Marxism would be called pure thievery.

In terms of trickle-down wealth, we can look at the Kardashian wedding and PGA tournaments. Liberals see waste and a lot of money flowing around that they would like their hands on. Conservatives and capitalists realize that the exchange of money helps empower people with income and pride. A fancy wedding is more than a beautiful ceremony. Expert service personnel of lace designers, seamstresses, caterers, flower arrangers, cake maker, gifts and their makers, photographer, on and on to the delivery people and limo drivers and wait staff are earning a living.

Professional Golfers' Association events have money flowing through its own design. Liberals see and smell the money and want it in taxes to dole out how they see fit. The exchange of money through just one tournament is an economic boost all around. In addition to the top golfer winning $1 million plus, money is exchanged to the staff of the golf course, restaurants, transportation of rental cars to private jets, signage companies, advertising venues and more. Liberals want people to picture the rich sitting on piles of money, but the fact is that the PGA gives to charity while also providing fantastic competition and beautiful scenery. Government does not provide this. The free market does.

To preserve our freedoms and way of life, true conservatives should be voted in with the majority to make the necessary changes. The only thing we can do about a Marxist Pope is to prove him wrong.

Leaders Lead, Pretenders Don't

December 5, 2013

The news on Obama's signature healthcare legislation is more embarrassing with each passing day. Obama had not met with the person in charge of Obamacare in the past three and a half years. Once Obama signed the legislation into law, he went golfing, went on lavish vacations and attended celebrity parties at the White House. He never got involved or checked up on the status of Obamacare. The IRS visited the White House hundreds of times but no visits from the Health and Human Services Secretary are recorded. How is this possible? Obama must not understand how businesses work. Businesses just don't happen. People are creating, organizing, taking action, managing, planning and just basically working. At the top of the business is a leader, whether that title is owner, CEO or president, who leads and directs the people.

A leader whose reputation hangs on this law should have followed it closely and been involved in every aspect. Obama's only contribution to Obamacare (and still is) is that of a used car salesman trying to convince us to sign up. His latest sales pitch is uber embarrassing; he called on bartenders to spread the word through Happy Hours. And if people do sign up, the security of their personal information has not been addressed by the website designers. In response to the IRS targeting of American citizens, Obama claimed that he heard the news like we did, on TV. Now, his statement is completely believable. He isn't leading this nation. He is pretending to lead our nation completely uninvolved in the actual governing.

Obama has three more years as our President, and he is already talking about his dream job. After the presidency, he would like to host ESPN SportsCenter's Top 10 list. With a teleprompter, he will do a fine job. For the present, however, our healthcare industry is falling apart due to Obamacare. How disconnected can a person be to his actions and inactions? Perhaps he would like a career change sooner than later. If he won't go willingly, dereliction of one's duties is grounds for impeachment.

I Want to Hear "I'm Sorry" from Millennial Know-It-Alls

December 10, 2013

Besides an "I'm sorry for helping to elect Obama for president", I want to hear why Millennials listen to a stranger's promises over their conservative parent's advice. We parents know history and his type of BS. Many of us saw straight through the smooth-talking teleprompter speeches. Truthfully, all it took were two Obama off-teleprompter phrases to size him up, wealth redistribution and fundamental transformation. With the internet, know-it-all Millennials could ask themselves why they were not open to conservative thought and searching for true information over campaign rhetoric.

Obama campaigned like no one else using the tech world of social media to reach targeted markets. He came across as cool and hip and did admit to being part of a Choom Gang. Think his type of cool is still cool in the White House? Please tell us it wasn't all about the free birth control. That's really embarrassing if this is why he won the election. As for adult liberals? I do not understand your support of this administration.

Obama had zero experience in the business world yet railed against successful business. What on earth is wrong about success? Changing the business of healthcare takes more than hope. The Millennial know-it-alls who fell for Hope and Change never questioned what this stranger was actually promising. Now that Millennials have elected an economic destroyer of our country, it's time to work harder than ever to reach a modicum of success. Millennials, especially those complaining about their fast food jobs, go find your lives. Pick up and go where there is work. Stop wallowing in your minimum wage jobs and go follow the fracking in North Dakota, Pennsylvania, Ohio and Texas. Please don't wait until you're 30 to wonder why you're still living in your parents' basement.

We now have to work with the cards Millennials helped deal. I am happy for those who are making a success out of their lives. Just remember, the President you helped elect who constantly harps on success is now harping on your success. You will and are being targeted in his wealth redistribution schemes. That's something else about youth who forget to consider other age brackets while voting. The youth become the old. Then again, know-it-alls knew that and would have considered others than just their own feelings when voting.

Hope and Change Has Transitioned into Rapping for Obamacare

December 13, 2013

Obama hoped the youth would fall for his teleprompter speeches and is now changing our country of many options into a government dictatorship with his Obamacare marketing in full force. The rapping of another acting Obama, the YouTube video contest and the #GetCovered are cringeworthy to anyone who follows the healthcare fiasco. The enrollment reports around 350,000 people signed up for health insurance. This includes the people who added a policy to the shopping cart, looked at the price and said no way. The billions of taxpayer dollars spent on a website and marketing schemes caused five million canceled policies. Millions of these taxpayer dollars are being handed out to Obama supporters posing as Navigators - and, yes, there still are Obama supporters and they are being rewarded well.

The United States deserves a fiscally conservative leader in the White House instead of this rabble-rouser who moves onto the next big thing. With healthcare on its way, the talks of amnesty are already being revisited. No one knows the exact number of illegals in this country, but the word is anywhere from 10 to 30 million to double that. If amnesty happens, all these illegals will be granted citizen rights of Obama freebies. Add millions more to Medicaid and watch the health insurance premiums skyrocket to anyone left paying.

Obamacare depends on the young and healthy to start paying into the system and thus the push of rapping and social media marketing. It's fair to assume that Obama believes this type of marketing will work because he was reelected a year ago by the young foolish crowd. The payment system of the website does not work, and insurance companies have not been informed who has even applied. It's almost two weeks before the New Year and insurance companies have been told to cover people on January 1 who will have paid as of December 31 and have partially paid. This is not how business works.

To top off this mess, a two-year budget has passed the House that includes funds for Obamacare. Instead of standing up for a conservative fiscal budget, the politicians get to celebrate a nice holiday at home. After the break, they are going to hear it from not only the lost individual policy holders but the newly dropped group policy holders. The ONLY politicians standing up for the average American are the Tea Party candidates.

The cringe-inducing marketing will end when Obamacare becomes our only viable option. Just think, if half of Americans do not have acceptable health insurance, Uncle Sam collects roughly $15,500,000,000 on April 2015. The first year's fine is $95 or 1% of income and half for children. The real change happens when government health insurance is deducted directly from the paychecks of anyone still working and government decides who gets what healthcare at what cost.

Obama's Selfie with His White Man's Overbite

December 16, 2013

In the photograph seen round the world, Denmark's blonde bombshell Prime Minister Helle Thorning-Schmidt is sandwiched between British Prime Minister David Cameron and Obama grinning his white man's overbite. Urban Dictionary defines this look as a 'derogatory term used to describe the facial expression white people make while dancing'. It's the look that Billy Crystal mastered in *When Harry Met Sally*. Of all places, our dear President catches a selfie with The Look in South Africa during the memorial service for a greatly admired black leader. Oh, the irony and the disgrace.

Truth is, Obama's mama was a white woman and he was raised by his white grandparents in Hawaii. We don't hear much from Obama about his white experience. Obama's claim to fame is that of first black president of the United States but that title isn't entirely true. Little Barry wasn't raised in the hood any more than Paula Deen was. On the other hand, Paula Deen grew up Baptist in the southern state of Georgia specializing in southern comfort cookin'. Her home catering business was called The Bag Lady. She has more in common with poor Southern blacks than Obama has. His whiteness slips out occasionally and displays for the world to see and hear. Anyone remember Obama discussing agricultural issues during his 2007 campaign with farmers? "Anybody gone into Whole Foods lately and see what they charge for Arugula?" "I mean, they're charging a lot of money for this stuff." The boys and gals in the hood can't relate.

About Obama's blackness or whiteness, as our President, it is his duty to protect the United States. He's failing miserably at uniting us but doing a bang-up job at dividing us – as in divide and conquer. If he could appreciate his whiteness as much as his blackness, the United States would be in a totally different place than where Obama is leading us.

237

Congratulate Yourself – You Survived Five Years of Obama

January 2, 2014

With the advent of 2014, we say goodbye to 2013 which can best be summed up as the Year of the Lying Obama - so many lies, so many scandals and so little media attention. The one big lie that the media cannot hide is Obamacare. Obama's intention of insuring 30 million uninsured is not coming to fruition. Instead, many including yours truly were given the option of increased healthcare premiums or astronomically increased premiums to transition to the superior Obamacare standards. And I was one of the lucky ones. Six million policies were cancelled. I think there was a simpler way to insure 30 million rather than mess with the rest of America, population approximately 315 million.

Obama wanted the insurance companies to call them transitioned policies, but people are a wee bit smarter when served cancellation notices. The even unluckier ones were told that their jobs were no longer in the budget and lost more than just healthcare. They lost their means to pay for food, mortgage, autos and insurance for homeowners, auto and flood. The cancellation of employer group coverage is just beginning.

Obama's media is telling us that the economy is turning around. Really? For whom does this apply? Because the middle class is now hit with sky high healthcare premiums, the threat of sky high flood insurance premiums, the threat of increased property taxes to pay for lifetime government pensions, increased interest rates thanks to the retired Dodd-Frank duo, out of control education costs and increased energy prices.

Increased prices don't just happen. Many of these are directly related to do-gooder liberal policies and plain ole political greed. The energy price increase is a joke. We've been told that $10 gallon of gas would be good for us because we would drive less and save us from burning up the world. In what world are these people living? The cruise ship stranded in Antarctica stuck in ice wasn't really a cruise ship. It's a Russian ship filled with climatologists studying melting ice due to global warming. No melting ice here. No worries for the lying liars who will continue pounding us with global warming/climate change reports and scenarios and then tax us to the point that people won't be able to heat their homes in the freezing cold. The truth is that America is teeming with oil just waiting to be drilled.

2014 may uncover even more grievous lies. How much more America can take will depend on the American resolve. We have survived the past five years of Obama with three more to go. Life is about to get harder with the enactment of

Obama laws and regulations that were put off until 2014. Just be prepared and carry on. This too shall pass.

Abortions for $1 per Month Upset the Little Sisters

January 6, 2014

What a deal! Obama's upgraded health insurance standards include a $1 per month premium fee, surcharge, tax or whatever name makes you feel best to pay for abortions. That simple little fee structure has upset a small group of frumpy, humpbacked nuns from the Little Sisters of the Poor who are making a stink over their religious beliefs. They want nothing to do with providing employee health insurance that charges a measly $1 per month for doctors to rip babies out of their mothers. That dollar would be trading their souls notwithstanding all the souls and lost lives of the babies. These American citizen nuns share the absolute belief that abortion is wrong. Somehow those humpbacked nuns have reinforced spines of steel that guide their moral compass.

Every Obamacare policy purposely charges one dollar monthly for abortion costs - another broken Obama promise. When all health policies transition to Obamacare by 2015, Obama scores up to hundreds of millions of dollars for the abortion industry. Back during the original promotion of Obamacare another set of nuns became politically active supporting the healthcare law. These self-named Nuns on the Bus stated that they were fighting for the election's cult topic of social justice. These politically active nuns would also have been aware that the Democrat platform supported abortion. Unlike the Little Sisters of the Poor, the Nuns on the Bus sold their souls by ignoring the abortion issue, that topic Pope Francis declared that we discuss too much.

Catholics and Christians alike are being forced by big government to go against their religious beliefs. Big government is just comprised of other American citizens with the power to force their beliefs on the rest of us. Guess what? We don't have to take it thanks to the Constitution of the United States. We should follow in the steps of the Little Sisters of the Poor. For those who claim to be Catholics or Christians, know your moral compass. Abortion is wrong. We cannot support Obamacare.

Progressivism v Capitalism Defined in Aesop's Fable of the Wind and Sun

January 9, 2014

Obama's claim of shame is the unfairness of capitalism and the fairness of progressivism with its kinder, more humane policies. The Aesop Fable of the wind and sun differentiates these two ideologies. To determine which is stronger, the wind and the sun challenge each other to cause a traveler to take off his coat. The wind starts blowing and then blows as hard as it can, but the traveler holds on tighter to his coat. The sun comes out shining and the traveler removes his coat. The moral of the fable is that kindness effects more than severity.

Obama's progressivism is the forceful wind effecting change in our lives. Government control starts with a nudge and then uses force. In Obama's case, he had to lie to be in position to control us. Take meat eating for example. Liberals don't want people to eat meat. The reasons do not matter, but liberals believe eating meat is murder and contributes to global warming. First, vegetarianism is promoted as a nicer alternative to eating meat. Meatless Mondays are promoted and scheduled in public school cafeterias. Children are indoctrinated with the horrors of slaughterhouses and the inhumane treatment inflicted on animals. Public announcements inform us of the unhealthiness of cholesterol found in a juicy burger. Despite all this information, people continue to eat meat. For our own good, liberals then go on attack mode. Protests are organized to shame people for eating meat. Farmers are visited by regulatory agencies. Then the force comes to all through higher taxes, more regulations, fines and the power of government agencies to price everyone out of production and purchase. Voila. We eat less and less meat until it is unaffordable to purchase any at all. Substitute meat eating with guns, private health insurance, 60-watt incandescent light bulbs, 16-ounce sodas, SUV's, conservative values, oil, business profits, Christian religion, etc. Liberals will blow like the wind to change us as to how the bureaucrats see fit.

Conservatives leave the vegans alone AND leave the meat eaters alone. Conservative government for meat eating is minimal and relegated for the safety of humans. Capitalism allows people to offer and purchase vegan dishes and meat choices. Conservatism is the more humane and kinder ideology that allows personal choices whereas liberalism forces bureaucrat choices. It is time to choose which ideology you want your children to live under – conservatism with the freedom of capitalism or liberalism with the depressed freedom of progressivism.

The Fallacy of Greed, Profit and Equality

January 10, 2014

I cannot live off the land. I don't farm or milk a cow. I don't spin cotton and sew my own clothes. I don't chop wood. I didn't build my house. I didn't invent the internet. I purchase all that I need to live a comfortable life while others do the work for money. I don't expect anyone to give me what I want for free, so I send my husband off to work five days a week. If I need more money, I'll send my husband out to get a second job unless I can think of some other way…

240

It is a fallacy that profitable businesses are greedy. The presidents and CEO's of the large corporations whom Obama calls greedy have a huge responsibility to keep their companies fiscally sound. (Now if those CEO's are criminal such as Enron, that's another story.) Investors, employees and consumers count on these rich, old white men to keep the companies profitable. In some cases, the rich, old white men are women or young, hip guys and gals, or black or Latino or Asian or whatever age or race who has climbed to that position of leadership. Companies that do not make a profit go out of business and people lose their jobs, including the rich, old white men.

People invest in businesses and do not expect their government to interject that at some point, they've made enough money. In most profitable industries, competition enters the market and profit and prices are lowered. The Occupy crowds against greedy business owners and corporate wealth were protesting something that naturally occurs. The market evens out on its own. The irony of the protesters against greed is that they are the greedy. They feel entitled to demand what someone else has earned.

Everything people depend on from food, clothes and the smart phone comes from the work of someone or some corporation. These items do not get in their hands by goodwill. Equalizing everything and everyone by government force is neither feasible nor desirable. Equality would be quite boring. There would be nothing to strive for. The United States is lucky to have the wealthy to look up to and have that hope that we, too, can one day have as much money as we want. What would be the fun of winning the lottery if you are forced to give it all away? In America, you still have the choice.

Disciplining Little Suzy in Our Schools

January 12, 2014

Apparently, progressives see disparity in the number of black children being disciplined over the white children as something to correct. Attorney General Holder has stated that it is unfair that black school kids are punished more than white kids. Here's what my school district has come up with. Teachers perform morning mismatched socks' inspections and report the offenders although socks were not addressed in the school rules. Offenders will face punishment and disciplinary action. The little blue-eyed blond Suzies and Johnnies like to wear mismatched socks.

The school intelligentsia has devised another solution to this disparity at the urging of Holder. Stop disciplining blacks who cause trouble. Teachers have been told that they are not to call security for help with bad behavior if the perp is black. They are not to call the police that may saddle black students with criminal records. In the world of progressives, it is the disciplining that is wrong, not the actions of the wrong doers.

My school board ignored this new discipline rule. Warning had gotten out about a potential confrontation at a high school basketball game and a black teenager with a gun. When the teen arrived at the high school, he was tipped off upon seeing an overwhelming presence of police and kept the gun in the car. Police questioned him and found a loaded .38 pistol in the car parked outside the gym. It's illegal to have a gun on school property and he was booked. According to Holder, another black teen and his two accomplices are now facing criminal records because his newest urging was ignored.

The disparity of disciplining black school children and white school children coincides with the rate of black crime in America. The Obama administration wants to make this a racist issue while the rest of America wants to reduce crime overall for the safety of everyone. America is in a dangerous place when our attorney general who is the main legal advisor to the government with executive responsibilities for law enforcement is Eric Holder.

I've Been Guilty of Liberal Thought on War but No More

January 13, 2014

So the politicking will continue that liberals oppose war and conservatives are warmongers. As a conservative, I hate war and how the Iraq and Afghanistan wars are maiming our military. To me, the fighting and injuries seem senseless in that the fighting continues and more of our men and women never return home or return without limbs.

I went to see the movie *Soul Survivor* and felt honored to visually experience this Afghanistan operation gone wrong. A team of four Navy SEALs runs an Afghanistan operation that left three of them dead. They didn't stand down when it would appear hopeless to civilians and they didn't abandon one of their own. They had a job to do and they did it. The US Navy SEALs are well-equipped and uniquely trained in enemy combatant. These are real men who take pride in their country and pride that they accomplish what they set out to do or they die trying.

To describe the fighting, death and injuries as senseless or hopeless is to misunderstand the military. Our men and women follow orders given to them by our government and fight for our country. To die defending our country is contrary to hopelessness. Navy SEAL Mark Luttrell says it best and I thank him for educating me on my ignorant thinking. Interviewed by CNN Host Jake Tapper who asked about the feeling of hopelessness and senseless death, Marcus Luttrell responded, "Hopelessness never came into it. We never felt like we

242

were hopelessly lost or anything like that. We never gave up. We never felt like we were losing until we were dead." "We spend our whole lives training to defending this country, and then we were sent over there by this country. ...it went bad for us over there, but that was our job. That's what we did. We didn't complain about it."

Conservatives' Fight for Individual Rights Applies to All Americans

January 15, 2014

Discussions of individual rights with dyed-in-the-wool liberals are mind-numbing. The latest is the right of contraception without having to personally pay for it. Back in 2012 during a primary debate, liberal moderator George Stephanopoulos asked Romney out of the blue if states have the right to ban contraceptives. Romney questioned if he's asking constitutionally because no one is talking about taking contraceptives away. Stephanopoulos reworded about privacy rights and Romney again replied that no one is talking about banning contraceptives. The relentless mass media talking points followed that conservatives are against contraceptives which transformed into conservatives against women and then conservative's War Against Women. And single women helped reelect Obama demanding how they needed their contraceptives. This is the same playbook that the Democrats successfully used in 1987 to stop legal scholar Robert Bork from being elected to the Supreme Court. Interestingly, in the 1800's, states did ban contraceptives. Legally, they have the right. They also have the right to approve contraceptives. Romney's question was a plant, and Democrats had their talking points. I understand politics is about positioning and winning. But how many lies and borking are we to take?

Conservatives are standing up to a much larger battle than the primarily pop culture sex and drugs individual rights. The God-given individual rights as stated in the United States Constitution are being violated for all Americans. We now have a president who publicly stated that our Constitution is a flawed document that fails to state what the government should do on our behalf. By executive orders, executive actions and claiming to not know what government agencies are doing, Obama is ruling like a tyrant. He announced that he will bypass congressional legislation for our own good. Liberals have no problem with this because Obama's doing it for us.

Obama has already put in place emergency control over the internet by executive order. Our National Security Agency (NSA) has a million plus square feet of data storage in Utah that monitors our emails, cell phones, internet searches and electronic data down to bookstore purchases. Our Department of Justice acknowledged this surveillance as an over-collection of domestic communications. Through Obamacare, our health will be monitored by our government to add new decrees for our own good. This government is working

243

on monitoring our energy usage in our own homes by Smart Meters and on the road by monitoring the number of miles we drive.

Citizens that value their liberty, freedom of speech and religion need to demand that this monitoring and government overreach stop. Once freedoms are gone, they will not be easy to get back. Who has the power to stop this?

FEBRUARY 2014

Government in Nancy Pelosi's Own Words, "It's not my responsibility."

February 4, 2014

Democrat Senate Majority Leader Nancy Pelosi was instrumental in getting Obamacare passed with the most moronic words ever spoken about a major policy, "We have to pass the bill so that you can find out what is in it." Americans willfully entered into a contract for their healthcare without knowing the facts about the contract. To these American citizens who voted to reelect Obama to guarantee that this bill moves forward, you reap what you sow; you entrusted our personal healthcare to a politician's campaign promises. YOU voted for the new, improved crappy, expensive healthcare. Yes, the politician is a liar, but you own it for believing Obama and for listening to Pelosi. Pelosi tells us how the policy is solid but it's just not her responsibility for the execution of the policy.

Although Pelosi was indispensable in passing the crap, making the crap work just isn't her thing. This is overgrown government wasting our tax dollars with layer upon layer of government bureaucrats all unaccountable to the American people starting at the top. We are left with a grand vision without execution or competence. It appears that it is ONLY private business which strives for success and held accountable to their customers and investors. American citizens do not work to support our government through taxes to provide for our needs. Our economic system of capitalism works to do that.

America once had a president who understood government's position in our lives and said that government is not a solution to our problems; government is the problem. I hope for change as many did with Obama except that my hope is for Americans to soon realize how dangerous an overpowering government can be. For die-hard Democrats, prophetic words were spoken in 1962, "I didn't leave the Democratic Party. The party left me." Ronald Reagan

244

Proof of Racism of the Tea Party, Finally!

February 11, 2014

National Association for Advancement of Colored People (NAACP) protesters are asked if the Tea Party is racist. They answer with an unequivocal yes. Black conservative media host David Webb then asks for examples of racism. Blank. Silence. Nothing. We all heard repeatedly that people who don't support Obamacare are just plain racist against a black president. The facts that insurance companies cancelled millions of policies and that people were separated from their doctors have nothing to do with it.

Obama uses his favorite word 'unequivocally' to explain his big lie of keeping your doctor if you like your doctor. Obama inserts his fancy word to dress up, "I lied" to "The way I put that forward unequivocally ended up not being accurate." It's like putting a bow on dandelions. People kinda don't notice the absence of roses or they are getting used to the dandelions. Back in 2010, people did notice the lack of roses in Obama's policies and formed the Tea Party to protest. Not one example has ever been uncovered that proves Tea Party members dislike the new healthcare law because Obama is black.

Conservatives have unequivocally attempted to repeal parts or all of Obamacare. Obama has stated that he would veto all attempts to fix this law and then he changes the law on his own. The latest change calls for a delay for the employer mandate until after the 2014 elections and possibly past the 2016 elections. Obama signed this law back in March of 2010 and now America will have to wait six years for complete implementation. The voice of the Tea Party may not even be necessary to turn Senate seats. Most Americans hate Obamacare and are ready to turn against the Democrats. Most Americans are not racist, and neither was the Tea Party, ever, unequivocally – a word that we have learned to hate when uttered by Obama.

A Man Who Lies to Your Face Will Lie about Anything

February 13, 2014

Obama looked the American people in the eyes and lied about our health insurance – that pesky product that helps us pay to save our lives should we fall ill. Our President lies about anything and everything. Who lies about a video as an excuse for standing down to a terrorist attack that leaves four Americans dead including our ambassador? Who claims that the IRS abuse of conservatives is inexcusable, follows it up with an investigation by a donor, and then has the gall to claim not a smidgen of corruption here? I feel sorry for all of us who live through these Obama years hearing lie after lie. It's deranged if not downright painful.

I hear fellow Americans complaining about being disenfranchised with America and I am the first to rail into them. America is great. The person elected to run America is horrid. Be disenfranchised with him. It would be nice to find a way to stop him, impeach him, just get him to step down as soon as possible or speed up to 2016. The November 2014 elections are nine months away and will be pivotal in determining our future. Let's hope the lies of Obama and his liberal sycophants overpower our Santa Claus government. Americans are not only listening but painfully experiencing liberalism in all its ugliness.

The Obamacare debacle defines the liberal Democrat agenda. The website can be ridiculed forever but it is the product and pricing that are outrageous. It is unaffordable for the young, unaffordable for the middle class and cuts off enrollees from the best specialists and hospitals. The liberal agenda of total government control of our healthcare through single payer is not what Americans want. Obamacare is a test run of how ordinary citizens are treated to medical care when the government is involved. Obama was not elected to turn us into wards of the state and steal our independence to provide for ourselves.

Who is promoting abortions and denigrating marriage on Valentine's Day?

February 14, 2014

Make no mistake. Our government wants you to dismiss marriage and have abortions. Minority House leader Pelosi asks on Valentine's Day, "Why would anyone get married?" Planned Parenthood, uber liberal organization heavily supported by the Democrat Party, is advertising abortions for Valentine's Day. Anyone remember Michelle Obama lecturing us that we have to change our history and traditions? Can any liberal reasonably explain why our government promotes abortion and denigrates marriage?

The answer pertaining to government's involvement is and forever has been to follow the money. These two agendas go hand in hand hurting Americans. Marriage is the stabilizing force in civilized living. Pelosi is reaching out to her base of single women that may not be receiving a bouquet of flowers and a box of chocolates today. Planned Parenthood is reaching out to the same base of people for monetary gain and to normalize promiscuity in the single lifestyle. Both hurt the institution of marriage which leads many to a life of poverty. Democrat party policies actively keep people in the poverty class once they arrive.

These new views on our lifestyles can be counteracted by teaching that a) abortion is directly related to the killing culture by stopping a beating heart and b) marriage is much, much more than a piece of paper. Marriage brings a man and a woman together, encourages them to stay together and is the best option to bringing kids into the world. The kids that are getting lost to us today are the

246

ones who fall for the soon-to-be legal pot, free birth control, abortions and promiscuity. Marriage will seem like an unattainable goal for the unworthy and not worth pursuing. The people who profit from these lost kids, and in turn lost adults, are the Democrat party politicians. Their jobs will be secure taking care of these failed lives that they themselves encouraged. And Planned Parenthood pays the politicians back with millions in campaign funds.

The Sun Barreling Down on You as Dangerous as a Nuclear Bomb

February 17, 2014

Secretary of State John Kerry announced that global warming is a weapon of mass destruction. I'm fairly certain that American citizens are more fearful of a nuclear bomb than the sun barreling down on them. Once Air Force One and the runway were de-iced, Obama jetted off to California to focus on his global warming agenda. California has a drought problem directly resulting from Obama's EPA's diligence in saving the smelt fish. Water was diverted away from the farmland back into the ocean. Obama created his own 'fact' for his settled science of global warming.

Liberals have always loved to spend our tax dollars. A great funding source for our politicians is higher energy taxes – every bit of energy we use to fill up our cars, heat and cool our homes, turn on a light bulb, etc. Private enterprise is finding huge energy sources here in America. Conservative Republicans want to support these businesses, bring prices down and build up the tax base by exporting and leaving capitalism to work without government interference.

The Liberals scare us relentlessly using global warming as the catalyst to justify higher taxes. We are being asked if we want Smart Meters on our houses to help us monitor our energy usage. I think the government wants to monitor our usage so it can regulate our usage. You flush the toilet too much, run your shower too long, clean too many loads of laundry, you are going to hear it from the energy police and pay more for it. We're going to find tracking devices on our cars for the government to monitor and regulate our mileage. This is where we are heading. This concept of government control is hard to grasp for overall decent people who would never consider taking advantage of others. America has problems that really need resolving and world issues that need the focus of our politicians. Real problems and real solutions are being ignored. Vote liberals out whenever you have the opportunity.

Presidential Contender Ted Cruz Rises above the Vitriol

February 18, 2014

The November 8, 2016, elections cannot come soon enough. The liberals have already promoted and bashed Chris Christie. Now they have turned their venom on first term senator Ted Cruz. An ABC reporter on the Stephanopoulos show suggested that Cruz needs a food tester because he is so hated in the Senate.

Establishment Republicans are unhappy with Cruz challenging the party line voting. Former New Hampshire Republican Chair Fergus Cullen commented on his filibusters, "For him to do this after being in the Senate for one year, he's obviously not preparing himself for a long career in the Senate." Although meant derogatorily, Cruz may have a shortened stay in the Senate because he will be living in the White House. Americans are ready for a leader who will lead.

Cruz had the foresight of the damage Obamacare would impose on our country and filibustered for 21 hours. During these hours, he read *Green Eggs & Ham* to his daughters for their bedtime story. Democrats will use this to depict Cruz as stupid and for wasting time. In Cruz's cleverness, he knew this story applies directly to Obamacare – shoving something down our throats while telling us we will and should like it. In the story, Sam-I-Am tries to convince a furry creature that he will like green eggs and ham if only he will try it. The creature replies over and over again that he does not like it.

Democrats were counting on us liking Obamacare once we tried it. We are constantly being bombarded with the greatness of Obamacare. Now Democrats face an election where their story and reality never meet. Ted Cruz was correct in his warning about Obamacare. Ted Cruz has such an impressive background. Here is factual history on Ted Cruz:

- High School Valedictorian
- Princeton cum laude
- Harvard Law School magna cum laude
- Top Speaker Awards at the US National Debating and North American Debating Championships*
- Princeton's highest-ranked debater at the World Universities Debating Championship*
- Senior Thesis on separation of powers and the stop against an all-powerful state
- Harvard Law Professor quote, "Cruz was off-the-charts brilliant."
- Named by *American Lawyer* One of 50 Best Litigators under 45
- Fun Cruz quote, "I'm Cuban, Irish, and Italian, and yet somehow I ended up Southern Baptist."
  *No teleprompters required

248

Millennials Have Never Been Taught This Basic Rule of Life

February 20, 2014

It is the answer my sisters and I received often from my parents to many of our questions. How much money do you make? How much money do you have? How much do you weigh? The answer was always, "It's none of your business" except when the word 'damn' was inserted in there.

As kids, we just wanted to know. What was the big deal? The big deal is that the information is private unless the person wants to share that information. It didn't matter what we wanted. In my family, the parents made the decisions about how to budget and spend the money. Government could never tell my parents that their children deserved more allowance because they could afford it. Imagine if the government stepped in and decided that we kids did deserve more of our parents' money! I think we would have liked it and accepted our free money with our hands out.

Obama has decided to be the wealth redistributor. He has decided who has too much money. Our President is teaching us that taking from the rich and giving to others is fair. The others are liking it; it's free money to them. The Millennials hear how much CEOs make and see money flowing through their bosses' cash registers. They were never taught that how much anyone else makes is none of their damn business. The CEOs who run billion-dollar companies have huge responsibilities to their employees, customers and investors. If low level employees want more money, they should make themselves invaluable, gain experience and move on if they want more than is offered.

A younger relative of mine complained how much money his boss was bringing in and that he deserved more benefits. I asked him if he knew how much money his boss paid for taxes and expenses – social security, unemployment, health insurance, property, flood, state, liability, monthly utilities, loans, attorney and equipment. He had no idea. He bought into the lies of Obama telling him to get his fair share. Millennials have not been told that the only moral way to get their fair share is to go out and earn it. Keep in mind that if they start their own businesses, their budgets must now include government standard health insurance and increasing hourly pay to all employees – whether they can afford it or not.

249

Federal Communications Commission Overseers in the Newsrooms

February 21, 2014

Federal Communications Commission (FCC) was formed in 1934 with the stated mission to make available nationwide and worldwide wire and radio communications services at reasonable charges. The FCC's What We Do statement is 'Leadership for consumers, public safety, accessibility, competition and technological and economic opportunity.' The FCC's 2014 budget estimate of $359 million with 1,821 employees is entirely funded by regulatory fees.

Always curious, I checked my phone bill to see how much in fees I am personally funding the FCC. My monthly charge for basic landline service that only allows incoming calls and local calls is $35.80. Government fees and taxes add up to 36% or $12.88. As far as my wireless and satellite bills go, the taxes seem low, but the bills are so high that it's safe to say government fees are built into the costs. It's time to have an overseer of these government entities and weed out the waste. These FCC guides were listed on the website. Guide on how to report a lost or stolen mobile device. Answer: Call your service provider. Guide on Sports Blackouts, when a sports event that was scheduled to air is not aired. Answer: Contact the broadcasting station who has the broadcasting rights. Guide on steps for consumers when their phone company may end service. Answer: Start looking for another carrier immediately. I would prefer not to be charged for this poppycock.

If only this was the worst of it. The FCC devised a plan to send in government monitors, overseers, or buttinski into newsrooms across America to study Critical Information Needs, the new catch phrase of the Left designed by the Left, totally Orwellian and unwanted. The FCC responsible for doling out broadcast licenses wants to know how stories are prioritized and the status of a station's bias. Obama's contempt for Fox News is well documented. It would be no surprise to hear the FCC's findings on unacceptable news reporting. Then again, White House Senior Advisor David Axelrod said that Fox News is not really a news station. First Amendment freedom of the press is a sticky issue for the Obama administration. For us, we get to pay for newsroom government spies in exchange for purchasing the services of land line phones, wireless, cable and satellite. In the end, we will be paying for monitored news, the news Obama wants us to hear.

250

Obamacare Has Frightened the Middle Class – a Huge No No in Rules for Radicals

March 9, 2014

The Holy Grail of progressives is universal healthcare, beginning with Obamacare – destroy health insurance companies and set the path for single payer government-run healthcare. Our dear leaders exempted themselves. Recall Lincoln's famous phrase from his Gettysburg Address to ensure the survival of America's representative democracy, "...government of the people, by the people, for the people, shall not perish from the earth." Progressive control of government draws a distinct line between the governed and those doing the governing. All the talk about social and economic justice is hogwash. The governing wants the middle class to merge with the poorer class. That's all social and economic justice really is – a deep chasm between the governed and the governing, a direct opposite of our representative democracy of which Lincoln spoke. Progressives cannot be honest about this.

What was the Democrat's response to job loss and decreased hours due to the cost of Obamacare? We should be thrilled not having to work so much and getting more time for family, artwork and poetry, yet still have healthcare. Harry Reid declared us lucky to be free agents. As a matter of fact, if we don't work at all, we can sit back and collect a monthly stipend along with free healthcare. A question one might ask at this point is what happens when we get tired of artwork and writing poetry?

Obamacare was a pre-planned disaster for our medical care from the start. Pelosi knew that. That's why she asked us to pass the damn thing before we could find out what's in it. Obama knew it, too. He had to lie about keeping doctors and policies to get it passed. A little too much of Obamacare has been enforced that Americans are now aware of what it is – one expensive mess which we want repealed.

Liberal progressives have been following Saul Alinsky's Rules for Radicals. They messed up on one rule big time – how not to frighten the middle class while pushing for the radical transformation of society. They have frightened us, and we will revolt with our vote come November 2014. We, too, follow rules. And the rules of the United States are written in our Constitution and the Bill of Rights, the first ten amendments to the Constitution. We want our government back.

Obamacare's Irony of Success

March 13, 2014

The Obama administration has declared success as seven million enrollees by the end of March 2014, never mind the 30 million uninsured as the reason for Obamacare. Six million have lost their health insurance policies. If this group signs up for Obamacare, success could be obtained by enrolling just one million out of 315 million Americans. Ta-Da.

Large number of individual Americans would consider Obamacare a success if the 30 million uninsured were insured and that the rest of us could afford the insurance and keep our doctors. Others would never consider Obamacare successful for the sole reason of being forced to fund everyone else's abortions. The true irony of Obamacare's success is that the more people find out about this law by being an actual enrollee, the more no one wants it. Despite the irony, the Obama administration is hellbent on getting the numbers up and proclaiming Obamacare a success.

The administration has refused to announce even two weeks early as to how many people have enrolled. It has been reported that 4.2 million have signed up, as in shopped on the website, placed a policy in the shopping cart and may or may not have clicked to make the purchase or payment. Implementation of Obamacare was designed to begin after the 2012 election. For me, that was receiving a letter in 2013 from my health insurance company stating the cost to transition to Obamacare would be nearly six times what I pay for my catastrophic policy. Obama can continue to peddle this law as affordable but that doesn't make it so any more than we can keep our policies, doctors and specialists. The latest marketing ploy to get young people to sign up and pay for an Obamacare policy involves Obama acting in a comedic skit with Zach Galifinakis. Not funny. At all.

Harry Reid, the leader of the Senate, told Americans who are having critical issues with Obamacare that they are liars. On the floor of the Senate, he proclaimed that the horror stories heard all over America are untrue. On November 4, 2014, we Americans can kick Harry Reid out of the majority and announce to the world that we don't want to be lied to, patronized, berated or falsely marketed to by our government. Success is all how you look at it.

What to Do, What to Do with Aborted Babies

March 24, 2014

A very disturbing expose in Britain by Amanda Holden addresses this issue titled 'Exposing Hospital Heartache.' Thanks goes to drudgereport.com for headlining this story. No doubt, viewers of cable news channels MSNBC and CNN will not hear this story. Parents of stillborn or miscarried babies were promised that their babies' remains would be cremated. And the promises have been kept, sort of. Their babies were thrown away with other rubbish in 'waste to energy' plants to help heat a major government-run hospital. The aborted babies were treated like the trash their own mothers treated them. Is it a big deal for the aborted babies to be incinerated along with the other power-generating rubbish?

Hillary already has her liberal progressive answer, "What difference at this point does it make?" Please recall, liberals are 'known' for being nicer and the fighter for the little guy. Maybe the bodies of aborted babies deserve the respect that was denied to them in life. Liberal's actions obliterate their reputation. The little guy actually is the little guy – the baby that cannot defend him or herself to live. It is callous and heartless to throw dead baby bodies into the trash. It is even more callous and heartless to let young women think that their babies are worthless and encourage abortion.

How in God's name that killing one's own baby as a choice has become a popular liberal mantra really doesn't have an answer. Abortion will continue to be a choice for many young women as long as the liberal rhetoric rings through their ears. It is as if the Nike slogan runs through their heads, "Just Do It." Imagine these women coming to their own conclusions that their babies are worth more than trash. In this screwy world, the only way may be through a marketing campaign that could be named, "Your baby is worth more than trash."

APRIL 2014

I Don't Believe that Obama Doesn't Get Why We Don't Want Obamacare

April 3, 2014

Obama stood in the Rose Garden April Fools' Day claiming the success of Obamacare while at the same time saying that he just doesn't get why people are opposed to healthcare for all. Perhaps he doesn't get it because he doesn't get the American people. We are opposed to Obamacare because it is overpriced and forced upon us. It is not a product to peddle to us by pleading, using humor or pestering us until we guilt into the purchase. Obama sold his great healthcare fix by outright lies, buffoonery and flippancy all at a great cost to the taxpayers.

Obama, our liar in chief, claims success with 7.1 million enrollees. Per the law, over 300 million people should be paying the mandate, tax, or fine of $95 or 1% of income for not purchasing the healthcare that the Dems chose for us. The fine jumps to $325 or 2% of income in 2015 and $695 or 2.5% of income in 2016. Fines may or may not have been delayed until after the 2014 and 2016 elections. Per Obamacare at Obama's whim, his union buddies, Congressional buddies and good friends are exempted from the mandate, maybe Obamacare insurance altogether. Word has spread that Obamacare insurance is not welcome nor accepted at many of the great hospitals and specialists – the same hospitals that Obama and his buddies will be welcome. If we really want the great hospitals and specialists, we can pay for them with cold, hard cash.

I do not believe for a moment that Obama doesn't get it. The only people who don't get it are the low information voters who hear only what Obama wants them to hear. I heard a teacher (union!) complain that his healthcare was going up $10. I asked if he had any idea of what non-union workers were facing. No clue. They will hear that Republicans are opposed to healthcare for all, the rollout was a bit messy, and that they are free of job lock, the security of a job. They will hear that Obamacare has increased benefits such as free birth control and that costs are down. They will not hear that the healthcare insurance costs are budget breaking to working Americans, the rollout was an immense embarrassing debacle, and that insurance plans are no longer private but total government intrusion.

We will be forced to live with this law for the next three years. The Democrats want us to move on, stop whining and accept this law of the land. That's not going to happen. The whines are going to become roars during the 2014 and 2016 elections. Obama will have single-handedly destroyed the Democrat Party with this progressive liberal ideal of government-run healthcare.

Politics doesn't affect you?

April 24, 2014

A conversation with a new acquaintance went something like this: "I don't pay attention to politics because it doesn't affect me. My life goes on as it always has." As the progressives stealthily and fundamentally change the United States, for her, life is pretty much the same. Her two grown daughters with their young children live on and off with her as they move in and out with new boyfriends. She is a hard worker and recently accepted a promotion with increased pay and benefits. She doesn't want much, just to help her family and have them near. Things are a bit more expensive but rising prices are expected. And her two daughters were able to save money to pay for their priorities, boob jobs.

Politics is so intrinsically intertwined with our lives that its power is easily overlooked, unchallenged and unquestioned. The average person has no direct power over the political sway. However, without being informed, an unqualified person could be elected who does not hold our values dear. The main problem today is that people lack values and thus no values get passed on to their children. I met a young woman from a small town and asked what she does for fun. Her answer shocked me. She goes to the strip bars and drag shows on the weekends with her mother and aunt. The Obama administration and fellow progressives have worked diligently on this lifestyle. Sex, perversion, abortion, free contraceptives, legalizing pot, denigrating marriage between a man and woman and deleting Christianity from the Democrat platform. Think these are not affecting our lives? Are people seriously brain dead to support this?

Aborted babies go somewhere. The little dead bodies and body parts have been tossed into a United States waste-for-power facility to provide electricity for Oregon residents. Gosnell and his dead babies are the byproducts of the abortion industry here in the United States. Legalizing pot has now mutated into releasing drug dealers from prison. Free contraceptives have encouraged sexuality resulting in pregnancies and non-intact families. I have yet to hear from any gay marriage supporter which parent they would pick to have never known. Gay marriage does sentence children to lives without a father or a mother.

According to progressives, we should not want a lot of money, for rich people are evil. Our long-term civil servants are getting vastly wealthy off their political positions. The Clinton's, Nancy Pelosi, Harry Reid, John Kerry, Al Gore and the Obama's have pushed the position of envy while stuffing their own coffers. These politicians teach us to hate big oil companies for making money. Big oil companies give us jobs, add to our mutual funds and save us from freezing in the winter and overheating in the summer. One of these groups has evil tendencies and it ain't the oil companies.

Progressives have the incredible White House power for over two more years. They are not going to fade away gracefully and definitely not going away with their tails between their legs. We will find out how evil progressives really are. How low can this political group go? Will it be a planted dirty bomb going off in an urban area scaring the bejesus out of us? If it is, Obama may have to save us with his promised civilian army more powerful than our military and remain in power.

Hillary's Grandbaby Doesn't Deserve the Gosnell Treatment

April 27, 2014

Hillary Clinton, 2009 Margaret Sanger award winner, received news that she is to be a grandmother sometime in late 2014. Margaret Sanger founded Planned

Parenthood to improve the quality of the human species where there is no need for the elderly, disabled, infirm or blacks. I assume Hillary does not believe this, but she did accept the award based on someone who did. In accepting the award, Hillary said how the award is tied into the economic and political progress for all women and girls. Planned Parenthood has evolved into abortion clinics in mostly urban areas where lots of black babies die.

In Philadelphia, the black doctor Kermit Gosnell ran the Women's Medical Society, sounds so noble. He is now in prison for murdering one patient and two babies in his clinic. When Hillary received her good news, did it faze her that many women like her were denied such news by her political actions? It is as doubtful as Hillary asking Chelsea how her fetal tissue is growing. It is also doubtful that Hillary would suggest aborting her grandchild.

President Obama backed out as the keynote speaker for Planned Parenthood's 2013 "Time for Care" gala. He did speak at a smaller venue, congratulating award winners. One of the awards handed out was the "Care. No Matter What" award for protecting women's health care. All these nice sounding names tied to the dirty, baby-killing industry are disingenuous: political progress for women and children, Women's Medical Society, Time for Care, women's healthcare and Care. No Matter What.

Hillary should be talking about how joyful babies are especially in a marriage with a young mother and her husband. After all, Hillary's grandchild does not deserve the Gosnell treatment and neither does anyone's baby. Were Hillary to get a conscience, she would acknowledge that the abortion industry has to go. Progress for women and girls would be the absence of abortion mills in their neighborhoods.

Let the Public Fire the Clippers Owner, by Kithy

April 29, 2014

Everyone has dealt with a bad boss at some time or another. You either put up with it or quit when you can. The man who was supposed to win a lifetime award from the NAACP, presumably because he has raised a lot of black people out of poverty, is now not getting the award, and people are calling for him to step down from a business that he owns. Did he not do those things that made him a candidate for the NAACP award after all? No, he said some offensive things. Ok, very offensive. So, he's a jerk inside. Lots of people are jerks. Should things they own be taken away because they are jerks? If he cannot get people to work for him, or to see his games and he has to sell his business because all of a sudden it is no longer profitable, that is just. But to have someone tell him he cannot own a business because he's a jerk is NOT JUST. I am so tired of the offensive police going after CEO's and now owners. Be offended. It's not the end of the world. There is no law stating that you cannot ever be offended. I'm offended by everyone's lack of common sense and kowtowing to offended people. I'm offended by rights being taken away because someone else was offended. I'm offended that you think you have a right to not be offended.

MAY 2014

Obama and His Scandals: Obamacare, Benghazi and the IRS

May 10, 2014

Let us not forget how the Obama administration works. Lies, lies and more lies passed throughout the mass media. We are subjected to avoidance, delays, obfuscation, denials and attacks. And then nothing. Life goes on and starts to normalize while Obama's real agenda progresses. Three exceptions have emerged: Obamacare, Benghazi and the Internal Revenue Service scandals.

American citizens are dealing with the effects of Obamacare. As bad as this bill is, the main item of cancelling millions of group policies has been delayed until after the 2014 election and possibly the 2016 election. The original upset over individual policy cancellation has died down but not forgotten. The Lie of the Year will forever be out there: you can keep your policy and doctor with savings of $2,500 per year. No one messes with people's healthcare and gets away with it, not even Obama.

Half-truth investigations into the terrorist attack on Benghazi have been declared over. Instead of moving on, Republicans set up a special committee to get to the truth, not the Obama administration story. An internal email was the catalyst that has already proven that the administration was involved in covering up the truth. Will we also get the facts on gunrunning through Benghazi to al Qaeda militants?

Obama's outrage following the IRS apology for targeting American citizens ended in an investigation that found a smidgen of mismanagement. The House voted to hold the top IRS official in contempt and with 26 Democrats voted for a special committee to investigate the targeting.

Obama's elections were based on lies. He knowingly lied about keeping health plans and doctors. He knowingly lied about al Qaeda attacking the Benghazi embassy while declaring that al Qaeda was on the run. He knowingly lied that the Tea Party was dead while siccing the IRS on them. Had Americans known the truth, would we have a different president with stronger leadership skills, more knowledgeable about foreign policy helping to stabilize our world, and bringing stronger business skills promoting jobs and careers?

257

That's the effect of lies. What difference at this point does it make? We are stuck with the Obama administration. Even when the special councils and committees come to their conclusions, which will be damning, what then? Obama's sycophant attorney general will refuse to follow the law and throw them in jail where they belong. But we will know the truth about the Obama administration, and this will be out there for history.

Obama's War on the Working Poor, by Kithy

May 13, 2014

I am fed up with Obama's war on the working poor! I am sick of paying double for every grocery item I buy on a regular basis. I am sick of paying almost $4 per gallon for gas, which I buy every week. Before Obama, we paid less than $2 per gallon for milk and for gas. We paid 50 cents for a candy bar. Now, I'm hearing that the price of beef and pork is supposed to skyrocket! I heard that electricity is the next everyday expense that is increasing. No wonder people want $10 an hour for their wages. Obama's policies destroyed our budgets by making everything we buy on a regular basis much more expensive than it was. Can we get rid of all the ridiculous policies that are increasing our prices? Can we get rid of Obamacare, Dodd-Frank, and coal destroying, life smothering EPA regulations, NOW?!!! We need relief from idiotic government policies NOW!!!!

JUNE 2014

Obama Doctrine: Plan for Nothing

June 6, 2014

The best descriptive name for the Obama doctrine is Plan for Nothing. Obama wowed enough of the electorate with his so-called fabulous oratory skills, only present with teleprompters, to become our president. What he did next was amazing. He traveled on the taxpayer dime, golfed and continued campaigning with his teleprompters. What else is there to do when you don't plan for anything? It is a shame that the presidency bores Obama as can be seen with his teleprompter speeches resembling ping pong matches and sounding more wooden.

On the foreign front, and this is true – not sarcastic - the Obama administration came up with the Lead from Behind doctrine. In essence, his leadership style includes tagging along and making a comment every so often. I have officially renamed his doctrine Plan for Nothing. The Benghazi disaster presented itself at such an inopportune time for Obama's reelection campaign that he ignored it to resolve itself. Well, it did resolve itself with the murder of four Americans.

258

Instead of planning retribution, Obama went on the cover-up mode. Unfortunately for Obama, pesky Americans demanded the truth about dead Americans; they just would not accept his story about a YouTube video.

To subside the Benghazi frenzy and closing in on the truth, Obama released the last Afghanistan American soldier prisoner and brought him to celebrate him at the White House Rose Garden. Obama claimed that the US does not ever leave our men and women in uniform behind. Could he really snub Benghazi like this? Unfortunately, again, for Obama, this certain soldier he was celebrating did leave his post, abandoning his fellow soldiers of whom six lost their lives searching for him. Despite this, Obama didn't plan for any backlash from Americans and topped it off by swapping five leading Taliban terrorists for our one deserter. He knows he will not be questioned; he is black after all with a funny sounding, Muslim name. We are diverse!

At a most dangerous time in our lives with terrorists feeling emboldened, Obama continues to gut our military, even to the point of diverting military funds toward climate change. Obama must feel no compunction to behold his oath of protecting Americans. If he would, his main goal would be planning for the safety of Americans. But, hey, Obama chooses open borders, gutting the military and releasing leading Taliban terrorists. What can go wrong?

Cringing When I Hear People Still Support Obama

June 7, 2014

Obama is like a child in an adult's world. He wants his way and goes about it all wrong. He supports socialized medicine, but he lies directly to our faces to impose it on us. There really are enough morons who would have voted for socialized medicine. It's free for everyone after all, right? He wanted to be reelected so badly that instead of telling the Americans that al Qaeda attacked our embassy and killed our ambassador, he made up an idiotic story about a YouTube video. The morons could have been told the truth and they really wouldn't have cared. The embassy is far away, right?

In the world leader arena, Obama fumbles around like a puppet. He whispers to Russian President Medvedev on a hot mic that he will be more flexible on dismantling our missile defense with Putin after the election. Cuz Putin will be nice if he kowtows to him, right? Now that Putin has stepped all over Obama, Obama ignores him at the D-Day remembrance like a spurned high school crush.

Sequestration was all the rage for a while. Obama warned us of the disasters heading our way if Republicans wanted spending cuts to his trillion plus annual budget. Sequestration went through with barely a blip except for what Obama did to our veterans. This we cannot forget or forgive. Elderly veterans who had stormed Normandy visiting DC's WWII outdoor memorial were deliberately obstructed by barricades which were set up due to sequestration cutbacks. Obama acted like a spoiled brat closing off the outdoor memorial and wanted everyone to see what power he had. Truly shameful. And then the veterans climbed over the metal parade barriers. I am surprised Obama did not throw them in jail.

Obama's signature legislation Obamacare was a joke from day one. His photo op surrounded with people in white doctor coats was preceded by his administration handing out white doctor coats. When asked how many signups on day one, the administration just couldn't tell us. They just didn't know. Judicial Watch found out by using the Freedom of Information Act that of all the 310 million Americans, just one person signed up on the first day. To this day, we Americans have not been told how many people are paying Obamacare premiums. See, if you don't pay your premium, Obama really can't count you in his eight billion total.

It has been a sad six years in America listening to the outright lies from our president with media types parroting this information. Journalists can no longer claim to be the media, just supporters propping up this juvenile president.

Obama Doesn't Understand that Superpower Status Is Earned

June 8, 2014

The United States of America is a relatively young country that has earned superpower status through her people's character, leadership, hard work and integrity. Contrary to Obama's thinking, America did not plunder other countries to become a superpower. When Americans were called to war, Americans young and old left home and family for foreign land not knowing if they would return. Many did not return but they left this earth safer for their families and progeny. This applies to World War I, World War II, North Korea, Vietnam and the Persian Gulf Wars. The wars in Iraq and Afghanistan in defense of our country were in hopes of spreading democracy and in turn diminishing terrorism.

America has never fought in a war to plunder the land and dictate to a country how its people are to live. America has fought wars to protect others from dictatorship earning the title of superpower. President Obama has publicly stated that we are no better than any other country and that is the way it should be, all the while perfectly aware that countries imprison gays for being gay, treat women as property, marry off young girls as sex slaves, commit mass murders of their own people, imprison or execute political dissenters, force children into military, control all media, and rule by fiat.

260

Citizens of these dictatorial countries are not allowed the opportunities of greatness. They are not allowed to improve their lives, start a business or strive for something/anything. Something that Millennials and young people may not grasp: all people do not have cell phones, able to take fish-face selfies, and many never will. Third world status happens because of bad and immoral leadership. America has grown into a superpower of international influence militarily, economically, and morally because of great leadership. It is simply incredible.

Obama cannot grasp this concept. He has bought into the theory that other countries are poor because America is rich, and that America is at fault. As our president, he may start comprehending that superpower status does depend on the direction of a country's leadership. Obama has demeaned himself by bowing to and bargaining with dictators, and demeaned our country, not only by proclaiming to the world that America is no better than anyone else, but by hurting our country internally. Internally, Obama has been hurting us economically by growing government, stifling business growth, stalling individual growth by promoting welfare and freebies, promoting drug usage and the list goes on and on.

Obama made himself irrelevant as a superpower leader and is now being treated on the international front as irrelevant. He himself has given his power away and is experiencing what happens when the superpower slot is open for the taking. We Americans will be vulnerable to attacks on all fronts by countries that will take advantage of weakness. Obama should have played the strategy board game of global domination called Risk in his youth. He would have learned that the weak lose and the strong survive. He has put America in danger with his deranged superpower theory.

Illegals and the Republican Party

June 11, 2014

America is a country with borders including 1,951 miles with Mexico. Our southern states near Mexico are being flooded with illegal immigrant children unaccompanied by parents. Our Department of Homeland Security is directly involved in dispersing these children by bus and plane from Arizona to Texas to New Mexico. Photos of warehoused children that our federal government did not want you to see have surfaced. The governors of these states are left with a humanitarian crisis: thousands of Spanish speaking children with just the clothes on their backs. Obama's response is asking for $1 billion of our taxpaying dollars, lawyering up the children and telling the governors to take care of the children being dumped in their states.

Moderate Republican's response has been to promise legislation on amnesty on our country which is already drowning in welfare recipients. Democrats will

261

fight for amnesty for 'the children' which many will be of voting age in 2016. How convenient to use and abuse the children for the good of both the children and the Democrat party. Anyone who cheered Obama on his proclamation of fundamentally changing the United States should be cheering loudly right now. If millions of illegals receive amnesty, Obama will have turned America into a majority welfare state.

Although our Constitution proclaims the right to life, liberty and the pursuit of opportunity; a welfare state prohibits this. Obama and his fellow progressive Hillary will need more of our tax dollars to pay for welfare. And then will need even more of our tax dollars down the road. Educating our new Americans with the Common Core agenda and medically treating with free healthcare costs lots of money. With open borders, courtesy of office-holding Democrats and Republicans, more and more illegals will continue entering our country. Who or what is to stop this from happening?

Republicans found out last night. House Majority leader Eric Cantor lost his primary reelection bid to Dave Brat, Tea Party candidate who campaigned on closing the border. Cantor told Neil Cavuto recently that something has to be done with the illegal children. Obama must have heard him and responded by the children dumping. I feel for Cantor having to negotiate with Obama and toeing the line on immigration, but he should have represented his conservative base with the focus on closing the border.

Conservative patriots know better than trusting Obama to have our country's best interests at heart. What kind of a person, much less president of the United States, promotes dumping illegal immigrant children in our country without thinking past our goodwill? If Republicans want the Senate in 2014 and the White House in 2016, they had better listen to their conservative base. Stop the bantering with promises of partial amnesty. Stop using Democrat's tired, used-up phrase of doing things for the children. And, most of all, start realizing that the Tea Party is the base of the Republican party.

Obama's Plan for Amnesty

June 13, 2014

No one knows how many illegals are in the United States because they are pouring in by the day aided by the Obama administration. Are they expecting amnesty? Republicans continue to talk about passing an immigration bill. To encourage a bi-partisan bill, Obama will threaten to declare amnesty. After all, he has to do something about the children he just encouraged to land on our doorsteps. If the Republicans fall for this and send any type of immigration bill to the Senate, it will be corrupted into a full-on amnesty bill anyway.

All revenue generating bills must start in the House of Representatives. Does anyone recall H.R. 3590, the Service Members Home Ownership Tax Act? Think this little tax bill has nothing to do with you? The House bill originated in 2009 to amend the Internal Revenue Code of 1986 to modify the first-time home buyers' credit in the case of members of the Armed Forces and certain other Federal employees, and for other purposes. The Senate received it, renamed it, rewrote it and called it the Patient Protection and Affordable Care Act, better known as Obamacare.

Prior to Teddy Kennedy's untimely death, the Senate had the votes to pass Obamacare. Scott Brown won the Teddy Kennedy seat promising to vote against Obamacare. The Senate deemed Obamacare passed without holding a vote. I doubt the 33,000 pages of law and regulations have any mention of the first-time home buyer's credit, any more than a Republican House immigration bill will resemble the final legislation.

Let Obama threaten amnesty all he wants and when he pushes too far, file the case for impeachment immediately. And have an arrest warrant for Attorney General Holder for dereliction of duty for refusing to act lawfully. We can no longer pretend that Obama will not cause irreversible damage to our country in the next two and a half years. I know this is wishful thinking. Who could tell the first black president that he is wrong and in contempt of our immigration laws?

How do you like your fundamental transformation so far?

June 17, 2014

A Chicago community organizer states that he is five days away from fundamentally transforming the United States while still a candidate for the presidency and he never gets questioned on just what type of transformation he's talking about. Not one person who voted for Obama ever found the answer to this question prior to placing a vote for him. Not one journalist questioned him on this transformation. Evidently, people were not curious about a community organizer's plans prior to placing him in the most important leadership position in the world.

History will not be kind to describing the American voter. Ignorant, uninvolved, and uninformed come to mind. Unfortunately for the United States, people are granted the right to vote even if they possess these qualities. Obama, who had the hubris to believe that he could be elected president of our great nation, knows the American people. They are not very smart, and when nudged with political correctness, can pretty much be controlled. He's black with a Muslim name after all. These Americans will congratulate themselves for supporting diversity.

263

Six years into the community organizer's presidency has not been kind to the United States on all facets dealing with the economy, healthcare, energy, military and foreign policy. The obvious, in-your-face disasters/scandals have become ignorable because they have become the norm. One thing not debatable is that community organizers thrive on chaos. Obama is on his path to fundamentally transforming the United States as promised. The disasters, scandals, and turmoil are not detrimental to his plan as far as he can see. They are his plan.

Not Much Left for Obama to Lie About

June 20, 2014

Al Qaeda is on the run. The only involvement I had with Acorn was doing some stuff with the justice department. You can keep your doctor and you can keep your health plan. Obamacare will lower premiums by $2500. There is not a smidgen of corruption at the IRS. Our border is more secure than it has in years. Benghazi was about a YouTube video. No family making less than $250,000 a year will see any form of tax increase. I didn't set a red line; the world set a red line. My budget will cut the deficit in half over 10 years. The NSA is not abusing its power. I've done more for Israel's security than any president ever. GOP wants dirtier air, dirtier water and less people with health insurance. No federal dollars will be used to fund abortions. I'll make it impossible for congressmen to slip in pork barrel projects. Obamacare fee is not a tax. Greedy doctors amputate legs and take out tonsils for more money. My Recovery Act has saved or created over 150,000 jobs. I am not somebody who promotes same sex marriage. I will have the most transparent administration in history. Lobbyists will not be a part of my administration. When a bill lands on my desk, the American people will have five days to review it before I sign it. I only learned about Veterans Affairs wait list by watching it on TV.

And the most egregious: I do solemnly swear that I will faithfully execute the Office of President of the United States, and will to the best of my ability, preserve, protect and defend the Constitution of the United States.

Thank you, President Obama, for spying on our emails!

June 21, 2014

We will never know if Obama would have won the 2012 presidential election had the conservative viewpoint not been silenced by the IRS. President Obama told Fox News political commentator Bill O'Reilly with a laugh that there was not a smidgen of corruption in the IRS. The congressional investigation committee asked for the IRS tax-exempt department head Lois Lerner's emails

264

over a year ago. This week we learned that the emails disappeared due to a computer crash. Fine, the emails can be recovered from the server. Alas, the server was reused and wiped clean. Fine, the emails can be recovered from the receiving end. Alas, unbelievably, the receivers of the emails lost their emails in the same computer crash.

The emails and our other social media correspondence have been recorded by our very own NSA, National Security Association. This is what we learned from NSA computer specialist contractor Edward Snowden who claimed that his sole motive for leaking surveillance program documents was "to inform the public as to that which is done in their name and that which is done against them." Snowden didn't realize at the time that this information will be used FOR us, not AGAINST us.

The IRS can claim that their emails are lost forever but according to Snowden, these emails may have been recorded and filed safely away by our very own NSA. Obama has been criticized for this privacy intrusion but now we can thank him for leading us to the truth about his involvement in silencing the opposing political party by the use of a federal agency for his own gain.

If Liberals Get Their Way

June 24, 2014

Obama is just a front man for the liberal ideology which he has bought hook, line and sinker. Liberalism is basically a belief that the uber educated know best about how everyone should live so they get to dictate to the rest of us how to live. Obama got elected on his smooth teleprompter-reading speaking voice and the perfect crease down his pant leg, not because of his description of the fundamental transformation of the United States. Had Obama claimed that he wanted to take opportunity away from the regular folk, Obama's description for the rest of us not included in his fellow ruling elite, he would have been describing liberalism. If liberals get their way in the form of a complete transformation, the following is our new world:

- Government will have complete say in our healthcare in the form of single payer government-run healthcare.
- We will be priced out of oil and gas for our cars and homes. The north will not be able to heat their homes in the winter and the south will not be able to cool their homes in the summer.
- Our children will be ingrained with government ideas through Common Core of group think instead of independent, critical thinking.
- Completely open borders will overrun social services and invite terrorists to live among us.

- Government will want more money until there is nothing left to give, 40%, 50%, 70% until your paycheck belongs to the government.
- Our military will be minimized, and our sovereignty will be in peril.
- We will be left with an unimpeded government because liberals will continue to use government agencies to silence any opposing view.
- Such a government will become more and more corrupt with power; it didn't get to this position honestly and will not rule honestly. You will not be able to vote them out.

One of Obama's first actions in DC was to discontinue the voucher system where poor black children were finally able to get a decent education and were thrown back into the inferior public schools. Does anyone have to ask where Obama sent his children? Liberals claim to care for young children and single women. This is but one example that clearly states their true intentions: keep the poor children down while handing their moms a welfare check. And keep the teachers' union money coming their way.

Conservatives do not cater to a specific group. They don't want gays, blacks, Latinos, single moms, and Millennials. Contrary to Democrat talking points, conservatives do want to take care of the needy. What conservatives care about are Americans. If any of these groups want to be catered to, they won't find it in conservatism. What they will find is the rule of law, constitutionally protected rights and unlimited opportunity to pursue dreams. A conservative government will never tell its people that they've had enough success. A conservative government will provide the opportunities to reach the American dream of owning a home, raising a family and enjoying the fruits of one's labors. It surely isn't to work to provide the government elite our tax dollars to do as they please.

JULY 2014

If I Don't Like You, I'm Going to Call You Racist

July 11, 2014

Obama's legacy is race-baiting political mobs. Dems call people names such as racist, homophobe or something equally disparaging as a tactical strategy to destroy someone. Call someone racist or homophobe, and he will be fired or at least ostracized. He will back down, for fear of consequences of false name-calling. How do we fight back against this strategy? Maybe we could ask for more details when someone/some group is called racist. Nah, that won't work, because the false name caller will make up false details. And, the destroy mob won't listen past the name calling, anyway. Once you are labeled, the target group has already decided it's true. Maybe we could start talking about the differences between racism and name-calling as a strategy. Sometimes, truth will make a difference. It is now common knowledge that name-calling is just a strategy- it does not matter whether it's true or not. The only outcome acceptable to the name callers is that they win by trashing someone's reputation and take out an opponent. Mother Teresa would not be safe in this environment.

Nothing's Fair in Obama Land

July 26, 2014

They cheered for Obama when he proclaimed that he was five days away from fundamentally transforming the United States of America. The transformation is right in front of anyone's eyes that are open. Our country is being flooded with illegal immigrants who are being shipped all over the states. Think shipping illegals to states and districts short on Democrat voters has any effect on elections? Democrats fight to end Voter ID laws. How can illegals partake in elections if they are required to prove their citizenship? In this new transformed America, aside from the flooding of immigrants, nothing is fair anymore. It isn't fair that some kids are smarter. It isn't fair that a Little League team is better than another team. It isn't fair that some people make more money. It isn't fair that everyone doesn't have a house. It isn't fair that blacks are jailed more than whites. And it sure won't be fair if illegals are denied the same rights as Americans.

Illegals have been dealt a poor deck while Americans have it easy. News to many Americans. Obama feels it is his job and duty to switch the decks rather than share what made America successful. And those less fortunate are pouring across our borders. Obama ignores immigration laws for Catch and Release. America's poor, minorities and Millennials must be asking themselves, "What about me, President Obama?" The cheering fools who helped elect him chanting Fair Share are now being neglected. Obama knows this better than anyone – America is the land of opportunity. He also knows that these fools squandered their opportunities and believed in someone who never believed in them.

Obama used his supporters to do what he set out to do, transform our country. This need for transformation makes no sense. Obama has been living the American dream, reaching successes and destinations that most only dream of. He was brought up with leftist hatred (Frank Marshall Davis) and sought out leftist hatred in college all the while enjoying the abundance that America offered him. The American people are finding out that by not appreciating the gift that is America that she may no longer exist for them.

United States of America in 2014

August 5, 2014

The United States of America's Declaration of Independence was signed 1776. Our country which started with 2.5 million people in 1776 is now 238 years young with 320 million people. It is incredible that in a little over 200 years that our country's citizens have invented electricity, automobiles, internet, smart phones and medical miracles. Where we are today is embarrassing and history will write us down as fools as having lost the greatest country ever.

What have we done lately? What are our accomplishments to brag on centuries from now? It seems like our only important achievement is that we have a black president with his fawning celebrities. Civil Rights Leader Martin Luther King is rolling in his grave as well as most past presidents. Take away the color of this president and judge him on his character and actions. We have a man who brags that he leads from behind on the world stage. We have a president who golfs with his buddies, headlines fundraisers and pretends that by eating a cheeseburger he's just a normal guy with no cares in the world. This is his facade for ignoring his position as leader of the superpower.

And it leaves the United States right where Obama said we belong – as no better than anyone else. Obama is dead wrong for he now betrays our allies and allows Muslim radicals and communist dictators to cause chaos in the world without restriction. Israel is fighting for her survival while the Obama administration supports Hamas financially and by decrying Israel's attack on children. Instead of building up our military strength during these dangerous times, Obama is firing thousands of army captains, majors and experienced senior military commanders and generals.

If an enemy wanted to destroy the United States of America, getting rid of our military commanders would be a great place to start. Strangers would also storm across our borders overwhelming our border agents, police and military. It is getting more and more difficult to enjoy everyday life knowing that soon we could lose our country all because a black man elected president does not like the United States.

Racist Cops of Ferguson, Missouri

August 17, 2014

We are to believe the race baiters that two black teens were walking down the middle of a street when a police officer told them to get to the sidewalk. The police officer started getting out of his car. Since he was too close to the teens, his door bounced off one of them. The officer got mad. While still in the car, the officer put Michael Brown in a headlock and shot the teen. Michael Brown put his hands up in surrender and yelled, "Hands up, don't shoot." The officer then proceeded to shoot the teen with ten bullets killing him.

Black citizens got mad and supposedly peacefully protested the police until cops turned up in military gear. The protest turned into looting and burning down a business. The storyline morphed into the teen who died was a gentle giant who was soon to head to college. Graffiti was sprayed that the only good cop is a dead cop. So, it all comes down to racist cops against blacks who receive no justice and no peace. In a civil society, evidence, truth and justice come forth in a court of law. In the race-baiting society that we have become with our president's urgings, the belief that white cops kill black teens overpowers any and all facts which are slowly emerging.

Michael Brown had committed a robbery an hour earlier of a box of cigars. A video shows the theft and Michael's strong-arm behavior toward the business owner. A police officer drove along two people walking down the middle of a street and told them to get out of the street. Common sense tells us that the officer would have told two green Martians the same thing. All Michael had to do was walk to the side of the street and the incident would have been over.

However, the officer did observe that the descriptions of Michael and his friend were those of the robbery. The officer's story is coming out that Michael charged him in the car, a fight ensued over his gun and the gun discharged. Michael taunted the officer with his hands in the air and asked him if he was going to shoot. The officer had the gun pointed at Michael. Here's where Michael had a second chance by keeping his hands in the air and taking his punishment for the robbery of a box of cigars. Instead, he charged the officer who he had just punched in the face and fought for his gun. The officer responded with gunfire and Michael ended up dead.

A week later and the protests and marches have grown. A dozen businesses have been vandalized and looted with over $5 billion in damages including a Walmart, AutoZone and a QuikTrip. The officer's story has no effect on the racist cop storyline. The officer is white. The professional race-baiters are ginning up the base of the Democrat Party by spreading the story of the racist white man keeping the black man down. All the while, generations of blacks have been kept down by the Democrat Party. Keep them on welfare, keep the schools dumbing down, get them smoking dope legally, promote their abortions, and most of all, keep the policies that tear into the family unit. If the black women don't need their black men, who does?

SEPTEMBER 2014

Golfing while the USA Burns

September 3, 2014

The modern equivalent to 'Fiddling while Rome burned' may soon be 'Golfing while the USA burns'. Obama has been receiving intel reports for the past year on the dangers of the growing Islamic terrorist threat. Two American reporters have been beheaded abroad and Obama openly admits that he has no strategy yet to combat this heinous threat. Obama has pretended long enough that this threat does not exist or that it's so far away, it couldn't possibly affect us. Islam extremists have taken over Tripoli International Airport and Obama has known for two weeks that commercial airliners are allegedly missing while the September 11 anniversary approaches.

Obama gave a speech yesterday Labor Day in his community organizer, rabble-rousing dialect. 'Gave' is over-generous. He ping-pong read the teleprompter as if he was reading it for the first time. He realizes he no longer has to waste time practicing his speeches for his base voters. In preacher mode, he said that watching TV is a downer these days and that the world is much less dangerous now than ever. If only Congress would help him, he can make companies pay higher wages. Notice to Obama: we Americans are sick of your schtick. You are a danger to the security of the USA and should have never been allowed near the White House.

If Sergeant Tahmooressi Was a Black, Deserting Gun Smuggler, He'd Be Free

September 6, 2014

Marine Sergeant Tahmooressi served two tours in Afghanistan and is now rotting in a Mexican prison since March 31, 2014, on weapons charges. A 911 call collaborates his story that he crossed the Mexican border accidentally with three registered guns. Our President brags about his power with the pen and phone. In this case, all Obama has to do to free him is to pick up the phone. This shameless president went to Mexico to meet with the Mexican president and did not mention our fellow marine.

Obama negotiated with terrorists to release five Guantanamo prisoners for one deserter who he then paraded around the White House. Obama stuck his black finger into the Ferguson mess to stir up racial tensions for a black thug who was killed for charging at an officer after he had already smashed in his eye socket. Obama stirred up an anti-gun campaign by his Mexican gunrunning scheme called Operation Fast and Furious. Two thousand guns were lost in this

270

operation sting, but some were traced back to the bodies of dead Mexicans and our own border agent. Obama can't find it in himself to help a non-deserter who fought for our country who is white and loves guns. This innocent man could rot in Mexico for years or until another Reagan comes along and demands his release.

Michelle O's Failure as a Nutrition Dominatrix Leads to Better Government

September 6, 2014

Michelle O's failure as a nutrition dominatrix is going to be Obama's main contribution to better government. Through all fault of her own ideology, she has made the government plan so awful that the people are choosing to drop the government handouts and do it themselves. That is called conservative government – not the awful part but the independent part. And the best part of her failure is that she has single handedly taught almost every public-school child in America what happens when the government becomes the dictator.

Michelle's policy stated that all schools participating in the free and reduced lunch program adhere to strict limits on fat, sugar, carbs and sodium. And the government money flows their way. She must have pictured in her mind that the good school children across our land would enjoy munching on cardboard while becoming slim and trim. She didn't consider before hoisting her menu upon our children that they wouldn't eat it because it tasted bad. Our children either went hungry or brought their own lunches. They learned to make their own peanut butter and jelly sandwiches. By not paying for the cardboard lunches which hurt school cafeteria budgets, schools are starting to drop her program.

Michelle wasn't happy to just ban the grilled cheese and pizza lunches. She also banned the fundraising bake sales, banned the Snapple and Coke vending machines and replaced vending chips with bags of edamame. Not only did snack sales reduce, the kids resorted to criminal snack behaviors becoming snack smugglers. By not paying for the cardboard lunches and in turn hurting school cafeteria budgets, schools are dropping her program foregoing the federal government handout and funding their own programs. Michelle's government failure is our government success. Teach the kids young and you have them for life.

271

The Murder of Brendan Tevlin by a Jihadist

September 18, 2014

Pelosi says that civilization as we know it today would be in jeopardy if Republicans win the Senate. This garbage came directly from the mouth of the leading United States House Democrat. Let's talk about Brendan Tevlin who has not been mentioned by our President or other Democrats who still cannot utter the phrase Muslim Terrorism.

Tevlin, a 19-year-old white college student of the University of Richmond, was sitting at a stoplight in New Jersey and was shot eight times, normally a sign of a targeted killing. His killer admitted to three other murders in Washington State to avenge the deaths of Muslims in the Middle East. There's another story of a teenager shot eight times in Ferguson, Missouri, and the media, community organizers and the President couldn't say enough about this particular incident. The story was totally perverted from a thug charging a police officer to white police officers shoot black men. Tevlin's murderer is a black Muslim and confessed to the random murder in the name of Allah.

Terrorism on our soil should be a main topic of discussion for our politicians. It's not. We are still told that Islam is a religion of peace. Obama plans to grant amnesty to illegals after the midterm elections. Terrorists have left evidence on the Mexican border that they are here. Democrats do not deserve to be in power on grounds of neglecting their duty to protect our country from terrorists. Before Obama throws a few bombs around in the Mideast, our own shores should be purged of anyone involved in radical Islam. Mosques and jails should be infiltrated, and radicals should be escorted from our country before they kill more innocent citizens. Brendan Tevlin will not have died in vain if we do whatever it takes to protect our civilization from terrorists. First, we must protect ourselves from Democrats. RIP, Brendan.

OCTOBER 2014

The Obama Presidency of Incompetents

October 1, 2014

Barack Hussein Obama is a superbly unqualified leader to be running the most powerful country in the world during these perilous times. Adding to the detriment of our safety and security, Obama is a consummate liar. Six years into his presidency, we find that everyone around him is also an incompetent, compulsive liar. This is not only difficult to listen to; it is supremely dangerous. While Ebola and Islamist terrorists are invading the world, we're told that neither is a threat to us, and we should stay calm and wash our hands.

The death of Osama bin Laden ten years after his terrorist plot of killing over 3,000 people on US soil led Obama to claim triumph that the Islamist terrorist group al Qaeda was dead. This ignorant statement can only be made from someone who doesn't understand leadership and basic group dynamics. A new leader will always step up from the lack of leadership. Obama's ideology led him to remove all US troops from Iraq against all recommendations and warnings from the military generals on the basis that we Americans are tired of war. Leaders do what is right – not lead on feelings and wishes that the war is over.

Obama's decision led to the rise of the Islamic State of Iraq and Syria (ISIS), a terror group known for slaughtering and beheading its enemies. Obama, in his detached way, said that ISIS is not Islamic. ISIS asked lone wolves to behead the enemy and shortly after, an Islamist convert beheaded a woman in Moore, Oklahoma, shouting Islamic phrases. The Obama administration will not declare that the terrorists we are fighting are Islamist, or that we are fighting a war against them.

On another front, Obama claimed that the deadly Ebola outbreak would not reach our shores. He then sent 3,000 of our troops into the heart of Africa where the Ebola outbreak is killing thousands of people. A Liberian traveled to Dallas, went to the hospital a week later, was sent home and returned by ambulance two days later infected with Ebola. We're told not to worry and that we should wash our hands. A major safeguard in quarantining arriving airplane passengers from infected areas was non-existent. Who knows what safeguards are in place for our troops. The competency of the Obama administration is questionable. Now the United States is on watch for Ebola cases to start spreading through our country.

Amnesty, Front and Center. Ya want it or not?

October 19, 2014

The thousands of innocent children crossing our borders from South and Central America have been welcomed and shipped all over our United States. Let's pretend this is the reason that hundreds of American children across the United States have gotten the enterovirus resulting in illness, paralysis or death. Let's pretend that one or more of the children and, let's be real, any of their relatives illegally crossing our borders with them, have Ebola or a third world disease. And this person is shipped to your neighborhood infected without anyone's knowledge and now attending your child's school. The danger of potential threats of deadly viruses should stop all Americans in their tracks to demand our borders close. The only teeny-tiny positive news out of the Ebola scare is that we're not hearing about ISIS 24/7. However, evidence of Muslim clothing and copies of the Quran have been found at our southern border. How's that amnesty support looking? The only option in our power to possibly stop amnesty is to vote Republican November 4, 2014.

There is absolutely no excuse for our President to be pushing amnesty unless he hates the American people and intends to keep one campaign threat – to fundamentally change America.

NOVEMBER 2014

Obamacare Architect Ridiculing the American People

November 15, 2014

Obamacare architect Jonathan Gruber, professor of economics at the Massachusetts Institute of Technology, is busted on video claiming that Obamacare passed because of the stupidity of the American people and their lack of economic understanding. Gruber stated on video that Obamacare would have never passed if people were told the truth. He claimed that anyone who understands economics would know that any taxes on insurance companies will be passed on to individuals. President Obama was aware of this each time he lied to the American people on keeping your doctor, your plan and saving $2500 per year. House Speaker Pelosi knew this when she said that we had to pass the bill to find out what is in it. Either the mainstream media are included in the stupid Americans or they were also aware of the truth. I'm going with stupid.

The American people were told a pack of lies so Obamacare could become the law of the land. It is designed for healthy people to pay for unhealthy people by the government redistributing the wealth, more like lack of wealth after six years of Obama-control. There are no built-in cost controls except to hold back on treatment decided by cost control bureaucrats. If your doctor tells you that you need X operation or you will die, Government Bureaucrat has the authority to tell you what your government dollars will or will not pay. In a sense, if you pay for your medical costs out of your pocket, you can keep your doctor. Even liars sometimes inadvertently tell the truth. To people who claim that their healthcare is just fine, most of the law has been delayed until 2018. That's also Gruber's point – the law will be imbedded by that time and nearly all employer sponsored plans will be taxed. Note: I found out post article that you cannot pay cash for your doctor because I asked when my doctor's office told me they no longer accepted my Obamacare insurance. And they would not take me as a patient without insurance.

It's All about the Skin Color in Ferguson

November 16, 2014

Can someone please tell the black agitators in Ferguson that we have a black president, a black attorney general, black generals in the military, etc? Don't they know the glass ceiling broke already? This outrage over cops killing blacks should be redirected to solving the problem of letting black (and white and every color in between) teenagers think they can smoke pot all day, steal things they want and get away with it without repercussions. Of course, cops should not kill innocent people. No one wants to hear that justice was already served. But when someone breaks the law and tries to take a gun from a policeman, charges at him, and then gets killed for that, what would you call it?

Note: Thomas Sowell recently wrote an article, and he is black, and he used the word black as a description, rather than African American. The black kid from The Cosby Show would rather be known as full blooded American, because that is where she was born. Since the race card is being used here, the major identifier/description happens to be skin color.

Ferguson Chaos Obama Lives For

November 22, 2014

Obama has had six years in the most powerful office and black communities have not improved. Our President purposely preys upon those stupid Americans that he and his administration have labeled as critical to their power causing unbearable grief upon a community. The opportunity presented itself on August 9 when Michael Brown was shot and killed by a white police officer in the town of Ferguson, Missouri. Had the legal system proceeded as law dictates and without interference from Obama and his attorney general Eric Holder, this incident would have gone down in history as a tragedy of one more black teenager killed in America. Obama could have called on young black men to obey the law and respect the police. He did the opposite.

The race-baiting crowd jumped at this incident without any regard for the facts. Ferguson is still overrun three months later by outside agitators including the Black Panthers, communist groups and Al Sharpton himself carrying a new title, Key Ferguson Obama advisor. The Black Panthers are advocating the killing of police officers and other white people; two members were arrested for purchasing pipe bomb explosives a day ago. Obama has the power to put an end to this phony outrage and violent protests, but instead, the violence and rhetoric are increasing as the Grand Jury decision nears.

America does not have a president. We have a racist thug taking up residence in the White House. He is a disgrace to the office inflicting untold damage on this country. The expected riots in Ferguson and beyond can rightfully be pinned on our President. The evil Obama lives for may all come to a head very shortly in Ferguson.

DECEMBER 2014

Anarchy Could Unleash Obama's Civilian National Security Force

December 1, 2014

The race-baiting has been amped up as predicted. Al Sharpton, Obama's key advisor for black and white relations, preached to a crowded church revving up the black community with a warning to whitey not to take off the gloves. He basically threatened whites all over this country that the black fight for justice is just beginning. He should have preached that anyone who roughs up a police officer, tries to grab the officer's gun, later charges at the officer, risks getting shot by the officer. Members of the Friendly Missionary Baptist church listened to very unfriendly preaching and the growing lie that Michael Brown was executed by a white officer while on his knees begging for his life.

The anarchy is spreading past Ferguson. Violent and non-violent protests have spread to cities all over our country leaving strong feelings of unease. Five members of the St. Louis Ram's football team came out onto the field with their hands up, a disgraceful act towards the police who work to secure the fans' and players' security and towards the fans who paid good money that pays their salaries. Malls were closed due to anarchists at the beginning of the holiday shopping season. The newest protest is the die in where large crowds of protesters lie down blocking paths and roads. Photographs have been posted online of bussed in crowds of paid protesters – these are Obama's anarchists that show up whenever, wherever to cause chaos.

This is President Obama's legacy as the first black president. His goal of tearing apart the United States is coming to fruition via the black thug who beat up a white police officer. Just maybe, Obama will finally have his anarchy across our nation that leaves him no choice but to call for the unleashing of his civilian national security force. This would be his private force as powerful as our army as promised in his July 2008 speech that would give him control over all of us.

The anarchists should be controlled and punished before they truly become unmanageable. In hindsight, Ferguson businesses should have hired private security guards who would have defended their properties. They unwisely depended on local and state government who stood down at the expense of private business. The aftermath could have been ugly but violent criminal behavior is unlawful and always ugly.

2014: The Year of the Stupidity of Americans

December 31, 2014

Obama's agenda continues to progress because of the stupidity of the American voter. How stupid are the American voters? So stupid that they don't even care that they are called stupid. The Gruber videos should have brought down the Obama administration, but the stupid Americans ignored the videos, accepted his apology for speaking off-the-cuff, or they possibly never saw the videos. Americans (stupid ones) who still rely on what has been known as mainstream media and 'comedians' definitely never saw the videos. This disgraceful media has been hiding the truth about the Obama agenda from day one.

Obamacare architect Gruber said it best. On the videos, he boasts that passage of Obamacare depended on the stupidity of the American voter. The law would have never passed had Obama admitted that the law required a huge tax on the middle class. Gruber boasted that Obamacare's main tax is an "exploitation of the lack of economic understanding of the American voter." Obama claimed that there would be no taxes on the middle class, just a Cadillac tax on business. Alert to stupid Americans, who do you think is going to pay this tax and who do you think pays for all those who get free Obamacare health insurance? Answer is you. Money does not appear magically to pay for doctors, nurses and hospitals.

The same time that Obama was touting the Affordable Care Act, Obama was told by Gruber that you cannot mandate insurance that's affordable. The ONLY way to control costs would be to deny treatment. Obama got around that with another little white lie – tell patients that surgery doesn't do any good so if you really want it, you have to pay full cost. Anyone recall Sarah Palin talking about Death Panels? Here you are. In Gruber's own words back in 2009, "I'm amazed politically that we got this bill through."

JANUARY 2015

Obama and Muslim America

January 16, 2015

The Islamic State has vowed to conquer America and our President welcomes the Muslim Brotherhood into OUR White House. We hear about Obama working with CAIR and promoting mainstream Muslims. CAIR sounds so

277

caring, but a little research shows that the acronym stands for Council on American-Islamic Relations, a group with ties to Islamic terrorism. Obama's attorney general Holder has busily fought local ordinances to favor Muslim infiltration. An all-American town 30 miles south of Nashville fought the building of the Islamic Center of Murfreesboro but lost. Now stands a mega mosque in a town of 100,000 citizens of which 25,000 are now Muslim. Research on the number of mosques within the United States is difficult to find. I've read anywhere from 1200 to 2000, 80% built in the last decade.

Since 2011, the FBI no longer has permission to monitor mosques for radicalism. Surveillance of mosques has proven successful in preventing terrorist attacks but is prohibited by Dictator Obama. These next two years will be a trying time for America, as her leader has claimed that the Muslim call to prayer is the prettiest sound on earth. When we start hearing the Muslim call to prayer, I fear the United States is in the Muslim takeover phase from the inside. I found out that Hamtramck, a town near Detroit, Michigan, has been hearing the call five times a day for the past decade.

Lies and more lies are what we hear from our President about Islam. It is Obama who slipped in an interview and said, 'my Muslim faith.' It is Obama who said that Islam has always been a part of America. It is the Islam faith that states that a son of a Muslim man is Muslim of which Obama's father was a Muslim. Above all, Muslims can lie to non-Muslims. From an informative website thereligionofpeace.com, "There are two forms of lying to non-believers that are permitted under certain circumstances, *taqiyya* and *kitman*. These circumstances are typically those that advance the cause of Islam - in some cases by gaining the trust of non-believers in order to draw out their vulnerability and defeat them."

No Empty Chairs for Clint Eastwood

January 19, 2015

Clint Eastwood, director of *American Sniper*, filled cinemas with a record-breaking January weekend set to pull in over a $100 million. *American Sniper* has more patriotism in two hours than seen by President Obama in six years. The script was being written before the ending which I will not reveal. Cowboy wannabe Chris Kyle joined the United States Navy SEALs after 9/11 to protect and serve our country.

In a foreshadowing event, Kyle's dad explains that there are three types of people: the sheep, the wolf and the sheepdog. He said to never be the wolf. Kyle became the protective sheepdog and became known as Legend with 160 confirmed kills in the Iraq War. When asked if he ever regretted killing so many, he said that he did it to protect his marines and only regretted the lives he could

278

not protect. His conscience was clear because he killed evil. In contrast, Hollywood's mindset and the liberal elite question if we should be celebrating a killer.

Eastwood's filled seats bring us back to his empty chair speech at the 2012 National Republican Convention. Instead of a boring, scripted teleprompter speech, he got three points across: not everyone in Hollywood is on the left, Obama broke a lot of promises, and people should feel free to get rid of any politician who's not doing a good job. He accomplished this by speaking to a stool which represented an invisible Obama. He was excoriated by the Hollywood left and the liberal elite for being an old, out of touch, rambling white guy. Eastwood was 82 years old at the time and considered himself to be the average Joe Citizen.

Now age 84, Eastwood is obviously not an out of touch, rambling white guy with his hit *American Sniper*. Following the terrorist attack in a Parisian concert hall where 130 were murdered, Obama has proven himself wholeheartedly to be out of touch. His advice to prevent terrorist attacks is for Europe to better assimilate Muslims. Wolves are never going to be nice to sheep.

FEBRUARY 2015

Republicans Should Show Obama's Transparency

February 2, 2015

Candidate Obama harped on our $9 trillion debt and promised to cut it in half. Now he's sending Congress his annual budget for 2015 totaling $4 trillion which will result in our debt closing in on $20 trillion. Republicans should be the bearers of transparency and present this budget to the people and ask for our input. We should be asked how we feel about Obama's request to spend $4 trillion of our hard-earned tax dollars. Let Obama find out how we feel by watching TV as he has claimed on other pertinent issues. What an embarrassment and disaster to the United States. I hope one day we will find out what was so important to increase our debt by $11 trillion.

Living Through the Worst President Ever

February 6, 2015

Congratulations are in order. We get to witness and are living through the worst president ever of the United States. Business owners are getting crapped on because they want to make a profit and provide for their own families and employees. They did not realize that they are also to provide for every illegal

279

and third world person who crosses our border. Students are getting crapped on because they wade through the new history of self-defeatists. Instead of learning how great our country is, they are learning the leftist progressive view on how horrible we (and they included) are. Our military is being crapped on at every turn. Our worst threat is Islamic terrorism and yet the most despicable Islamic leaders are let out of Guantanamo prison. Is our military supposed to go back out risking lives to recapture these terrorists when they reenter the war?

Sane people will say that Obama broke the last straw off the camel's back yesterday when he compared the burning alive of the Jordanian pilot to the Christian Crusades. The king of Jordan started immediately bombing ISIS targets. When the latest of one of ours was beheaded, our President spoke a few platitudes and minutes later was playing golf, makes for a very introspective video. The Islamic threat to our lives and the civilized world is staring us in the face, yet our President threatens about global warming and the need to close the terrorist prison. Unforgivably, Obama is attempting to minimize the danger by claiming that a thousand years ago Christians protected themselves by committing atrocities. Then again, if the call to Muslim prayer is the most beautiful sound on earth as Obama has said, maybe we should all be Muslim. That would be quite a transformation of the United States as candidate Obama promised.

Obama and his Peaceful Diplomacy

February 26, 2015

ISIS continues to behead foreigners, enslave young girls and massacre Christians. Obama's response is that we need peaceful diplomacy. And this is how I picture Obama's diplomacy: Obama sits at the head of a boardroom table speaking of the ills in the world and how his guests must account for their own fault in Mideast terror. Obama speaks about the peace-loving Muslims never touching on the topic of Islamic terrorists. Obama asks for input, disagreements, anything. Silence follows and he ends his professorial dissertation with, "Now that's how you have peaceful diplomacy. Thank you." Then he heads to the golf course with the Muslim Brotherhood after a brief press conference declaring the success of his international peaceful diplomacy. His administration cleans up the boardroom and removes his guests: the decapitated heads of American James Foley, Japanese Kenji Goto, Ghanaian Matthew Ayariga, French Herve Gourdel, British David Haines and a couple of Egyptian Coptic Christians.

Corruption's the Problem, Not Capitalism

March 10, 2015

Capitalism is fundamental to the American dream. Corruption is killing it. Democrats have convinced the uninformed, Millennials, and Occupying types to believe that capitalism equals greed. Ask them what they think, and they will repeat that word for word. Capitalism is our successful economic system which is the opposite of socialism. Capitalism provides a free marketplace for goods and services with the added benefit of careers in all aspects of industry: clerical, shipping, manufacturing, development, engineering, management, technology, marketing, sales and supply. No one has ever mistaken a communist country such as Cuba of being an economic powerhouse. No American citizen has ever abandoned homeland US on a homemade raft to live the Cuban dream.

Any and every economic system is fertile ground for greed, for it is in human nature. Greed can be found in the capitalist system which is based on a profit motive because the system builds wealth. Business owners' dreams do not include doling out profits to line the pockets of politicians. Take the auto industry in Detroit, formerly nicknamed Motor City, the original home of the Big Three auto manufacturers. The city of Detroit is a failed city. The capitalist auto industry did not fail due to the greed of CEO's. Its failure, along with the city of Detroit, can be blamed on the greedy union officials and politicians with their corrupt policies, demands, fraud and outright thievery.

Following the money in politics is a must to figure out agendas. This is true for individual industry regulations and for Democrat pet causes of abortion, global warming carbon credits, and pot legalization. The wordsmith marketing of killing babies, getting your kids high, and raising energy rates and taxes has attracted loyal supporters. And in all these, corrupt politicians crave the power and money that go hand in hand.

The continual beating of drums against capitalism is paving a way towards communism. Don't believe for a second that it is about fairness for everyone. It is the corrupt politicians' paths to unheard of wealth for themselves who see the hard work of capitalists and their employees as a power grab. Once in charge, the politicians steal the wealth until it runs out. Ever wonder why communist countries turn into third world hellholes with wealthy communist leaders?

Minorities Should Open Their Eyes

March 30, 2015

President Ronald Reagan said it best, "…the nine most terrifying words in the English language are I'm from the government and I'm here to help." The Democrat Party has the reputation of standing up for the little guy and helping fight against the evil Republicans. Liberal progressive policies sound like they are helping minorities, but history has shown that it is precisely these policies that have hurt minorities. Minorities need to open their eyes as to what is behind the helpful sounding government policies and their effects.

Take the minimum wage law, for example. In his recent article 'Ruinous Wage Compassion', economist Thomas Sowell wrote about the first minimum wage laws in the construction industry with the Davis-Beacon Act of 1931. The law was to prevent contractors from basing their bids on cheap labor, guarantee fair competition and protect workers with higher wages. Sounds great so far. Sowell pointed out that whites only unions were losing federal public works projects to contractors that had black workers who were paid less. Instead of lowering their wages to compete in the free market, unions pushed the minimum wage law. The contractors with the black workers could no longer bid competitively and the blacks were out of jobs. The whites only unions got the jobs and could continue to pay artificially higher wages while bragging about them.

The same scenario is playing out right now with calls for protecting workers with higher wages. Many minorities are working in the food industry which averages 1 to 3% profit margins with about one third of budgets going to labor. When businesses such as restaurants are forced to increase their labor budgets, they offset this business expense with additional revenue, often raising prices and by reducing entry level jobs. If customers refuse to pay the higher prices, the restaurants close and the jobs are gone.

Liberal progressives have a way of marketing their policies to sound favorable while fully aware of the detrimental effects. Their policies have focused on abortions, legal pot, free apartments for young women with children and without husbands, expanding welfare and cancelling education vouchers. History shows that these policies have been devastating to the minority communities socially, morally, economically and educationally. There is no reason for minorities to be living negligible lives when America has so much to offer. It starts with the realization that liberal progressive government hurts them and that the alternative is conservatism.

APRIL 2015

We Have Found the Weapon of Mass Destruction

April 1, 2015

If you take the time to look around and see what is happening, you will notice the devastation left by Obama's community organizing, policies, and leadership. Devastation is all over American towns. Police officers shot point blank, blacks playing the knockout game (physically knock down white people), a zoo, state fairs and malls closed on account of mob violence, Republican governors disparaged over fake grievances, and a dozen dead, 31 wounded at Fort Hood by a Muslim US Army Major. The most notable change to America is the influx of foreigners and Obama's policies of spreading the poor around our country. Could this be the cause of a dozen American children dead from third-world diseases? Obama's fight to end Voter ID is directly correlated to an increase in votes for Democrats. Obama always hedges his bets and gets away with blaming voter suppression on Republicans. See, those crazy Republicans think only citizens should vote, and a requirement to vote should be a Voter ID.

Obama's devastation abroad is as abhorrent: four dead Americans at our Libyan embassy, sending community organizers to Israel with the goal of ousting Israeli Prime Minister Netanyahu, and after failing, Obama leaked Israeli secrets to her enemies, and Obama claiming the killing of Osama bin Laden as his victory which will always belong to US Navy SEAL Team Six. One month later, thirty Americans, mostly members of US Navy SEAL Team Six, were killed in an ambush, likely aided by the leak from the Obama administration. The spread of ISIS is on Obama's hands, and with his open border policy, we have no idea who is illegally crossing our borders. Abroad, ISIS has been responsible for the massacre of Christians, other minority religions and anyone non-Shiite. Presently, Obama is farting around with the Iranians who do not play community organizing games when it comes to nuclear proliferation. And this is not the end of Obama's terror. We have found the weapon of mass destruction and it is Obama.

Millennial Malaise

April 7, 2015

A common phrase I hear from Millennials is that it's all good. Millennials have no idea how liberal policies have invaded our lives and country or they really don't care. I have been told by a Millennial that politics has no effect on her life personally. I was twenty once, also, with the same thinking. In reality, it is politics that have shaped mindsets and guided our paths in life. Many have the attitude that there really isn't a great future for them. This malaise has been ingrained in them ON PURPOSE politically by a leftist mindset based in communism, a community-based mindset over individual independence.

Increasing policies and regulations touch every aspect of everyday living: how the internet runs, what is promoted on social media, healthcare, pricing of consumer goods and to the simple - banning of cheap light bulbs and how long a shower to take. Politics determines how much government control over our lives that we are willing to tolerate. A leftist government will touch on things we cannot imagine such as the air we breathe.

Millennials need to know that if they had moral guideposts with strong backbones and beliefs, the constant political marketing ploys would have little effect on them. For example, young girls have dreamed of having their own families one day after falling in love and getting married. The goal is to leave their parents' rule, become independent and form their own family units as a mommy and daddy raising their own children. Millennials have been corrupted into believing that marriage is nothing more than a piece of paper. Strong family units have morphed into unwed mothers and derelict fathers. Somewhere along the line, the family unit has become whatever you want it to be and "It's all good." This didn't just happen on its own.

That line, where the political progressives moved in with their ideology and invaded the young girls' dreams of a stable family life, was crossed. It started with promoting the 60's free-for-all sex, abortions, divorces on demand, two mommies, etc. The radical feminism was a political agenda which diminished the family and the need for husbands or men in general. The norm of the stable family unit was mocked and discarded as old-fashioned. Women were told to go out and get their power jobs and leave the raising of their kids to someone else. Democrat policies embraced these changes and provided the condoms promoting sex out of marriage, legalized the abortions, promoted daycare and provided the path to living as single moms. The Democrat progressives continue to provide the means for people to stay home collecting welfare benefits and smoke pot all day, truly generating wasted lives that will never stand up to a growing, powerful government.

The alternatives for Millennials to leave this negativity and malaise are to purposely lead conservative lives and find the best conservative candidates for office. The progressive left is leading our country into communal living, communal transportation, centralized government rule, nationalizing business, taxing anything they can get away with, and eroding hard-fought constitutional rights. Millennials have fallen for this garbage and actively support it. The liberal catch phrases such as humanist, diversity, social justice and fairness are all based in communism. The Democrat party that is now led by liberal progressives wants a communist America. If this sounds foreign, study the history of Cuba and Venezuela. Read up on George Orwell's *Nineteen Eighty-Four* and Ayn Rand's *Atlas Shrugged*. Politics is all about accumulating power

284

and we may still have the right to vote in the type of power that made America great. However, when a country has purposely been invaded by illegals, handed freebies and allowed to vote, we can end up living in a one-party rule that tosses out our rights along with the Constitution. Once freedom is lost to a dictator government, we cannot just vote freedom back.

MAY 2015

Why I Haven't Written in a While

May 11, 2015

What more is there to say about President Obama and his destruction of our country? For a couple of weeks, I tried to avoid any news and enjoy my life and my family and experience the goodness and competence of our local hospital due to a family member's surgery. My daughter is in competitive golf with high hopes of playing college golf, my son is excited about leading his brass section in his ROTC band and searching for the right college and my husband is growing junior golf in the area. I have an idyllic life. And then in the background is a grumbling of our country falling apart.

I hear the news: our First Lady stoking the racist flames, police shot in multiple cities, the burning of Baltimore by black thugs, war preparation of China, Islamist jihadists in our country and a flattened football. I expect no good news coming out of the Obama administration. His term cannot end soon enough – January 2017. I just hope our country survives this President and his purposeful destruction, because our country and individual citizens are just plain the best.

Proof of Obama's and Hillary's Lies. Anyone offended?

May 20, 2015

Long-awaited emails are trickling in thanks to FOIA, the Freedom of Information Act. The emails clearly state that ten days prior to the attack killing our Benghazi ambassador, the administration knew that a revenge attack was imminent. Obama and Hillary did nothing to protect our ambassador, and when he was killed, the unbelievably idiotic story may have already been concocted that a YouTube video-maker made Muslims mad causing the attack.

Obama lied because he must have thought Americans would connect the dots that his foreign leadership decisions led to the four Americans dying in Benghazi. If Americans knew the truth, they might not want him president. Ditto for Hillary. If Americans connected the dots on her response to the 3am telephone call to action and that she failed to act, they would not want her as president of their country either. Her advertisement from her failed presidential campaign asked us who we want answering the White House phone at 3am. Truth is, their supporters and the media would not have cared less about the truth. If Obama and Hillary were so fearful that if Americans knew the truth that they were unelectable, then just maybe they should not be president. Our President is a proven liar about American deaths. Hillary is also a proven liar and Americans can keep her from becoming president.

The unavoidable truth is that Obama has lied to the American people plenty: the stimulus, the student loans, the shovel-ready jobs, Obamacare and Islamic terror. Obama had to lie to the American people to get passage of the bills. His Obamacare consultant Gruber was caught on video claiming how stupid Americans are and confirmed that the healthcare bill would not have passed had Americans been told the truth. But Obama named it 'Affordable Healthcare Act' and claimed that he was just trying to help us, and it passed. Private lenders have been kept out of the student loan business. And his naïve, avid supporters claim that Obama is trying to help but those darn Republican obstructionists are making it hard for him.

If you are not offended, you might want to look in the mirror and ask yourself why you don't mind being lied to or called stupid. Both are stupendously offensive. Obama and his wife keep pulling the racist cards hoping to keep Americans quiet, at least through 11:59am January 20, 2017. Americans are waking up to the dangers of a growing, all intrusive government along with the dangers of an inept president. These Americans are just hoping to survive the Obama years.

JUNE 2015

With Regulations Come the Compliance Check Inspections

June 23, 2015

The FDA has spent close to $200 million since 2010 on compliance check inspections for underage tobacco purchases. A pack of cigarettes is just one product under the FDA's authority of compliance check inspections. And the FDA is not the only agency responsible for compliance checks. There are generally two responses to these checks. 1) It's good to keep cigarettes from being sold to those under 18 and 2) that's a lot of taxpayer money wasted on an unnecessary program.

Business owners are not purposely selling cigarettes to anyone under 17, not because it's the law but because no mom or dad wants to see 10-year-olds smoking. But the FDA program cannot hire 10-year-olds to purchase cigarettes. The legal minimum age to work is 16 so these purchasers of cigarettes for the

286

FDA are 16 or 17, many of which look beyond the legal age of 18 to purchase. Many businesses have been or are going to be receiving letters stating that they illegally sold to minors and either receive a warning letter, a fine, or lose their permits to sell cigarettes.

A liberal, progressive government is the nanny state. With this present administration and its ever encroaching nannyism, taxpayers are forking over a lot of their paychecks for government garbage. And plenty of this garbage works against the taxpayer. This nonsense has to stop. We can take a stand and vote it out or it can fizzle out on its own because in the end, our government will be bankrupt. And teens will continue attempting to purchase cigarettes before turning age 18, that is unless they turn to legal marijuana if it is easier and cheaper to buy. Easy access to pot is another story – why would a government want wasted potheads in its citizenship?

What to Do with the Supreme Court Verdicts

June 27, 2015

Subsidies remain for Obamacare despite wording of the law. I hope the proposed bill by Representative Babin called SCOTUScare Act passes: The Supreme Court justices and their employees should be forced to enroll in Obamacare. Let's go further. Congress and their employees and Michelle Obama should be pressured to enroll in Obamacare. When that doesn't work, they should be nudged and eventually forced to get their health insurance through the federal exchanges. It is unseemly that the people foisting this horrid law on the American people have exempted themselves from it. This would lead to the expeditious road of repeal, unless its self-destruction comes first.

Announced today, gay marriage is the law of the land. I am sure a lot of nice same-sex couples are thrilled that they can be called married. Now that gay marriage has become a law, it is time for the Church to stand up for the Sacrament of Marriage reserved for a husband and a wife. Divorce lawyers will soon be busy with gay couples.

Here's the tricky part of gay marriage. Lesbian gay marriage activist Masha Gessen states on video what is behind the fight for gay marriage. It is to redefine the traditional family and to end the institution of marriage. "The institution of marriage shouldn't exist." This woman is filled with vengeance for anything traditional and fighting to destroy the family and goes hand in hand with Obama's promise/threat to change our history and our traditions.

287

Ya catching on to what the transformation of America is all about?

July 11, 2015

Obama did not lie to us about his fundamental transformation of America and changing our history and traditions. It's not enough that slavery was abolished in 1865 and that blacks have had the rights to life, liberty and the pursuit of happiness granted in the Constitution for 150 years. A segment of society wants to erase all history of the confederacy. Statues, monuments, and flags should come down. Street and school names should change. Talk includes changing the name of our country's capital Washington, DC, because George Washington owned slaves. My prediction is that Mount Rushmore will be blown up and reduced to a pop culture monument. If progressives get their way, it will be rainbow colored less anyone forget about gayness and sexual deviancy screwing over marriage.

On the rainbow front, traces of Christianity are fading. Public school children already have Winter Break, no longer Christmas vacation. Parental forms will no longer ask for names of mother and father because that would offend the gay couples. Future marriage licenses will no longer have husband and wife because that would offend the gay couples. The term husband and wife will become offensive. Marriage can no longer be assumed to be man and wife. Businesses will have to change their couple events to be inclusive. Children will be forced to learn that gay families are just like the traditional Christian family. I know Millennials who are supporters of gay marriage despite their religious affiliations stating that it is wrong. Why follow religion when everything is about feeling good and just? America is being transformed and will continue down this path as long as our citizens fall for the progressive rhetoric. The only alternative is voting in true conservatives.

Aborted Babies Butchered for Baby Parts

July 23, 2015

Planned Parenthood's Director of Medical Services describes how she is able to butcher babies to preserve their baby parts in order to sell them, livers being the most desirable. THIS IS TRULY INDEFENSIBLE. Abortion has been OKed because the thing being destroyed is not a baby but just baby tissue. How on earth can baby parts be harvested for resale if the thing being destroyed is not a baby itself? Well, the liberal elites are still attempting to defend abortion as a woman's right. Ladies, it is time to stop buying into the lies of abortion. A beating heart is stopped. Your rights end when someone else's begins. How does this not make sense?

Young and older ladies have supported the abortion industry because they have been programmed to believe that a baby growing inside of their bodies isn't a baby at all. I'm not even sure if they buy this argument – I think they just appreciate the ability to get rid of a problem or embarrassment without thinking about guilt. Those who vote Democrat for their social values are now condoning the selling of baby parts. Why not use aborted babies to make a few more bucks? They just get thrown out with the trash or incinerated to help generate power. Yup, that also is true here in America.

The Middle Class Is Shrinking to Becoming the Lower Middle Class

July 23, 2015

Obama's government is destroying the middle class. I visited a friend today and was greeted by a foreclosure notice on the front door, one less family able to continue a middle-class life in today's America. It is not surprising, considering the major costs for the middle-class life.

$1500 mortgage on an average home of $200,000 accompanied by $2,400 property tax, $2400 home insurance, $2000 flood insurance

$800 monthly car payments for a two-car family accompanied by $2,800 annual auto insurance

$8,200 private school tuition for one child

$12,000 Obamacare mandated health insurance accompanied by $10,000 deductible

$500 monthly cell phone, cable, internet and electricity

Total Annual Expenses for a Middle-Class Family:

- $18,000 Home
- $12,400 Auto
- $8,200- $16,400 Private School for two children   .
- $12,000-$22,000 Health Care
- $6,000 Cell, Cable, Internet & Electricity

$56,600 is needed to live the middle-class life in America. When the mortgage is paid, the total lowers to $38,600 annually. Another $10,000 is needed for electricity, gas and food. An income of $50,000 gross, $60,000-$75,000 net, is needed to make it in the middle-class. To survive these times of layoffs and job eliminations, struggling families need to cling on to the lower middle class, never give up hope of improving their lot, and keep on keeping on: downsize, budget reduction and increase income – whatever it takes to avoid joining the welfare state. The middle class cannot be lowered to the welfare state which would cause an eventual destruction of our economy and country. America needs to survive the Obama years.

AUGUST 2015

Rubio, a Politician, Finally Said It

August 17, 2015

Republican presidential candidate Marco Rubio finally said something about abortion that I have wanted a politician to say. All life in-utero should be protected, including the innocent babies conceived by rape. Most politicians parrot what pop culture comes up with such as abortion is OK if... People who believe that abortion is wrong should believe that it is wrong in all cases.

It is time to educate the public that what they have been conditioned to believe about abortion is not only wrong, but morally inhumane. What has been accepted is pure marketing lingo, women's rights and a choice. A child of rape is as good as a nothing. This political season is the time to bring on the Planned Parenthood videos along with a video of an abortion. I prefer a simulation, but I assume the real footage is available.

People are not stupid, but they are lazy. They have been too accepting of liberal garbage without having to think and learn. The surgery by itself is gruesome. A doctor who has taken the Hippocratic Oath takes instruments to dig a live baby out of a mother's womb. It can take a strong suction to break up the baby parts, a scalpel to puncture the head and now it takes a skilled surgeon to keep the baby as intact as possible so the baby parts can be sold, almost like delivering a live baby. The surgeons in the videos talk about baby parts, not fetus parts.

Ask liberals if they would ever consider aborting growing puppies in their doggies and you won't get an answer. It is too gruesome to consider dead puppies. But ask about abortion in general, and the answer you'll get is blah blah about choice, fetus or women's rights. They were obviously never taught that their rights end when someone else's begins. Thank you, Marco Rubio.

Republican and Democrat Parties Stumped by Trump

September 8, 2015

Republican presidential candidate Donald Trump continues to lead the polls for the GOP Presidential nomination. Not surprising that the Democrat bashing of Trump has begun along with the Republican guard trying to expedite his downfall waiting to pour money into Republican presidential candidate Jeb Bush, brother of former president George W. Bush. So far, Trump has stumped both.

Not so for conservatives and a growing contingent of blacks and others usually uninterested in politics. Trump attracts attention, talks bluntly and has never backed down from the sycophant media. We have learned that Trump will not allow the Democrats to lead the conversation. Trump leads the polls because he has proven leadership qualities. We conservatives can picture our country heading away from disastrous liberal progressive policies.

The GOP has won election after election ignoring most every pledge made to its constituents. The Republican congress and Republican-backed judges have backed down from fighting Obama's policies and lawless executive orders. We conservatives are sick of this. We will not stand for a Republican Party candidate who is wishy-washy when it comes down to basic conservative beliefs. We will not vote for Jeb who has sided with open borders and Board of Education's Common Core. Carly tripped over conservatism with her comments on real climate change. Carson's view on more government-regulated healthcare ending private health insurance companies is anti-conservative.

Conservatives are happy to have Trump attract attention away from the false Democrat promises. The Democrat Party will look foolish claiming to be the party for the middle class and workers when it is Trump who has generated the very jobs that allow workers to be middle class. As Trump attracts Obama voters to see and understand conservatism, they too will see and hear another Republican presidential candidate, conservative, Ted Cruz.

Has Obama committed treason with Iran Nuclear Agreement?

September 12, 2015

Treason is a violation of allegiance to one's sovereign country. Obama's Iran Nuclear Agreement strengthens the world's most dangerous terrorist organization and accepts Iran's word that they will not build nuclear weapons for ten years. Iran has called for the death of America for years and is a fervent supporter of ISIS, the group responsible for mass executions, beheadings and calling for attacks on our soil. The agreement grants Iran production of intercontinental ballistic missiles, recognition on the national stage as a peaceful nuclear nation, and access to $150 billion. Obama declared that the $150 billion economic boost would increase Iran's nefarious activities and anticipates such activity to benefit under the nuclear agreement. Obama refuses to use the word terrorism which is exactly what he means.

Unbelievably, the billions of dollars aiding terrorism are not the worst of it. Political commentator Charles Krauthammer's September 10, 2015, column cites the agreement's provision that commits our nuclear experts to teach Iran on how to protect against sabotage through training courses and workshops. It also states that should Israel attempt a cyber attack on Iran's nuclear abilities, we will work with Iran to stop Israel from protecting herself. How is it not treasonous to support Iran who supports ISIS, both of whom are intent on destroying America?

Hillary's Right about Something: It Is Time for a Woman President

September 17, 2015

Republican presidential candidate Carly Fiorina would make an excellent president of the United States. She will not waste time defending her looks nor will she entertain political correctness in replacing a man's face for a woman's face on the ten-dollar bill. Carly understands that our nation is failing in character and will not allow any corporation to kill babies on her watch and treat them as a chop shop. She dares Obama and Hillary to view video footage of a live baby, heart beating and all, about to be harvested for his or her brain. See, Obama has said that God has blessed this company called Planned Parenthood and Hillary continues to cheer on said company despite video proof of baby butchery happening across the United States. Abortion is no longer a Democrat or Republican issue; it is the scourge of our nation.

The pundits are already coming after Carly as aloof and uncaring because of her strength. Her strength comes from her experiences. She has lived the American dream from being a secretary to becoming a CEO of a multinational corporation. She has experienced the effects of drug and alcohol addiction on a family ending with the knock on her door of two policemen informing her of her daughter's death. She has experienced reconstruction surgery from a double mastectomy. She is a serious candidate and truly a person who, like Donald Trump, is a citizen and leader not of the political class. Hillary is right: the time has come for a woman president; she is wrong in thinking the United States needs a lying, political hack like herself. It can be Carly Fiorina's time.

Trump Got the Muslim Question – The Presidency Is His if He Wants It

September 20, 2015

Republican presidential candidate Trump had a question and answer session in which a concerned United States citizen stated that we have a Muslim problem. The citizen went on to say that our current president isn't even a Christian. His ultimate question pertained to training camps and how they want to kill us. Trump is under fire from the pundits on all sides for not stating that Obama is a good Christian. Hillary naturally went into a tirade about Republicans and their hateful, untrue rhetoric. Republican presidential candidate Christie stated that he would have corrected the US citizen that Obama is a Christian. Also, Republican presidential candidate Marco Rubio said that he, too, believes that Obama is a Christian because he said so.

Those responses knock Christie and Rubio out of the presidential race. Here are two worthy political candidates for president who do not get the Muslim issue. Fact one is that Obama was born of a Muslim father. Fact two is that children of a Muslim father are, by birth, Muslim. Obama penned a book called Dreams from My Father – A story of race and inheritance. Never does it mention that a dream of his Muslim father was for his son to denounce Islam and convert to Christianity.

Islam is a tricky governmental religion all tied into one – the religion cannot be truly separated from its government. It is by its nature anti-American. By law, Muslims are allowed to lie to infidels in order to defeat them and to advance the cause of Islam. Muslims even have a fancy word for this type of lying called Taqiyya. The biggest lie that Americans have heard repeatedly is that Islam is a religion of peace. What is happening in the Mideast is the opposite of peace – mass killings, beheadings, and rapes ad nauseam. The refugee crisis has become a Muslim invasion on non-Muslim countries. Muslim leaders are calling for the raping of non-Muslim women. Children from these rapes, again by law, are Muslim.

If Trump answers to the concern of American citizens honestly about Muslims, he will absolutely become our next president. Americans with their eyes open are seeing the Muslim invasion here in our country with the help from President Obama. Christianity and Islam do not mix and never will.

Trump Has Failed on Muslim Political Correctness

September 21, 2015

According to TV media, Republican presidential candidate Trump has committed Muslim PC failure. Progressives expect and come close to

293

demanding that Trump make a statement on Obama's Christianity. Trump said that he will not defend Obama. The liberal progressives including TV media will remain flummoxed when the polls rise for Trump. The media ignored the concerned citizen's question on Muslim training camps within our borders. An internet search on most search engines (Google is questionable) results in information on Islamic training camps, now up to 35, within our borders that the FBI has known about for decades.

Concerned citizen is correct. We have a Muslim problem. I have noticed that many gas stations around town are now owned and run by Muslims, abandoned strip malls are now homes to Muslim community centers and that run-down areas are becoming Muslim enclaves. Sharia law has become an issue in cities across the United States, some voting it as lawful, others not, some voting to ban foreign law, some not. The largest enclave of Muslims in the United States is Dearborn, Michigan, where 30% of its 98,000 population is Muslim. The city council has voted in Sharia Law 4-3. For Trump to claim that Obama is a Christian has absolutely nothing to do with our Muslim problem. We just need Obama out of office and a real man or woman that will stand up for our Constitution.

OCTOBER 2015

My Ideal Presidential Candidate

October 3, 2015

I would like to believe that we will have a fair election come November 2016 and my vote will count. That depends largely on illegals and their illegal voting permissible by the Obama administration and fraudulent voting like the dead. Howsoever, I continue to dream of my ideal presidential candidate who will be a true leader, believe in America and her Constitution, and respect all American citizens. My candidate will:

- Turn the political system on its head – no more wealthy front groups determining our political candidates without transparency

- End nonprofits such as Planned Parenthood – tax dollars will no longer fund businesses that in return funnel money back to the politicians or line their own pockets
- Defund the ridiculous – no more tax money on politicos' pet causes that a private investor would never consider

- End crony capitalism – bonus for explaining where Obama's trillion-dollar taxpayer funded stimulus went

294

- Protect and strengthen American sovereignty and her Constitution against foreign law, particularly Sharia Law

- Strengthen our military and reverse what Obama has wrought – bonus for rehiring the leadership Obama dismissed

- End the IRS, EPA, and Department of Education, to start with

- Break up the liberal hold on our public universities and their outrageous costs

- Bring common sense back to our primary education system by actually teaching reading, writing, arithmetic and history

- Exhibit strong international leadership, respect our allies, and fear our enemies

- End regulation nation and free American businesses from government intrusion

- Stop the illegal alien invasion and adhere to immigration laws

- End federal funding of the Catholic Church so that its future leaders will not be bought by politicians

- Nominate constitutional conservative judges

Kudos to Trump, America will be great again. The Republican presidential field of 16 is full and nearly each and every contender has a chance to rise above and become our candidate. Here is the list: Jeb Bush, Ben Carson, Chris Christie, Ted Cruz, Carly Fiorina, Jim Gilmore, Lindsey Graham, Mike Huckabee, Bobby Jindal, John Kasich, George Pataki, Rand Paul, Rick Perry, Marco Rubio, Rick Santorum, and Donald Trump.

Obama Spreading Terrorism throughout Our Land

October 9, 2015

We have a president who has been warned that Islamic State jihadists are hiding among the Syrian refugees with the goal of killing us. He has also been warned that the Muslim migrants are ditching their identification and that they cannot be vetted. Yet, he says we will fly in 3,000 Syrians and resettle them across our country, increased that to 10,000 and again increased the number to 200,000. With Obama spreading terrorism throughout our land, shouldn't he be imprisoned with treason, the crime of betraying one's country? The fear of being labeled a racist has kept every politician's mouth shut from attacking Obama.

Trumped by Common Sense

October 14, 2015

Kudos to Republican presidential candidates Donald Trump and Ben Carson for representing common sense in America. Americans are ready for the end of being pushed and pulled by the media, the political ruling class, political correctness and all the idiocy that these bring into our lives. Trump and Carson continue topping the polls while Hillary's poll numbers drop AFTER the media pushes more of her on us through the talk shows and the pop culture iconic TV show Saturday Night Live.

Americans understand that the media duped them into believing Obama's rhetoric against the 1% that Hillary and Bernie continue spewing. The social justice bullshit 'We are all equal/Share the wealth' is commie lingo for no one gets ahead but the ruling class and friends. Everyone else is used as lemmings towards this end. What is difficult to believe is that the world is filled with such greedy, selfish people who crave this type of power. Oh, wait, history HAS shown us that social justice is founded in communist lingo and these leaders rule as greedy, selfish people turning their citizens into slaves for the government rulers.

Obama proved this with his first major action for shovel ready jobs that we heard over and over to pass the Stimulus. The video showing Obama laughing about the lack of shovel ready jobs is so hilarious. The one trillion dollars of our taxes promised for this program went to his donors as payoffs for electing him. His shovel ready jobs Stimulus should be renamed the Trillion Dollar Giveaway in the history books.

At a Q&A for political action group No Labels, Trump had to deal with a plant in the audience who stated that he isn't a friend of Woman. This is the kind of moronic PC attack that continues to be pushed by the media to destroy Republican candidates. Trump and Carson can be trusted to continue with common sense making these typical media attacks powerless in determining our elections. Americans are listening.

The Holy Grail to Fixing Climate Change

October 21, 2015

Democrat socialist presidential candidate Bernie Sanders has a fan that wants money out of politics so we can finally focus on what's important – climate change. It is true that people with vast amounts of money have bought politicians. What is beyond absurd is that climate change is not about money. If people want to believe that driving a big car heats up the earth's temperature, they can stop driving cars. If people believe eating meat supports greenhouse gases, they can go vegan. Green has become their religion and it is what excites them. I almost hate to burst these naïve greenies' bubble. But really, feel-good time is over, and it is time for a little research, starting with ShoreBank and the Chicago Climate Exchange, CCX.

The Holy Grail to fixing climate change is the trading of carbon credits. Never mind that carbon credits are not an actual physical thing. Money would flow to the estimated tune of $10 trillion a year through the CCX exchange through ShoreBank earning their investors billions of dollars ANNUALLY. What politicians do you think have their hands in these two entities and might you get a bit cynical about global warming/climate change as an issue at all? Are you going to continue to support these same politicians including Obama who campaigned about capitalist greed and fairness? Or do you believe Obama is doing this to give you your fair share? Do you think $10 trillion passing through a bank will have any effect on our climate at all? I am sorry. I am going to burst your bubble. You are being used, and to some us, it is quite obvious.

$3,248,723,000,000 Federal Taxes Collected for Fiscal 2015

October 22, 2015

That's what $3.2 trillion dollars looks like and the reason the Democrat Party is called the party of tax and spend, truly not the party of hope and change. Change is not what the Obama administration spent or even left us because $3.2 trillion was not enough. An additional $438,900,000,000 was spent, running a deficit of $438.9 billion. When our government spends money, it is supposed to help and protect us. Can anyone honestly say that we got our money's worth from spending a grand total of $3,687,623,000,000?

This number should anger Americans. Politicians, who are just ordinary Americans, are using the government power against its citizens, playing with our economy as if there is a never-ending supply of money. Politicians need those tax dollars, fees, and fines rolling in to build up to trillions of dollars. Republicans and Democrats used to balance each other out. No longer. The old Republican guard goes along to get along. Republicans do have a challenging act when our president threatens to cut our military pay if he doesn't get his way. That's just plain nasty to use our military as blackmail.

The time has come to throw the old guard out of power. This is the reason that Trump has led the polls for the Republican presidential candidacy for the entire campaign season. Hillary's gearing up to use her millions of fundraising dollars to smear his reputation as a businessman and will say and do anything for power. For that, Biden is standing in the wings to continue the tax and spending should she fall. Trump will continue to tell us like it is.

Conservatives Holding onto the Republican Party by a String

October 30, 2015

Republican political action committee (PAC) money in the hundreds of millions is behind Jeb Bush. Jeb is running an embarrassing campaign. As the GOP candidates strengthen as a group and party, Jeb chooses to henpeck a younger, more popular candidate Rubio; this is not the way to endear yourself to the electorate. This campaign is not like campaigns in the past. We Tea Party conservatives know what we want and politics as usual is out. We will reject the old Republican guard's handpicked candidate no matter how much money is behind him. We have zero trust that Jeb will work for the people and 100% belief that he will protect the old Republican guard's power and privileges.

This power just passed the Bipartisan Budget Act of 2015 handing Obama a blank check to spend as much as he wants in his last year of office. Tea Party conservatives want nothing to do with Republican leadership that has ceded to Obama's demands resulting in an $18.1 trillion national debt with a year to go. Jeb's only hope is to separate himself from the Republican guard which he can't. Either way, the PAC money may jump to Rubio and sink his campaign also. The only viable candidates for conservatives are Donald Trump, a successful businessman who knows the ins and outs of the elite, and Ted Cruz, an extremely smart conservative leader in the Senate. The Republican Party was meant to be conservative, not a party highjacked by crony, self-serving politicians.

NOVEMBER 2015

Obama Claims ISIS Contained

November 14, 2015

Our President who has the ultimate duty to keep us safe claims that ISIS is contained. On the very same day, Paris is attacked by ISIS leaving carnage

298

throughout the city. Obama thinks and acts in terms of his liberal agenda. As our Libyan embassy in Benghazi burned from an al Qaeda attack, Obama claimed that al Qaeda was on the run. This lie about being such a strong leader helped him with his reelection. The ISIS lie is to help him spread Syrian refugees throughout the United States. The Drudge headlines today read that Syrians are beginning to arrive in New Orleans and that Obama is accelerating the admission of Syrian refugees. Information was just reported about the Paris attackers – one was a Syrian refugee. Anyone still confused about our President and his intentions for the future of our country?

Obama Responsible for Cusp of WWIII

November 24, 2015

It is a pity for the entire world that Obama has never understood the greatness of America. Previous presidents focused diligently on keeping the world a safe place for all. Obama has led the world closer to WWIII than ever before because of his dangerous worldview that America should not lead. It is not ironic that he campaigned on diplomacy and ending wars. It is blatant stupidity. Our safety and security rests on a man who has no concept of America's place as a leader in the world.

Obama's embarrassing Lead From Behind leadership has allowed extremely dangerous terrorist groups to grow and threaten the entire world. Our traditions of celebrating Thanksgiving, Christmas and New Year's Day will now be accompanied by a global travel alert of terrorism courtesy of our State Department. Obama's response to Islamic terrorism? Blame Republicans for causing fear, focus on decimating our energy sectors via climate change and deny that he ever received intelligence on the threat. The global travel alert may as well be a global terrorist alert from here on out. Coordinated terrorist attacks as in Paris are likely to occur here in the United States. Obama's lack of concern for ISIS may ultimately be the cause of World War III.

Climate Change Taxes Will Cure Terrorism

November 28, 2015

The global cooling, then global warming and now climate change taxes were all designed as vehicles for wealth redistribution on a major scale. It could almost be classified as ironic because dumb Americans would have voted straight out for wealth redistribution. As long as it is thievery of someone else's money, it's all good. It is not ironic because the point of these scare tactics was to make an elite group of people very wealthy. Yet the poor still wait for their chunk of

Obama money. Maybe that's the irony – the wealthy get wealthier and the poor get poorer – exactly what Obama claims he is against.

Americans are coming to the truth that radical Islam is a threat to western civilization. The political elite came up with a new excuse to push climate change taxes – climate change causes terrorism. Obama is meeting right now at the Climate Summit in Paris trying to take wealth out of America and hand it to other nations, thus increasing temperature, wait, reducing temperature, no, reducing terrorism. Whatever. What difference does it really matter? Politicians want to tax our energy significantly and they need justification for it.

Obama is pushing for a Muslim invasion of our country whether terrorists are mingled in with the rest. He could easily be tried for treason and convicted in a sane world. But he has drummed up so much chaos in our own country based on race and has built up the social injustice meme as insurance. When politicians get behind an agenda, citizens have to start asking themselves who benefits, how they benefit, how much they benefit, and who pays what price. When these questions go unanswered, politicians can take you to the cleaners, as in third world living conditions. Questions for the ages: Why would an American president want terrorists on our soil? Why would this same president be hellbent on ruining the American economy?

DECEMBER 2015

Obama Has Had Three Strikes, He Should Be Out

December 10, 2015

Obama would not be our president if we followed the rule of baseball, three strikes and you're out. Our leader did not anticipate the threat, lied about the threat, and denied the threat. Obama received intelligence reports on the growing Muslim terror threat. As ISIS grew into a world threat, Obama blew it off as a JV (junior varsity) team. One strike. Before the most recent terrorist slaughters in Paris, Obama told us that ISIS was contained. Two strikes. Obama denied that the San Bernardino Muslim jihadi attackers, Syed Farook and Tashfeen Malik, who shot and killed 14 and injured 22 at a work Christmas party, were Islamic terrorists. Three strikes.

Americans no longer believe what Obama says or trust that he will keep our country safe. He is absolutely the wrong leader to deal with Muslim terrorists. He stills claims that Islam is a peaceful religion and that we cannot deny Muslims' freedom of religion. Islam cannot be separated from its own government. The two are intertwined and can never be Americanized as in separation of church and state. America has two options: give Muslims the right to impose their will on everyone or end Muslims' rights because others' rights need to be protected. Freedom of religion should exclude a religion that is its own government. Islam needs to be redefined as a government just as much as it is a religion.

Thank God for Donald J. Trump

December 10, 2015

Progressive liberal politicians take liberally from people's paychecks and then hand it over even more liberally to non-workers (the poor) and their friends (crony capitalists.) The poor are promised lots of free stuff and the friends get plenty of government positions and free money in the name of grants. Check out the government fraud and waste websites which list this idiocy. One example is a National Science Foundation grant of $1,300,000 to study if a koozie keeps a beer cold. Liberals then claim to support the sciences with X numbers of dollars.

Conservatives rightly claim that this is waste and expansion of government. Aside from this NSF study being completely unnecessary, any college student with ten extra minutes can figure out if a koozie helps keep a beer cold and would do it for a free can of beer. What politicians had the gall and arrogance to pretend to use our tax dollars this way? Any excuse to pay back their political donors.

Politics has turned into one big scam after another. Politicians used to be called public servants. They worked for peanuts for the good of the country while also working their real jobs. It has turned into a circus of huge political donors investing money in politicians with the expectation of greenbacks. This political campaign season proves that people are fed up. Thank God for Donald J. Trump. His popularity is no surprise to all the people across our country whose lives have been turned upside down by liberalism and dirty politics. The jig is almost up on the political establishment's domain, Democrat and Republican.

Republican Establishment Supported Rubio's Amnesty Bill and Ryan's Budget Deal

December 19, 2015

Conservatives voted in Republican politicians handing them majorities in the House and Senate to fight the liberal, progressive agenda. Paul Ryan, the new speaker of the House, signed the OK for Obama to continue paying for Muslims' permanent resettlement, Planned Parenthood's butchery of babies, and for influx of illegals at our southern border. What Ryan has unleashed is a resolute goal of conservatives – deny the establishment its pick for president, be

301

it Jeb Bush or Marco Rubio or Chris Christie. We want our country back along with the rule of law and our Constitution.

Rubio helped write the bill to grant millions of illegals amnesty. Had Ted Cruz not challenged the bill by writing an amendment prohibiting citizenship to the illegals, amnesty would have increased the Democrat voting bloc and crushed any Republican vote in the future. The establishment only wanted amnesty IF the illegals could become citizens and vote against conservatism. The bill died. Rubio took a huge risk charging Ted Cruz as a supporter of amnesty. The spotlight is back on Rubio and there is no doubt that he helped write the amnesty bill. Conservatives cannot vote Rubio. That leaves only two possible candidates: Trump or Cruz. Rubio, you're out.

Mayor of New Orleans Wants to Remove Historical Confederate Monuments

December 19, 2015

Mitch Landrieu, Democrat liberal, white mayor of New Orleans, declared 100-plus-year-old historical monuments as public nuisances. City Council members voted to have General Robert E. Lee, General P.G.T. Beauregard and Confederate President Jefferson Davis come down. Landrieu claims that the monuments reinforce the Confederate ideology of slavery. What Landrieu and fellow white liberals fail to recognize is the importance of the history behind our country. The monuments represent the history of the south.

Black African chiefs went around kidnapping fellow Africans and selling them to black buyers who would then sell them around the world. African chiefs made tons of money out of the slave business for 500-1000 years. The Emancipation Proclamation of January 1, 1863, by Republican President Lincoln declared that all persons held as slaves shall be free. Some blacks did return to Africa and resettled on the Western coast called Liberia where they had to deal with primitive savages and deadly diseases. For others, America was their only homeland and they made their way in America.

Slavery did bring blacks to America but within 100 years of our country's birth, slaves were freed and free to all the Constitutional rights and opportunities of America. The monuments are historical, but the blacks today have never experienced slavery. Their ancestors suffered but this suffering brought their progeny freedom from all that slavery entailed. The historical monuments are a reminder to the South's past and should not be swept away as if it never existed.

History brings us to the present and what Landrieu should be focusing on which is the city of New Orleans where a young black couple anticipating their son's birth was murdered while sitting in a car. He should be focusing on the carjackings that occur repeatedly throughout the city. He should be focusing on the armed robberies in the restaurants. He should be focusing on the schools and why high school students cannot read. He should be taking care of the citizens of New Orleans and not wondering which monument is next. Talk is already touching on Jackson Square and the monument of President Andrew Jackson and the Battle of New Orleans. Landrieu is a disgrace.

Hillary and Americans Differ on What Qualifies as Egregious

December 20, 2015

The Hillary Clinton campaign has accused the Bernie Sanders' campaign of criminal behavior and an egregious breach of data and ethics. The DNC, Democratic National Committee, hired an incompetent vendor in charge of the campaigns' voter databases and the firewall failed to keep the Clinton's database private. Sanders' campaign was able to view Clinton's voter database. How easily Clinton can accuse others of criminality yet fail to acknowledge her own actions of truly egregious behavior. She has the gall to call her campaign data breach as damage that cannot be undone.

Egregious defines as extraordinary in some bad way as in egregious mistake and egregious liar. Americans have not forgotten Clinton's private server. Highly classified government intelligence was opened to international hackers. Clinton lied through her teeth that she never used her server for classified information. To American citizens, data breaches related to our national defense and the lying about it qualify as egregious behaviors.

Any other Clinton behaviors that qualify as egregious? Perhaps Benghazi, the US Embassy under her watch. Clinton convinced many that she was the right person to answer a 3am call to duty. The call came to help our Libyan ambassador and fellow Americans. All they got was a busy signal during the 8-hour attack which resulted in four dead Americans. Also, unforgivably, she met the family members at the site of their loved ones' coffins placing the blame on a YouTube video.

The Clinton quote during the House Oversight Committee hearing presents her character quite clearly. "What difference at this point does it make?" They are dead already – move on to what's important to Hillary – her quest for the presidency.

Political Review for Dense Relatives

December 26, 2015

More than a few of us had political discussions with the younger generations over the holidays. I hope the majority of us did not bash our heads into the wall. The younger relatives of voting age that I spoke to are feeling the Bern, as in Democrat socialist presidential candidate Bernie Sanders. The word socialism does not scare them because Bernie talks right to them. For some reason, an old, grumpy white man proudly spouting off socialism speaks their language – free college, free healthcare and punish the 1% for being wealthy. Yikes.

Into Obama's eighth year in office, we have no jobs and massive student debt accompanied by economic inequality. My relative blames... the Republicans for voting against Obama's agenda. When I asked if Obama had any blame, incredibly the answer was no. What is failed to be recognized about Obama is that he lies. His policies are named exactly the opposite of what they do. His words shift all blame from his policies to his opposition. To pass his policies, he claimed the opposite of what they would do. A couple of specifics:

Student Aid Bill of Rights or Obama's Student Loan Forgiveness Program: Obama passed this bill to make college more affordable, help students avoid default and strengthen the economy. Sounds great. What it does is encourage students to borrow excess money, get worthless humanities degrees and seek nonprofit jobs. Since these low-paying jobs make it impossible to pay back loans, they won't have to pay them back (forgiven). Tons of federal tax dollars flow to the universities, the students pretend to borrow it, and the true taxpayers are on the hook for the bill. The universities have federal dollars flowing in and have no incentive to reduce college costs. Competition from competing colleges is a non-issue. Yet, the students who borrow private money have high interest rates up to 8% on extremely overpriced tuition.

Patient Protection and Affordable Care Act or Obamacare: Obama promised to increase quality and affordability of health insurance, lower the uninsured rate and reduce healthcare costs. States who set up their own health exchange would get federal subsidies and states who opted for the national healthcare exchange would not receive federal subsidies towards the cost of health insurance. Who would forego a state exchange? More than half the governors did on the basis that a state healthcare exchange would cost an unknown amount of money to operate, had rules that hadn't been fully written and would force states to pay for Medicaid expansion. How are the state exchanges doing after receiving $5.4 billion in federal grants as we end 2015? Hawaii is the latest state exchange to go bust despite receiving $205 million. Oregon has gone bust despite receiving $305 million. Not one single state exchange has survived. As these states transition to healthcare.gov, millions of more federal dollars will be spent on the funding.

304

On the consumer end, the health insurance is virtually useless because the costs and deductibles are in the thousands of dollars. This bill practically got passed and built momentum because of the promise of free birth control. Does it really have to be said that nothing in life is free? An annual doctor's visit is approximately $100. But it's free with Obamacare. That's after paying the monthly premium. We were also promised a free colonoscopy, but that is only a preventative colonoscopy. If the doctor clips a little polyp, the free colonoscopy turns into a bill of over $800. Healthy people would rather pay for the $100 annual and their own dollars for birth control with a major medical policy as insurance. Obamacare fines people for doing this for it is against his law.

Obamacare is even worse on the business end. Republicans fully funded Obamacare yet Obamacare is falling apart on its own. Why have a reason to blame Republicans for its failure? Democrats have become this fascist, socialistic machine which claims to support the worker and punish the rich. When politicians claim to be able to pay for their utopian policies, they mean that the taxpayer pays it. The 1% uber wealthy cannot support the remaining 99% of the citizens.

The fancy terms of federally financed, federal grants and federal subsidies all come from the same place – the taxpayers' wallets. The younger generation can support Bernie and feel the Bern. Unfortunately, the burn they will be feeling is in their wallets with a lower standard of living. The younger generation may want to research Hillary's healthcare act that she wanted to impose on us in the 90's.

America's Most Admired Woman of 2015

December 31, 2015

The joke is on us. Hillary has won her 20th coveted title of America's most admired woman of the year. Apparently, no other admirable women exist in America. She deserves the label of America's most admired woman who gets away with cheating, lying and staying out of jail. And she sure wins for being pertinacious. There is no way she will be voted into the presidency except by fraud or with the help of Obama's transformation of our country. I hope after this next year of primaries that she settles into grannyhood and steps into the background. For that, even she would earn my admiration.

My pick for America's Most Admired Woman of 2015 goes to Elizabeth Hasselbeck, a young mother of 3 children under age 10 with the coveted job as one of three anchors on Fox and Friends cable news show. She is on top of her profession with a nice salary, opportunities for fabulous experiences, and engagement in the day to day political news. And she is stepping down to be a mommy. For her to realize how much her children need her, her husband needs her, and that motherhood trumps all else, I truly admire her.

Elizabeth is about to step into daily battles with three little people who will not always respect her, who will fight with each other, and wear her down as a person. And she will know that she has earned her title of mom every minute of every day. Moms are often just present doing the daily grinding chores of cooking, dishes, laundry, chauffeuring and house-cleaning. Who chooses this over a dream job? A mother does. It often comes down to just being there and being available.

American women have gotten so far off track in what can be a simple path to a fulfilling life of motherhood. The conservative path is date, marry, sex, then kids. Pretty straightforward yet difficult in our permissive culture. Feminism has worked relentlessly to condemn conservatism as old-fashioned. Feminism has promoted free-for-all sex – a life of hookups, contraceptives, abortions and single motherhood. The dad figure is taken out of the equation. Single moms work to make a living and often have their children raised by someone else. And this is a step up from living off welfare. On the other spectrum, married women have been treated as lazy outcasts when they do not have a career, relegating their children to daycare.

Kudos to the women who are stay-at-home moms. It makes all the difference in the world to the little people who count on you most. Kudos to Elizabeth Hasselbeck for providing a fabulous example for mothers everywhere – America's Most Admired Woman of 2015.

JANUARY 2016

Why trust a liar just because he cries while talking about gun control?

January 5, 2016

Obama wants gun control and is passing his very own executive orders while openly crying. The tears kinda really looked fake, as if required to help us feel sympathy and to help us believe that Obama has our best interests at heart. We the people believe in our Constitution with the Second Amendment on gun ownership. No tears are going to change this. If Obama wanted simple background check loopholes fixed, he should go through congress. We the people believe that we have elected reasonable politicians who would work with Obama on simple fixes. But Obama cannot include his extra measures to gun control that our reasonable politicians would vote yes. He reverts to his need for executive control with his pen and paper. One of these little measures includes ordering doctors to report any mental problems of their patients to the FBI and if they own a gun. According to Obama, extremists should not own guns. Obama has already said who he thinks are crazy, dangerous or extreme - Tea Party, soldiers, Christians, Republicans, climate change deniers - anyone who opposes his ideas. Sounds and feels like our government does not have our best interests at heart and that we are nearing communist control. In Obama's world, opposing opinions are not allowed to exist.

Obama's Failed Fast and Furious Designed to Lead Us to Gun Control

January 15, 2016

Fast and Furious, Obama's gun smuggling, tracking operation in 2009, put guns into the hands of criminals for years to come. 2,000 guns from the United States traveled to Mexico into the hands of bad guys who ended up killing an ICE agent, a Border Patrol Agent, a Mexican police chief and bodyguard, and 200 confirmed killings in Mexico including Mexican children shot at a birthday party. Agencies involved included ICE, ATF, FBI, DEA and the IRS. Obama denied knowing anything about this gun smuggling operation involving a neighboring country. According to Obama, five major agencies went rogue leaving him in the dark. Obama has proven to be a serial liar. He did know, and instead of counting the body bags his operation left behind, he was counting on a smooth passage to gun control.

This operation was designed to prove how bad the gun situation is in the United States and that we the people would agree to give up our guns. Now, six years later, Obama cries for the children of gun violence and passes gun control all by himself. We are to believe that his tears were for the children – a play by liberals used over and over again. Obama didn't cry for the Mexican children shot at a birthday party by guns traced back to his operation or for the hundred's dead because of guns he put into the hands of criminals. This is a beginning to gun control, and like Obamacare, it will be implemented little by little until it may be too late to turn back.

United States' Most Dangerous Year – 2016

January 15, 2016

Obama spoke his last State of the Union giving us a rosy picture of his accomplishments. In listening to Obama, one would never guess that terrorism is a threat to the world. The history of Obama on terrorism is that he makes a statement and then the opposite occurs. His State of the Union (SOTU) statement on terrorism claimed that he averted World War III. This should be a concern for all Americans. It is as close to a tell that we are on the verge of WWIII there is. And it is all due to Obama's direct actions – not from his lack of leadership skills.

Obama has deliberately lowered our country's standing in the world along with our security. Obama was well-aware that Iran had taken control of two navy boats and ten US sailors as prisoners while boasting of US power. This is the same Iran officially deigned a state sponsor of terrorism, the same Iran that Obama bragged about working out a nuclear deal and the same Iran soon to be receiving $150 billion from us. Nothing about this makes sense. Our Navy sailors were unprotected in small river boats within three miles of Farsi Island, the home of an Iranian naval base. On the surface, it appears to be a set up to benefit Obama's reputation. On the other hand, it could be possible that Obama wanted to provoke Iran.

United States is in a horrible position of having a president who may or may not want our destruction. We know his goal for his presidency is to fundamentally transform America. We do not know how far he is willing to go. It is obvious that Obama is not concerned about protecting us from terrorism and that terrorist acts may go unpunished. Iran received a thank you from our Secretary of State John Kerry for its latest provocation. Possible scenarios for 2016 include more terrorist attacks on our soil. On top of terrorism, Americans fear purposeful damage to our economy, food supply, energy supply, monetary systems and health system courtesy of our president. And if the worst occurs, Obama will pull his Orwellian tactic – act angered followed by placing blame on his biggest enemy, the Republicans. May we all survive 2016 with an intact United States.

Cruz Cruising to the White House

January 17, 2016

Campaigning for the Republican nomination, Cruz did cut down New York by claiming Trump has New York values. So what? In the past ten presidential elections, New York has only supported one Republican candidate for president, Ronald Reagan. That means New York voted for Jimmy Carter, Michael Dukakis, Bill Clinton 2X, Al Gore, John Kerry and Obama 2X – all horrid, liberal progressives, with the exception of Bill Clinton who ruled by poll numbers.

Trump can easily win New York in the primaries, but is he a Ronald Reagan? Cruz is Reagan-like. However, if there is a match-up between communist Bernie Sanders and Tea Party Conservative Ted Cruz, Sanders will win New York. Trump is trying desperately to hurt Cruz with citizenship questioning and lying about a loan disclosure. New York Trump is bullying a true conservative and it will hurt him. There is a devastating video clip from *Meet the Press*, 1999, in which Trump says that he is for partial-birth abortion. If Cruz continuously runs this clip, Trump is toast. Trump is an interesting contender because he has attracted a significant percentage of Democrats and Independents. He could lose the conservative vote by hitting hard on Cruz and it will all go to the victor.

My Pick: Ted Cruz and Carly Fiorina – but will it matter?

January 29, 2016

I have solidified my picks for the next president and vice president of the United States: Ted Cruz and Carly Fiorina. The United States needs a conservative constitutionalist as our president to save our country. Cruz's history speaks for himself, and Carly, every word and statement that comes out of her mouth confirms that she is a fighter for the ideals of the United States. The Democrat and Republican political establishment and elites have set our country on a disastrous path to bankruptcy, open borders, and government control. Cruz looks us in the eyes and tells us exactly what will happen under his watch.

Trump 'Make America Great Again' fans – take a look at the YouTube video of Harry Reid behind the mic stating that he is pulling for Trump. As he said this, ultra-lib Chuck Schumer is kicking him in the leg, warning Reid to shut up before he messes up the Republican primary candidacy of Trump. As a conservative, I want nothing to do with a Republican presidential candidate who has had a fundraiser for Reid in the past, has stated he is pro-choice and for partial-birth abortion just four years ago, and is already stating that he will negotiate with ultra-libs such as Nancy Pelosi and Reid.

On the reality side of this election, will the Republican candidate matter? Obama is working to make sure a Republican does not have a chance of being elected. The Obama administration's White House Task Force on New Americans is working on legalizing citizenship for legal permanent residents beginning in Los Angeles. Our public libraries will be set up with citizenship corners to hold citizenship classes. Our law states that non-citizens cannot vote in federal elections, which are punishable by imprisonment or removal from the United States. Back in 2011, there were 13 million legal permanent residents. Five/six years later the number may have mushroomed past 20 million.

I was warned that the election of Obama meant that Republican votes will not count in future elections. If the illegals, permanent legal residents, and non-citizens cast votes, a Democrat majority will form. Combine this with additional fraud, Bernie fans may get their wish - a socialist country beholden to the government and away from a representative government. Communist governments don't let the other side win. For now, I have my dream ticket of Cruz and Carly.

What Millennials' Support of Bernie Tells Us

February 1, 2016

Millennials' support of Bernie tells us that they didn't learn anything in high school about economics, English, politics, math, history and government. It is quite sad, but they are falling again for the person railing against success in any shape or form with the rhetoric of demonizing the 1% super wealthy. When questioned about support of Bernie with a microphone in the face, it comes down to free stuff, particularly college and healthcare. Here are the lessons Millennials have yet to learn. Economics: There is no free lunch. English: Lunch, in this context, is a metaphor for anything. Politics: Promises of free health care and college are false. Math: The costs of health care and college are expensive. History: Taxes are extremely high to pay for free health care and college, as high as 90% of paychecks. Government: When taxes are high, government controls nearly every aspect of our lives. You see, you will have no money to do anything extra.

Millennials have taught us that to prevent future generations from believing in a 74-year-old socialist, our schools have to teach basic knowledge which leads to critical thinking. Progressives have crept into the education arena and have been in charge of our children from ages 5 to 18 to 22 for decades. Our schools need an overhaul and focus on what is imperative – developing the brains of our children, not pushing the ideology of a party. A critical thinker may be inclined to research where one could easily deduce that a Democrat socialist is a progressive is a communist. A critical thinker may ask how much free stuff really costs.

Liberals and Republicans to Blame for Over-Spending, Credit Downgrade

February 18, 2016

President Bush added $4 trillion to our nation's debt bringing it to $9 trillion. Candidate Obama claimed in his snarky, off-putting way that adding $4 trillion to the debt was irresponsible and unpatriotic. He went on mocking Bush on taking out a credit card from the Bank of China in the name of our children. Candidate Obama then promised to cut this debt in half. With the remaining year to his presidency, Obama has already doubled the debt past $18 trillion. Why didn't our elected representatives hold the Obama administration accountable? That was their job.

The United States has nothing to show for this debt, NOTHING except a downgraded US credit rating for the first time ever. Look around at the decay.

We do have a possibility of going bankrupt and of living in a third world country. Compare this debt to personal debt. At some point, the shell game is over, and the debt comes due. Obama spent our country into oblivion and in the future, he will claim that the fault lies with those darn obstructionist Republicans. If only the Republicans HAD stood up to Obama, we would not be in this position. The spineless Republican political elites have earned zero respect from their electorate. No wonder Trump has stayed on top of the presidential contenders. He wants to make America great again because it is not anymore. He could have it in the bag by announcing that he would appoint Ted Cruz as the next Supreme Court Justice.

American's Anger Should Focus on a President Cruz

February 28, 2016

Anger towards the tone-deaf political elites of both parties has been focused on electing Trump. Trump keeps repeating what the people want to hear and it is starting to remind me of candidate Obama. It's giving me the feeling of uneasiness. Obama wasn't questioned on ANYTHING of substance. Neither is Trump. In the latest debate, he stated that his healthcare plan was to cross state lines. He said there was nothing to add to that. He brags that he will get things done – again, familiar words of Obama. His braggadocio is starting to sound just that – a lot of hot air. Trump is the dealmaker, but that does not define his values and conservatism. The position of Secretary of State or a new business deal committee seems better suited for the Donald.

The presidential race has come down to Trump or Cruz. Cruz won in Iowa despite saying that he would end corporate loopholes and subsidies, including paying corn farmers to produce ethanol fuel that gunks up our motors. Cruz stands on his values and does not waiver. Trump favors the ethanol subsidies. We do not know if subsidies are something Trump favors or if he thought it was the political thing to say. The bottom line is that Cruz will end subsidies and Trump will not.

The political elite are beginning to stand behind Trump which tells us that Cruz is the one they fear as president. Trump brags that he can make deals with anyone including his friends on both sides of the parties. That is exactly what we do not want. The cronyism and special favors are exactly what Trump is talking about – deal making. Talk about the power that Trump, the political elite and the big corporations will have over the little people. He brags that he knows them all and will work with them. We want someone who has our values and stands up for them. The New York values Trump has held for over 50 years are not our values. Only one person has our values.

311

Had it not been for Senator Cruz, Rubio and his Gang of 8 would have passed amnesty of over 12 million illegals and put them on a path to citizenship. Trump talks about deporting all illegals and bringing the good ones back. That is Trump's plan as we have heard repeatedly. Trump admitted on the debate stage that he hired illegals because no Americans wanted the jobs. He's double talking; he's going to send them away, but they are needed for American corporations. We really do not know where his values lie.

Cruz is a staunch defender of our constitution. If another progressive ideologue finds his or her way onto the Supreme Court bench, we can kiss our liberties goodbye. We have no idea of the type of person Trump wants on this bench. We certainly have a clear idea of who Cruz would nominate as a Supreme Court justice. With Cruz as president, we can have complete faith that he will find the best person suited for the lifelong position.

Cruz has said that he will end the IRS and the following State Departments: Energy, Education, Commerce, and Housing and Urban Development. These wasteful bureaus have expanded government reach and Cruz is determined to close them down. Trump hasn't mentioned closing any agencies or bureaus. Trump has only repeated the line that he is going to make America great again. Sounds like rhetoric that has no direction behind it. We know how Cruz will make America great again. He will cut down the size and power of the political elite's power bases. Of course, they hate him. Trump said at the debate that Cruz's colleagues hate him and will not endorse him. Imagine having a president who we no longer question the political motives behind each action. Ted Cruz is exactly who we are looking for as a president.

MARCH 2016

Establishment Politicians May Be Playing Double Jeopardy with Trump

March 4, 2016

Prior to Super Tuesday, establishment Republican Chris Christie endorsed Trump. We can assume that was to help Trump shore up more delegates on Super Tuesday. Trump didn't do as well as expected with Cruz winning three states and Rubio winning one state. Maybe the support of the establishment hurt Trump. The establishment Democrat horrible Harry Reid even stated that he liked Trump the best because he could work with him. This surely hurt Trump more than help.

The next move the Republican establishment took was to trot out Romney who was rejected by the conservative Republicans. Romney railed against a Trump presidency and how Americans are being played as suckers. This criticism of the public would and has resulted in a backlash against Romney and a clamoring of

312

support FOR Trump. Perhaps the establishment Republicans were shoring up support for Trump because they may have finally understood how hated they are.

Reid has now come out railing against Trump calling out the establishment Republicans for creating Frankenstein. Could this be double jeopardy by both parties of the establishment elite? In short, first they are against Trump over Jeb. Then they are for Trump over Cruz and Rubio. Now they claim they are against Trump when Cruz has an opportunity to overtake Trump. The establishment HATES the idea of Cruz who is in the chase for president. The establishment politicians know they are hated all around and now we know who needs to be president.

Ode to Millennials on Bernie Sanders Democratic Socialism

March 29, 2016

Big difference between socialism and conservatism. Conservatism supports the freedom of individuals to go for it. If a person has a great product, service or idea and turns it into a profitable company, yay for that person. Expand, hire more workers and be successful. Lots of choices for consumers. Socialism says boo for that person for making too much money. Companies close leaving less or no choices for consumers. Government's claimed goal based on any brand of socialism is to weaken profitable companies and increase the power of the working people. What the hell do these workers know about running a profitable company and how would they accomplish this? Pure ignorance rules the day. Take Apple and kick out the CEO/owner who has the knowledge and ability to run the company, purely for the reason that the owner is making too much money. What do the 'workers united' know about running Apple? The company will die along with the jobs and products. It is a utopian dream that it will remain running and profitable. The same goes for a hospital, an airline, an oil company, etc.

When the adults in the room talk about the ignorant Millennials, this is what we are talking about. None of this socialist talk about workers uniting, greedy corporations, social justice is new. It is stale, old socialist, commie talk no matter who is saying it, even a grumpy, frumpy grandpa-type old white guy. Naive Millennials will respond that they do not want to run the companies, they just want to redistribute the wealth. That, my little friends, is stealing. Imagine that you have a cupcake business and your hard work pays off. People love your cupcakes and pay you for them. The socialist government you voted for takes your profits to give out free stuff to others. Ya going to continue working really hard when you are not rewarded for it? The answer is no, and that answer is the same for anyone with a successful company, no matter what size.

Not Impressive for Trump to Win Blue States over Cruz

April 21, 2016

Trump is winning blue states over conservative Cruz – the same states that Hillary and even Bernie would win. The election is shaping up that neither Trump nor Cruz will win majority of delegate votes prior to the Republican convention. Many of the headlines and talking heads are blowing off Cruz and crowning Trump as the Republican candidate. Cruz has a very good chance of winning the second vote at the convention – his ground game, knowledge of the delegate process, and his steadfastness on constitutionalism give him the advantage.

This is a very exciting election that began with seventeen candidates. Trump has led the pack, but the direction was always leading to a Trump versus a conservative. Establishment politicians had no chance this election season. Conservatives are beyond furious over the Washington politicians bowing to Obama. Furious does not even define how we are feeling. Leftist politicians are now fighting for men in dresses to use the same female bathrooms as our young daughters. Hillary, Bernie and Trump are PC on this point. The end game will be non-gender bathrooms if one of these is elected. Why Obama is fighting for something this controversial nearing the end of his term is odd.

Trump is not winning majority of the red states; Cruz is. Republicans, Independents and some Democrats are getting very tired of the direction of the United States. The Rule of Law has been ignored far too long. The anything goes faux revolutionary grievances can be put to bed with Cruz. Police and military will be respected. The Black Lives Matter crowd will not be allowed to burn down blocks of cities. The president will treat LGBT, feminist and minority groups as Americans and not pit these individual groups against the norm. Criminal illegal aliens will not be allowed to roam free in the United States. American Muslims will follow the United States Rule of Law, not Sharia. As Cruz has said, he does have conservative views but that he will not impose his views on us. States will have the rights to decide their laws, not five lifer judges. Finally, the citizens of the United States have the opportunity to vote for an honest, law-abiding, brilliantly smart politician and citizen for the most important job in the world.

Media and Obama-Style Rhetoric Helping Trump

April 28, 2016

If Trump becomes the Republican presidential candidate, once again, the media and Obama-style rhetoric 'Make America Great Again' helped make it happen. As a viewer of Fox News, it was clear that every utterance of Trump was the election news. I favored Trump for his assistance in clearing out the establishment candidates. I also welcomed Trump's style of bashing political correctness. But Trump's non-conservative leanings keep coming to light – his New York values seem real. Few details emerge on his foreign policy which is summed up in two phrases: Build a Wall and Destroy ISIS. After Trump won the northeast liberal states, Fox News' Bill O'Reilly declared Trump the winner. Sean Hannity tried to hen-peck Cruz into talking about Trump's meme of Cruz as a cheater. Hannity could have talked about all the delegates and states that were coalescing behind Cruz. Other major media outlets ran headlines that Cruz was defeated.

Cruz is running a fantastic campaign and working for every delegate he can, plus he just chose my pick for VP, Carly Fiorina. In the earlier debates, Fiorina was the one person that could be counted on for straight-on, biting attacks on Hillary. Both candidates are conservative, very intelligent, and would make great leaders of the United States. Cruz can and will win a contested convention. As much as Trump and Fox News want this primary election over, rules apply. The rule is to reach majority of the delegates – not close to, or the most, but to reach the number of 1,237. The election is now up to the Hoosiers of Indiana. No pressure.

MAY 2016

Thoughts on Cruz Suspending Campaign

May 4, 2016

Republicans had a constitutional conservative presidential choice in Ted Cruz who would have brought back law and honor to our country. They blew it; Cruz bowed out this evening. The current president disregards our Constitution with the assistance of Republican Representatives and Senators. The anger directed at the Republican establishment is palpable. Republican voters feared another establishment candidate and when political outsider Trump entered the race claiming that he would make America great again, they jumped to him.

Trump's popularity soared when he ignored political correctness, especially on illegals and Muslims. The media including the talking heads of Fox News hung onto every word that Trump uttered which often included derogatory remarks

315

about his fellow candidates. Fox News all but ignored the other candidates including Cruz who is on video from 2012 talking about building a wall. One of Trump's popular campaign promises is to build a wall. Cruz became Trump's main competition and when they debated one on one...oh, right, they didn't. Trump could have been clobbered by Cruz and may have been outed as less knowledgeable on the issues. News outlets could have reported on policies and backgrounds of Cruz and Trump. Instead, we got to hear Trump call Cruz 'Lyin Ted', unhinged, desperate and wacko. Up to the very last day of Cruz's campaign, Trump tied Cruz's dad to Lee Harvey Oswald – absolutely nothing to do with policy and the direction of our country. And then Indiana voted for Trump over Cruz, who is uncannily intelligent, honest and a truly good person.

Now the election moves to the phase where the media turns against Trump, the Republican candidate, and supports the Democrat candidate. Cruz warned us that Trump was part of the hated establishment. Now the media will report on Trump's funding of Democrat party politicians, his New York values, his failings, etc. With a President Trump, it appears that the crony Washington party will continue when we had the candidate who would have broken it up. Americans missed the obvious that Cruz was the answer to their anger. The one thing that Ted Cruz can never admit is that he got along with the establishment. If he did, he would be lyin'.

Why the Conservative Candidate Cruz Failed This Time

May 15, 2016

Senator Ted Cruz failed to win the Republican primary for 2016. Hillary or whatever Democrat candidate must fail this year so if it is the Donald, so be it. We know what we will get with a Hillary or Democrat president – more of the Obama agenda and horrific Supreme Court Justices. In retrospect, some reasons Cruz didn't cinch the nomination:

- Tea Party favorite Rubio went all in for amnesty siding with establishment Republicans; he helped taint conservative politicians across the board.

- Republican politicians failed to defund Planned Parenthood, a company caught manipulating abortions to obtain intact baby parts and then selling them.

- Republican politicians failed to defund Obama's agenda on bringing in illegals and Muslims and dispersing them across our nation.

- The Cruz-Kasich alliance lost the PR meme to Trump who accused them of colluding.

- Cruz lost the meme on freedom of religion to instilling his religion on everyone.

- Every word Trump uttered became the election news, ignoring the competing candidates -- we noticed, Fox News.

- Cruz should have demanded a debate with Trump. Tag-along Kasich would have had to be invited and ignored.

- Cruz let Trump continually brag about the idea to build a wall when he could have aired his 2012 video on building a wall.

- Cruz should have countered the Lyin' Ted with alleged Trump lies.

A Trump-Cruz debate was needed. Cruz could have been creative and defined their differences on his own terms. Since Trump refused to debate Cruz, Cruz should have had the debate with a Trump fill-in. It could have been a SNL-style debate but totally scripted by Cruz resulting in a YouTube video sensation. This debate would have been the most entertaining and informative on the issues. As a Cruz supporter, the fat lady hasn't completed her song leaving a smidgen of hope for Cruz to become our nominee. Hope is a good thing.

The Good News about Trump

May 18, 2016

Trump supporters will not be swayed by anything Hillary or any Democrat will throw at Trump. They are loyal and nothing will keep them from voting for their candidate. Nothing. The negative advertising will be in the hundreds of millions of dollars and not one dollar will convince a Trump supporter to vote Democrat. The negative advertising will convert Democrat voters to wonder why they shouldn't vote for Trump and then they will. Hillary and the Democrats will find out that Trump earned the top Republican slot.

From the beginning of his candidacy, Trump talked about the illegals. Then an illegal killed an innocent American Kate Steinle on a San Francisco pier. Trump talked about the Muslims and how we don't know enough about them. Then Muslims committed murders against their co-workers in San Bernardino, California. Trump said that we should stop letting Muslim refugees in because they could be terrorists. Then Muslim refugees slaughtered Parisians at a concert. Trump was always one step ahead of events, by chance, but they were big events, even huge as Trump says.

Hillary's baggage should have kept her holed up at her home but since she has the gall to run for president, Trump will open her baggage for all to see. Despite my ideal candidate being Cruz, perhaps Trump is the person for our times. In this day and age, the tweet gets the worm. The Democrats have become so nasty that it takes a tough candidate like Trump to maneuver through the bullsh#t. Go get 'em, Trump, and may the best man win.

JUNE 2016

Muslims are the Bigoted, Racist, Homophobes – Not the Republicans

June 17, 2016

Liberals claim to love the Muslims and the gays. Liberal leaders are at a crossroads because their leadership has resulted in the largest mass murder targeting gays on American soil at the hands of a Muslim. Muslims are taught to hate gays and kill them. Muslims who kill gays are not radical; they are devout. Obama and Hillary have said they will continue the immigration of Muslims from terrorist countries by the tens of thousands despite the odds that terrorist attacks will increase.

Liberal supporters find themselves at a crossroads: are the socially agreeable policies worth the threat of more Muslim attacks? I don't know why liberal leaders are so intent on bringing more Muslims to the United States. It could be that Barrack Hussein Obama who grew up in Muslim schools is sympathetic to Muslims. Is his fundamental transformation to revert the United States from a Christian nation to Islamic? Has Hillary sold her soul to the Muslims just to increase her bank account? Nothing logical explains the danger that their leadership has wrought.

Gays have the option of joining conservative Republicans. According to the meme of liberal leadership, we are supposed to be the bigoted, racist, homophobes. The truth is we knew you in high school before you came out of the closet. We admire your creativity and carefree ways. We also never think of your sexuality any more than you think of ours. The mass murder of your fellow gays hurts us because we are all human. Many Republicans are the most accepting and welcoming of all. Conservative Republicans want security and economic stability so that all can prosper. We are sorry that you are an enemy of the Muslims, but we do have that in common – we are all infidels to them.

318

Trump Is Being Carrie Underwooded

August 11, 2016

Carrie Underwood won a TV singing show, became the darling of country music and miffed the seasoned veterans who had put in their time in the biz. Trump is being Carrie Underwooded by the political elite. He came into a new arena without putting his time into the system and jumped ahead to the ultimate prize of presidential candidate. This wasn't supposed to happen to an outsider.

The voters chose Trump by the millions precisely because he was not the system. He's a self-made businessman who sees the danger that progressives such as Obama and Hillary have wrought on the United States. Why on earth are our kids being taught to hate the United States? Why on earth are blacks torching cities hating on police? Why on earth are men now welcome in girls' bathrooms? Why on earth are Muslims and their Sharia laws besting our Constitution? Why on earth are all the government agencies under Obama performing disgracefully and illegally – the VA, EPA, IRS, HUD, Departments of Education, Health and Human Services, Defense, Homeland Security and Customs and Border Protection? Perhaps the citizens have finally had enough corruption, cronyism and progressivism and have hope that a successful businessman can clean it up. In other words, we depend on Trump to lead America in making it great again.

The media and political elites can throw inane intimations at Trump waiting for something to cause the Trump meltdown. Newsflash – the meltdown isn't going to happen. The millions of citizens that voted for Trump are waiting to cast their votes again in November. And it can't get here soon enough. We are tired of the progressive chicanery that is tearing our country apart. We have tired of waiting for our established politicians to turn this around. No matter how much Trump is Carrie Underwooded, we stand behind him.

The Deplorable Democrats

September 13, 2016

Democrat presidential candidate Hillary Clinton called out half of Trump supporters as belonging in a basket of deplorables. We all know who the deplorable one is when a political party candidate considers a quarter to half of the US population as deplorable. This presidential candidate should have no right to be in contention to lead our nation after rattling off the opposing party's supporters as being every derogatory comment on the tip of her tongue as factual – racist, sexist, homophobic, xenophobic, Islamophobic and you name it. For you Deplorables who don't realize what you are, xenophobic means fear of people from other countries.

I for one am sick of hearing her name and having the news revolve around her. Her name has been shoved in our faces for over two decades as the smartest woman in the world. But hell, she did leave the White House dead broke and convinced people to support her nonprofit to the tune of hundreds of millions of dollars. Secretary of State John Kerry must have thought she was clever; he funneled around $10 million in tax dollars to his own daughter's nonprofit. These smart Democrats are downright deplorable and need to be kicked out on their asses.

Unfortunately for Hillary, she may be taken out on a stretcher. This candidate is so power hungry for the ultimate position of leading the United States that she continues to trot her sick self out in public pretending to be presidential material. She is downright selfish. Videos show her freezing up, having seizure-like episodes and being shoved into her van with feet dragging, possibly signs of the neurological disease, advanced Parkinson's. It would be refreshing for Democrat supporters to turn against this candidate and send her into retirement for the good of the nation.

Recap of her accomplishments:

- Carpetbagging New York elections, riding her husband's coattails to position of senator

- The red button to restart Russian relations imprinted with the Russian word peregruzka which translated to Overcharged instead of Reset.

- Being Secretary of State – leaving the Mideast in flames and migrants over-running European countries

- Claimed Ted Kennedy's children's CHIP program as her own

- Claimed to work for vets, as all politicians claim

- Women's rights which boils down to funding the top abortion provider who sells baby body parts with hundreds of millions in tax dollars that are funneled back as donations to Democrat candidates

- Supports gay marriage/LBGT while accepting millions in support from countries that stone gays/LBGT and toss them off roofs to their deaths

A Smug, Lying, Power Hungry, Indebted Woman Wants to Be President

October 1, 2016

Trump is hugely correct on this point. Without the media behind H (I can't even stand to see or hear her name), she would not have a chance of being near the White House, again. The truth on this woman is frightening. It should be laughable that she is this close to the presidency. But this is liberal progressive media-backing of a deplorable candidate as a thoughtful, caring grandmother politician. Smart thinking Americans must ask themselves – why the hell would we want to put this smug, lying, power hungry, indebted woman to her powerful crony friends and foreign countries in charge of our lives? November 8th is the time to show the political elite and media where they can stick it.

H will continue Obama's legacy of lining donor friends' pockets at our expense. This is criminal and should be punishable by jail. We don't need another super-indebted president handing out taxpayer money to her friends via cooperation of her justice department. In addition to the money, H is far from being a friend of the American public. She will continue to promote anti-American security laws and regulations. Americans deserve better than open immigration and a blind eye to Islamic terrorism.

Americans know why the political elites and the media want and need H. It is all about the corrupt power that they are used to and crave. Trump is our chance to break up this powerhouse of corrupt politicians and media. We have had enough and want true leadership that is of the people, for the people, by the people. One necessary leadership quality of successful people is that they surround themselves with the best. Successful businessman Trump has a history of assigning the best and brightest to necessary positions. We already know who H will surround herself with – her biggest donors who paid to play. The United States does deserve better than this corrupt woman, right?

The Elite Still Think We Care What They Think

October 10, 2016

Trump will win the presidency. This will be despite everything thrown against the wall at Trump: media-backing of H, elite Republican politicians trashing Trump, Trump's locker room talk videos, non-issues such as O's (I can no longer bear to see or hear his name, either) birth certificate, Trump's taxes and sure more to come before November 8. Even fraudulent voting will not topple Trump. It would have to be a lot.

321

Trump is the end of liberal progressivism in America. Trump will bring the end of political correctness, the end of political elite power, the end of sending our tax dollars as thanks to donors, end of fake racism and police hatred, end of LGBTQ in our faces, end of government positions going to donors and friends, and finally, the end of the Clinton machine. Trump will bring business sense to the national budget, tax reform and regulations. He will surround himself with quality leadership bringing strength to our military and competence to government entities such as EPA, IRS, and Homeland Security. Our Justice Department and Supreme Court will follow the law and our Constitution. When the economy recorrects from zero percent interest rate, Americans can feel some sort of relief that a successful, competent businessman is in charge.

Americans are no longer allowing the powerful media and political elite to determine our future. The ones left behind will be those who continue coddling progressive values such as denigrating whites as privileged, actively promoting welfare as a way of life, promoting victimhood to minorities as a right to destroy communities, teaching feelings over knowledge, and trying to convince Americans that Islamic terrorism isn't a problem. We want America back strong and sane. We want our patriotism to shine. We want to feel safe. We want our children to know the America we know. With Trump, Americans will know that the United States is run by a president who has their best interests at heart.

Number One Reason Americans Plan to Vote for Hillary

October 17, 2016

The number one reason Americans plan to vote for H: the plain and simple truth is their ignorance. Pop culture and a liberal media have guided these sheep into believing and supporting the indefensible. It truly is a shame when the ignorant have no clue how ignorant they are. H supports the following:

- Obamacare. Obamacare architect Gruber on video calls American citizens too stupid to understand simple economics and that Obamacare would have never passed if Americans knew this was just a huge tax.

- Planned Parenthood. Top abortion company in the world, is caught selling baby body parts for profit. In a civilized world, it would have been closed down immediately.

- Muslims/Open borders. As Muslims commit terrorist acts one after the other, Democrat politicians ask us to look the other way. Hillary runs on bringing millions more to America and is on video calling for open borders.

- The Clinton Foundation is built on millions of dollars funded by the Mideast.

- Democrats have encouraged Black Lives Matter thugs labeled as innocent black youth being killed by police to ensue race riots.

- Democrats support public teacher unions to the point of closing charter schools proven to be beneficial to the education of minorities and push poor curricula.

The ignorant are like sheep. They follow a herd as if they do not possess a single brain cell and are led to continue supporting smooth-talking leftist politicians. The architect of Obamacare calls you stupid? You find out in America people are selling baby body parts? Unvetted Muslims are coming to America and committing terrorist acts? Your presidential candidate is indebted to Mideastern countries where Islamists call for world domination? Blacks are killing our police because they have a grievance? Successful charter schools are closed? Americans supporting Democrats are complicit with all the above.

Everyday Americans are hurt by these policies, and badly. Hillary supporters should ask themselves why on earth am I listening to her spew her garbage when all we get out of it is garbage. No matter how many times she states that she is for children, for women, for minorities, blah, blah, blah, question the above and ask yourself if this woman who defends these deserves your vote as president of the United States. This woman will be dangerous with power.

NOVEMBER 2016

Words of Walter Scott from 1808 Describe this Election

November 3, 2016

This presidential election season comes down to Electoral College votes Tuesday night. The United States will have elected a successful businessman or a lifelong, crooked female politician. The momentum is with Trump despite H having practically been coronated while picking out Oval Office drapes.

H already played the typical destroy Republican cards that worked on Romney – doesn't pay taxes and hates women. Trump still stands surrounded by pumped up crowds. H's VP pick draws maybe 30 to an event. H isn't doing much better. She has tried to duplicate O's exact wording about closing down the coal mines; he is applauded, and she is disparaged. She has tried the tax the 1% and fairness for everyone as O did; no one believes her. It's quite surprising to her that it just isn't working this time around; O had it so easy.

Julian Assange via WikiLeaks and James O'Keefe via hidden videos have been exposing the truth on Democrats for which Americans are forever grateful, and yet the perverted husband of H's confidant Huma may ultimately bring her

323

down. Of course, it is Huma's fault for using her home computer for classified State Department business. H's classified emails intermingled with his sexually explicit emails were only found because Huma's squirrely husband Anthony Weiner is being investigated for sexting sex scandals.

The best words to depict this election were written in 1808 by Walter Scott. "Oh, what a tangled web we weave...when first we practice to deceive." H is guilty of lies, deception and much worse, as well as the Democrat machine – the political elite, mainstream media, the crony capitalists, the foreign donors, Wall Street, Big Banks and other low-level political hacks. Thank you, Julian Assange and James O'Keefe. This election is our chance to rid the world of H's corrupt influence that has been going on for far too long. Go, Trump, and make America great again.

We Love Trump

November 11, 2016

Election night had us on pins and needles. The thought of the Clintons back in the White House disgusted us and the continuation of the progressive liberal assault on our country petrified us. Could conservatism finally win in this PC world of snowflake Millennials, militant gays and paid anarchists? Would the silent majority pull an offset or had liberalism set in? At 1:37am CST on November 9th, we were rewarded with the election of Donald J. Trump as president. The silent majority had enough, enough of the left stream media, celebrity interjection, political elite with their corruption, cronyism and lies, endless taxation, policies named for exactly the opposite of what they do (Affordable Care Act – yeah, right), political correctness police, erasure of Christianity from our lives, schools' liberal indoctrination, destruction of our healthcare, immigration influx, Muslim tolerance, assault on our police, Black Lives Matter destructive riots, Common Core education, disarming of the military, climate change fraud, encroachment of the EPA, the new normal malaise, the list could go on and on. And the power of these will soon end, some by the stroke of President Trump's pen.

Trump may have been the only person to have been able to take on the media, the Clinton regime and the Obama regime. He was the right person for the right time to take them on. He did it. He broke through the madness and can now clear out the garbage of our government. He was confident to be himself without fear of the PC world. He took the shots and arrows for us and kept standing.

Because of Trump, many of us can rest without the worry of what Hillary had planned for our nation. He has earned our trust and has lifted the chains of liberalism from us. We wait anxiously for his inauguration on January 20, 2017. May God bless Trump and his family, and may God continue to bless the United

States of America. And may the misguided come to understand America and know what it means to be free.

If Journalists Reported the News, They Wouldn't Be Surprised about Trump

November 23, 2016

America has gloriously been delivered the gift of Trump to stop the liberal progressive assault. The leftist media has been reporting Democrat talking points for decades as the news and apparently ignored the real-world news. Unfortunately for H, the news that did get through was Obama claiming (threatening to the majority) that his policies were on the ballot.

Falling behind in my newspaper reading, I glanced over the headlines for the week prior to Trump's victory. I found absolutely nothing on why to vote for H. The headlines ran from "Hillary has a 98 percent chance of winning" to "How will Trump supporters handle his loss" to "What does Trump do after the election." America, due to her freedoms, has the free internet where blogs, social media, Twitter and videos showed a completely opposing story of the election. Compared to the internet, the reporting from the mainstream media reads more like satire.

A post-election article being shared on social media reports that Trump supporters are regretful of their votes. This is so far from the truth that it continues to read like satire. There is palpable excitement in any leak of Trump's cabinet. So many qualified, reputable, experienced people are being vetted. The socialist PC'ers have no more say; the adults are back, and it feels like divine intervention. H's cabinet would have been picked by going through the Clinton Foundation donor log. Nightmare.

Mainstream media and liberal education policies have nearly destroyed parts of the younger generations. The Millennials believed every word of the mainstream media and are having meltdowns as if they were snowflakes. The uneducated are taking the Soros-funded, rioting protest jobs. Meanwhile, businessman President-elect Trump is making promises on bringing jobs back to America. How hopeful is that, little snowflakes and rioters? When you make more money, you can give more to charities. You can go travel and have a life instead of focusing on your feelings. Government was not made to bleed dry the workers to give to the non-workers. People revolt to that and win elections - if the majority hasn't been transformed into third world poor. Journalists should be reporting that the nation's peaceful revolt is over. The silent majority has spoken with clarity. Trump is the 45th president of the United States.

The Adults Are Back in Charge

January 11, 2017

Obama faded with his fifty-minute farewell address last night followed by Trump's press conference in the morning in which he shined. The end of the Obama years is so close. Obama boasted about the power of his pen rather than work with Congress and focus on relationship-building. A nasty memory of Obama meeting with congressional leaders pretty much sealed his fate. Our elected official spoke up and Obama responded with, "I won." Much of his agenda will be simply reversed with Trump's pen. Obama never seemed to understand that the office of the president did not come with dictatorial powers. As the Trump administration is about to begin, the children are packing up and moving out with their victim-pushing, race-baiting, political correctness, and overall amateurish agendas. The adults are back, and the United States' citizens can rest assured that our country will have the best and brightest in charge of our future.

The left has been bombarding us these past eight years with hypocritical sayings which were often blatant lies. The latest, and to be sure Obama's administration is behind it, is the Fake News. He and his minions brainstormed to come up with the Fake News meme on why Trump got elected. Trump and the electorate checkmated Obama this time having already pinned the real fake news on Obama and his media. Obama has been successful for eight years claiming one thing but meaning another. He must think that this strategy will continue working for him, but he is wrong. The jig is up. Obama and his administration have relied on these childish tactics – use of celebrities, repeat lies, refute lies when the time comes, make up stories, and move on to the next disaster. If Americans wanted this to continue, H would be president. Americans are sick of the Obama administration lies, not to mention its treasonous policies and agendas – that's taken for granted.

Trump has already brought his knowledge of the business world to the benefit of manufacturing jobs back in the USA. His cabinet will be filled with excellent generals, businessmen and women, trusted politicians, brilliant minds and experts in their fields. The name of the game starting January 20 is the rule of law and constitutional rights, which is a huge change from the whims of liberal ideologues focusing on which sector to decimate.

Trump, the Only Man Who Couldn't Be Beaten

January 26, 2017

The long awaited, glorious moment arrived as President-elect Trump put his hand on the Bible and recited the presidential oath. The relief that the Obama era concluded with America standing is indescribable. The fear that the middle class with its conservative values would be wiped away from an H presidency was very real. For eight years, the United States has been run by an Orwellian administration with lies so big and ridiculous. Names given to bills were outright opposite of what the bills did. The socialist agenda of government control was incrementally erasing our freedoms. Liberal supporters including the media never blinked an eye. The irony of the media support with fake poll numbers and false narratives of a nearly guaranteed H presidency landslide aided in a Trump win. And now the fawning media have to deal with Obama's antithesis in Trump. God willing, political correctness will become a distant memory.

A few days into the presidency of Trump feels like a new era in America has taken hold. The nasty women can march all they want dressed up as vaginas, but they have been marginalized by the citizens who voted for Trump. Black Lives Matter is on notice that police lives do matter and that rioting can now lead to ten years in jail. Free rides of setting fires and vandalizing property in the name of racism will no longer be tolerated.

A lesser man than Trump could not have pushed through the onslaught as he did and survive. The anarchists who want the United States destroyed from the inside out are real and come in all types of forms, mostly funded by the evil Hungarian-American George Soros, original Jewish name Schwartz. The most unfortunate are the women who marched in the name of equality; they are the clueless puppets of evil yet think they serve a noble cause. They may one day understand that Trump rose out of Obama's liberal mess to save their sorry asses. Liberalism lost this time; conservatism won.

What the hell was the Women's March really about?

January 26, 2017

Many social media discussions and articles have been trying to get to the bottom of this so-called march. Trump had been president maybe 24 hours and protest marches occurred across the United States for what reason? A long social media debate came down to equality and, not kidding, one of the issues was that women's dry-cleaning costs more than men's. To which I inquired, "What was the percentage of women who marched because their designer silk blouses cost more at the cleaners than a man's standard cotton shirt?"

327

An interesting take by American Thinker's Doris O'Brien's article Progressives' Post-election Guilt Therapy is that liberal women feel guilty for not getting Hillary elected. This is likely true for the Bernie supporters who didn't vote, but this guilt has turned into a Trump hate-fest. The garb of the march was a square pink hat that was supposed to look like a pussy cat's ears in reference to Trump's locker room talk caught on video. They really got him this time, an alpha male to another male bragging what you can do to women when they know you have money. Actually, the hats just really looked dumb and Trump is president. If the point of the pussy hat and a major reason for the march was to hate on Trump for treating women badly of which he was never accused, why no hatred for Hillary who took on the job to denigrate the women abused by her husband Bill Clinton? The truth of the matter is that liberals truly hate the opposition and Hypocrite is thy name. See, Bill Clinton raped women and Hillary disparaged them – not her husband.

The fall-out from the march came from the marchers with their vulgar signs and costumes and Hollywood elite speakers who disgraced themselves and their liberal causes. Trump supporters were and will always be extremely loyal to Trump; he has saved them from an Obama third term via Hillary. These women marchers unknowingly strengthened conservatives' resolve to never let these people be in charge again. It is conceivable that not one person in the United States was proud of this display and persuaded to join the likes of them. Good luck, Democrats. You reap what you sow. With eight years of Obama's lessons in divisiveness, these women learned really well. Your constituents' anger and hate are in stark contrast to conservatives' optimism and love. They never saw the silent majority coming and now they have become stark-raving mad.

Why all the protests?

January 31, 2017

Trump was elected by his silent warriors. We blogged, we posted on social media, we supported the Tea Party, and on November 8, 2016, we elected our person. Very organized protests across the country started the day after Trump's inauguration and it appears that the protesting will continue whatever Trump does. The Left's views are the opposite of the rest of the country. Why protest post-election? The Left lost. Wait for the next election.

The Left was living in its liberal-made bubble with fake accolades, fake news, and fake polls while their countrymen were suffering. Local hospitals are closing, fed-up doctors are choosing early retirement, small businesses are looking at doubled labor costs and rising insurance rates. Middle-class families are trying to figure out how to afford going to doctors and how to pay for health insurance. Families are drowning while the Left continues to promote a phony world of fairness. These families' hope is in Trump to change the course.

About that fake news, H, awarded Most Admired Woman of the Year for the 20th time in 2015, still couldn't cross the line to the presidency. I know we good little people of the United States were supposed to drum this into our heads and automatically elect her president. We chose Trump because it no longer works that way. Enough of us decided that the Left is completely out of touch with reality and this overboard promotion is pure craziness. Plenty are holding on with their protesting but when the jobs open because of Trump's policies, they, too, will leave and go to work.

Here's to Trump obliterating the liberal agenda and getting this country back on its conservative, independent way of life. The dreams of open borders, denigrating capitalism and harping on queerness and climate change are dying. The protesting won't bring it back. Liberals, this time you lost big. You know it and we know it. We love Trump and trust that he has the backbone to ignore your protesting tears and propaganda.

MARCH 2017

The War on Trump

March 3, 2017

One can almost feel pity for the progressive left whose dream of a socialist USA is disappearing with every Trump executive order. Despite the lefts' best efforts, the USA is still made up of citizens who know the meaning of freedom and independence and also know how socialism would kill both. This is no exaggeration as I am sure Bernie fans remain 100% clueless; it is mindless to even try to educate them. However, the evil progressives are trying to make a stand with a war on Trump and Trump must win.

The election of Trump meant that Obama failed at his transformation. Obama's success depended on H to finish it off. The progressives are mad as hell that Trump could come in and take that all away from them. The left is trying to bear down on a phony Russian voting fraud story. The next accusation by the left should be greeted by announcing the investigations on the Clinton Foundation, her voter fraud, and the many miss-dealings of Obama. The citizens deserve to know what Obama did these past eight years with an accounting. What was so important that caused an extra $10 trillion in debt to the USA? How much of the $10 trillion is in the hands of Obama's friends' pockets? Progressives should be the ones on defense, not the other way around. Daily announcements on the regulation rollbacks, the dismantling of Obama executive orders and the advancement of conservative ideals would remind progressives that they continue to lose.

The media such as Fox News and its reporters continue to react to the left's fake news. Fox News could be directing the news and ignoring the false accusations of the left. Why is it that we hear Stolen-Seat Senator Al Franken accuse Trump's Attorney General Jeff Sessions of anything without evidence? Why repeat the hateful words on Trump spewed from the ladies on the TV show The View? It's mind-numbing to the point that Fox News fans are going to turn it off. Trump and his administration have all the means to direct the news. Keep telling us what you are doing, how you are doing it, what needs to be done, and why it needs to be done. The citizens who elected Trump trust him wholeheartedly. There is no reason the left determines the discussion of the day. The left lost the election and should be treated as such. They also need to admit that they lost fair and square.

Good riddance, Obamacare

March 24, 2017

This past Fall, my Obamacare Health Maintenance Organization (HMO) health plan required permission from my primary care physician to grant me approval to visit two specialists. HMO is the dreaded health plan that treats everyone like a child and has been around for too long. But to get subsidies for healthcare, the HMO was my only option. I got the approval and my doctor's office contacted the specialists. I got calls from them and when they found out my plan, they both refused my insurance. I really wanted to visit these local doctors and I asked if I could pay cash. Surprising to me, both said, "No." I assumed this was because the law requires us to have insurance and the doctors can only see patients that have insurance. Built into the law is how much insurance will pay the doctors. Not enough to take the business, apparently. The faster this asinine law dies, the better.

The vote on the first of three phases for changing the healthcare law was postponed, blocked by the conservative contingency. The word is that the new plan is Obamacare-lite with the government's hand central to the law. Prior to Obamacare, it was legal to google health insurance, pick a website and purchase health insurance through the website. Due to American ingenuity, there were true marketplace websites that compared companies and prices. I had a major medical policy for my two children and me for $150/month. Obamacare made this illegal. Everyone who did not receive insurance from their employer or could not pay full price for health insurance had to go through the government website to receive subsidies. My policy for a family of four is $1,676/month without subsidies, about $1,000 less with subsidies. The true cost is thousands more with the deductibles.

The vote may or may not happen today March 24, 2017, to change the law. We wait patiently for the death of Obamacare either by the Republican's plan or by its own death spiral. How mad I will be if I cannot call up a specialist doctor and make an appointment.

MAY 2017

Trumped Up Charges on Our President

May 17, 2017

Sane people see right through the leftist media who keeps hammering, keeps hammering and keeps hammering to end Trump's presidency. The gleeful looks and hysterics when they think they have finally nailed something against Trump are outrageous. The trumped-up charges of treason are actually covering up other treasonous acts. Trump is smart and not anything close to the stupid dolt the media depicts him. These charges will not hold for long. The truth has a way of coming forward. We conservatives are waiting for the day that the criminal acts of H, O, Lynch and their deplorable cohorts are proven beyond a reasonable doubt and result in prison time – no more half-ass investigations resulting in nothing. In the meantime, the chants of "Lock her up!" at Trump rallies always make me smile.

These true deplorables are trying to impeach Trump before the truth comes out about their illegal activities. I believe that the crimes they have committed while they were in power and to stay in power are beyond reprehensible. H allegedly said that if that effing bastard wins, we all hang from the nooses – her ranting after a Matt Lauer interview in which he dared ask about her judgment on using a private server for classified State emails. An H presidency would have all but guaranteed that their secrets remain safely hidden. Trump destroyed this guarantee while also impeding the progressive march to an all-powerful government over its citizens. Impede it is but not a complete end to their agenda. In the middle of the night in protective gear, New Orleans Mayor Mitch Landrieu dismantled Southern heritage and history by taking down three impressive, bronze monuments. These communists behind the progressive and liberal labels have taken command of the Democrat Party and are deliberately destroying our country and everything that has made it great.

Trump supporters are counting on Trump to fight this evil with every breath he takes. When younger relatives claim that socialism is fine, I want to slap them in the face and, like Cher in Moonstruck, yell at them to snap out of it. We need Trump to fight. And one more thing, it has been said that Trump rarely sleeps, maybe four hours per night. He is working tirelessly around the clock protecting our great country and great things are already happening. Make America Great Again. MAGA.

TRUMP'S PRESIDENCY

November 2018

When Trump and his lovely wife Melania rode down the escalator of Trump Tower to officially announce his candidacy for president July 2015, he garnered immediate attention and support that has never wavered. President Trump is doing a fabulous job wiping away Obama's legacy of executive orders and job-killing regulations with a stroke of a pen. I suppose when arrogant Obama was bragging about his pen, he never considered what a President Trump could also do with a pen. The Left paints Trump as a loud, obnoxious buffoon who incites chaos and violence and claims that he doesn't know what he is doing as president. From what I have observed, the polar opposite is true. His straightforwardness is refreshing. His political instincts and common sense are dead on. He's putting his business smarts to work on conquering his agenda.

In interviews from decades back, Trump explained what was happening in foreign trade and other countries ripping us off. He garnered great respect from the likes of talk show hosts Oprah, Colbert and Letterman. These pathetic leftists now treat Trump like a pariah. As far back as 1980, Rona Barrett asked him about running for president, as did the great Oprah.

Trump's background as a successful real estate developer also includes host and producer of the popular reality TV show, The Celebrity Apprentice. He brought celebrities of all backgrounds together in which he showed respect for each and every one of them, even when firing them with his catch phrase "You're fired." The theme song of the show was For the Love of Money, and for the ten years plus, no one complained about how rich he was but praised him for how charitable he was. No one ever charged him with racism or sexism or any ism. The celebrities won money for their chosen charities and were always gracious in return. Trump's temperament was steady throughout his show and he was always a decisive, level-headed decision-maker, respectfully taking input from his Board.

At the 2011 White House correspondents' dinner that he attended, the host said that he was surprised that Trump was running for president because he thought he was running as a joke. Trump sat through it and when he was elected president, instead of attending the 2017 Trump-bashing dinner, he celebrated with a 100-day rally in Pennsylvania. He warned us that we would get tired of winning; that's never going to happen. The Left has not stopped mocking Trump and it has gotten so vicious. The Fake News is nastiness and negativity 24/7 and has gotten so boring. Today's late-night comedians have forgotten to be funny and have lost viewers for life.

The silent majority that lived through the Obama years could not wait to vote for Trump. We have total respect and confidence that he is doing all he can to Make

America Great Again, MAGA. What he does is out of concern for the average citizen, although he does not accept 'average' as a description for anyone. (He tells a woman this in a video.) He fights the unrelenting liberal onslaught that reports news on Trump that is mostly negative. Doesn't matter to his supporters and is even producing a movement called #WalkAway. Democrats who see through the hatred and vitriol of the Left have walked away to Trump's Republican Party.

Trump supporters know that this fight for our country and culture is real. Our young people cheer when historical monuments are toppled over and our flag disrespected on a national level. With our younger generation voting in socialists, watching cable news shows featuring known communists, and fighting to keep our borders open, we see total corruption of what America is and where she is headed. Trump has altered our path and we can see a positive future.

President Trump has been extremely successful in trade deals with countries all over the world, bringing back jobs and manufacturing, showing respect for our military and police, moving the US embassy in Israel to Jerusalem, cancelling the tax/fine/mandate of Obamacare, and passing major tax reform called Tax Cuts and Jobs Act, all this in less than two years. Obamacare will die but Republican Senator John McCain just could not grant the needed vote to repeal Obamacare, still smarting from Trump saying that he didn't consider McCain a war hero because he got caught. McCain died hating Trump and wasted his funeral with his final dissing of Trump.

Each Trump success brings on more Left hatred. Here's a despicable example of what Trump has faced. The impeccable Brett Kavanaugh, who Trump nominated to the Supreme Court of the United States, should have been confirmed with a simple vote. The Democrats didn't want a conservative to replace Justice Kennedy who was often the deciding Democrat/liberal vote. Kavanaugh found himself in a confirmation process resembling a political circus in which he basically went on trial defending himself from uncorroborated allegations and accusations from grandstanding liberal Democrats. A California professor Christine Ford accused him of a sexual attack while at a high school party in the 80's but could not remember when, where, with whom, any details, and caught in lie after lie. A few more women came forward, one claiming that Kavanaugh took part in gang rapes. Only two outcomes were plausible, either Judge Kavanaugh gets confirmed or his career is destroyed, possibly facing a criminal trial. Leftists showed no concern for the defamation of a man with proven credentials, proving that they will destroy anyone who gets in their way.

Trump did not waver his support and Kavanaugh held his ground. It was absolutely disgraceful that only one Democrat voted to confirm. Republican Senator Susan Collins made the final vote to confirm with a very brave speech. After the confirmation, the woman admitted that she made up the gang rape

333

story to keep him off the Court. Not a peep in the news about Dr. Ford except that $1 million was raised for her through a GoFundMe website. Young liberals now claim that we have a rapist on the Supreme Court. This opposition is what Trump and Americans face daily. Elections no longer matter. Truth and facts no longer matter. Trump endures this type of treatment day after day. Thankfully, he is a fighter and a beyond confident alpha male.

The United States has been known for its peaceful change of power for presidential administrations. This ended with the election of President Trump. The Left, who was as close as ever to changing our country to a socialist hellhole, decided that Trump should be impeached; Hillary was supposed to be crowned queen. Trump's pick for Attorney General Jeff Sessions stepped aside by recusing himself and let a phony Trump-Russian collusion investigation precede. For two years, the Left reported on this, antsy that something will be found to get rid of President Trump. It has yet to wrap up. Somehow, Democrats won the House in the midterm elections. (lousy Republican marketing) Who knows what will happen now, but the Dems are threatening thousands of investigations, indictments, and whatever can bring down Trump. No talk of partisan policies or working for the American people. It sounds like we are in for a terrible two more years of liberal hate.

About the midterm elections, Democrats tried to steal Florida. A week post-election, Democrats keep finding votes. How about that? If you don't win, "find" boxes of votes and recount until you beat the Republicans. Rumors abound of non-citizens voting, dead voting, and poll worker fraud. The sad part, Democrat leaders and supporters are fine with stealing elections from Republicans. It happened before with the Al Franken Minnesota Senate seat and his miraculous find of enough votes to beat the Republican post-election, producing the needed Senate vote to pass Obamacare. We have faith that Trump will do his best to get ahead of this garbage and corruption.

The youngest member to be elected to the House is a New York Millennial Democrat Socialist who is totally ignorant about the rule of law and of economics. She ran on free healthcare for all because it will be cheaper. She didn't understand why she was being questioned on how to pay for it. She and her supporters are, without a doubt, pure proof of the dumbing down of our schools; she has an economics degree from Boston University. It will be amusing yet sad following her political career. Ultra-socialists Beto and Gillum came close to winning the Texas Senate seat and the Florida governorship. If the Left continues to get its way, America will decline rapidly.

What I have observed about Trump is his steady Eddie personality, no gratuitous grins, no need for fake indignance, no playacting of his feelings, and no need to lie about his policies. Trump can never be accused of being a phony. He is confident in who he is and never feels the need to seek acceptance from others. As a businessman, he is a thinker and has no use of wasting time on frivolous feelings such as being offended. Millennial snowflakes should take note. I doubt he has ever referred to a self-help book and questioned if he is good enough or what his future will be. He is a creative visionary and a problem solver. He makes things happen when others do not even see the path. He says what he means, and he means what he says. There is no need for him to nudge us, push us to think his way, or convince us that he is correct. He is correct and knows that we feel the same way he does. He loves America, unlike his predecessor. We know that if you want to fundamentally change our country, you do not like our country. We know that if you want to change our history and traditions, you do not like our history and traditions.

I also see a man who is extremely kind and courteous. His simple acts of kindness present who he is. When Kim Jong-on seemed a little lost at the North Korean summit, Trump guided him respectfully to the correct door. At a ceremony to honor a gunned down New York city cop Miosotis Familia, her petite mother hugged and held onto Trump and he kissed her forehead and her hand. It was heart-warming. At a signing for the Right-to-Try bill (terminally ill patients can seek experimental drugs), a young boy moved in to hug President Trump and Trump gave him a big hug back, kissing him on his head. A young boy wanted to mow the White House lawn and he was allowed. Trump went over to talk to the young boy who was determined to do his job more than converse with the president. The respect veterans have for Trump is a beautiful thing. They give him serious hugs, no simple pats on the arm or back. These veterans realized what Obama was about and they seriously support Trump, truly grateful for his leadership.

The Left will surely misconstrue this as idiotic idolatry, but they are wrong. Their focus is simply on hating Trump. I will never understand nor respect support for liberal policies, especially selling aborted baby parts and importing Muslims. With almost two years in office, President Trump is beloved, and I predict will go down as the best president ever. The educated liberal Democrats will not understand this version of Trump for they have blind hatred for the man. It is almost jealousy, but they think they are better than him, and secretly believe they deserve his success and what he has, including his smarts. The very poor may like Trump but will not vote for him for fear of losing their freebie benefits. The younger Democrat Socialists don't have a clue about politics but think they know it all. They sure are virtuous in their feelings. A perfect example of the liberal greenies just happened with the California fires. The greenies love the earth more than anyone else, so they think. When forest rangers wanted to do their jobs of controlled burns, the know-it-all environmentalists sued so no trees or brush could be hurt, or possibly a mouse – because they care more about animals, too. The brush and dead trees became kindling, grew into an inferno, spread and burned down complete towns and killed many people and animals. The forest rangers wanted to prevent this with the burns but were stopped by the law. Facts don't matter to liberals. The truly smart, knowledgeable experts are ignored.

Democrats are beginning their posturing for a 2020 presidential run. Hillary seems to be first in line. Something to be said for persistence. As long as she is alive, she will run. I can already feel who the Democrats want – Michelle Obama. She is on the covers of the magazines, promoting a book, and touring the country with a Listening/Conversation tour. No word has been reported about the tour (it's very hush hush and I will not pay $200 to see her!) except that prices are extremely high, $200 to $12,000?? A Trump/Michelle Obama debate? I cannot imagine what she would say besides Trump is a white supremist nationalist who hates her because she's black, lest anyone forgets her skin color.

The Tea Party changed the course of this country and will always stand behind our President. Obama, in his quest for power, elected Trump. America's future depends on President Trump draining the Swamp faster than the Left can hinder or stop him. So far, he has been three steps ahead of everyone. And since he is known to sleep only 3-4 hours a night, it's like getting two terms for one. MAGA and for 2020, KAG.

ACKNOWLEDGMENTS

I want to thank my guest authors for their terrific articles,
Kithy for her economic smarts and common sense,
Tbird for her well-researched articles & for winning "Shortest Article",
and for the fabulous contributions from CWK, SH and TH.
Why not their real names? Just because and for the same reasons Trump
supporters didn't put stickers on their cars or signs on their yards.

Acronyms

401K	retirement investment plan found in IRS Taxation Code subsection 401(k)
AARP	Association of American Retired Persons
ABC	American Broadcasting Company Television network
ACORN	Association of Community Organizations for Reform Now
AK47	Avtomat Kalashnikova model 1947
ATF	Bureau of Alcohol, Tobacco, Firearms and Explosives
ATM	Automated Teller Machine
BO	Barrack Obama
BS	Bullshit
CBO	Congressional Budget Office
CCX	Chicago Climate Exchange
CEO	Chief Executive Officer
CHIP	Children's Hospital Insurance Program
CLASS Act	Community Living Assistance Services and Supports Act
CO2	Carbon Dioxide
COBRA	Consolidation Omnibus Budget Reconciliation Act
DC	District of Columbia
DEA	Drug Enforcement Association
DNC	Democratic National Committee
DOE	Department of Energy
DVR	Digital Video Recorder
EPA	Environmental Protection Agency
ESPN	Entertainment and Sports Programming Network
FBI	Federal of Bureau Investigations
FOIA	Freedom of Information Act
FOBO	Friends of Barrack Obama
GDP	Gross Domestic Product
GM	General Motors
GOP	Grand Old Party
H	Hillary
HHS	Department of Health and Human Services
HUD	Housing and Urban Development
ICE	Immigration and Customs Enforcement
ID	Identification
IPAB	Independent Payment Advisory Board
IPO	Initial Public Offering
IRA	Individual Retirement Account
IRS	Internal Revenue Service
ISIS	Islamic State in Iraq and Syria
KAG	Keep America Great
LGBTQ	Lesbian, Gay, Bisexual, Transgender and Queer
MAGA	Make America Great Again
MAW	Most Admired Woman

NAACP	National Association for the Advancement of Colored People
NASA	National Aeronautics and Space Administration
NSA	National Security Association
O	Obama
OBL	Osama bin Laden
PAC	Political Action Committee
PBS	Public Broadcasting Service
PC	Political Correctness
PGA	Professional Golfers' Association of America
PLUS	Parent Loan for Undergraduate Students
PR	Public Relations
PRISM	Planning Tool for Resource Integration, Synchronization and Management
PTA	Parent Teacher Association
RNC	Republican National Committee
ROTC	Reserve Officers' Training Corps
SCOTUS	Supreme Court of the United States
SEAL	US Navy Sea, Air, and Land teams
SOTU	State of the Union
STOCK Act	Stop Trading on Congressional Knowledge Act
TBA	to be announced
TV	television
UN	United Nations
US	United States
USDA	United States Department of Agriculture
VA	Veterans Administration
VP	Vice President
W	George Walker Bush

ABOUT THE AUTHORS

Carol Headrick resides in Slidell, Louisiana, with her husband Jimmy, son Jared and daughter Josie, all living at the mercy of Chihuahua Suzy and cockatiel Bird. She grew up in St. Louis Hills with her four sisters and graduated from Bishop DuBourg High School, Mizzou with a business degree and Saint Louis University with an MBA. She has enjoyed being a stay-at-home mom and volunteering as a PTA president, band mom and golf mom. She helps Jimmy run junior golf tournaments.
contact: carolhead64@msn.com

Kathleen Tompkins resides in Wentzville, Missouri, and with her husband Rick, raised five sons and a daughter. Kathleen graduated from Cor Jesu Academy and Mizzou with a business degree in economics. She has enjoyed being a stay-at-home mom and is now working as an underwriter.

Mary T. Hardy resides in Ballwin, Missouri, and with her husband Ken, raised four sons and a daughter. Mary graduated from Southwest High School, the University of Missouri-St. Louis with a business degree and Saint Louis University with a law degree. She has enjoyed being a stay-at-home mom and now works on her art.

All three are very proud Deplorables and always will be.

Made in the USA
Monee, IL
16 December 2023

49461684R00208